OTHER BOOKS BY EDMUND PHELPS

MASS FLOURISHING

MASS FLOURISHING

How Grassroots Innovation
Created Jobs, Challenge, and Change

EDMUND PHELPS

The 2006 Nobel Laureate in Economics

PRINCETON UNIVERSITY PRESS

Princeton and Oxford

Requests for permission to reproduce material from this work should be sent to
Permissions, Princeton University Press

Published by Princeton University Press, 41 William Street, Princeton, New Jersey 08540
In the United Kingdom: Princeton University Press, 6 Oxford Street, Woodstock, Oxfordshire OX20 1TW
press.princeton.edu

Jacket design by David Drummond, Salamander Hill Design

Willa Cather epigraph courtesy Knopf/Random House.

Jackie Wullschlager epigraph from *Financial Times*
© The Financial Times Limited 2013. All rights reserved.

Hunter S. Thompson epigraph reprinted with the permission of Simon & Schuster, Inc.
from *Songs of the Doomed*. Copyright © 1990 Hunter S. Thompson.

John Rawls epigraph reprinted by permission of the publisher,
from *A Theory of Justice: Revised Edition*, p. 4,
Cambridge, MA: The Belknap Press of Harvard University Press, Copyright
© 1971, 1999 by the President and Fellows of Harvard College.

ISBN 978-0-691-15898-3
Library of Congress Control Number: 2013936720

British Library Cataloging-in-Publication Data is available

This book has been composed in Calluna with Filosofia and DIN display by
Princeton Editorial Associates Inc., Scottsdale, Arizona.

Printed on acid-free paper. ∞
Printed in the United States of America
1 3 5 7 9 10 8 6 4 2

CONTENTS

PREFACE

Wʜᴀᴛ ʜᴀᴘᴘᴇɴᴇᴅ ɪɴ ᴛʜᴇ 19ᴛʜ ᴄᴇɴᴛᴜʀʏ that caused people in some
countries to have—for the first time in human history—unbounded
growth of their wages, expansion of employment in the market economy,
and widespread satisfaction with their work? And what happened to cause
many of these nations—by now, all of them, or so it would appear—to lose all
that in the 20th century? This book aims to understand how this rare prosperity was gained and how it was lost.

I set out in this book a new perspective on what the prosperity of nations
is. Flourishing is the heart of prospering—engagement, meeting challenges,
self-expression, and personal growth. Receiving income may lead to flourishing but is not itself a form of flourishing. A person's flourishing comes from
the experience of the new: new situations, new problems, new insights, and
new ideas to develop and share. Similarly, prosperity on a national scale—
mass flourishing—comes from broad involvement of people in the processes
of innovation: the conception, development, and spread of new methods
and products—indigenous innovation down to the grassroots. This dynamism may be narrowed or weakened by institutions arising from imperfect
understanding or competing objectives. But institutions alone cannot create
it. Broad dynamism must be fueled by the right values and not too diluted by
other values.

The recognition by a people that their prosperity depends on the breadth
and depth of their innovative activity is of huge importance. Nations unaware
of how their prosperity is generated may take steps that cost them much of

their dynamism. America, judging by available evidence, does not produce now the rate of innovation and high job satisfaction it did up to the 1970s. And participants have a right not to see their prospects of prospering—of self-realization, as John Rawls termed it—squandered. In the past century, governments sought to move the unemployed into jobs so they could prosper again. Now there is a larger task: to reverse losses of prosperity among the employed. That will require legislative and regulatory initiatives having nothing to do with boosting either "demand" or "supply." It will require initiatives based on an understanding of the mechanisms and mindsets on which high innovation depends. Yet surely governments can do it. Some began clearing paths for innovation two centuries ago. These thoughts were on my mind when I conceived this book. I believed the sole problem was the terrible unawareness.

Eventually I began to sense another kind of problem: a resistance to modern values and modern life. The values that supported high prosperity ran up against other values that impeded and devalued flourishing. Prosperity has paid a heavy toll. Questions are being asked about the sort of life it would be best to have and thus the sort of society and economy to have. There are calls in America for traditionalist goals long familiar in Europe, like greater social protection, social harmony, and public initiatives in the national interest. These were the values that have led much of Europe to viewing the state in traditional, medieval terms—through the "lens of corporatism." There are calls too for more attention to community and family values. There is little awareness of how valuable modern life, with its flourishing, was. There is no longer in America or in Europe a sense of what mass flourishing was like. Nations with brilliant societies a century back, say, France in the Roaring Twenties, or even a half-century ago, say, America in the early sixties, have no living memory of wide flourishing. Increasingly, the processes of a nation's innovation—the topsy-turvy of creation, the frenzy of development, and painful closings when the new things fail to take hold—are seen as a pain that upstart materialist societies were willing to endure to increase their national income and national power, but that we are unwilling to endure any longer. The processes are not seen as the stuff of flourishing—the change, challenge, and lifelong quest for originality, discovery, and making a difference.

This book is my response to these developments: It is an appreciation of the flourishing that was the humanistic treasure of the modern era. It is also a plea to restore what has been lost and not to reject out of hand the modern values that inspired the broad prosperity of modern societies.

I first set out a narrative of prosperity in the West—where and how it was won and how to varying degrees it has been lost in one nation after another. After all, much of our understanding of the present comes from trying to put together some pieces of our past. But I also study cross-country evidence of the present day.

At the core of the narrative is the prosperity that broke out in the 19th century, firing imaginations and transforming working lives. Widescale flourishing from engaging, challenging work came to Britain and America, later to Germany and France. The step-by-step emancipation of women there and, in America, the eventual abolition of slavery, widened the flourishing. The making of new methods and products that was part of this flourishing was also the major part of the economic growth that coincided with it. Then, in the 20th century, flourishing ultimately narrowed, and growth slipped away.

In this narrative, the historic run of prosperity—from as early as the 1820s (in Britain) to as late as the 1960s (in America)—was a product of pervasive indigenous innovation: the adoption of new methods or goods stemming from homegrown ideas originating in the national economy itself. Somehow the economies of these pioneering nations developed dynamism—the appetite and capacity for indigenous innovation. I call them *modern* economies. Other economies gained by following the modern ones in their slipstream. This is not the classic account by Arthur Spiethoff and Joseph Schumpeter of entrepreneurs jumping to make the "obvious" innovations suggested by discoveries of "scientists and navigators." The modern economies were not the old mercantile economies, but something new under the sun.

Understanding the modern economies must start with a modern notion: original ideas born of creativity and grounded on the uniqueness of each person's private knowledge, information, and imagination. The modern economies were driven by the new ideas of the whole roster of business people, mostly unsung: idea men, entrepreneurs, financiers, marketers, and pioneering end-users. The creativity and attendant uncertainty was seen through a glass darkly in the 1920s and 1930s by those early moderns, Frank Knight, John Maynard Keynes, and Friedrich Hayek.

Much of the book is occupied with the human experience in the innovation process and the flourishing it brings. The human benefits of innovation are a basic product of a well-functioning modern economy—the mental stimulus, the problems to solve, the arrival of a new insight, and the rest. I have sought to convey an impression of the rich experience of working and living in such an economy. As I considered this vast canvas, I was excited to realize that no one had ever depicted what a modern economy felt like.

My account of the phenomenon of dynamism recognizes that myriad economic freedoms are a key element—freedoms that we have our Western democracy to thank for. So are various enabling institutions, which arose in answer to business needs. Yet the rise of economic modernity required more than the existence and enforcement of legal rights and more than various commercial and financial institutions. My account of dynamism does not deny that science has been advancing but does not link prosperity to science. In my account, attitudes and beliefs were the wellspring of the dynamism of the modern economies. It is mainly a culture protecting and inspiring individuality, imagination, understanding, and self-expression that drives a nation's indigenous innovation.

Where a country's economy becomes predominantly modern, I argue, it goes from just producing known, specified goods or services to dreaming up and working with ideas about other things to try to produce—goods or services not known to be producible and perhaps never before conceived. And where an economy is pulled back from the modern—denied its institutions and norms or blocked by curbs or inhibited by opponents—the flow of ideas through it narrows. Whichever direction the economy is pulled, toward the modern or the traditional, the texture of working life is profoundly changed.

Thus the history of the West set out here is driven by a central struggle. That struggle is not between capitalism and socialism—private ownership in Europe rose to the American level decades ago. Nor is it the tension between Catholicism and Protestantism. The central struggle is between modern and traditional, or conservative, values. A cultural evolution from Renaissance humanism to the Enlightenment to existentialist philosophies amassed a new set of values—modern values like expressing creativity and exploring for its own sake, and personal growth for one's own sake. And these values inspired the rise of modern societies in Britain and America. In the 18th century they fostered modern democracy, of course, and in the 19th century they gave birth to modern economies. These were the first economies of dynamism. This cultural evolution brought modern societies to continental Europe too—societies modern enough for democracy. But the social disruptions brought about by the emergent modern economies in those nations were a threat to traditions. And traditional values—putting community and state over the individual and protection against falling behind over going ahead—were so powerful that, in general, few modern economies made much headway there. Where they made or threatened to make deep inroads, they were forcibly taken over by the state (in the interwar years) or hobbled by restrictions (in postwar years).

Many authors allude to a long struggle to free themselves from received wisdom, and I had to escape from a forest of unrecognizable descriptions and inapplicable theories to be able to talk about the modern economy, its creation, and its value. There was the classic formulation by Schumpeter—innovations are sparked only by exogenous discoveries—and the neo-Schumpeterian corollary that innovation could be increased only by boosting scientific research. These two views assumed as a foregone conclusion that a modern society could do without a modern economy. (No wonder Schumpeter thought socialism was coming.) There was Adam Smith's concept that people's "well-being" derived from consumption and leisure alone, and thus their whole business life was for these ends, not for the experience itself. There was the neoclassical welfarism of Keynes, in which failures and fluctuations are the main modern ills to be combated, since the challenges and ventures responsible for them have no human value. This was followed by the neo-neoclassical view, dominant in business schools today, that business is about risk assessment and cost control—not ambiguity, uncertainty, exploration, and strategic vision. There was the Panglossian view that a nation's institutions are not a concern, since social evolution produces the most needed institutions and every nation has the culture that is best for it. If this book gets at all close to the truth, all these ideas of bygone times were false and harmful.

The book devotes many pages to admiring descriptions of the experience that the modern economy offers participants. It was, after all, the marvel of the modern era. But that tribute invites the question of how this modern life, which the modern economies made possible, compares with other ways of life. In the next-to-last chapter I argue that the flourishing that is the quintessential product of the modern economy resonates with the ancient concept of the good life, a concept on which many variations have been written. The good life requires the intellectual growth that comes from actively engaging the world and the moral growth that comes from creating and exploring in the face of great uncertainty. The modern life that modern economies introduced perfectly exemplifies the concept of the good life. That is a step in the direction of justifying a well-functioning modern economy. It can serve the good life.

Yet a justification of such an economy must address objections. An economy structured to offer prospects of the good life, even to all participants, could not be considered a just economy if it caused injustices in the process or provided the good life in a way deemed unfair. The less advantaged and indeed all participants suffer—from workers who lose their jobs to entrepreneurs whose companies are ruined and families whose wealth takes a huge hit—when a modern economy's new direction turns out to be ill judged or very close to being a racket, like the housing boom rigged up in the previous decade. Governments fail to govern the distribution of the benefits of a modern economy—the primary one being the good life—in a way that is as favorable to the less advantaged as it could be. (But that may be the fault of the government more than of the modern economy.)

The last chapter sketches a conception of an economy that is modern but also just in going as far as feasible to provide prospects for the good life to the participants whose talent or background renders them less advantaged than the others. I note that a well-functioning economy of the modern kind can be governed in accordance with familiar notions of economic justice, such as focus on the least advantaged. If all are keen on the good life, they will be willing to take the risks of large swings to have that life. I also add that a justly-functioning modern economy is to be preferred to a justly-functioning traditional economy—an economy based on traditional values—under a wide variety of conditions. But what if some participants have traditional values? In an introductory exploration one has to stop at some point. But this much is clear: Those in a nation who want to have economies of their own, based on their traditionalist values, ought to be free to set them up. Yet those who aspire to the good life have the right to be free to work in a modern economy—not to be confined to a traditionalist economy, bereft of change, challenge, originality, and discovery.

It may seem paradoxical that a nation would countenance or even strive to make more effective a kind of economy in which the future is unknown and unknowable, an economy prone to huge failures, swings, and abuses in which people may feel "adrift," or even "terrified." Yet the satisfaction of having a new insight, the thrill of meeting a challenge, the sense of making your own way, and the gratification of having grown in the process—in short, the good life—require exactly that.

MASS FLOURISHING

Advent of the Modern Economies

It is true that modernity was conceived in the 1780s. . . . [But] the
years 1815–30 [are] those during which the matrix of the modern
world was largely formed.

PAUL JOHNSON, *The Birth of the Modern*

O VER MOST OF HUMAN EXISTENCE, the actors in a society's economy seldom did anything that expanded what may be called their economic
knowledge—knowledge of how to produce and what to produce. Even in
the early economies of Western Europe, departures from past practice that
might have led to new knowledge and thus to new practice, or innovation,
were uncommon. Ancient Greece and Rome made some innovations—the
water mill and bronze casting, for example. Yet it is the dearth of innovation
in the "ancient economy," especially over the eight centuries after Aristotle,
that is striking. The Renaissance made pivotal discoveries in science and art
and brought riches to royalty. Yet the resulting gains in economic knowledge
were too meager to elevate the productivity and living standards of ordinary
people, as the historian of everyday life, Fernand Braudel, observed. Familiarity and routine were the rule in these economies.

Was that because the actors in these economies did not desire to depart
from past practice? Not exactly. Humans, it has been found, were exercising imagination and displaying creativity as long as a thousand generations
ago.[1] Participants in the early economies, we can safely assume, did not lack
the desire to create—they invented and tested some things for their own use.
But they lacked a capacity to develop and provide new methods and products
for society: early economies had not acquired institutions and attitudes that
would enable and encourage attempts at innovation.

1. Researchers at the University of Tübingen recently unearthed some flutes fashioned from
bones by the cave dwellers that colonized Europe 35,000 years ago. Nicholas Conard and colleagues reported the find in 2009 in the science magazine *Nature*.

The highest achievement of these early economies was the spread of commerce within each country and the spread of foreign trade with other countries. The commerce of 14th-century Hamburg and 15th-century Venice—two prominent city-states—stretched along Hanseatic trade routes, the Silk Road, and ocean lanes to increasingly far-flung cities and ports. With the establishment of the New World colonies in the 16th century, commerce spread within nation-states and foreign trade increased. By the 18th century, most notably in Britain and Scotland, most people were producing goods for the "market" rather than for their families or towns. More and more countries exported and imported at significant levels in distant markets. Business still involved producing, but it was also about distribution and trade.

This was capitalism, of course—to use a term that did not exist in those times. More precisely, it was *mercantile capitalism:* someone with wealth might become a merchant, investing in wagons or boats to transport goods to places where prices were higher. From about 1550 to 1800 or so, this system was the motor of what the Scots called a "commercial society." In Scotland and England, at any rate, many admired this society unreservedly, while others felt it lacked "heroic spirit."[2] In the mercantile age, though, these societies were certainly not lacking in aggressiveness. Merchants were pitted against one another in the struggle for supplies or market share, while nations raced to establish colonies. Military conflict was rampant. Perhaps with little to challenge people's minds and to tempt big leaps in their business, the heroic spirit sought outlets in military ventures.

In the mercantile age, to be sure, business life exhibited a good deal less of the familiarity and routine that had been so pronounced in the middle ages. Finding and penetrating new markets—and being found and penetrated—must have provided bits of new economic knowledge from time to time. No doubt expansion of commerce often turned up a new opportunity for domestic producers, or a new opportunity for foreign competitors—thus new knowledge about what to produce. Such gains could be public knowledge, falling into the laps of people "in the business," or could be hard-won and remain private knowledge. Less often, perhaps, the stimulus to switch to producing a good

2. Adam Smith in his *Lectures on Jurisprudence,* given in Glasgow in 1762–1763, saw "disadvantages" of the "commercial spirit." "[T]he minds of men," he wrote, "are contracted . . . education is despised or at least neglected, and heroic spirit is almost utterly extinguished." (See Smith, 1978, vol. 5, p. 541.) In his 1776 classic *The Wealth of Nations* he says that "in barbarous societies . . . the varied occupations of every man oblige every man to exert his capacity. . . . [Thus] invention is kept alive" (p. 51). Adam Ferguson in his 1767 *Essay on the History of Civil Society* quoted admiringly the American Indian chief who said, "I am a warrior, not a merchant."

not produced before might lead to advances in how to produce. By how much, though, did economic knowledge increase in the mercantile age?

Economic Knowledge in the Mercantile Era

Some scraps of early data from England's economy are revelatory. Increased knowledge of what to produce can be supposed, other things unchanged, to pull up productivity—to pull up output in relation to labor input. So if this know-how in the hands of the economy's participants, whether it was private knowledge or public knowledge, grew appreciably over the mercantile era, this would be manifested by *increased* output in relation to labor input between the era's start around 1500 and its end around 1800. If we see little or no such improvement in the relationship, that would be reason to doubt that there was important growth of production know-how during the mercantile era. What, then, does the evidence show?

Output per worker in England did not increase at all between 1500 and 1800, according to the estimates by Angus Maddison in his 2006 volume *The World Economy*, a trusted source. However, population, and thus labor force, increased enormously over that span—recovering from losses from the bubonic plague, or Black Death, of the 1300s. Conceivably that pulled down output per worker, through "diminishing returns," enough to mask an upward pull on output per worker exerted by increasing knowledge, if there was any. However, decadal estimates by Gregory Clark show that output per worker was as high in the 1330s and 1340s, when population had not yet fallen much below its pre-plague peak, as it was in the 1640s, when population was nearly back to that previous peak. Some rare micro data suggest that output per farm worker was no higher even in the 1790s than in the early 1300s. Another study comes up with a one-third increase over that span.[3] It is safe to conclude that available farming techniques did not improve

---

3. A study of grain output in England's Ramsey Estates found that average rates of output per man-day between 1293 and 1347 "either surpassed or met the literature's best estimates for English workers until 1800." See Karakacili, "English Agrarian Labour Productivity Rates" (2004, p. 24).

A broader study reports no reductions in the labor required for threshing, reaping, and mowing. Yet its findings on overall productivity suggest that over a 4½-century span knowledge of how best to use farm workers did increase somewhat. Workers produced 58 bushels of grain per 300 man-days in the early 1300s and 79 bushels in the 1770s. But this is a meager gain over so long a period. See Clark's 2005 working paper, "The Long March of History," figure 3 and table 6. Clark's figure 8 shows a single upward shift from the 1640s to the 1730s in the output-per-labor relationship—by about 20 bushels.

much over almost five centuries. (Yet measuring output per worker, product by product, misses the continual gains in aggregate output per worker from shifts of labor to production where prices or productivities are higher. In this respect, wages are more informative.)

Real wages per worker—the average wage in terms of a basket of consumer goods—reflects, among other things, knowledge of how to produce and what to produce. Start-up projects to develop new methods or products would create jobs and that would pull up wages sooner or later. New methods also tend to exert an upward pull. Did the mercantile economies see a strong lift in real wages, which would be consistent with important increases in economic knowledge? In English farming, real wages, like output per head, were falling during the first half of the mercantile age, 1500 to 1650, owing to population regrowth after the plague. Wages rose from 1650 to 1730, though about half of that gain was lost by 1800. The net result was that wages in 1800 were lower than in 1500. However, wages in 1800 *were* higher than in 1300—about one-third higher. But is that gain large enough to confirm increased economic knowledge through English innovations in products and methods? First, real wages were greatly increased by declining prices of imported consumer goods and the "arrival of new goods such as sugar, pepper, raisins, tea, coffee and tobacco," as Clark in his 2007 book records (p. 42). So the one-third gain in real wages is not a sign of English innovation so much as evidence of discoveries by navigators and colonizers. Second, 1300 marked the end of a century of wage decline. Real wages in 1800, as Clark's table 4 shows, were lower than in 1200! It is safe to "split the difference," agreeing that England saw little progress in wages from the middle ages through the Enlightenment.[4]

We must conclude that the mercantile economies brought strikingly few advances in economic knowledge even in their heyday from 1500 to 1800. As population increased dramatically in the 18th century and still more over most of the 19th, with population levels setting record highs every year, it might be supposed that the fixity of land must have slowed the rise of productivity that growth of economic knowledge would otherwise have brought. But as Britain's population grew rapidly, its economy devoted itself more and more to manufacturing, trade, and other services, which were activities

---

4. It is true that wages (and output per worker) in 1200 may have been pushed a little above the 1300 level by an abundance of land that was never matched again—a time when a Robin Hood could enjoy an entire forest. But land could hardly have been appreciably scarce in 1300 either. In neither period was labor pressed against the land. So there is no compelling reason to rule out 1200, with its good wages, as the base year from which to make comparisons.

requiring less land than farming did. For this reason, population growth mattered less and less for growth of wages and output per worker. The belief that rising population prevented or severely limited productivity and wages, thus thwarting and masking a rise of economic knowledge, is not persuasive. Something else was limiting growth of wages and output per head.

The remarkable similarity of economic development across the mercantile world is also a clue to what was driving them—and what was not. We now know that in the mercantile era 11 countries (or regions that become countries) were in the same club with respect to output per capita and wages per worker: Austria, Britain, Belgium, Denmark, France, Germany, Holland, Italy, Norway, Sweden, and Switzerland. (Even in the 1200s and early 1300s, England was not the backwater next to the European continent that it was thought to be.) By 1800, America had joined the club. We could say that these nations and others marched to the same drummer, though in a ragged way: each had its own fluctuations around roughly the *same trend path*—with Italy in the lead position in 1500 and Holland by 1600 (until the early 1800s). That fact suggests that their modest upward trend was the product of mercantile forces—global and felt about equally, at least within the club—not nation-specific forces.[5]

Anyone living in those times might have forecast that, once commercialization had spread as far as it could go, the national economies would settle into the routine of old, albeit in a more globalized way. As it turned out, however, the mercantile era would not be the last stage of economic development—not for these developed parts of the world, at any rate. In several of the commercial societies, the economy, while still engaging in commerce and trade, would soon take on a new character. Something happened that was strange for its time, something that would change everything.

Signs of Exploding Economic Knowledge

The indicators that were surprisingly trendless from 1500 (by some measures even from 1200) to 1800 took an astonishing turn within just a few decades. From the 1820s to the 1870s, Britain, America, France, and Germany broke out of the pack one by one. The trajectory of these countries' two indicators— output per head and the average real wage—was a phenomenal development in the history of the world.

5. The standard source is the rough estimates, drawn from a range of data, by Maddison, *The World Economy* (tables 1b and 8c).

Output per head in Britain, according to present-day measurements, began a sustained climb in 1815 with the end of the Napoleonic Wars and never turned back. It grew spectacularly from the 1830s through the 1860s. Output per head in America is now viewed as having gone into a sustained climb around 1820.[6] In France and Belgium, it began a bumpy ascent in the 1830s, with Germany and Prussia following in the 1850s. These extraordinary climbs are indelibly associated with the first scholar to dig them up, the American economic historian Walt W. Rostow. He dubbed them *take-offs*—take-offs into sustained economic growth.[7]

The average real wage generally followed suit. In Britain the daily wage in the crafts for which we have data began a sustained rise in 1820 or so—not long after the time that output per worker took off. In America, wages took off in the late 1830s. The countries that saw, one by one, an explosion of their productivity saw an explosion of their real wages. (Chapter 2 will quantify the ascents.) The wage take-offs were discovered in the 1930s by Jürgen Kuczynski, a German economic historian of Polish birth. An extreme Marxist, he saw in the transformed economies only "deterioration of labor conditions" and "increasing misery." Yet his own data, even after his adjustments, reveal wages to be taking off strongly by the middle of the 19th century in all of the countries he studied: America, Britain, France, and Germany.[8]

The countries pulled one another along. With the quickening of the four lead countries' growth in both output per head and wages, every other

6. An attempted climb in 1800 ended in a crash. Despite years of fast growth until 1807, all of that growth and more was soon lost and was not regained until 1818. In contrast, the years from the mid-1830s to the mid-1840s showed a slowdown but no loss of previous gains. See the 1967 paper by Paul David, "The Growth of Real Product in the United States before 1840."

7. The chief work is Rostow's 1953 *The Process of Economic Growth*. See also his 1960 *The Stages of Economic Growth*. His discussion, involving "linkages," of the causes of the take-offs was difficult and did not win over the profession. (That explanation of the take-offs does not resemble or appear to anticipate the one given here.) After a stint in the government in the 1960s he was not invited back to Harvard. Yet he deserved more recognition than he got, if only for calling attention to the take-offs.

8. Kuczynski's early research is in his *Labour Conditions in Western Europe* (1937) and *A Short History of Labour Conditions* (1942–1945, vols. I–IV). In a life suitable for a film noir, he was not afraid of controversy. He made several novel adjustments to the raw wage data he had compiled, which succeeding investigators could not replicate. Yet, even his real wage for Britain "net" of lost time in unemployment goes from 57 in the "trade cycle" 1849–1858 to 99 in the cycle 1895–1903 (vol. I, part I, p. 67). The estimates cited above, however, are drawn from present-day sources: the 1995 international tables by Jeffrey Williamson et al. and tables by Broadus Mitchell, Paul Bairoch, Gregory Clark, and Diedrich Saalfeld. (Kuczynski's calculations portrayed the nations he studied as starting off highly unequal and finishing the century with roughly equal wage levels, thanks to technology "transfer" and migration of workers. Calculations by Williamson show less convergence, even some divergence among the four nations.)

member in the pack was able to grow faster simply by continuing to trade with the leaders and by stepping up trade to capitalize on emerging differences—in short, by swimming in their slipstream, like fishes behind a whale.

The pioneering observations of the take-offs, made by our two Galileos of modern economic history, Kuczynski and Rostow, crystallized the extraordinary journey that the West embarked upon in the 19th century. What, historians and economists asked, were the origins of these unprecedented phenomena? Economists turned to traditional economic thought.

Many traditional economists supposed that the answer lay in the sharply increasing stock of *capital*—plant and equipment—in farms and factories during the 19th century. But capital formation could not plausibly explain—even in part—the ascent of output per capita in the United States from the mid-19th century into the 20th. In fact, the rise of capital and land in use accounted for only one-seventh of this rise.[9] The growth of capital in the 18th century may have been sufficient to explain the somewhat meager and fitful growth of productivity in that period. But the growth of capital in the 19th century, though hastened, could not have powered the ascent of productivity and wages. Owing to diminishing returns, sustained growth of capital cannot singlehandedly yield sustained growth of output per worker and the average real wage.

Sensing that difficulty, some other traditional economists suggested that the answer lay in *economies of scale.* As labor multiplied and capital kept up, they suggested, output per worker (and per unit of capital) increased.[10] But the near-tripling of productivity between 1820 and 1913 in America and Britain is far too large an increase to attribute to economies of scale resulting from the expansion of labor and capital. And if such an expansion worked wonders in that period, why did a similar expansion from the 1640s to the 1790s have no comparable effect—or, in fact, any effect? Moreover, if economies of scale raised productivity and wages so significantly, why did they

9. The span analyzed, 1869–1878 to 1944–1953, had the earliest start date possible with the U.S. data available to researchers at the time. Today, one could make rough calculations from as early as 1840 without much change in the results. See Abramovitz, "Resource and Output Trends in the United States since 1870" (1956).

Historical research on Britain concluded that although the lion's share of 18th-century growth there was due to growth of capital rather than of knowledge, in the 19th-century growth it *was not.* See Crafts, "British Economic Growth, 1700–1831" (1983, p. 196). McCloskey's remark, quoted below, appears in this paper.

10. This thesis was advanced in 1969 by an important economic theorist of yesteryear, John Hicks, in one of his lesser works, *A Theory of Economic History.* The theoretical work on how integrated markets work out these scale economies was initiated by Paul Krugman in his 1992 book *Geography and Trade.*

not provide the same effect in Italy and Spain? Those countries' excess populations fled to the Americas, North and South, in search of better economic opportunities. Furthermore, achieving new economies of scale must have been harder over the 20th century in the take-off economies. The increases in labor and the resulting increases in capital that could feed new economies of scale subsided. Yet output per worker and wages kept right on growing over most of the 20th century—right up to the early 1970s. (Productivity rose at a blistering rate between 1925 and 1950, even during the Great Depression of the 1930s, then again from 1950 to 1975.)

Other traditional economists supposed that the answer lay in ongoing expansions of commerce within countries and expansions of trade among countries over much of the century—the shifts of people out of self-sufficiency and the creation of new canals and railroads connecting markets. Of course, the broader horizons added to the knowledge in economies—the take-off economies and the others—of what to produce and even how to produce. But we have been here before. If *all* the commercialization and trade from medieval Venice and Bruges to 18th-century Glasgow and London was not sufficient to lift output per worker and wages, we can hardly believe that the last expansions of commerce and trade in the 19th century increased productivity and wages so spectacularly. Moreover, even if commerce and trade were important to one or another take-off economy, they could not power the boundless growth of output and wages that appeared to be unfolding. Trade as an engine of growth runs out of fuel once globalization is total.

Almost nothing in the social world is absolutely certain. But it would appear that only increasing economic knowledge—knowledge of how to produce and knowledge about what to produce—could have enabled the steep climb in national productivity and real wages in the take-off countries. As Deirdre McCloskey put it, "ingenuity rather than abstinence governed." And, we might add, ingenuity rather than trade.

With time, the modernist emphasis on increasing knowledge—and the presumption that there is always more knowledge to come—triumphed over traditional emphases on capital, scale, commerce, and trade. But where did that knowledge come from? Whose "ingenuity" was it?

Finding the Wellspring of Economic Knowledge

Most historians coping after Rostow with the phenomenon of take-offs had no philosophical qualms about accepting the possibility that the mind can produce new ideas and that new knowledge may result. Further, if much of the future knowledge of consequence for society was not inevitable, or determinate, the future of society was not determinate. And what is indeterminate is unforeseeable, as Karl Popper wrote in his 1957 book against "historicism"—the view that the future grows determinably out of the historical situation.

However, even these historians, though not wedded to historical determinism, based their view of economies—19th-century economies and the take-off economies included—on an 18th-century conception handed down by Smith, Malthus, and David Ricardo. In that classical conception, a "market economy" was always in equilibrium. And, in equilibrium, this economy incorporates all of the world's knowledge potentially useful to its working: if the world discovers a new piece of knowledge, these market economies act at once to make use of it. In this view, there is no room for discovery within a nation's economy—no room for what we may call *indigenous innovation,* or home-grown advances in economic knowledge—since, in this view, the economy is already as knowledgeable as it can be. A nation has to look outside its economy—to the state (the legislature or the crown) or privately endowed nonprofit institutions, at home or abroad—for whatever ideas or findings might bring it new economic knowledge. It follows on this view that the onset in the 19th century of unremitting growth in productivity and wages reflected some new external force rather than a new force in the economy itself.

This view of economic history was explicit in the works of the last generation of the German Historical School of Economics. They regarded all material advances in a country as driven by the force of science: the discoveries of "scientists and navigators" external to the national economies. Without these godlike figures, there would be no material progress or anything else to exclaim over. The dazzling Austrian economist Joseph Schumpeter, not yet 30, added just one new wrinkle to the school's model: the need for an entrepreneur to develop the new method or good made possible by the new scientific knowledge.[11] In what became a hugely influential work published first in

11. The school grew famous and influential in Europe and America for its underlying theme that institutions are of central importance for economic performance—a theme going back to Wilhelm Roscher and even Marx. In the early 1900s the leader of this school, the German Arthur Spiethoff, and his Swedish successor, Gustav Cassel, were upstaged by the last member, Joseph Schumpeter. (Other notables were Werner Sombart, Max Weber, and Karl Polanyi.) Yet Spiethoff was important. The great British economist John Maynard Keynes traveled to Munich in 1932 for the *Festschrift* celebration marking Spiethoff's retirement—an occasion organized by Schumpeter.

Austria in 1911, he set out the dogma of the school, which may be fairly paraphrased as follows:

> What is knowable at present in the economy is already known. So no originality is possible within the economy. It is discoveries outside the economy that make possible the development of any new method or good. Though the opening of such a possibility is soon "in the air," its realization, or implementation, requires an entrepreneur willing and capable enough to undertake the demanding project: to raise the capital, organize the needed start-up company, and develop the newly possible product—"to get the job done." Though the project is onerous, the likelihood of the new product's commercial success—the likelihood of an "innovation"—is as knowable as the prospects faced by established products. There is no chance of misjudgment, provided there is due diligence. An expert entrepreneur's decision to accept a project and a veteran banker's decision to back it are correct ex ante, even uncanny, though ex post bad luck may bring a loss and good luck an abnormal profit.[12]

Thus Schumpeter proposed a way to think about innovation while barely departing from classical economics. The two pied pipers, Schumpeter with his scientism and Marx with his historical determinism, profoundly misled historians and the general public. Economics remained mostly classical throughout the 20th century.

Difficulties with this mode of thinking quickly appeared. Historians relying on the German theory realized that by the time of the take-offs, the great navigators had nearly run out of navigable routes to discover. Historians depended on "scientists" to link the take-offs to the step-up in the pace of scientific discovery over the period of the Scientific Revolution from 1620 to 1800, which includes the Enlightenment (defined as the years from 1675 to 1800 or so). Some scientific successes of that period remain legendary: Francis Bacon's 1620 *Novo Organum,* setting out a new logic to replace Aristotle's *Organon* [*Logic*]; William Harvey's brilliant analysis of the "motion of the blood" in 1628; Anton Leeuwenhoek's work on microorganisms done in

---

12. These propositions express the main themes in Schumpeter's 1934 *The Theory of Economic Development* and the 1912 German edition from which it was drawn, *Theorie der wirtschaftlichen Entwicklung.* Thus it serves as a window onto Schumpeter's theoretical perspective in the 1900s—a decade or two before the "moderns" of the interwar years, notably Friedrich Hayek. Influenced by Hayek's work, Schumpeter came around in his 1942 *Capitalism, Socialism and Democracy* to believing that companies in the business sector, not just scientists in royal courts and universities, could be creative in conceiving successful innovations. In his mind, though, they needed industrial labs employing scientists to do it.

1675; Isaac Newton's 1687 mechanics; Pierre Simon Laplace's mathematics work around 1785; and Eugenio Espejo's 1795 work on pathogens. Is it plausible, though, that the findings and subsequent research of a handful of scientists in London and Oxford, and a few other sites, were the forces that propelled the explosive take-offs into sustained growth?

There are ample reasons to be skeptical of this thesis. It boggles the mind to think that the scientific discoveries during and after the Enlightenment had applications so comprehensive and profound as to triple the take-off nations' productivities and real wages in less than a century—and in *most* industries, not just a few—when all the world's past discoveries could do almost nothing to raise productivity. For one thing, the new scientific findings were just additions to a vast storehouse already there. Newton himself insisted that he and all scientists were "standing on the shoulders of giants." For another, the new findings may have had scant applicability to the economy's production; the scientists' discoveries enabled new products and methods only accidentally. Furthermore, most innovating—obviously in entertainment industries, fashion, and tourism—is remote from science. Where it is not, innovation often goes first: the steam engine preceded thermodynamics. The historian Joel Mokyr found that in cases in which entrepreneurs could have used some scientific understanding, the innovators typically ventured ahead of science, using their hunches and experimenting accordingly.

Schumpeter's scientism goes on to credit science with the rise of economic knowledge right through the 19th century. But this is equally problematic when tested against another kind of evidence. Any important new piece of scientific knowledge is accessible in scholarly publications at little or no cost—it is for this reason that it is called a public good. Scientific knowledge, therefore, tends to be roughly equalized across countries. So if we were to accept advances in scientific knowledge as the major explanation of the huge increases in economic knowledge in the take-off nations, it would then be very hard to explain the mounting disparities (starting from rough equality in 1820) in economic knowledge over the 19th century—the Great Divergence, as it has been dubbed. It would be necessary to string together a half dozen ad hoc explanations to account for Britain's early, unsustainable lead, followed by America's durable lead, Belgium's and France's advances, and Germany's progress late in the game. It would be necessary to explain from the perspective of scientism how America left France in its dust, then blew past Belgium and finally overtook Britain, when America was the country least schooled in science and, being exceptionally far geographically from the others, had least access to scientific discoveries. It would be an even greater challenge to explain how the Netherlands and Italy remained at the starting gate, despite their sophistication in science. (Schumpeterian historians might hypothesize that those two nations fell short in entrepreneurial spirit and financial expertise. But Schumpeter himself could not have expressed such doubts after building his theory on the zeal of entrepreneurs and the knowledgeability of financiers.)

We must conclude that advances in science could not have been the driving force behind the explosion of economic knowledge in the 19th century.

Some historians give the credit to the inventions of the applied scientists emerging during the Enlightenment—the most famous being the headline inventions of the so-called First Industrial Revolution. In Britain, examples include Richard Arkwright's 1762 water-powered spinning frame; the 1764 multispool spinning machine credited to the humble Lancashire weaver James Hargreaves; the improved steam engine designed by the firm of Boulton & Watt in 1769; the method for producing wrought iron from pig iron developed by the iron mill of Cort & Jellicoe in the 1780s; and the steam-powered locomotive invented in 1814 by George Stephenson. In America, John Fitch's 1778 steamboat comes to mind. There is no reason for these historians to focus on headline innovations, however. The advances too tiny to be recorded may well have added up to an amount of innovation—measured by the gain in output or wages—far larger than the total innovation prompted by the standout inventions. We may assume that the historians of the Industrial Revolution recounted the headline inventions only to make vivid the restless inventiveness that began to spread in Britain starting in the 1760s. But can we really interpret these inventions as drivers of advances in scientific knowledge—advances scored on the ground, rather than in the ivory tower? And were they drivers of the explosions of economic knowledge in the 19th century?

A point against this thesis is the fact that nearly all the inventors, even the headliners, were not trained scientists, nor were they even particularly well educated. Watt was the exception, not the rule. Arkwright was a wigmaker turned industrialist, not a scientist or engineer. Hargreaves, a Lancashire weaver, was of humble background—too humble to have invented the spinning machine. The great Stephenson was virtually illiterate. Paul Johnson observes that the vast majority of inventors were born poor and could afford little education. It was enough to be creative and smart:

> The Industrial Revolution, which first developed in the 1780s when
> Stephenson was a little boy, is often presented as a time of horror for
> working men. In fact it was the age, above all, in history of matchless

opportunities for penniless men with powerful brains and imaginations, and it is astonishing how quickly they came to the fore.[13]

This characterization of the headline inventors undoubtedly also applied to inventors of the myriad advances in methods that, being tiny, went unsung. So if the historians pointing to the famed inventions thought that their inventors were vessels bearing new scientific knowledge to the fertile field of 19th-century economies, they were sadly mistaken. Furthermore, this scientism does not explain why the explosion of inventions began early in the 19th century, and not before or after, and why the explosion occurred in some high-income nations and not others.

Some might think to say that gifted inventors, even if untrained, were adding to scientific knowledge when their tinkering led to an invention. But these inventors did not create *scientific* knowledge any more than bartenders inventing new drinks create chemical knowledge: they lacked the training to do so. An addition to scientific knowledge occurred if and when trained theorists managed to understand why the invention worked. (It took a musicologist to see how Bach's cantatas "worked.") If an invention at the proof-of-concept stage went on to be developed and adopted, thus becoming an innovation, it did create *economic* knowledge. (Failure also added knowledge of a sort—the economic knowledge of what apparently does not work.)

To regard inventions as the driver of economic knowledge is misleading by suggesting that they are exogenous forces acting on the economy. (Even an accidental discovery happens and has impact only if the discoverer is in the right place at the right time.) The inventions made famous by the major innovations they led to were not prime causes—not thunderbolts from outside the economic system. They were born out of perceptions of business needs or an inspired sense of what businesses and consumers would like to have—all drawn from the innovators' experience and guesswork in the business world. James Watt may have been a pure engineer at heart but his partner, Matthew Boulton, demanded a steam engine that would be widely useful. Invention and the curiosity and ingenuity behind it were nothing new, after all. What

13. Johnson, *The Birth of the Modern* (p. 188). Few would want to question the judgments made by this polymath in any of his several fields. Yet it is highly eccentric to conceive of the First Industrial Revolution as starting in the 1780s rather than the 1760s and unusual to conceive of it as stretching to the 1820s. (Some of the most important inventions and succeeding innovations of the Second Industrial Revolution, starting with the Bessemer process and the Siemens-Martin open hearth processes, were significantly science-based. But even here scientific advances were not generally the drivers of the inventions and certainly do not account for the greater part of aggregate innovation.)

was new, and tied up with the deeper causes, were the changes that inspired, encouraged, and enabled people to invent on a mass scale.

The headline innovations rarely move the mountain that is the economy. The brilliant innovations of Britain's 18th-century textile industry led to great gains in output per worker but, the textile industry being a small part of the economy, could not cause more than a very modest increase in output per worker in Britain's economy as a whole (so modest that output per worker barely increased, if at all, from 1750 to 1800). In the same vein, the economic historian Robert Fogel shook up his fellow historians with his thesis that American economic development would have proceeded as well without the railroads. The fruits of the Industrial Revolution are all one-off—one-time events rather than manifestations of a system or a process. They do not explain either the spectacular take-off in Britain or later take-offs. As Mokyr wrote, "[t]he Industrial Revolution itself, in the classical sense, did not suffice to generate sustained economic growth."[14]

We must conclude that neither the stirring voyages of discovery nor the splendid discoveries in science and the headline inventions that followed could be the cause of the steep and sustained climbs of productivity and wages in the 19th century in the take-off economies of Western Europe and North America. Rather, the explosions of economic knowledge in the 19th century must be the effect of the emergence of an entirely new kind of economy: a system for the generation of endogenous innovation decade after decade as long as the system continues to function. Only the structuring of these economies for the exercise of indigenous creativity and pathways from there to innovation—for what has come to be called "indigenous innovation"—could have put these nations on steep paths of sustained growth. If there was a fundamental "invention" here, it was the fashioning of economies that drew on the creativity and intuition that lay inside them to attempt innovation. These were the world's first modern economies. Their economic dynamism made them the marvel of the modern era.

---

14. He adds:
    It is easy to imagine the economies of the West settling into the techniques [of producing throstles, wrought iron, coke-smelting, and stationary steam engines] that had emerged between 1750 and 1800 without taking them much further. Such a development would have paralleled the wave of inventions of the 15th century, with the printing press, the three-masted ship and iron-casting settling into dominant designs and the process of improvement slowing down to a trickle subsequently.
See Mokyr's 2007 Max Weber Lecture, "The Industrial Revolution and Modern Economic Growth," p. 3.

We do not have to infer from data on productivity growth the presence (or absence) of dynamism—as physics inferred the existence of dark matter and dark energy. The revolution in the societies possessing take-off economies went far beyond the unprecedented phenomenon of sustained—and apparently sustainable—growth. As pioneering entrepreneurs multiplied, ultimately overshadowing merchants, and as more and more people were tinkering with methods and products or dreaming up new ones, the experience of work changed radically for increasing numbers of participants. From retail trade to textiles to Tin Pan Alley, masses of people in society were active in conceiving, creating, evaluating, and trying out the new and learning from the experience.

In this way, the modern economies brought to a society something of the "heroic spirit" that Smith hoped to see, such as standing out from the crowd and rising to a challenge. These economies also brought to ordinary people of varying talents a kind of flourishing—the experience of engagement, personal growth, and fulfillment. Even people with few and modest talents—barely enough talent to get a job—were given the experience of using their minds: to seize an opportunity, solve a problem, and think of a new way or a new thing. In short, dynamism's spark created modern life.

These modern economies, present and past—their rewards and costs, the preconditions for their rise, how some of them were unseated, their justification, and now, the weakening among the remaining ones—these are the subject of this book.

PART ONE

THE EXPERIENCE
OF THE MODERN ECONOMY

He was . . . a prey to homesickness for his own kind, for his own epoch, for European man and his glorious history of desire and dreams.

WILLA CATHER, *Death Comes for the Archbishop*

CHAPTER ONE

How the Modern Economies
Got Their Dynamism

The secret of brilliant productivity will always be discovering new problems and intuiting new theorems, which open the way to new results and connections. Without the creation of new viewpoints, without positing new aims, mathematics would soon exhaust itself in the rigor of logical proofs and begin to stagnate, as it would run out of content. In a way, mathematics has been best served by those who distinguished themselves more by intuitions than by rigorous proofs.

FELIX KLEIN, *Lectures on Mathematics in the 19th Century*

P ART ONE SEES THE FIRST MODERN ECONOMIES as lying at the core of the modern societies that arose in the West early in the 19th century. Their unprecedented dynamism was mirrored by dynamism in other realms of society as well. The narrative describes how these economies changed not only living and working standards but also the very character of life: dynamism manifests itself in manifold ways. The narrative goes on to examine how and why these history-making economies came about.

A modern economy, as that term is used here, means not a present-day economy but rather an economy with a considerable degree of dynamism— that is, the will and the capacity and aspiration to innovate. One may ask, then, what makes a modern economy modern, just as one may ask what makes modern music modern. If a national economy is a complex of economic institutions and a fabric of economic attitudes—an economic culture—what structure of these elements equipped and fueled the modern economies for dynamism? To begin, it is necessary to be clear about the concept of dynamism and its relation to growth, with which it is often confused.

Innovation, Dynamism, and Growth

An innovation, to repeat, is a new method or new product that becomes a *new practice* somewhere in the world.[1] The new practice may arise in just one nation, before it spreads, or in a community that cuts across nations. Any such innovation involves both the *origination* of the new thing—its conception and its development—and the *pioneering adoption*. Thus innovations depend on a *system*. Innovative people and companies are just the beginning. To have good prospects for innovation, a society requires people with the expertise and experience to judge well whether to attempt development of a new thing; whether a proposed project is worth financing; and whether, when a new product or method is developed, it is worth trying.

Until recent decades, the innovation system was supposed to be the national economy. To innovate, a nation had to do its own development as well as its own adoption. But in a global economy, in which national economies are open to outside developments, the development could take place in one country and the adoption in another. If an innovation, joint or singlehanded, is then adopted by another country, that adoption is not regarded as an innovation—not from a global perspective. Yet selecting foreign products that would have good prospects of acceptance at home might require as much insight as selecting among new conceptions to develop. The distinction between innovation and imitation is basic, but the line between may be fuzzy.

We must also understand the concept of an economy's dynamism. It is a compound of the deep set forces and facilities behind innovation: the drive to change things, the talent for it, and the receptivity to new things, as well as the enabling institutions. Thus dynamism, as it is used here, is the willingness and capacity to innovate, leaving aside current conditions and obstacles. This contrasts with what is usually called vibrancy: an alertness to opportunities, a readiness to act, and the zeal to "get it done" (as Schumpeter puts it). Dynamism determines the normal volume of innovation. Other determinants, such as market conditions, may alter the results. And there can be a drought of new ideas or a gush of them, just as a composer may have a dry or fertile spell. So the pace of actual innovation may exhibit marked swings without any change in dynamism—in the normal tendency to innovate. Post-war Europe saw a

---

1. This usage is not universal but is increasingly common. An example is Denning and Dunham, *The Innovator's Way* (2010). To economists, ever since Schumpeter's 1912 work, an innovation has meant a new practice, not just a new development. (For him, development and adoption went hand in hand, both being a sure thing.) Scientists tend to call the invention of a new method or product an innovation whether or not buyers are found for it.

sprinkling of innovation in the 1960s —the bikini, the Nouvelle Vague, and the Beatles, for example. By 1980, though, with wealth having recovered to its old level relative to income, innovation had fallen back. It became apparent that the dynamism of Europe had not recovered, even partially, to its healthy level in the interwar years, although that became clear only with mounting evidence.

One way to measure this dynamism is to gauge the aforementioned forces and facilities—the inputs producing dynamism. Another approach is to gauge the size of its estimated output: the average annual volume of innovation in recent years—the growth of total GDP not attributable to the growth of capital and labor—after allowance for unusual market conditions and after deducting the "false innovations" copied from other countries. The decadal average income earned by those in the innovation process, if we could observe it, would be a crude measure of that "output." Or we could size up many strands of circumstantial evidence: new firm formation, employee turnover, turnover in the 20 largest companies, turnover of retail stores, and the mean life of a product's universal product code.

The economic growth rate of a country is *not* a useful measure of dynamism. In a global economy driven by one or more economies of high dynamism, an economy with low or even no dynamism may regularly enjoy much the same growth rate as that of the highflying moderns—the same growth rate of productivity, real wages, and other economic indicators. It grows that fast partly by trading with the highflyers but mainly by being vibrant enough to imitate the adoptions of original products in modern economies. Italy provides a nice example: from 1890 to 1913, output per manhour there grew at the same rate as in America—it remained 43 percent lower, neither gaining nor losing ground in the *league tables* (the rankings of countries by the relative levels of their productivity (e.g., output per hour worked) and real wages), but no economic historian would suggest that Italy's economy had much dynamism at all, let alone the American level.

An economy with low dynamism might for a time show a faster growth rate than a modern economy does with its high dynamism. A transient elevation of the growth rate could result from any of a number of structural shifts in the economy, such as an increase in vibrancy or an increase in dynamism from low to not-as-low. While the economy is moving up to a higher place in the league tables—a partial "catch-up" to the modern economies—it will be growing at the normal, global, rate plus a transient, which fades away as the destination nears. But even a growth rate that is the world's highest should not suggest that the economy has just acquired high dynamism, let alone the highest. Sweden provides a good example. It held the world cup for the championship growth rate of productivity from 1890 to 1913. It started a raft of new companies, several of which endured and became famous. But it did not appear to acquire the high dynamism of America or, say, Germany. In ensuing decades its growth rate dropped below that of America and not one new firm has entered the top 10 on the stock exchange after 1922 even to this day. Japan's high growth from 1950 to 1990 is another example. Many observers inferred high dynamism, but this streak of growth reflected not the advent of state-of-the-art modernity throughout Japan—no such transformation occurred—but rather the chance to import or imitate practices pioneered for decades by the modern economies. The world-record growth in China since 1978 is the latest example: while the world sees world-class dynamism, the Chinese discuss how to *acquire* the dynamism for indigenous innovation, without which they will be hard pressed to continue their fast growth.

So a nation's "dynamism" is not a new word for a nation's productivity growth. Its own dynamism is not necessary for its growth if the rest of the world has dynamism—vibrancy is enough; and it is not sufficient if the nation is so small that its dynamism cannot go far. Dynamism over an appreciable part of the world leads to global growth, barring bad luck. The modern economies, with their high dynamism, are the engines of the growth of the global economy—today, as in the 19th century.

So, although the growth rate of productivity in an economy—say, output per manhour—over a month or even a year is no indicator of its own dynamism, we might think that the *level* of its productivity relative to the levels abroad would be an indicator. It is true, with few exceptions, if any, that the economies with productivity levels at or very close to the top level owe that position to a high level of dynamism. Yet a low position of a country's productivity level may reflect low dynamism *or* low vibrancy or both. So the relative level of productivity is not an altogether safe indicator of an economy's dynamism.

To gauge more deeply an economy's dynamism, we have to look under the hood to see what there is in the structure of an economy that might strongly nourish or inhibit dynamism.

Inner Workings of the Historical Modern Economies

Schumpeter's near-classical theory, with its concept of punctuated equilibrium, blocked all thoughts of a modern economy—an economy generating economic knowledge through its own talent and insight into the business of innovating. The dominance of this theory has had consequences: to this day, policymakers and commentators do not distinguish between modern economies, less modern ones, and nonmodern ones. They see all national economies, even exemplars of modernity, as essentially machines for producing products and doing so more or less efficiently at that—though some have natural handicaps or costly policies.

But if we just look, we can see the distinctive stuff that modern economies are made of: It is *ideas.* The visible "goods and services" of the national income statistics are mostly embodiments of past ideas. The modern economy is primarily engaged in activity aimed at innovation. These activities are stages in a process:

- conception of new products or methods
- preparation of proposals to develop some of them
- selection of some development proposals for financing
- development of the chosen products or methods
- marketing of the new products or methods
- evaluation and possible tryout by end-users
- significant adoption of some new products and methods
- revision of new products after tryout or early adoption

In an economy of substantial size, there are gains in expertise from a Smithian division of labor, and innovational activity is no exception: some participants work full-time in a team conceiving and designing a new products, some work in a financial company picking new companies to fund, some work with a start-up entrepreneur developing a new product, some are employees specializing in evaluating new methods, others specialize in marketing, and so forth. No less important, in an economy of dynamism, some portion of most participants' time is spent looking at current practice with the expectation that a new idea will occur for a better way to do things or a better thing to produce. This patchwork of activity is the *ideas sector.* In an economy high in dynamism, the idea-driven activity might amount to a tenth of total manhours worked. However, the work of investing in new ideas and new practices—though it may crowd out work in some familiar lines of investment activity—may spark a boundless amount of investment activity aimed at producing facilities to make the new products. The result is a strongly positive effect on employment. (Innovative activity in particular and investment activity in general are far more labor intensive, hence less capital intensive, than the production of consumer goods: food production, for example, uses much capital, such as wire fences, and much energy; energy production also uses much capital, such as derricks, dams, and windmills.)[2]

How do these modern economies *work*—those of the 19th and the 20th century too? We may begin at an almost physiological level, rather like Henry Gray's *Anatomy* (1862). We see in these modern economies multiple lines of innovative activity. These are parallel efforts, which represent the competition of ideas. In an economy of appreciable size, new commercial ideas are hatched every day, mostly inside enterprises. Development of such ideas will generally require enterprises with the right expertise. Among the projects with an eager entrepreneur, not all will find financial backing. Capital flows only to those projects judged by an entrepreneur and a financial backer to have good prospects of development and marketing. Among the projects carried forward, not all will manage to embody the idea in a product that would be cheap enough to be marketable. Among the new products brought to the market, sales or orders will come in only for those judged by end-users—managers or consumers—to be worth the risk of a pioneering adoption. Only a small proportion will show signs of wide enough adoption to continue production or to warrant stepping up production to break-even or profitable levels. This *selection mechanism* may leave one idea standing where there were thousands to begin with. (A study by McKinsey estimated that, from 10,000 business ideas, 1,000 firms are founded, 100 receive venture capital, 20 go on to raise capital in an initial public offering of shares, and 2 become market leaders.)

We can picture the corresponding competition going on in a socialist economy: the "enterprises" are state-owned, and the backing comes from a state development bank. We can also picture the corresponding competition in a corporatist economy: the enterprises, though under private ownership, are state-controlled, and their finances are allocated by state-controlled banks. However, the modern economies of the storied past possessed neither one of these structures. The modern economies of the past two centuries—primarily those of Britain, America, Germany, and France—were, and to varying degrees still are, specimens of *modern* capitalism.

In these real-life modern economies—and in any modern-capitalist economy—decisions to provide capital for the first steps toward innovation are made predominantly by investors, financiers, and share buyers drawing

---

2. The Austrian-born Fritz Machlup did some early work on measuring the importance of the industries aimed at producing new economic knowledge. The estimate above is not a precise calculation but is not just an impression either.

on their own private wealth or by managers of financial companies under private ownership. The collected investments and loans of these "capitalists," some of them with very small wealth, determine which directions, among those presented, the economy will embark on. Decisions to take the initiative of planning and seeking finance for development of a new idea are made predominantly by producers—managers by trade—starting a private venture or acting within established private enterprises. To distinguish producers of such undertakings from producers of established products, the former are called *entrepreneurs*. Typically, the entrepreneurs also bring some capital to the new undertaking. Both a project's entrepreneur and its investors stand to gain whatever pecuniary returns the project might bring and suffer the loss should the returns be negative. Of course, these returns are not determined in isolation: such projects compete against others, driving down the private returns and driving up rents to land and wages to labor. The pecuniary return is not unimportant to an investor with a large stake or to an entrepreneur—their livelihoods and standard of living may be at stake. An entrepreneur may need the prospect of winnings to obtain the moral support of family members.

The prospect of profit, which entrepreneurs and investors share after paying creditors, is not the only prospective return factored into the decision to start a new undertaking. Both entrepreneurs and large-stake investors favor projects that excite their imagination and enlist their energies. They may also want to play a part in the development of the community or the nation.[3] (Some entrepreneurs and financiers create enterprises primarily for the satisfaction of producing a social benefit—on top of whatever pecuniary return may be expected. These "social entrepreneurs" may coexist alongside the classic entrepreneurs, whether or not they are financed by the state. To the extent that this parallel system has dynamism, it helps make modern economies modern.)

It is unfortunate that most discussions, except for trivial distinctions like that between ships and factories, do not distinguish modern capitalism from

---

3. Do entrepreneurs generally receive large nonpecuniary returns? Schumpeter was skeptical. He writes poignantly of the successful entrepreneur who finds that admittance to polite society will not be one of the rewards. He also thought that the average realized pecuniary return of entrepreneurs was below normal: they were too sanguine or paid a steep price to have some fun. Now there appears to be a consensus that, even in the unromantic 20th century, modern entrepreneurs as a group find big nonpecuniary rewards—"the time of their lives," as some put it; but perhaps at some cost to their cash flow. None of this matters for how the modern economy *works,* however.

mercantile capitalism (also known as early capitalism or commercial society). Modern capitalism built on early capitalism, of course. The latter solidified property rights; won acceptance of interest, profit, and wealth-building; and taught the social value of individual responsibility. Mercantile capitalism also gave birth (in Venice and Augsburg) to banks that lent to or entered into business. But modern capitalism is as different from mercantile capitalism as innovators are different from merchants. The mercantile economy was about the distribution of products to consumers. (To exaggerate slightly, men and women scooped up nature's crops and took the excess supplies to market to exchange them for excess supplies of other crops.) Modern capitalism introduced innovation into capitalism. Entrepreneurs soon put merchants in the shade. As new practices welled up, many guilds founded in medieval times could not enforce standards. The state could not issue charters fast enough to meet the exploding demand.

Even more unfortunate, economies around the world that repress competition by limiting entry to the well-connected and do nothing else that might encourage or facilitate innovation are being seen as examples of capitalism by those suffering hardships in those economies as well as those who run the economies. (The American economy is seen as an "exceptional" case of capitalism.) In northern Africa, a tightly connected ring of politicians, elites, and the armed forces keep the business sector for themselves: outsiders are not licensed to enter industries in competition with incumbent enterprises. These economies are said to be "capitalist" on the thought that "capital" is in charge—the wealth of the oligarchy of the ruling families. But a hallmark of capitalism is that the capitalists are independent, uncoordinated, and competing with one another: no monarchy or oligarchy is in charge. And a hallmark of modern capitalism is that it permits and invites outsiders with a new idea to seek capital from capitalists willing to place a bet on the proposed project. These oligarchic economies are more accurately viewed as a kind of *corporatism,* a system in which the business sector is under some kind of political control.

This chapter began by asking what structure "equipped and fueled" the modern economies for dynamism. The discussion so far has cast some light on how the modern economies are equipped to select among new ideas for development and adoption. But what fuels the creation of new ideas?

The very concept of new economic ideas has been foreign to the rising numbers under the spell of scientism, which came to rule academia in the 20th century—not to mention historicism, which ruled out any new ideas! As noted in the Introduction, the German Historical School supposed that only scientists have new ideas, which, after testing, often add to scientific knowledge. That theory never worked well: from the time of Columbus to Isaac Newton's era there was little innovation and between the steam engine and electric power there was no epochal scientific advance. But the failure of a theory is not enough to stop it. Schumpeter, some 30 years after his first book, reaffirmed that only scientists can have ideas, allowing that they could have their ideas in the great industrial labs, such as DuPont.[4] The popular theory today is neo-German: gifted conceivers of new technology "platforms," such as Tim Berners-Lee, creator of the World Wide Web; Jack Kilby and Robert Noyce, the builders of the microchip; and Charles Babbage, inventor of the computer, are thought to provide the underlying advances that make possible successive waves of applications. This scientism easily persuaded the public. No one had to ask where scientists and engineers "get their ideas," since everyone knew they got their ideas from their observations in the lab and the findings reported in research journals. The investigators and experimenters are immersed in their science and engineering fields—though no more than entrepreneurs and financiers are immersed in their fields.

But the advent of the modern economy brought a metamorphosis: a modern economy turns people who are close to the *economy*, where they are apt to be struck by new commercial ideas, into the investigators and experimenters who manage the innovation process from development and, in many cases, adoption as well. (In a role reversal, scientists and engineers are called in to assist on technical matters.) In fact, it turns all sorts of people into "idea-men," financiers into thinkers, producers into marketers, and end-users into pioneers. The driving force of the modern economy in the past two centuries is this economic system—a system built of an economic culture as well as economic institutions. This system, rather than the brilliant *personaggi* of the popular theory, generates the modern economy's dynamism.

The modern economy, then, is a vast *imaginarium*—a space for imagining new products and methods, imagining how they might be made, imagining

---

4. See his 1942 monograph *Capitalism, Socialism and Democracy*. The brilliant 1912 book with which Schumpeter made his name portrayed his subject as an infallible machine, one that had no creativity but could promptly and faultlessly seize every opportunity for profitable investment soon after it arose. The 1942 book with which he closed his career went further in concluding that corporate managements could promptly and faultlessly seize opportunities for technological advances. That led to the question, if corporate managements could do it, why not state agencies and socialist enterprises? That may have deepened Schumpeter's feeling at the end of his career that the Western world was on an inexorable "march into socialism."

how they might be used. Its innovation process draws on human resources not utilized by a premodern economy. In Schumpeter's theory, premodern development draws on the capacities of premodern entrepreneurs to organize the projects made possible by outside discoveries—he spoke of human resources like hustle and the determination to "get the job done." As modern theorists have said, *modern* entrepreneurs are business owners or managers who, in the face of not very much real knowledge, micro or macro, demonstrate "a capacity for making successful decisions when no obviously correct model or decision rule is available"—nor can be—as a 1990 essay by Mark Casson put it. This capacity, which relies on financiers as well as entrepreneurs, is recognized to require the resources called *judgment,* or acumen—judgment about the unknown likelihood of things—and *wisdom*—the sense that there are forces not even conceived of, called the unknown unknowns. This judgment involves imagining in an effort to foresee the consequences of alternative actions. This entrepreneurial capacity is *modern entrepreneurship*. But it is not by itself a source of radical change or even novelty. It is not the same as *innovatorship*.

The indigenous innovation process of the imaginarium draws on a different set of human resources. A basic resource is the *imaginativeness*, or *creativity*, to conceive of things not conceived already that a firm could try to develop and market. There cannot be much departure from present knowledge if no one can imagine the existence of another way or another goal, or if no one can imagine the chance of beneficial outcomes. Imaginativeness is fundamental to successful change, as David Hume saw in his profound work so fundamental to the modern era.[5] The innovative capacity also requires *insight*—insight into a new direction that might turn out to meet desires or needs that could not have been known before. That insight is often called strategic vision—an intuition we cannot explain and a sense of whether other enterprises will be adopting the same strategy. Steve Jobs owed his huge success to his creativity and deep insights. Curiosity to explore and the courage to do something different must also be mentioned.

Yet no imaginarium will be present in economies where people are not motivated and encouraged to innovate or are not in a position to innovate.

---

5. Hume's great themes—the necessity of imagination for discovery or change, the importance and legitimacy of sentiment or "passions" in human decisions, and the danger of depending on past patterns to hold up in the future, all in his 1748 masterpiece *An Enquiry Concerning Human Understanding*—can be seen as prefiguring the modernity to come, in which imagination would run wild, the growth of knowledge would be rampant, and the future would be barely recognizable.

The fuel on which this system operates is a mixture of pecuniary and non-pecuniary motives. Pecuniary rewards make a difference: The prospects of significant money are apt to be helpful in persuading one's family to support the effort one may have to put in. So few participants in the economy will be available to conceive and develop a commercial idea if not legally free to monetize it—to sell it to an entrepreneur for a share of the resulting profit or, in the case of patentable concepts, to collect the royalties under the patent or sell the patent to others. Entrepreneurs and investors will not develop an idea if they are not legally free to start a firm, break into an industry, sell their shares in the firm later (nowadays in an initial public offering), and close down the company in the event that buyers do not turn up. Entrepreneurs have to know that potential end-users are free to abandon a current method or product in order to cast their lot with a new method or product. Without the incentive of such pecuniary protections and inducements, most entrepreneurs will draw back from undertaking such ventures, no matter the non-pecuniary rewards.

Some nonpecuniary motives, or drives, are also important—perhaps critical—for the functioning of the modern economy. To function, the modern economy feeds off a motivating economic culture as well as pecuniary incentives. High dynamism in a society requires people who grew up with attitudes and beliefs that attract them to opportunities that they expect will excite them with their novelty, intrigue them with their mysteries, challenge them with new hurdles, and inspire them with new vistas. It requires people in business brought up to *use* their imaginativeness and insightfulness to achieve a new direction; entrepreneurs driven by their desire to make their mark; people in venture investing willing to act on a hunch ("I like the cut of her jib"); and many end-users—consumers or producers—with the willingness to *pioneer* the adoption of a new product or method whose expected value is not knowable beforehand. This requires drives such as aspiration, curiosity, and self-expression. High dynamism in the system requires high dynamism in all its parts.[6]

6. Various observers have written on the subject. In Somerset Maugham's 1929 story, "The Man Who Made His Mark," a man fresh out of a job, noticing that the neighborhood has no tobacconist, has the drive to restart his life by opening a tobacco shop there. End-users, too, must share in the dynamism of Maugham's tobacconist. What became known as the Nelson-Phelps model of the adoption of an innovation, published in 1966, was an early attempt to highlight end-users in the innovation process, such as farmers risking adoption of new seeds and fertilizers. The focus there was on the importance of end-users' education. Amar Bhidé in his 2008 book focused on the need for "venturesome" end-users.

Innovating also draws on people's observations and personal knowledge. New business ideas come only to those who have been observing at close hand some area of a business, learning things about how it works and giving some thought to the possible size of the market for a new sort of product in that area or to the prospect for a better method of production; plausible business ideas rarely come to those remote from any business. People situated in some area of the business sector will gain knowledge and see opportunities that they would not otherwise have been aware of—or have known existed.

Hitting upon an idea for better use for retail space or a better route for delivering packages is not exactly what we mean by innovation. Yet, it may be argued, the detailed business knowledge that inspires new ideas for business investment also inspires ideas that may lead to business innovation. (Similarly, the attitudes that help stir the formation of new investment ideas also stir ideas for innovation.)

So there is an obvious answer to the question of where business people's ideas for innovation come from: they come from the business sector. Business people draw on their personal observation and private knowledge, in combination with the shared pool of public knowledge (such as economics), in coming up with conceptualizations that lead to a new method or product that might "work"—much as a scientist, immersed in his or her own experimental data, specialized expertise, and general scientific knowledge, arrives at a new formulation or hypothesis to be tested, which might add to scientific knowledge. Business people and scientists alike draw on private knowledge, based on individual observation, as well as on the public knowledge of the community to which the individual belongs. (Yet scientists will undoubtedly go on believing that business people get their ideas from outside business, just as most people say that composers get their ideas outside music. Giving the lie to this common illusion, Robert Craft reported an exchange between reporters and Igor Stravinsky: "Maestro, can you tell us where you get your ideas?" "At the piano," Stravinsky shot back.)

Friedrich Hayek, the Austrian-born economist who loomed large in the Austrian school, was the first economist to view economies from this perspective. His seminal works from 1933 to 1945 see producers and buyers in the complex economies around him as having valuable practical knowledge about how best to produce and what best to produce. Typically, such knowledge, being local, contextual, and kaleidoscopic, cannot be easily acquired by or communicated to others: it remains private knowledge. (Even if all of it were all costlessly accessible—open to the public—it is too enormous to be comprehended, let alone assimilated.) Therefore such knowledge is, and remains, dispersed over the economy's participants, each industry having much knowledge unique to the industry and each participant some further knowledge unique to that individual or to a very few. This leads to two propositions: First, an economy of complexity gains critically from markets, in which individuals and companies can exchange goods and services with one another, so that the specialization of practical knowledge can continue—so one does not need to be a jack-of-all-trades with only the thinnest knowledge of any. When new knowledge is obtained in an industry, this is "communicated" to society through the market mechanism: a drop in price, or the like. Second, such an economy, if unimpeded, is an organism ever-acquiring gains in economic knowledge of what and how to produce (while also deaccessing old knowledge once it is of no further use). The right prices are "discovered" in the process. Every company or participant is like a forward observer, or scout ant, responding alertly with adjustments in the level or direction of production to observations and analyses of any local development. If the output of some product is increased, the reduced price on the market will signal the society that it now costs less than before.[7] This was Hayek's *knowledge economy.*

Yet this work of Hayek is not about innovations. It does not envisage indigenous innovations, which develop from ideas sparked by the creativity of participants in the economy. In a much-cited 1945 paper, he makes it explicit that he is discussing *adaptations*—"adaptations," he calls them, to "changing circumstances." These adaptations do draw on some of the human resources of modern entrepreneurship mentioned earlier: judgment, and wisdom, and the drive to make their mark.

There is an air of predictability about adaptations, unlike innovations. They do not involve an intuitive leap but are repercussions that would take place sooner or later, barring some other change that erased the need for the adaptation. And they will not go on long if "circumstances" should stop "changing." They are not disruptive: they bring closure to a disruption rather than causing

---

7. This work begins with Hayek's 1937 presidential address to the London Economic Club, "Economics and Knowledge," and ends with his much-cited 1945 paper "The Use of Knowledge in Society," which has the notion of "changing circumstances." These and other papers collected in his *Individualism and Economic Order* (1948) were conceived in the period from the 1920s until almost the 1950s, when socialism and corporatism were hotly debated by many European economists. The present chapter, though, is focused on how Hayek's views contributed to the understanding of modern capitalism. Chapter 5 takes up the debate over socialism and Chapter 6 the modern economy's struggle with corporatism.

new disruptions. In contrast, innovations (from *nova*, Latin for new) are not determinate from current knowledge, thus are not foreseeable. Being new, they could not have been known before. Yet many business people have the mistaken notion that innovation means going out to find out what their customers want. The fallacy that innovations are foreseen is criticized by Walter Vincenti:

> The "technical imperative" of the retractable landing gear is . . . after-the-fact. Designers at the time, by their own testimony, did not foresee it. . . . Innovators see where they want to go and by what means they propose to get there. What they cannot do, if their idea is novel, is *foresee* with certainty whether it will work in the sense of meeting all the relevant requirements.[8]

Being unforeseen, an innovation may be disruptive, creating a new jigsaw puzzle in which to fit the pieces—to which to adapt. Innovations are the happenings to which "adaptations" adapt. (A big adaptation that comes far sooner than supposed could be disruptive.) An innovation may be ephemeral, yet most innovations tomorrow stand on the shoulders of today's innovations. Cumulatively they drive the economy's "practice" on a path to ports-of-call that would otherwise have gone unseen. Thus innovations pass a more demanding test than adaptations do.

Innovations, while requiring the intellectual faculties of imaginativeness and insight to envision a new objective, may also require the boldness to venture into unknown territory and thus to go in a different direction from one's peers and mentors. This causes us to see innovators as heroes—putting creation ahead of their comforts and braving failure and losses. However, there is no reason to think that innovators love risk. The Minnesota innovators Harold and Owen Bradley said that an innovation springs from conceiving a new *model* of the business or of the world in some respect. So it may be that innovators, whether the founders of companies or gifted CEOs or the pioneer end-users, are driven by an inner need to demonstrate to themselves or to others the superiority of their understanding.

Henry Ford's quest for the mass-produced car is a paradigm case of innovation. In the 2011 lecture "Eureka," Harold Evans told the story:

> Many Americans believe Henry Ford invented the car. Of course, he was preceded in Europe and by others in America and even in his home town of Detroit. He said: "I invented nothing. I simply assembled into a car the discoveries of other men." In fact, he did do something startlingly new.

8. Vincenti, "The Retractable Airplane Landing Gear" (1994, pp. 21–22).

> Not so much in originating the automatic production line; an assembly
> line that multiplied milling productivity fivefold was devised by Oliver
> Evans in 1795 . . . Henry Ford's genius lay in an idea—the egalitarian idea
> that everyone should have a car.

Although some people did not view Ford as highly innovative, like Ford himself, his breakthrough was a farsighted vision of a new way of life, which he proved realizable. Another instructive story is America's glorious cross-country railroad. Evans's 2004 book *They Made America* discusses it:

> Theodore Judah, of Sacramento, had the boldness to entrepreneur and
> engineer America's first transcontinental railway. His wife Anna wrote
> that "it . . . show[ed] what was in the man . . . to grasp the gigantic and the
> daring." Detractors said that the idea had been around for years and it was
> "just a matter of time" till the railway was built.

As Evans remarks, Judah's engineering feat was felt by some to be too foreseeable to be classed as an innovation. Yet it was only the *attempt* at construction that was "just a matter of time." *Success* was in doubt. Many engineers thought that such a direct railway to northern California was not feasible. So the successful construction was by no means foreseeable. Judah had a stunning intuition and proved he was right.

Some innovations are accidental. Thomas Edison absent-mindedly created a filament out of some tarred lampblack in his hand, and Alexander Fleming made penicillin by mistakenly leaving a Petri dish uncovered. In the economy, too, there are countless examples of an undreamed innovation. There is always some "Side B" or low-budget sleeper that becomes an unimagined hit. Pixar was created to develop a new computing practice, but when a technician showed some visitors he could use the technique to make animated cartoons, their excitement turned the company into an animation studio. These accidental innovations were so novel that the conceivers did not even dream of the new product.

And virtually all innovations have an accidental or random element. Success in developing the new product and gaining adoption for commercial production is in part a matter of chance. The iconic TV interviewer Larry King commented more than once that his most famous guests all told him that their enormous success depended on a stroke of good luck. Yet the success or failure in attempted innovation is not like a lucky or unlucky flip of a known coin. Innovators travel on a voyage into the unknown, one with some known unknowns and some unknown unknowns; so they have no way of knowing whether—even with every lucky break—their creativity and intuition will deliver the innovation they hoped for. Hayek, coming finally to innovation in 1961, was dismayed that the American economist John Kenneth Galbraith supposed that companies knew what the prospects were for their new products. For Hayek, a company can no more *know* the probability of this profit or that loss on a new auto design than a writer of a novel can know what his or her chances are of making the bestseller list.

Oddly enough, economists left it to Hayek to tie up the rudimentary theory he missed starting—though he may have inspired it. In 1968 he sees economies—evidently referring to what is called here the modern economy—producing "growth in knowledge" through the operation of a method he dubs a *discovery procedure.* The term refers to the process of determining whether the imagined product or method can be developed and, if developed, determining whether it will be adopted. Through internal trials and market tests, a modern economy adds to its knowledge of what can be produced and what methods work, and to its knowledge of what is *not* accepted and what does *not* work.[9] It might be added that the advance of business knowledge may very well be boundless, since, unlike scientific knowledge, it is not limited by the physical world. It is the scientists who should be worried that their discoveries are coming to an end.

Another source of growth in this knowledge, though this one has limits, comes from correction: the fact that much of current knowledge is incorrect both at the micro level of particular products and the macro level of the whole economy.[10] Conditions and structural relationships are apt to be changing in not-yet-perceived ways. (Northrop, using a wind tunnel, found the added drag from a fixed landing gear instead of a retractable one was negligible; they did not realize the added drag was serious on the much faster planes.) In addition, observations of the economy are not outcomes of a controlled experiment; the data themselves are constantly changing as knowledge (and misunderstanding) change in the economy. So there is room in economies for insight into the mistakes of others.

The modern economy takes on "the problem of discovering—or inventing—possibilities and making good use of them," as Brian Loasby wrote.

9. Hayek's 1961 piece is "The Non Sequitur of the 'Dependence Effect'" (reprinted in 1962). The later paper mentioned is the 1968 "Competition as a Discovery Procedure" (published in English in 1978). A 1946 paper contains the first hint of this new chapter in Hayek's thought.

10. The notion of "changing beliefs" figures in Hayek's *The Counter-Revolution of Science* (1952). To really understand a social phenomenon, he writes, one needs to know "what the people dealing with it think" (p. 156).

The more an economy devotes itself to this activity, the more modern it is. An economy can have the vibrancy to formulate, the diligence to evaluate, and the zeal to exploit new commercial opportunities opened by external discoveries, which was as much as Schumpeter could see and thought possible. Yet the same economy or another economy may possess the creativity to conceive its own new commercial ideas in response to conditions or developments within it and have the vision (or intuition) to point that creativity in plausible directions. Creativity and vision are resources; they exist in all human economies. Yet historically some countries were unable or unwilling to deploy them and others drew back after earlier use. A modern economy unleashes creativity and vision yet manages with some success to harness it to the expertise of entrepreneurs, the judgment of financiers, and the gumption of end-users.[11]

The basics of the modern economy—how it functions as an innovation system—have been set out. Participants have new commercial ideas, which grow out of their deep engagement and long observation in their respective industries and professions. The process of development of new methods and products involves a variety of financial entities—angel investors, super-angel funds, venture capitalists, merchant banks, commercial banks, and hedge funds; it involves various sorts of producers—start-up companies, large corporations and their spin-offs; and a range of marketing activity—marketing strategy, advertising, and the rest. On the end-user side, there are company managers making pioneering assessments of novel methods and consumers deciding what new products to try out. Both are learning how to use the new methods and products they have adopted. By the mid-19th century, building blocks for a modern economy were in place in Britain and America, later in Germany and France:

> There was a swarm of entrepreneurs enjoying rights to hold property
> and do business, rights against the state, and the protections of contract
> law. These entrepreneurs, in companies or proprietorships they founded,
> were heavily engaged in tinkering with new methods and dreaming up
> new products. Banks seldom lent or invested in entrepreneurs without
> a track record. Family and friends often acted as "angel investors" to get

---

11. It is not controversial to say that the economies that have stood out for their extensive and effective use of creativity and judgment are those making heavy use of a relatively well-functioning "free enterprise," or "capitalist" system—whatever the social and political systems they operate with. They have been the great historical examples of modern economies—leaving aside the issue of whether they are the sole examples. Yet well-functioning capitalism could perhaps be superseded by some new form of the modern economy.

the entrepreneur's project started. Many new businesses had to plow back earnings if they were to expand. In England there were country banks supplying entrepreneurs with short-term credit and trusted attorneys accepting deposits from clients and lending long-term to entrepreneurs. And sometimes individuals became partners in a venture or put up the fee to buy patent protection. A few banks virtually went into business, as the Fuggers had done in south Germany centuries before—some advising and investing in whole industries. In America, country banks tended to be more entrepreneurial. New England businesses not uncommonly went into banking, even selling bank stock to finance their business ventures. Other banks lent to family and friends. (Not many of these proto-venture capitalists could take equity stakes, as today's venture firms do, until entrepreneurs created joint-stock companies that could issue shares.)[12]

The modern economy, seen as a vast, unceasing project to conceive, develop, and test ideas about what would work and what people would like, has had profound consequences for work and society. Its predecessor, the mercantile economy, offered little work and what there was offered a wage and little else. It may have been a relief from domesticity, yet it was tedious. In modern economies, work is nearly universal: economic inclusion is far wider than in mercantile times. This work is central to people's experience, particularly their mental life, and shapes their development. Thus the modern economy institutes a way of life. The fierce struggles over economic systems, which came to a head in the 20th century, were all about the human experiences that came with the modern economy and the loss of what had gone before.

A Social System

Most innovative ideas envision adoption by others, not just by the conceiver or entrepreneur. And a multiplicity of entrepreneurial projects is going on at any one time. Most of the fuel for the modern system—and the worst complications—derives from its operating in a society, not on a one-person island. The multiplicity of the actors, each acting independently, adds enormously to uncertainty in the economists' sense. Frank Knight, an influential

---

12. After nearly two centuries in which most knowledge of how the system worked was lost, a new literature has sprouted up, much of it spearheaded by Cambridge University Press. Chapter 4 on the historical origins of the modern economy conveys some of that. In the above paragraph, the pieces of the financial puzzle were put together by the late Jonathan Krueger, a student of mine at Columbia in 2010.

American economist, contrasted the known risk when a known coin is flipped, such as one known to be fair, with the unknown risk when an unknown coin is flipped, which he called *uncertainty*. He saw that business was rife with this Knightian uncertainty. He seemed to appreciate that this uncertainty is a hallmark of the modern economy.[13]

Uncertainty about the end results of an entrepreneur's project for a new product is in part the *micro* uncertainty about whether end-users will like the new product enough to buy it. The entrepreneur lives in fear that end-users will like it but will like some other entrepreneur's new product more. (Crusoe had only to fear that he himself might not like his new product.) Furthermore, the results of other entrepreneurs' ventures will affect the results of the entrepreneur's own venture. (The micro uncertainty about whether those other products being readied will be liked raises uncertainty about whether output and income in the economy will hold up. And that creates a *macro* uncertainty about whether end-users of a new product will be able to afford to buy it.) Thus, as John Maynard Keynes was first to see, the uncoordinated nature of the modern economy's entrepreneurial projects spawns a future unfolding in ways and magnitudes that are very indeterminate. The future, after any considerable length of time, becomes largely unknowable. About the future, Keynes wrote, "we simply do not know." In the space of a generation, an economy can take a shape that would have been unimaginable for the previous generation.[14]

For both Keynes and Hayek it was bedrock that new ideas are drivers of economic history—contrary to the stark determinism of, say, Thomas Hobbes or Karl Marx—because they understood that new ideas are unforeseeable (if they were foreseeable, they would not be new) and, being unforeseeable, have an independent influence on history. Yet the unknowability of the future makes

13. Knight's radical book, *Risk, Uncertainty and Profit,* was published in Boston in 1921, delayed for several years by World War I. (Another brilliant though less influential book on uncertainty, Keynes's *A Treatise on Probability* (1921), suffered the same delay.) An idiosyncratic thinker, Knight was fascinated with the proposition that if there were no uncertainty, there would be no genuine profit earned by businesses, only a normal return that could be thought of as required to pay the competitive level of interest to creditors.

14. See Keynes's *General Theory* (1936), with its allusion to Plato's "animal spirits." (Hayek's 1968 paper on the discovery procedure could have made similar points but it steered clear of them.) Ideas were never far from Keynes's mind, it seems. His greatest line was, "the world is ruled by ideas and little else." It was stated in his discussion of the hold that prevailing policy ideas have over nations. But Keynes's own career demonstrated that new policy ideas sometimes break in. Similarly, the ideas in business and finance, both old and new, dominate the directions and the swings in the business world.

all the more uncertain the consequences of developing today's ideas. Hence, any plausible projection of economic development in a modern economy is out of reach, just as Darwin's theory of evolution cannot predict evolution's course. Still, we learn some truths by studying processes for "growth in knowledge" and innovation: Failed ideas are not always valueless, since they may indicate where not to try any further. Successful ideas—the innovations—may inspire further innovations in an endless virtuous cycle. Originality is a renewable energy, driving the future in unknowable ways, creating new unknowns and new mistakes, thus new scope for originality. We will do well to study the fertile soil that high economic dynamism requires.

The modern system thrives on diversity within the society. How willing and able to innovate a society is—its propensity to innovate or, for short, its economic dynamism—obviously depends not only on the variety of situations, backgrounds, and personalities among potential conceivers of new ideas. (The entries into the music business of Jews in the 1920s and blacks in the 1960s are familiar examples.) A country's dynamism also depends on the pluralism of views among financiers. The more opportunity that an idea has to be evaluated by someone who can appreciate it, the less likely it is for a good idea to be passed up for funding. (To let the king pick all the creative projects for financing would be a recipe for making a monochromatic country.) Dynamism depends, among many other things, on the variety of entrepreneurs from whom to pick the one most in tune or most prepared to embody the new idea in a workable method or product. Clearly the pluralism among end-users is also important. If they were all identical, finding an innovation they would all like would be like precision bombing.

If all this diversity is important, we have an answer to a question avoided earlier: Historically, the system of creativity and vision described above— thus, growth in knowledge and innovation—exploded in the private sector, not the public sector. Could a comparable system for growth in knowledge and innovation function inside the public sector? Not if diversity among financiers, managers, and consumers is quite important.[15]

The success of this system depends also on the degree of interactivity within it. A project to dream up a new product typically begins with the formation of a creative team. A project to develop a newly conceived product for

15. Whether the presence of a really large public sector, marked by massive state purchases of goods and services for defense, the environment, and so forth that add up to half the GDP greatly impairs the economy's creativity and judgment, thus seriously reducing innovation and growth in knowledge, is another question. It is best deferred to the last two parts of this book.

commercial production or marketing typically begins with the formation of a company staffed by a number of people. Anyone with experience operating in a group understands that, generally speaking, groups are capable of producing a set of insights far beyond what the members would have been able to do working in isolation. The belief of some social critics that one can have a good career working at home neglects the value of being pinged by the ideas and questions of others—especially those we learn to admire and trust. And the belief that a company can place large numbers of its employees in solitary locations, such as their homes, without any cost to its innovation overlooks the importance of serendipitous interactions at the watercooler and luncheon meetings.

Interactions also enhance individual powers. When the principal horn player of Amsterdam's Concertgebouw Orchestra was complimented on the high level he had reached, he replied that he never could have done it without interactions with the rest of the orchestra. A team—a well-functioning one, at any rate—achieves not just the productivity from combining their complementary talents, as a classical economist would say, but also, in management theorists' terminology, the "superproductivity" that comes as every member of the group acquires a heightening of his or her talent, thanks to their mutual questioning and resulting gains in insight, and their urging one another on, a point emphasized by the management philosopher Esa Saarinen.

There is also interactivity over distance and time. The ideas of a society combine and multiply. A person's fertility in producing new ideas is hugely increased by exposure to recent ideas generated by the economy in which the person functions and, these days, the global economy. If isolated, the person might have a run of failed ideas at some point and be unable to generate any more. In *Robinson Crusoe* the economist-novelist Daniel Defoe shows us how pitifully few ideas Crusoe has without a society from which to take inspiration. The contention that to maximize its prosperity, a country like Argentina must remain agrarian rather than become urban, in view of its natural advantage in producing sheep, overlooks the fact that rural life is not conducive to the intellectual stimulation and wide-ranging interchange that contributes so critically to creativity.[16] Thus wide participation and the huge

16. In a 1940s debate, the Argentine economist Raúl Prebisch advocated taxes on agricultural output and import duties on manufactures. He was opposed by the Chicago economist Jacob Viner, a classical advocate of free trade and laissez-faire. Both Prebisch and Viner were too classical to articulate the gain in innovativeness that could be expected from urbanization. In their shared perspective, there was no such thing as creativity, engagement, and personal growth in a modern economy—there were only resources, technologies, and tastes, and the consumption and leisure they enabled.

agglomeration in cities of people in diverse pursuits serve to amplify the creativity of the system.

This chapter has viewed the anatomy and functioning of modern economies—the historical ones of the 19th and 20th centuries. In its first decades, participants had little sense that elements for a new system were in place and were quickly developing. But with the growing awareness of the modern system in which they were operating, there was a gathering sense that the new system was opening up fantastic possibilities. The next two chapters tell the little-known story of the gains in productivity and living standards the system brought—the material benefits—and the gains in the character of work and the meaning of life itself.

CHAPTER TWO

Material Effects of the Modern Economies

Babylon had her hanging gardens, Egypt her pyramids, Athens her acropolis, Rome her Coliseum, so Brooklyn has her bridge.

Banner at the 1883 opening of the Brooklyn Bridge

THOUGH WE IDENTIFY THE KIND OF ECONOMY a nation has by its structure, as in the previous chapter, its real meaning is in its consequences. The sustained growth of productivity that the arrival of the modern economy brought to several nations as early as the 19th century was a momentous consequence. Karl Marx, though he opposed the developing system he saw around him, did not think that this sustained growth was unimportant. In 1848, even before the modern economies were running at top speed, Marx, with productivity partly in mind, noted the "progressiveness" of the modern economies before his eyes.[1] As noted in Chapter 1 this productivity growth was of global significance, since the new methods and products could be adapted and used by other economies, even many very far from modern. It may very well be that some countries saw their early modern economies become less modern in the 20th century—France, it is fair to say, appears to have lost much of its dynamism some time after World War II. (A few economies, such as Germany's, verged on the *un*modern or *anti*modern in the 1930s.) Yet some other countries have seen their economies become more modern—Canada and South

---

1. Marx and Engels, *The Communist Manifesto*. It was in this pamphlet that Marx and Engels called the capitalism around them "progressive." But it is important to be clear that mercantile capitalism and the primitive capitalism before that were not "progressive"—not perceptibly from one generation to another, at any rate. The term capitalism has since come to mean any system but socialism—the economies of the Philippines, Argentina, the Arab states, and every country in Europe and Eurasia—no matter that nearly all of them have plainly been far from "progressive." To repeat, the present book terms *modern* any economy that is chronically, indigenously innovative, like the several that transformed Europe and North America in the 19th century, some of which are still somewhat modern.

Korea are clear examples. All in all, then, the modern economy lives on: several economies are making widespread efforts to innovate and are succeeding at it, under most market conditions at any rate.

The aim here is to get a sense of the force and effect of the dynamism of a well-functioning modern economy. A Martian landing on the earth would have little idea what to attribute to what. But the miracle-like arrivals of the modern economy, which were timed when not much else was arriving, make it plausible to attribute the differences between 19th- and 18th-century life to the birth of the modern. Examination of the magnitudes of those things attributable to the advent of the modern is the nearest thing we have to a laboratory experiment. We have to remember here that finally achieving high *levels* is not good enough if the levels are not growing. (People in the movie business used to say that "you are only as good as your last picture.") And *growth* is no compensation for being at abysmal levels.

Fundamentally we are interested in the consequences of the modern economy for human life, or more accurately, the life people live in society—in short, for social life. The data on output per worker and the average wage per worker are dry as dust: they do not adequately suggest life in the modern economies—what the (proceeds of) the output and the real wage came to buy in the space of a few decades and what the rewards were of the experiences that achieved that output and wage. We want a sense of how modern economies transformed work and therefore life—ideally a vivid and sweeping survey of the range of benefits and costs for the participants in the modern economies.

This chapter and the next argue that the modern economies and the modernity that brought them had deep consequences, most of them good. The present chapter takes up some of the modern economies' tangible effects—the "material pleasures and cares." The next chapter devotes plenty of space to the sweeping effects on intangibles—the intangibles that people live for.

A Cornucopia of Material Benefits

The climb of output per worker—so-called labor productivity or productivity, for short—brought about by the modern economies was sustained and remains so. In qualitative terms, the nations with modern economies (and with varying lags, those of other nations that are plugged into the global economy) went from a stationary state to explosive, boundless growth. Had the growth rate of productivity been only one-half of one percent per year or less, though, that growth might not have been widely noticed. At that rate, it would take a nation 144 years for its output per worker to double. The modern economies brought not only boundless growth: they also brought fast growth.

How high output per worker climbed over the so-called long century (ending in 1913 on the eve of World War I) is breathtaking. By 1870, total domestic output per capita in Western Europe as a whole had risen 63 percent above its 1820 level. By 1913, there was a further rise of 76 percent over the 1870 level. In Britain, the first rise was 87 percent and the second 65 percent. In the United States, the first rise was 95 percent and the second 117 percent. (Such climbs may not make much impression on today's readers after the even more spectacular growth in China between 1980 and 2010. But China had the opportunity to acquire and adopt a vast amount of production knowledge from overseas, while there was no third area from which Europe or America could have done that.)

The cumulative increase from the time of take-off to 1913—almost a tripling in Britain and a quadrupling in America—provided a standard of living for ordinary people that in the 18th century would not have been thought possible. The change in living standards had transformative effects, some of which are mentioned below. There was also an indirect effect: With an economy's aggregate output and hence income growing without bound, households' wealth will not regain its former size relative to income. People, who were not saving much at all in the old stationary state, began to save more and tried to earn more (to save still more) than they did in the 18th century so that their wealth would not fall further behind the pace—the pace of income growth. On this view, we should expect to find that participation rates in the modern economy are much higher than they were in the mercantile economy. Unfortunately, the data do not exist to test that expectation.

But wages, not productivity, are the single most important indicator of the material benefits available to those people coming into the economy without appreciable inherited wealth or the prospect of it. Adequate wages were—and still are—a gateway to important benefits. In the 19th century especially, though less so now, the *wage* that a person could earn was the main determinant of the primary goods that ordinary wage earners could afford—basic material goods, such as shelter and health care, and nonmaterial goods for which virtually everyone has a deep need, such as holding a job that is not dangerous or deadening, having a family, or having access to community life.

An increase in productivity is not a guarantee of increased wages, just as increased wages may occur without an increase in productivity. As noted in the Introduction, Fernand Braudel, the foremost French historian of the postwar period, found that even though the great explorers and colonists of the 16th century brought back cargoes of silver to their rulers, these revenues did not lift wages.[2] Although the wage per worker and output per worker are connected (someone once said that in economics everything depends on everything else in at least two ways), special factors can alter the channel from productivity to wages. But never mind. Modern economies raised the wages of working people, which stores of silver did not.

As the Introduction's discussion of wages implied, the advent of modern economies broke the gloomy pattern that Braudel had observed. (It was in the 16th century, as noted earlier, and in the 18th century, from 1750 to 1810, not modern times—the age of the modern economies—that wages were falling—in Britain, at any rate, for which we have data.) In Britain, daily wages per worker expressed in real terms, or purchasing power, in the crafts for which we have data started a sustained rise in 1820 or so—around the time that output per worker took off. (In America such early data are virtually nonexistent.) In Belgium, wages started such a rise around 1850. In France, wages took off soon after, playing tag with Britain's until 1914. In German cities, wages had been on a roller-coaster and went downhill again from the early 1820s through the 1840s, thus helping to set off the 1848 uprisings; a sustained rise began in 1860 or, according to another source, in 1870. So the real wages of building labor, factory workers, and farm workers in the modern economies took off with the take-off of productivity.

The question arising here is whether wages showed the same impressive ascent that output per worker did. Perhaps wages lagged behind productivity, as labor suffered a reduced share of the growing product. In fact, the nominal daily wage of an "average urban unqualified male" expressed in the local money did not just keep up with the money value of output per capita: It gained ground. From 1830, Britain's wage-productivity ratio, after losing a bit of ground until 1848 (that bad year again), more than caught up in the 1860s, fell off again in the 1870s, and finally surged ahead in the 1890s and was still further ahead by 1913. In France, the ratio followed a similar pattern.

2. Braudel, in his 1972 volume on the Mediterranean world, writes that the rulers exchanged their silver for spices and silks from the Far East rather than for the products made by European labor.

In Germany, the ratio, after remaining firm from 1870 to 1885, was some-what weaker in the 1890s but ended at a high water mark in the 1910s, until the war came. And these data overlook that workers were not buying units of the gross domestic product with their pay; to an important extent, they were buying imported consumer goods at prices that were collapsing as sup-plies were increasing and transport costs were decreasing. One British study concludes that "after prolonged stagnation, real wages . . . nearly doubled between 1820 and 1850."[3] The thought that, in the modern economies, wages lost ground to nonwage income cannot be supported. What happened to the wages of the less advantaged, or underprivileged, in these economies could be different, however.

In the public mind, the new system that the 19th century ushered in was an economy from hell for the less-fortunate workers who had to work in fac-tories, mines, and menial jobs. Some believe that social conditions scarcely improved until a century later, when socialist ideas changed Europe and the New Deal changed America. Literary works may have given that impres-sion. Often the dates are wrong, though. Victor Hugo's *Les Misérables* was focused on tensions arising in the years 1815 to 1832 from the Louis Philippe monarchy, not on the downside of the modern economy that reached France some decades later. Yet there are impressive works from the mid-19th century too. It is Dickens's microscope on London poverty in his 1839 novel *Oliver Twist* and Honoré Daumier's graphic depictions of the struggles of Parisian workers, which ran until 1870, that give us the impression that when produc-tivity took off, the great mass of working-age people were harmed by reduced wages—or, at best, remained for a long time just as miserable, unengaged, and unfulfilled as they had been before. That proposition needs to be tested.

One test of that proposition is to see whether so-called working class wages—blue collar wages for manual and other physical labor—were stagnant (or even falling) while the modern economies were taking hold and becoming more effective. So, it has to be asked, *were* wages for blue collar work in fact

3. Lindert and Williamson, "Living Standards" (1983, p. 11). Results on wages as a ratio to pro-ductivity are from Bairoch, "Wages as an Indicator of Gross National Product" (1989). If these are not grossly inaccurate data, one wonders how another scholar could have reached a rather different conclusion: "[T]he rise in living standards in [1815–1850] was almost undetectable; it is but one of many minor fluctuations in the course of seven centuries. The gains from 1815 to 1850 were a cycle—and a minor one at that—not a trend" (Allen, "The Great Diver-gence in European Wages and Prices," 2001, p. 433). The explanation is that only two of Allen's dozen cities, namely London and Paris, are located in the emerging modern economies of that period. Both London and Paris showed sharp wage increases.

stagnant or falling? The popular impression is that the least-skilled workers did see their wages fall over the 19th century as a result of mechanization—or fall relative to the wages of skilled labor, at any rate.

This is another misimpression, however. According to the British study mentioned previously, the average wage per worker outstripped the wage of blue collar workers by about 20 percent between 1815 and 1850. But much of that was a result of lagging wages of manual labor in agriculture, and hard times in agriculture cannot easily be blamed on the modern sector. British estimates from another source show that the average wage of all skilled workers in the nonagricultural sector climbed only a little more over that period than the average wage of unskilled workers—by 7 percent.[4] Clark's 2005 data on the wage per day of craftsmen and the wage of "helpers" in Britain's building trade show that helpers began to lose ground to the craftsmen in the 1810s—this after no trend up or down since the 1740s—but the data show that the tide turned in mid-century; helpers regained their former position by the 1890s and went on to gain more ground in the next decade. That was the impression in those times too. Prime Minister Gladstone, seeing the gushing tax revenues pouring into the government from all sorts of wage earners, commented in the House of Commons:

> I should look with some degree of pain, and with much apprehension, upon this extraordinary growth if it were my belief that it is confined to the class of person who may be described as in easy circumstances. . . . But . . . it is a matter of profound and inestimable consolation to reflect that while the rich have become richer, the poor have become less poor . . . [I]f we look to the average condition of the British labourer, whether peasant or miner or operative or artisan, we know from varied and incontrovertible evidence that during the last twenty years such an addition has been made to his means of subsistence as we may almost pronounce to be without example in the history of any country and of any age.[5]

In Britain, then, the modern economy did not aggravate wage inequality—not systematically and never in any permanent way. Marx, obfuscating the data, never did acknowledge the facts to which Gladstone called attention.

The belief that labor in general suffered in the 19th century relative to capital fares no better than the other misimpressions. Recently available data

---

4. Jackson, "The Structure of Pay in Nineteenth-Century Britain."
5. Hansard (1863, pp. 244–245).

show the daily wage per employed worker as a ratio to the national output per capita. In Britain, the ratio went up, not down—from 191 around 1830 to 230 around 1910. In France, the ratio went up from 202 around 1850 to 213 around 1910. In Germany, the ratio went from 199 in the early 1870s to 208 in the early 1910s.[6] A stylized portrait was drawn in 1887 by Robert Giffen, a journalist and chief statistician of the British government, using individual income data collected with the start of British income tax in 1843. These data show that aggregate income of the "rich" doubled over the next 40 years, but so did their number; the aggregate income of manual laborers more than doubled, and their number increased relatively little.

> The rich have become more numerous but not richer individually; the 'poor' . . . are, individually, twice as well off on the average as they were fifty years ago. The poor have thus had almost all the benefit of the great material advance of the last fifty years.[7]

The favorable movement of real wages, notwithstanding a lengthy low in the relative wage for unskilled work over several decades in the 19th century, can be supposed to have two benefits that are generally considered to be of social value. One benefit is that an increased general level of wages is liberating: it enables persons confined to the lower reaches of the available wages—unskilled workers, in the usual terminology—to move from work they previously could not afford to reject to work that is more desirable. A person working in the "domestic economy" as a homemaker or as paid help in other people's homes could afford to move to a job that is not so isolating; someone working in the underground sector could afford to take a job in the legitimate economy with its greater respectability and lesser dependency; someone could afford to leave a job in the business economy for one with initiatives, responsibilities, and interactions that make it more rewarding. Thus higher wages also result in what may be called *economic inclusion.* More people end up participating and contributing to society's central project and thus finding the rewards that could only come from such involvement. To describe and confirm the value of economic inclusion requires a discussion like that in the next chapter, so it cannot be elaborated just yet.

---

6. See the 1989 paper by Bairoch, "Wages as an Indicator of Gross National Product." The curious units in which this ratio is measured may be disregarded.

7. "The Material Progress of Great Britain." Giffen was immortalized in Alfred Marshall's textbook *Principles* (1938) for the "Giffen good"—a good that people buy more of the higher its price is. However, scholars have been unable to find this concept explicitly formulated anywhere in Giffen's works.

The increase in wages has the further social benefit that it reduces poverty and pauperism. Observations by two distinguished economists of their day confirm that a noteworthy decline of poverty took place in all the modern economies emerging in the 19th century—those for which we have data, at any rate. Speaking of the trends in England and Scotland, Giffen noted in 1887 the steady decrease in the number of paupers (individuals relieved of debts)—in the teeth of the fastest population growth on record—from 4.2 percent in the first half of the 1870s to 2.8 percent in 1888. To quote Giffen again, in Ireland, to which the modern economy came only later, "there has been an increase of pauperism, accompanied by a decline of population." Writing in the 1890s about America, David Wells in a couple of pages on "pauperism" notes that the "number of poor as a proportion of the whole population have been generally decreasing; and this, notwithstanding the very great obstacles in the way of . . . checking pauperism, in a country like the United States, which annually receives such armies of poor from European countries."[8] Another way to weigh the claim that the modern economy hurts the masses is to examine the somewhat surprising evidence on infectious disease, nutrition, and the resulting mortality. The story, like the above stories, is not one of linear progress. It shows societies flowering in the 19th century after the trials of Job in the 18th. Strikingly, smallpox deaths, which are mainly found among young children, rose over the 17th century up to the heyday of the commercial economy in the mid-18th century, when two-thirds of all children died before their fifth birthday. The cause of the smallpox epidemic could not have been the functioning of the modern economy, since it was hardly functional then. The cause was the rise of international commerce!—"the importation of more virulent strains with the growth of world trade." Then smallpox deaths began to recede. By the second quarter of the 19th century, child mortality had fallen by two-thirds. This appears to be more the result of the modern economy dating from the 1810s than from the first stage of the industrial revolution in the 1770s, which, as noted above, was largely confined to a single industry in a short time span.[9] As the modern

8. From Wells's 1899 book, p. 344. A polymath of his time, Wells, after his college years at Amherst, studied science with the naturalist Louis Agassiz in Boston, invented textile machinery, and was prominent in American policymaking even before his bestseller. He appears to have known only the material side of the economy and saw material progress as solely the application of science.

9. See the 2007 paper by Razzell and Spence, "The History of Infant, Child and Adult Mortality," p. 286. Data there show a faster proportionate decline of burials per child from 1790–1810 to the modern interval 1810–1829 than from 1770–1789 to 1790–1810.

economies gained force over the 19th century, the decline of smallpox intensified. Wells reports that "for 1795–1800 the average annual number of smallpox deaths in London was 10,180; but for 1875–1880 it was only 1,408."[10]

Infectious diseases affecting adults more than children also fell sharply in the 19th century. Wells writes that "plague and leprosy have practically disappeared [from Britain and America]. Typhus fever, once the scourge of London, is said to have now entirely disappeared from that city." As a result, mortality rates were steeply declining. "In London, the death rate, which had averaged 24.4 per 1000 in the 1860s was down to 18.5 by 1888. In Vienna, the death rate had been 41 and fell to 21. In European countries, the decrease ranged from one-third to one-quarter. In the whole United States it was between 17 and 18 in 1880."[11]

Was all this a credit to science? That does not appear to be expert opinion. Referring to the reductions in the gamut of infectious diseases in London—smallpox, "fevers" (typhus and typhoid fever), and "convulsions" (diarrhea and gastrointestinal diseases)—Razzell and Spence point to the public health and hygienic measures made affordable by higher incomes:

> Most of these were dirt diseases. [The fall of mortality] occurred equally amongst the wealthy and the non-wealthy population. . . . It is possible that a transformation of the environment had an impact on a number of diseases. . . . The replacement of woolen underwear by linen and cotton garments . . . and more effective washing—involving the boiling of clothing—were probably responsible for the progressive elimination of typhus as well as lice.[12]

Wells points to the better diet that came with higher incomes:

> Now, while improved sanitary knowledge and regulations have contributed to these results, they have been mainly due to the increase in the abundance and cheapness of food products, which are in turn almost wholly attributable to improvements in the methods of production and distribution. . . . The American is apparently gaining in size and weight, which could not have happened had there been anything like a retrogression toward poverty on the part of the masses.[13]

---

10. Wells, p. 349.
11. Wells, p. 347.
12. Razzell and Spence, pp. 287, 288.
13. Wells, pp. 347, 349. He calculates that a good diet required a small fraction of the daily wage of manual workers and marvels at the decade-long explosion in imports of tropical fruits and fresh fish from the north Pacific.

In these ways, the modern economy helped to reduce disease and mortality. The improvements in productivity made by the economy on a daily basis provided the wherewithal for families and communities to combat disease through private measures and public health measures. Improvements in hospital practice, such as the use of antiseptics, helped to reduce many infectious diseases. Moreover, modern hospitals are a part of the modern economy. The insights and learning occurring in hospitals and their diffusion throughout the healthcare industry were a notable part of the explosion of knowledge produced by the modern economies.

With the development of the modern economies and the productivity gains that traveled to various other nations, the world embarked on a virtuous circle. With lower mortality came a larger population of young people, thus more persons around who might invent, develop, and test new concepts, and thus another round of increased wages and lower mortality.

Not a Rose Garden

Readers surprised at the very good news on wages in the modern societies may be expecting that the record of the fledgling modern economies on employment and unemployment will provide a corrective. In 2009 a British journalist, Maev Kennedy, reacting to the century of British newspapers just put online by the British Library, suggested that "anyone overwhelmed by today's political scandals, wars, financial disasters, soaring unemployment and drunken feral children can take refuge in the 19th century—its wars, financial disasters, political scandals, soaring unemployment and drunken feral children." But it was the commercial economy of the 18th century, in creating the first large cities, that marked the birth of the phenomenon of mass unemployment. It marked the start of the migration of people from subsistence farming with only the occasional paid work, or "wage labor"—a life in which no one was unemployed—to urban life in which lacking a paid job meant having few alternative ways to earn one's bread and the roof over one's head. People had to self-insure against unemployment by saving enough for a rainy day, if they could. If they couldn't, there were the mutual aid societies (the *Verein*) to which craftsmen might go for help; and many could fall back on family or friends. State-run unemployment insurance programs came to the rescue in France in 1905 and Britain in 1911.

The rise of modern economies in the 19th century multiplied the number of cities, thus multiplying the number of people unemployed. By expanding

the part of the country that was urban, with its unemployment, and thus contracting the part that was rural, which had only underemployment, it inescapably increased the national unemployment. That was not unambiguously bad. For urban dwellers, there was the risk of being unemployed. There was also the chance of finding some of the benefits that drew people to agglomerate into cities. Many people fled farming for city life because it was a trade-off worth making.

We lack the data to tell whether the modern economy drove the average unemployment rate in existing cities above the average of a century earlier. However, the available data show increasing labor force participation rates over the 19th century (among women) and unemployment rates that were not larger than the rates in the present age, say, since 1975. A recent study of France found that "a change in direction, first discernible in the 1850s, occurred from the 1860s onward: there was a marked acceleration in the growth of [the number] *working* [despite] a sharp check in the increase in the working-age *population*."[14] The advent of the modern economy in France appears to have pulled increased numbers of working-age people into nonfarm employment, there being no known force in the farm sector giving them a push. As for Britain, the classic work by A. W. Phillips on unemployment in relation to inflation presented data going back to 1861. These data show no evidence of any upward trend in unemployment in the next several decades as the modern economic system spread wider and its power to create new knowledge, and thus change, increased. Moreover the path of the unemployment rate in the early period of the series (say, from 1861 to 1910) does not appear to be elevated by comparison to the period from 1971 to 2010, a span over which Britain has not been a front-runner in knowledge or invention relative to its peers. The lesson is that rapid growth of knowledge, thus productivity and wages, managed through one or more channels to hold down unemployment, which latter-day Britain, with a less inventive economy in a less creative society, has found it difficult to do. Myriad subsidies and state agencies succeeded in moderating unemployment among low-wage participants but not in turning back the tide.

Why, then, has a poor reputation shadowed the modern economies—those emerging in the 19th century and later manifestations? They were stuck with William Blake's image of the "dark Satanic mills" he saw dotting the landscape in 1804—a decade before the invasion of factories came. The drudgery and deprivation of rural work was mainly replaced by the tedium,

14. Caron, *An Economic History of Modern France* (1979, table 1.7, p. 19).

grime, and noise characterizing many or most factories. Charlie Chaplin's image of the assembly line in his 1937 film *Modern Times* looked more mindless than oppressive. In any case, the factory was not unique to the modern economies of the 19th century and the first half or so of the 20th century. Similar or worse factories appeared in some of the least-modern economies ever seen: in the Russia of Lenin and Stalin and the China of Deng Xiaoping, for example. Furthermore, the rise of factories is not an inherent accompaniment of a modern economy at any stage. The next country to make a break for modernity may very well skip factories and go straight to offices and interactive webcasting.

There may be another explanation. For us, even now in the twenty-first century, we can still be appalled by the filthiness and suffocating pollution in the fast-growing cities of the modern economies arising in the 19th century. But we forget to appreciate what it meant for people to escape from the wages of medieval times to incomes two or three times the medieval level, as most people in Britain, America, France, and the German lands came to enjoy in the 19th century. Income is such an abstract, lifeless thing. Yet higher income cuts the incidence of poverty.

To countries where it came and even, to some degree, to countries where it did not come, the modern economy brought immense material benefits: In raising wage rates, it provided increased numbers the dignity of self-support, it liberated them to get out into society, and it opened up city life as an alternative to rural ways. In raising incomes, it improved living standards in very basic ways, reducing risks of early death through disease, so that one might live to enjoy the new living standards. A new middle class arose that could dine out, go to the stadium or the theater, and introduce their children to the arts. (In America, it was said, there seemed to be a piano in every parlor.)

It might seem that, now, this "sustained growth" is no longer important. Higher income *is* less important to people today than it was when consumption and health conditions were so desperately low—as evidenced by the major shortening of the work day and work week between the 1860s and the 1960s. It is a central theme of this book that, for an ever-increasing number of people in the modern economies, continued growth of their wage rates and salaries is not among the most important things in their lives. Research a decade ago on "happiness," however, has stimulated a different thesis. It has concluded from household survey data that, after a point, persons higher up the income ladder did not report higher levels of "happiness"—a Buddhist-like state where no more consumption or leisure is wanted. And

this is concluded even though higher responsibility and greater scope generally come with higher income. (Subsequent researchers have argued from similar data that this conclusion is not accurate.) Whatever the truth of that thesis, we have always known that "money cannot buy happiness." Happiness is not yoked to income. Earning a high income is a means to satisfactions not classified as "happiness"; otherwise, people would not seek the increased income that does not bring an increase in their reported happiness. A shortfall of one's income is an impediment to key goals: to personal development and a gratifying life. It is a great achievement of modern economies that, over their long history, fewer and fewer participants were lacking the income to pursue their nonmaterial goals.

Of course, had the modern economy not arisen in the West, leaving only the mercantile economy of the baroque era, wage rates and incomes might have grown as a result of some of the scientific advances exogenous to economies that would have occurred—whatever those might have been. But wages and incomes would not have grown nearly as fast. If exogenous science had been the main driver of 19th-century growth in the select Western economies that saw rapid growth, those scientific advances would have caused a rising tide lifting all boats, including the boats of the Dutch and the Italians, who were relatively productive and sophisticated when the 19th century started. The fact is that, although nearly all the Western countries started in the same place around 1820, the material achievements of some countries went far beyond those of the others—namely the modern economies' towering achievements.

To conclude: This chapter has not only quantified the rapid growth brought to several countries by the advent of the modern economy. It has also found evidence that, in the countries in which it took root, the modern economy, through its ceaseless creation of new economic knowledge, changed radically the material conditions of life. The modern economies performed this feat by doing what they were well structured to attempt and to succeed at: by mass innovating.[15] The massive effort to innovate evidently

---

15. Referring to the "hundred years' peace" from 1815 to 1914, Karl Polanyí, brother of the brilliant Michael Polanyí, suggested that the paucity of wars, civil and foreign, had much to do with the cumulative rise of capital and productivity in that period. See his *The Great Transformation* (1944). This was odd on the level of facts alone, since America had its Civil War, Britain had the Crimean War and the Boer War, and France and Germany had their wars. The achievement of modernity is therefore all the more remarkable. From the perspective he took, he was unable to see that the challenges and the engagement brought by innovation must have had much to do with the long stretches of peace. His book is in major ways 180 degrees to the present book.

permeated nations from the bottom up. As befits the grassroots character of this innovation, some benefits, such as income, went equiproportionately to the less advantaged; some other benefits, such as health and longevity, went mostly to the less advantaged. As a recent American history of this development put it, it was an economic "revolution" and was "in many ways the best thing ever to befall the ordinary people of America."[16]

Material change is not the only feat of the modern economy, though. The immaterial, or intangible, world of experience, aspiration, spirit, and imagination was, for more and more people, no less radically changed. That is the subject of the next chapter.

16. See H. W. Brands's 2010 book, *American Colossus,* p. 606.

CHAPTER THREE

The Experience of Modern Life

Europe was transformed by the new experience of metropolitan life between 1860 and 1930. Expressionism was a visionary expression of what it feels like to be adrift, exhilarated, in a fast-paced, incomprehensible world.

JACKIE WULLSCHLAGER, *Financial Times*

Young America . . . has a great passion—a perfect rage—for the new.
ABRAHAM LINCOLN, "Second Lecture on Discoveries and Inventions"

WITH THE MODERN ECONOMIES CAME something radically new—modern life. The results in consumption, leisure, and longevity pointed to in the previous chapter were very large, a few of them large enough to make a difference for what people were able to do. With a longer life in prospect, people might be willing to prepare for careers requiring a larger investment. However, these material gains, although they changed the standard of living (and of working), did not change radically the way of life—did not change the "way we were." Of those material gains, perhaps the one that comes closest was the decline in child mortality. It must have reduced the heartache and fear in having children. But did it change fundamentally the experience of having a child and raising a child?

The radical significance of the modern economy in those cities or nations where it emerged lies in its nonmaterial results. It transformed the work and career of a large and increasing number of participants. Thus it was life-changing: the new experience of work in the modern economy and, with it, the new experience of city life changed the *character* of living, not simply the standard of living. Of course, the full effect took time to build up, and it reached some jobs later than others or never. So it would not be surprising if early observers took less notice of this effect than did later observers, who could hardly miss the new tenor of the times.

To be sure, some of the great economists of the modern age came to recognize that the work experience was central to the lives of the working population. Alfred Marshall, the leading British economist in the quarter-century from 1890, emphasized that those employed in modern business find that the majority of the problems they have to solve arise in the course of their *work* in the economy:

> [T]he business by which a person earns his livelihood generally fills his thoughts during by far the greater part of those hours in which his mind is at its best. During them his character is being formed by ... his work ... and by his relations to his associates in work.[1]

Very likely, there is some British understatement here, and Marshall welcomes the mental stimulation and mental exercise being offered in the jobs he sees around him. A few decades later, the Swedish economist Gunnar Myrdal makes a stronger point in his always explicit way:

> [I]t is a stock phrase ... in economics [that] consumption is the sole end of production. ... In other words: Man works in order to live. But there are many who live in order to work. ... [M]ost people who are reasonably well off derive *more* satisfaction as producers than as consumers. ... [M]any would define the social ideal as a state in which as many people as can live in this way.[2]

Marshall and Myrdal were departing from orthodox economics in recognizing that, for growing numbers of people, business life—figuring out how better to produce and pondering what might be better to produce—engaged the mind.

Marshall and Myrdal's observation is striking in a couple of ways. To have so emphasized the mental side of work, they must have understood that this aspect had been uncommon. People—most people, at any rate—do not derive comparable stimulus and challenge from a lifetime of child care or other

---

1. Marshall, famous for the eight editions of his *Principles*, made this remark in his more popular 1892 textbook *Elements of Economics*, p. 2. Born in 1842, he rose to great heights at Cambridge University, becoming the most accomplished and prolific economist of his time. His students, Keynes, Arthur Cecil Pigou, and Dennis H. Robertson, were to become the great Cambridge economists of the next generation. Marshall, having grown up in the urbanized section of London called Clapham, had the advantage, almost unique among Oxbridge dons, of seeing and sensing what work was like in the second half of the 19th century.

2. Myrdal, *The Political Element in the Development of Economic Theory* (1953, p. 136), translated from the 1932 German edition.

domestic activities. (Had they found the world packed with mental stimulation and challenge at every turn, finding the same in the workplace too would have been nothing to write home about.) They must also have understood it was something new under the sun. They tacitly assume that work in bygone times was not widely engaging, except maybe for the king's work to keep power. It is the mental stimulation and intellectual challenge of work in the modern economy that is rich with satisfactions, not the agrarian work of traditional economies. Marshall and Myrdal implicitly understood that intellectual involvement was going on in workplaces, but they left unspecified what the stimulants and challenges were.

Another World: Work and Career Transformed

The distinctive experiences of the modern economy come from its distinctive activity of creating, developing, marketing, and testing new ideas. In many occupations, though not all, the experience of work is transformed from the sameness, or *stasis*, typical in the traditional economies to the change, challenge, and originality found in the modern economy. With a little observation and more than a little interpretation we can identify some of the modern experiences, or categories of experiences—though some may escape us. Perhaps not all of these experiences could be called rewards (see below). And even the clear rewards are not sufficient for a well-functioning modern economy to be found just, though they may be necessary for a just economy (see Chapters 7 and 8). But first, the experiences.

With modernity came continual change, which contrasted sharply with the sameness and tedium of work in the traditional economies. Ceaseless change arriving from outside a company brought mental stimulation to the participants. When a new product comes along, a user or potential user of it may be stimulated to ask whether there could be some gain from using it in some way that is overlooked. A producer may be stimulated to ask whether there could be a way to improve or change its functioning. A traditional economy may well have some existing products that could have new uses or could be improved upon—and thus some unexploited possibilities remaining—so there may be some stimulation to be found even in traditional settings. However, the stimulation that comes from the stream of new products is far more powerful.

Another experience brought by the modern economy is the process of solving the new problems arising from efforts to create change from the inside. Although artisans and farmers were gradually surmounting age-old hurdles in ancient and medieval times, they had evidently run out of hurdles or solutions over the 16th, 17th, and 18th centuries. Several Schumpeterian discoveries had occurred earlier, and some more were to occur from time to time. Yet a country can count neither on the force and frequency of such discoveries, nor on being the country best placed to develop a new opportunity. Only a country's modern economy is capable of creating for its working-age people the endless succession of new problems required to keep their work challenging. Philosophers refer to the resulting "expansion of talents" as *self-realization* or *self-actualization*—the full realization of one's potential. Managements use the term *employee engagement* to indicate both that their workforce is stimulated by novel developments and absorbed by the problems presented to them. Marshall and Myrdal can be interpreted as having in mind these qualities of modern work.

Relatedly, there is the social experience of *interchange* with workplace colleagues in the course of their work. No doubt, interactions, as well as problems and problem solving, are present at home too, where a parent interacts with the children and other parents. But the modern workplace is constantly offering new interchanges rather than a recycling of old ones, which no doubt makes a considerable difference.[3] Interchange outside the workplace also develops in a modern economy. Companies that competed with each other, not just those buying from each other or from the same pool of labor or of capital, found it convenient to merge or collude. An employee gained in a variety of ways from taking part in shop talk after work. A company with better access to the industry's rumor mill would have a better idea what not to produce.

In another category are the experiences of directing or taking part in an innovative kind of initiative. For the entrepreneur or team leader and for others on the team too, such projects offer opportunities to inject one's own creativity and judgment into decisions—for *self-expression* or *self-affirmation*. For many people this activity is apt to result in a greater sense of accomplishment than mere problem-solving does. In the traditional economies of the

---

3. The value to people of both problem solving and teamwork in solving problems are themes inseparable from the pragmatist school of American philosophers—Charles Peirce, William James, John Dewey, and Josiah Royce—especially Dewey. (Later members were Stanford's Richard Rorty and Harvard's Amartya Sen.) Somewhere in Dewey's vast work is the image of a team of shipbuilders solving the problems of making a battleship. Dewey, an anticommunist yet a critic of U.S. capitalism, shared the socialist vision of enterprises in which the manager or at any rate the foreman is replaced with workers' meetings and consensus. Dewey supposed their decisions would be as good as the boss's.

mercantile age and earlier, work was largely routine, and, aside from the occasional fire to put out, the opportunity and the need to exercise initiative were only occasional.

Another category of work experiences is the most distinctively modern. In the modern economy, careers almost force participants on a winding voyage of *exploration*—a leap into the void. Some of the unimagined experiences people have and the challenges they meet in these careers may be the most valuable episodes in their careers—and are certainly the most distinctively modern benefits of the modern economy. In earlier economies, expeditions of discovery were exceptional: Marco Polo's journey to China and Leif Ericson's expeditions to Vineland, for instance. In the commercial economy of mercantile capitalism there was, here or there, a leap into the unknown that was a privilege reserved for a handful of people. In the modern economy, however, these modern rewards of *self-discovery* are endemic.

Some end results of work and career are also among the nonmaterial rewards of modern work. The modern economy makes it possible for participants to rack up *achievements*, achievements that are very visible. The gratification from such success is a not unimportant benefit of the modern economy. Such satisfactions were out of reach of all but a tiny minority in traditional economies, including the mercantile economies of the commercial age, since not much out of the ordinary was achieved—other than swapping goods at greater and greater distances. Yet some household surveys do not find that people look for jobs offering the prospect of achievement. They seek personal experiences and inner growth, so we must be careful not to overemphasize this aspect.

There is also the experience of *freedom*. For a classical economist, it would be double counting to count the material blessings of the modern economy opened up by its enabling institutions and encouraging culture, and then to add the blessings of the freedoms that enable people to produce these material benefits. But in any real-life modern economy—not a theoretical model in which everything in the present and the future is known—the actors may sense or entertain opportunities and dangers about which there is little or no public knowledge. Individuals' *freedoms to act* (or not to act) on their unique knowledge, judgment, and intuition may be indispensable to people's sense of self-sufficiency and thus self-worth. In this view, the freedom to take charge of one's own heading and make one's own mistakes is a primary good itself, one of huge importance.

The concept of *attainment* appears in some discussions of the rewards from work in modern times. Some material attainments, such as the wealth amassed by a person, do not belong in the set of end results from participation in the modern economy. Wealth is primarily a means to various benefits, most obviously to the material benefits noted in the previous chapter and also to various work experiences as well. (Households may save now to be able to afford to take a job later offering experiences at some cost in terms of lower pay.) Nonmaterial attainments, such as honors and influence accumulated, are also problematic. They suffer from being positional goods—they are precious only to the extent that some others do not have them. (It has been said that the happiness of the Nobel Prize winners is outweighed by the unhappiness it causes the runners-up.) Nevertheless, it is unreasonable to believe that a society has no appreciation for the attainments of its people—that it gains only to the extent that the pursuit of these attainments helps motivate risks and sacrifices that serve to generate some of the other nonmaterial benefits identified above.

How does it feel to be alive in a country with a modern economy? How in particular did it feel to participate in the modern economies that arose in the 19th century and in those that stayed modern in the 20th? Answers to the question require some imagination on our part. Evidence of the significance that the experience of work and career may provide does not stare us in the face. Yet pieces of evidence exist here and there, some of them directly observable and even measurable, others highly circumstantial and speculative. The importance of this experience is the focus here. And if it is important, there is some presumption that people have found it valuable.

On the significance of interchange, a feature of modern work, there is direct demographic evidence. In the mercantile economies it was the exceptional industry that became concentrated in one town or region. When keeping up with new ideas was not an imperative, most industries spread out over the land. When, during the 19th century, keeping up with new ideas became crucial for decisions, the landscape was transformed. People went where the ideas were, and there was much agglomeration. Companies in an industry herded together—French textile makers in Lyon, English metalworkers in Birmingham, and Italian clothes makers in Naples. Later, in the 20th century, there were the German film makers in Berlin, American car makers in Detroit, and so forth. Rural areas depopulated, and cities sprang up. Germany, in spite of little increase in population, went from 4 towns that qualified as cities in 1800 to about 50 by 1900. By 1920, Americans went from living predominantly in rural areas to living predominantly in cities. For the first time in history people could conveniently interact with one another for business, professional, or other reasons. And people took advantage of their new situation. There was an explosion during the 19th century (and a detectable rise earlier) in both Britain and France in the number of taverns and cafes where people might talk. What Marxians saw as overcrowding leading to urban misery was, from this perspective, in the interest of both labor and capital—up to a point, at any rate. (No company broke from the city with its workforce delighted to follow—not until some internet companies headed for the hills in recent decades.)

On another modern experience, the pleasure of encountering the new, particularly new problems and the satisfaction of solving them, there is direct clinical evidence of the craving for mental stimulation and problem solving among primates. Zookeepers have talked about their findings:

> Once animals at the Bronx Zoo spent their days in idleness and boredom, pacing their small cages, eating meals handed to them on a platter. That made for listless animals. As the study of wildlife and animal behavior grew, it became apparent that boredom undermined animals' health. . . . Nowadays, the animals stave off boredom. Since the mid-'90s, New York's zoos have expanded their definition of care to include the animal's mental state. . . . Basically, the purpose is to prevent boredom. But scientists have higher goals, Dr. Diana Reiss, senior scientist at the New York Aquarium, said. "We're asking: How can we give animals . . . the chance to make their own choices? To deal with challenges? To solve problems and use their brains? To teach them to learn for themselves?" . . . The zookeepers are experimenting with ways of reproducing the tasks, puzzles, . . . in the wild. These include using various toys, hiding food. . . . "Novelty is very important," commented Dr. Richard Lattis, senior vice president of Wildlife Conservation Society, which runs the city's five zoos and its aquarium. The problem is "we have to keep inventing new things. The animals get tired of the same old toys."[4]

Though the same experiments have not been performed on humans, we can be pretty sure that there is at least as much craving for more mental stimulation and problem solving among humans. Prison reforms decades ago suggested that when inmates were allowed to play chess or other games and to study books, the inmates were healthier, emotionally and physically. Some nations have experimented with a drastic curtailment of work. In continental

4. Stewart, "Recall of the Wild: Fighting Boredom, Zoos Play to the Inmates' Instincts" (2002, p. B1).

Europe, where half the men are retired by age 55 and women are retired even sooner than the men—no more change, challenge, or originality for them!—a physician reported that the mortality rate of his patients spiked up in the months after they retired.

There is also statistical evidence. In the 2002 General Social Survey, nine in ten of the American adults who worked more than 10 hours per week in 2002 reported they were "very satisfied" or "somewhat satisfied" with their jobs. Job satisfaction is less among those taking less enriching work, of course. Yet even among those who categorized themselves as working class, 87 percent reported they were "satisfied." It is still a logical possibility that people simply love to exert and to tire themselves, while there are no mental and intellectual rewards. But that case appears to be far-fetched. Had the surveyees responded that they were dissatisfied with their jobs, it would be problematic to argue that the mental and intellectual side of work was highly valued though outweighed by the pain of the hard work. However, the fact that people *do* report considerable satisfaction from their jobs in spite of any fatigue, stress, nuisance costs, and interpersonal tensions, is quite impressive. (This refutes Robert Reich, the former Secretary of Labor, who in a radio show with the present author in October 2006 erupted with "Americans *hate* their jobs.")

Perhaps these first observations make it reasonably clear that the advent of the modern economy was a godsend to people, delivering rewards known only to a fortunate few in earlier times—employee engagement, intellectual gratification and the joy of the occasional discovery. It might be worthwhile, then, to look at the advent of the modern through another lens.

Modern Experience Mirrored in Arts and Letters

Is there other evidence of the profound change that the modern economy brought to working life, thus to life itself? There is the literature and the arts in the age of the modern economy. We expect literature to illuminate aspects of life in our time that we may not have been very conscious of. "Yes," we say in response to the more resonant works, "that's how it feels." And the mere fact that some are writing novels and some are composing symphonies may be a sign that people are in an excited state and are trying to express and understand the new system that has transformed life, as Vargas Llosa has remarked. So it is reasonable to check the greatest fiction to see whether there are some hints there of how life changed with the emergence of the modern economies. Of course, few writers reflected in concrete terms on the experiences of work and career in their time. But what is there may be suggestive.

There have always been writers who write about adventure, even when there was little of it to be seen in the world. The leading countries of the Baroque era, with their mercantile economies and state-sponsored explorers, did not offer writers an experience of change, challenge, and originality to write about. In Spain, Miguel Cervantes's 1605 novel *Don Quixote* was, from a literary point of view, a satire on the romances that some popular writers attempted to sell to the public. But from another viewpoint its theme is the deprivations of a life without challenge and creativity. Quixote, stuck on the Spanish desert, could have no experience of modern work and career. With his "squire," Sancho Panza, the don is driven to invent chivalrous challenges and causes. When, bedridden, he announces that their adventures are over, Sancho bursts into tears, for he needed the fantasies too. In Britain, Daniel Defoe, equipped better by his imagination than his background in economics, was interested in innovation, but, to write about it, he had to set his 1719 novel *Robinson Crusoe* on an island far from sea lanes on which Crusoe, a shipwrecked seaman, was to be trapped for 28 years. There Crusoe does what he could not have done in largely premodern Britain. He lives a life of innovation, at first to survive, then because he could. He starts by working for months to build a boat, only to find it is too heavy to get to the water. (In Defoe's 1721 novel *Moll Flanders,* the adventuress steals a horse, then, not knowing what to do with it, gives it back.) Defoe has been called the poet of mistakes, difficulties, and setbacks.

When modern economies do sprout up, there are few writers conveying much sense of it. Yet three towering novels stand out as suggesting that something of epic importance has been occurring. The earliest of these is the 1818 work *Frankenstein; or, The Modern Prometheus* by Mary Shelley (born Mary Wollstonecraft Godwin). For Romantic poets and artists in Britain, the heroic figure of Prometheus symbolized the capacity for free will, creativity, and destruction. *Frankenstein* became the most influential version.[5]

---

5. The original tragedy *Prometheus Bound,* by the ancient Greek Aeschylus, told of the captivity of Prometheus and his eventual release by the omnipotent Zeus (Jupiter). In the 1820 dramatic poem *Prometheus Unbound* by Percy Bysshe Shelley, Prometheus frees himself by withdrawing a curse he had put on Jupiter, which causes Jupiter to lose his power and leave the world to a benign anarchy. Mary, living with Percy and Lord Byron, started her horror novel in Switzerland in the summer of 1818 and described Percy's drama in a letter that September. It is fair to say that her Prometheus story was, in part, a reaction against the "rational-humanism," as Muriel Spark terms it, of her atheist father, William Godwin, and that of her Christian lover and husband to be, Percy. In his younger years, Percy was called Viktor.

The author could not foresee the modern economy, let alone warn against it, but as the modern economy grew powerful, readers continued to be drawn to the novel, no doubt seeing parallels between the monster created by Dr. Viktor Frankenstein and the innovative companies created by entrepreneurs. When in James Whale's 1931 film version Dr. Frankenstein, seeing the monster move, cries "It's alive!" he could have as well been exclaiming over the nascent modern economy in Britain or America. A company is generally inclined to be kind to customers and employers just as the monster was usually kind. And companies are feared, just as the monster was feared. But was the novel an indictment of Prometheanism? Against the modern economy? The poet Percy Shelley, worried that his wife's novel would be seen as a warning against these developments, opposed any such interpretation in the preface he wrote for the book. Yet he had little reason to worry. The book does not attack innovation. It laments Frankenstein's inability and that of the townsfolk to accept the monster. And it asserts that science cannot duplicate the creative powers of human minds.

Another novel of the Romantic period that is a marker of the modern economy is the 1847 novel *Wuthering Heights* by Emily Brontë. The backdrop of the tragic love story is the tension between the rural life that imprisons Cathy and the irresistible force that pulls Heathcliff to the big city where important careers are made.[6] By the middle of the 19th century the dynamism of London had seized the imagination of the young generation, though some would have to remain behind. In the classic film version, as Heathcliff leaves Wuthering Heights, Cathy expresses the excitement—hers or perhaps her sense of his—in a single line: "Go, Heathcliff. Run away. Bring me back the world!"[7]

Charles Dickens had views on the world of work that were more complex than is widely appreciated. His power as a writer was such that he could arouse public sympathy for destitute orphans and unskilled workers oppressed by the mindlessness of the most routine factory labor—as he did in his 1837 novel *Oliver Twist* and in his 1854 novel *Hard Times*. Dickens's own harsh introduction to London when he was a boy of 12 gave him deep

6. Heathcliff, who was of Gypsy origins, may also have sensed that London, where business acumen counted, would offer chances of skirting the traditional prejudices of the rural areas. Mid-century London must have been a locus for economic inclusion as well as economic dynamism.

7. This is the 1939 version—Hollywood's golden year—produced by Samuel Goldwyn and directed by William Wyler with screenplay by Ben Hecht and Charles MacArthur. Merle Oberon and Lawrence Olivier played the lead roles.

insights into the burdensomeness of unskilled work. But he became sensitive to a growing range of problems in English society.

Even *Hard Times* is not concerned with the sorts of workers' suffering detailed by Mrs Trollope. . . . The novel's satirical focus is less industrial . . . more involved with those forces that would oppress individual and imaginative life. Stephen Blackpool's problems result not from industrialization . . . but from (in the first instance) the incapacity of the System, embodied in Parliament and the Establishment, to respond to the difficulties of his marriage; and (in the second instance) by his refusal to submerge his individuality in another dehumanizing system, Slackbridge's trade union.[8]

Dickens's views on industrialization changed too. By the 1850s he was delighted with the rise of new work opportunities across Britain while retaining a nostalgia for traditional life and an unsurpassed sympathy for the less fortunate. In his extraordinary night walks through the city he was fascinated by the vitality and variety he encountered—the "restlessness of a great city and the way in which it tumbles and tosses before it can get to sleep." In the 1836 work *Sketches by Boz* he describes the slow awakening of the city: shopkeepers, law clerks, office workers, and a new set of people entering by 11 o'clock: "The streets are thronged with a vast concourse of people, gay and shabby, rich and poor, idle and industrious, and we come to the heat, bustle and activity of NOON." After a second look at Birmingham factories he writes, "I have seen in [your] factories and workshops such . . . great consideration for the work people . . . I have seen the results in the demeanour of your working people, excellently balanced by a nice instinct, as free from servility on the one hand as from self-conceit on the other."[9] Nor was he as naïve as the solution George Orwell ascribed to him—to "give everyone turkeys." For example, Dickens warned factory operatives that a manipulative labor union organizer would use them to secure personal benefits or political ends that would not be beneficial to them.

Dickens came to see careers as a means, if not *the* means, to personal growth. His 1850 novel *David Copperfield* celebrates the development of David from childhood to maturity, contrasting it to the strategy of David's nemesis, the unctuous climber Uriah Heep:

8. Schlicke, *The Oxford Reader's Companion to Dickens* (1999, p. 294).

9. The first quote is from "Night Walks" in *The Uncommercial Traveller,* the second is from "The Streets—Morning," in *Sketches by Boz,* and the third is from a speech delivered in Birmingham on January 6th of 1853 and reprinted in *Speeches, Letters and Sayings.* These quotations also appear in Andrews, *Dickens on England and the English,* pp. 98, 84, and 69, respectively.

Heep's egocentricity prevents him from seeing work as a means of genuine liberation and self-affirmation. It is . . . David whose life assumes meaning because he finds the work that gives him both purpose and identity. The self-actualization that comes to David through his vocation as a writer constitutes Dickens's own endorsement of the worth of work. . . . [T]he oppressive situations Dickens opposed in so many of his novels were perversions of the work ethic. . . . [Dickens], the most striking nineteenth-century model for success through enterprising work, shared the basic assumptions that work is, in general, good and that workers are to be respected for their individuality and intrinsic worth.[10]

In Dickens's work, David is just one of many characters who take control of their lives. The richness and courage he saw in ordinary people is striking. So Dickens proves no less of a vitalist than Shakespeare or Cervantes.

A comparison of the writing of the mid-century novelist Charlotte Brontë, born in 1816, with that of the 18th-centuryish Jane Austen, born in 1764, may offer insight into the transformation of life in 19th-century England. Brontë's 1847 novel *Jane Eyre* can be read as the "story of a woman who succeeds in 'getting on.'" She strikes out courageously and independently and forges her own career, first as governess, then as an independent schoolmistress with her own business. . . . By the book's end, she has 'got on' very far, struggling against poverty and adversity for most of her early life, enjoying immediately none of the benefits of birth or patronage."[11] In contrast, in Austen's work, women's experiences are in the domestic economy, and her heroines look more toward marriage for their economic achievements. For them, money, which they legally had no right to in Austen's time, was basically an opportunity to raise their standard of living and social class: In *Sense and Sensibility* (1811), the Dashwood women, Elinor and Marianne, argue over the annual budget that will be required. Although many people in the present day and many contemporaries too, such as Samuel Coleridge in Britain and Thorstein Veblen in America, lamented the materialism in the mid- and

10. Bradshaw and Ozment, *The Voices of Toil* (2000, p. 199). Thus it would be wrong to view Dickens as writing about 18th-century or 17th-century capitalism as much as 19th-century modern capitalism.

11. Rick Rylance in *The Cambridge Companion to the Brontës* (2002, pp. 157–158) discusses the phrase "getting on" in the Victorian Britain of the 1840s. It meant making a success of one's life and was applied to a whole emerging class of "economically dynamic and socially mobile entrepreneurs." Interestingly, he comments that the literature seemed to disapprove of the changes in character that developed during the economic revolution though not objecting to the economic system itself.

late 19th century, evidence suggests that it was the 18th century in which the game of making money was an obsession. William Blake, the feminist writer Mary Wollstonecraft, and Thomas Carlyle were all contemporary critics of that materialism. In Austen's time, around the turn of the century, even a landowner of social rank has an intense interest in increasing the profits from land. But in her last novel, *Mansfield Park* (1814), making money begins to hold an intellectual fascination. Henry Crawford says that "the most interesting thing in the world [is] how to make money—how to turn a good income into a better [one]" (p. 226).

In the other countries where a modern economy had sprung up there are also literary works reflecting on the new business life, of course. In France, Balzac wrote approvingly for an entire volume on the phenomenon of the French cafes in the 19th century, and Émile Zola wrote about the changes taking place in Paris. In Germany, Johann Wolfgang von Goethe, the pioneering novelist of personal development, wrote with an eye on the new but his heart still in the old about the economic modernity arising along the Rhine in the 1820s. Thomas Mann's novel *Buddenbrooks*, first published in 1901, tells of four generations of a family, starting with the generation that made its fortune in business. The book charts the vitality that is lost as each generation moves farther from the world of business.

One would guess that America must have seen an outpouring of literature on the new economic life, since that life spread so far and so profoundly through the population. Americans were swept up in the movement to build new things, settle in new places, find adventure, test themselves, improve themselves, and get ahead. But for just that reason there were not many people who preferred writing about the new life to taking part in it. There was not much demand either. Had America been supplying as many new titles as Europe did, few of them would have found buyers willing to take time out to read them. Yet the novels by Herman Melville, the greatest master in 19th-century American fiction, hum with the undertones of the rising business world.

Two of Melville's major novels speak of confidence, trust, and uncertainty. In *The Confidence-Man*, his 1857 novel set aboard the ship *Fidele*, business is all about whether to entrust money to an entrepreneur or potential partner. As a friend of Melville's said, "[i]t is a good thing . . . and speaks well for human nature that it *can be swindled*." Melville's grand success in 1851, *Moby-Dick*, devotes pages to describing the processes of whaling, suggesting the excitement and indicating the hazards, which we understand are not at all quantifiable. The "whaling lines" in which the seamen may become caught, perhaps fatally, serve as a metaphor for the developments in which the actors in the economy may become disastrously entangled.[12] Although business life—the good and the bad—and the profusion of occupations made big impressions on Dickens, it took an American observer with a poetic voice to capture the fascination and suspense of the new life.

Washington Irving's *The Sketch Book of Geoffrey Crayon, Gent.*, well received in England and America in 1820, featured stories dealing with profound changes to cities. In "The Legend of Sleepy Hollow," some 25 miles up the Hudson River from New York City, Irving depicts a town isolated from the sweeping economic changes of America: Sleepy Hollow is where "population, manners, and customs remain fixed, while the great torrent of migration and improvement, which is making incessant changes in other parts of this restless country, sweeps by them unobserved." A relatively learned man— Ichabod Crane—comes to work and teach in this town of "listless repose" only to be eventually shunned by its superstitious and stubborn inhabitants. Irving subtly hints at his critical view of those who may have "understood nothing of the labor of headwork." Engagement in work is harshly contrasted with idleness, which Irving associates with lost opportunity and isolation from change.

The emergence of the modern economy drove change not just in literature but in painting as well. Until the 19th century, painting was generally static and picturesque, not only the bucolic canvases of Claude Lorrain or Thomas Gainsborough and the portraits of domesticity by Joshua Reynolds or Diego Velasquez but even in what Willard Spiegelman (somewhat unfortunately) terms "action painting":

> [A]ction painting—whether dealing with mythic, religious or historical
> events, and even if violent in content—often lacked real energy. In France,
> the gorgeous colors and symmetries of Poussin in the 17th century, the
> chiseled nobility of David in the late 18th century and the shellacked
> beauty of Ingres at the start of the 19th all gave way to the explosion of
> Romanticism.[13]

12. I am indebted to Richard Robb for general discussion. In a course at Columbia University, he has used the "whaling lines" metaphor to make vivid the hazards of making decisions in conditions of radical uncertainty characteristic of the modern economy. Regarding *The Confidence-Man*, the friend of Melville's quoted above was Evert Duyckinck, who commented in 1850 in the periodical *Literary World* on newspaper reports of people being taken in by confidence men.

13. Spiegelman, "Revolutionary Romanticism: *The Raft of the Medusa*" (2009, p. W14). The

In France this Romantic movement started in the 1820s with Théodore Géricault's tempestuous painting *The Raft of the Medusa,* in which, as Spiegelman writes, the wind-blown and sea-tossed survivors, sighting the rescue ship, express a range of emotions, "from eagerness and exultation to incredulity [and] hysteria." The huge canvases by Eugène Delacroix soon follow. On his 1834 painting *Arabic Fantasy,* E. H. Gombrich comments that "there is no clarity of outline here, no pose and restraint . . . , [no] patriotic or edifying subject. All the painter wants is to make us partake in an intensely exciting moment, and to share his joy in the movement and romance of the sea."[14] In Britain, J.M.W. Turner, in such epochal paintings as the 1801 *Dutch Boats in a Gale,* the 1842 *Steamship in Snowstorm,* and the 1844 *Rail, Steam and Speed,* evoked almost palpably the dangers and excitements of modern business ventures:

> Turner is an artist of anxiety, of restless turbulent motion, of a world that on the surface might look like the old, immemorial pre-industrial planet painted by the masters he sought to rival, but in reality is being shaken from its moorings by war, industry and revolution.
>
> This Romanticism . . . sweeps you away like a cork on a tidal wave. . . . [W]hile [the 17th-century painter] Van de Velde's sea piece *A Rising Gale* . . . paints a picture of the wild sea, [*Dutch Boats*] makes that model seem as quaint as a toy windmill. . . . Turner captures the motion and menace of the waves as paint—his paint is the sea, not a picture of it. He gives objects and energy physical reality . . . while Van de Velde seems just to be creating a virtual nature on a computer screen.
>
> Turner's painting makes you doubt the solidity of the ground beneath your feet. His earth is not a pre-Copernican platform but an orb spinning in space. . . . Turner, as his champion John Ruskin claimed, is the very definition of a "modern painter."[15]

The sea and trains became symbols of the kind of economy that had emerged

---

titular "Medusa" was a frigate that ran aground in Mauritania, leaving 150 clinging to a raft. This canvas by Théodore Géricault bids to be the earliest action painting of 19th-century Romanticism.

14. Gombrich, *The Story of Art,* p. 382. Gombrich embraces the 19th-century "revolution" in painting, though, noting the "two possibilities in Constable and Turner," he declares that "those who followed Constable's path and tried to explore the visible world rather than to conjure up poetic moods achieved something of more lasting importance." Of course, any self-respecting art scholar wants art to be a subject in itself, not just a branch of social studies. However, it remains true that the spirit of some great painters' works does reflect the spirit of the society in which they worked.

15. Jones, "Other Artists Paint Pictures, Turner Brings Them to Life" (2009).

in the century—powerful, dangerous, and too unpredictable to control, yet also fascinating and thrilling.

This Romantic movement in art, as is widely said, rejected the ordered equilibrium of 18th-century neoclassicism as mechanical and impersonal. The Romantics turned to the directness of personal experience and to individual imagination and aspiration. The parallel with the transformation of the economy is quite clear. The 18th-century economies, in which the timepaths of production, investment, and work might have been supposed to be largely determinate and thus largely knowable—apart from occasional exogenous shocks, such as the plague and finding the New World—gave way to modern economies in which what can be produced is constantly being uncovered by innovations and in which decisions on what to produce and invest in reflect the imagination of entrepreneurs. But the parallel goes only so far. Did these paintings up to the 1850s signal high engagement and deep gratification from work in the emerging modern economies? Did they reflect moments of happiness from landing the desired job or proving the worth of the new commercial idea? Apparently not. But they do represent the thrill of the opportunities and dangers of the new era.

Expressionism sought to capture other aspects of economic life not successfully represented previously. Vincent van Gogh, the forerunner of the Expressionists and another nominee as the founder of modern art, brought high emotion to subjects from everyday life in his incandescent work painted in Arles, such as *Sower with Setting Sun, The Painter on the Road to Tarascon,* and *Café Terrace on the Place du Forum,* all in 1888. In the last, the outdoor cafe in summer is as glowing as the night sky, and we want to be there chatting, drinking, and eating with friends. In his voluminous letters to his brother, van Gogh showed he understood something about the modern economies. As a daring innovator himself, he understood the need of people to create and to leave a mark by innovating. As a professional, he also understood that innovation cannot go far in the absence of possibilities of observing, and learning and taking inspiration from the innovative activities of others:

> Man is not placed on this earth to be happy; nor is he placed here merely to be honest. He is here to accomplish great things through society.[16]

The Expressionists, following up on the breakthroughs of van Gogh, were fascinated by the fast-expanding urban life. Before them, there were paintings such as Kruger's *Parade in the Opernplatz 1822,* in which a traditional subject, with its royal figures, is transformed into an image of a "modern crowd"

16. Van Gogh, *The Letters* (2009, p. 57).

composed of ordinary citizens and celebrities.[17] The Expressionist Ernst Ludwig Kirchner with his half-dozen paintings titled *Berlin Street Scene* between 1913 and 1915 struck a new note in conveying the vitality, glamour, and rush of the new city life at the end of the century. Later, however, Oskar Kokoschka and George Grosz were extraordinarily dark about the modern life around them, having survived the horrors of World War 1 and the upheavals in the 1920s. A sunnier side was presented in the Mediterranean region with the Futurist painters of Italy, who caught the quickened pace of Italian life. An early example, the 1910 work by Giacomo Balla *Dynamism of a Dog on a Leash* must be mentioned. Later, Gino Severini celebrated in 1915's *Red Cross Train Passing a Village* the breathtaking speed and sleek design of the modern trains coming into being in Italy. (In contrast, the painters who took the road of Constable—Paul Cézanne and the great Cubists—were more interested in space and perspective than in life in business and the city.)

There is little expression in the visual arts of a key dimension of living that the modern economies introduced. Business life used to be full of derring-do—of going "down to the boats and into the sea," as the Vikings did. With the modern economy, life was full of cerebration—of "I'm going up to the attic to think." In painting and sculpture there are some acknowledgments of the new mental life, however. A portrait painted around 1900 by a Philadelphia artist depicts a businessman apparently deep in thought. *The Thinker,* about the most well-known work in all of sculpture, was produced in 1889 by Auguste Rodin, progenitor of modern sculpture and widely appreciated for representing ordinary men and women. Maybe *The Thinker* was the mythic Prometheus, yet "promethean" has long been a term used to characterize the modern economies; no one made such a sculpture until the modern economies and, with them, modern sculpture came along.

We do not find in literature or the visual arts much appreciation for the interior satisfactions and gratifications that surely arose and spread first in the 19th century. In *Field Notes from Elsewhere,* his meditation getting to the bottom of life, the philosopher Mark C. Taylor asks in his next-to-last chapter, "why is it so hard to write about happiness?" He suggests that writers tend not to write when they are happy and when the happiness passes, as it always does, they deal with their unhappiness by writing about it. Maybe doing so helps them to work their way out of their unhappiness. Another reason may be that, although moments of joy, glee, or ecstasy may be possible to

17. Foster-Hahn et al., *Spirit of an Age* (2001).

represent if put in a particular context, unremarkable everyday satisfactions and gratifications from being engaged in projects—alone or in teams—do not lend themselves to representation by words or paint.

In contrast, it appears that music has proved better able to resonate with those interior feelings, with the internal dimensions of much of our experience. Music appears to have captured the experience of meeting problems and resonated with the obstacles and exaltation of creating. Perhaps this is because a piece of music may be a hundred stanzas and thousands of bars, while a painting is a single frame. So their capabilities are different.

No doubt, the product delivered by music is not a mere depiction of others' creativity, innovation, the ensuing struggle, defeat and triumph. The music is its own thing; with exceptions, it does not represent anything in the social world. What the composer expresses is the composer's own feelings about the composer's own effort to create and, with luck, to cause a musical innovation. And if perchance the audience "resonates" with the task and the struggle expressed, the composition becomes a commercial success.

Europe and America in the 19th century were alive with the sound of music, increasingly so over the century. Music was no longer a sort of treasure reserved for European bishops and princes. So-called serious music came to be embraced by the middle class from the business world, and so-called popular music could be accessed by the working class as well. The audience for music was strong in America. In 1842 Vienna's Musikverein was founded to support the Vienna Philharmonic Orchestra while in the same year the Philharmonic Society of New York was founded to create a high-level orchestra there. Yet in the 19th century the great producers of music, serious and popular, were all European. In the next century, though, America took the lead in popular songwriting and, by the 1930s, pulled its weight even in the music of the concert hall.

Something important must have been going on in music that struck a chord with the life of the times. It is clear now what it was. Composers in the Baroque and classical periods of the 17th and 18th centuries routinely drew on the stock of preexisting folk tunes for material and were formulaic in developing their themes—as routine and formulaic as the mercantile economies of that era. Working in this style, a composer of Joseph Haydn's musicality could produce more than 100 symphonies. The subsequent eras were all about tearing down these rules. A poll years ago asked musicologists to name the three most innovative composers of all time. The winners were Ludwig van Beethoven, Richard Wagner, and Igor Stravinsky. (There would surely have been no consensus on the fourth.) They all broke rules in musical composition between 1800 and 1910 in company with the rise of the modern economies and the high business innovation that resulted.

Beethoven, most loudly with his 1804 Symphony No. 3 (*Eroica*), introduced a way of innovating by leaving it to some extent undetermined how the symphony will develop—much as the path of the modern economies was to an extent undetermined owing to the possibilities of innovation that were left open to entrepreneurs and financiers. Beethoven can break into a new theme unpredictably—for example, the last movement of the Symphony No. 2, with its frenzied strings, seems chaotic, and Symphony No. 9 breaks rules to express disorder—just as an entrepreneur might unpredictably start the development of a new product. Of course, Beethoven was not inspired by vast commercial innovation: the modern economies were just beginning to be developed enough to be able to carry out successful attempts at business innovation. What seems likely is that Beethoven rocketed to success over ensuing decades because the experience of hearing his symphonies struck a chord among people who were experiencing innovation—their own and, mostly, those of others—in their own business lives. It was the educated bourgeoisie who hoisted Beethoven up on their shoulders. They celebrated him; he was not celebrating them.

The next generation of composers raised the celebration of the hero to a fever pitch. Robert Schumann's overture *Manfred* caught the spirit of Shelley's poem and the propulsiveness of his piano quartet in E-flat major—played at breakneck speed—brilliantly expressed the rush of his times. Franz Liszt broke new ground with *Les preludes* (*d'apres Lamartine*), an orchestral work not structured along classical lines, which he dubbed a "symphonic poem." The title is thought to refer to an ode by the poet Alphonse de Lamartine and an epigraph in the published score evokes that poem:

> What else is our life but a series of preludes? . . . [W]hat is the fate where the first delights of happiness are not interrupted by some storm, the mortal blast of which dissipates its fine illusions, . . . where the soul . . . on issuing from one of these tempests, does not endeavour to rest in recollection in the calm serenity of life in the fields? Nevertheless man hardly gives himself up for long to the enjoyment of the beneficent stillness which at first he has shared in Nature's bosom. . . . [W]hen "the trumpet sounds the alarm" he hastens to the dangerous post, whatever the war may be, which calls him to its ranks, in order at last to recover in the combat full consciousness of himself and entire possession of his energy.

(The electrifying trumpet call lets the audience know when "recovery" has come.)

Richard Strauss's symphonic poem *Ein Heldenleben* [*A Hero's Life*] is inspired by the ups and downs in the early years of a career—his own. His last opera, *Capriccio,* has a business setting: the theatrical business. With the character of the theater director La Roche, Strauss draws a convincing warts-and-all picture of a vain but great man. Yet, in that opera and some others, Strauss is primarily interested in dramatizing the heroine's quest for self-knowledge. Women as well as men must go into the world to find out who they are. By Strauss's time, modern economies had wrought a cultural and psychological revolution and were beginning to break down even age-old gender barriers.

Nineteenth-century opera reflected the new aspirations of people for liberation and self-expression. Richard Wagner and Giuseppe Verdi, both born in 1813, reflected the tensions and emotions raised by the modern social life developing around them. In Wagner, heroines are at the center and it is passion, such as love, that gives life meaning—nowhere more so than in his four-opera cycle *The Ring of the Niebelung,* which premiered in 1869. He does not assert that there are no passions in business or that meeting challenges, experimenting, and exploring in the business world cannot give life meaning. But the *Ring* cycle is also about the meaninglessness and possible downfall that await those who indulge in a single-minded, unbridled pursuit of material wealth or arbitrary power. The sought-after golden ring is cursed. The cycle also expresses foreboding as the old order of throne and altar is brought down by the arrival of industrial nations and the end of the Holy Roman Empire. When Wotan, ruler of the world, steals the ring from Alberich, who had himself stolen it, he undermines all the old treaties and obligations—it is everyone for himself. Yet Wagner is not a pessimist. The downfall of the gods in the *Ring*'s last opera represents, according to Wagner himself, the beginning of the modern world, where human beings will be freer than before to shape their destinies. And befitting an artist of his talent and daring, Wagner was not a social conservative. He may have been a socialist on some ethereal level but he was no corporatist: his only comedy, *Die Meistersinger,* pays affectionate tribute to the traditions of the medieval guild, yet he comes down on the side of the individual and openness to the new.

Later operas in Italy, notably Verdi's *La Traviata* and the *verismo* works of Giacomo Puccini and Pietro Mascagni that followed, dramatize the modern theme of emancipation from oppression and repression. In the 20th century, the jazzy compositions of Maurice Ravel, Darius Milhaud, and Jacques Ibert celebrate the freedom and sheer fun of modern life in France in those times. The rise of jazz in New Orleans and Chicago in the 1920s was an expression of individuality and an imaginative spirit.

Evolving in tandem with modern music, modern ballet offers a respite from opera's heroism and revenge. Marius Petipa, the French dancer who, after stints in America and Europe, ended up in St. Petersburg, created the modern ballet of ecstatic leaps and twirls in collaboration with Peter Ilyich Tchaikovsky. *Swan Lake,* in its original 1877 version, centers on the conflict between the upright and dutiful Odette, turned into a Swan Queen, and the glamorous woman of the world Odile, a would-be seductress of the Prince, in love with Odette. The ballet can surely be seen as an allegory of the moral tensions in modern life, where there are new hazards in commitment— though a virtuous path can offer rewards too, and virtue is its own reward. Yet ballet certainly had further to go in modern directions, and another Russian, George Balanchine, took it there as he wended his way from St. Petersburg to Paris to London to New York. His revolutionary works, from *Apollo* in 1928 ("I learned I too could simplify") and *Prodigal Son* in 1929, to *Agon* in 1957, and *Stravinsky Violin Concerto* in 1972, depicted elements of modern life—journeys without destinations, the strangeness of it, and its exhilarating moments. Russia's economy was far from modern then—it still is. Yet, soaking up the spirit of the West's modern cities from an early age, Stravinsky and Balanchine became modern giants.

One wonders whether the decline of modern art and music during the 1960s—when Ezra Pound's "Make It New!" was replaced by the endless loops of Philip Glass and the irony of Pop Art—and the decline of economic dynamism that was already visible across Europe and beginning to set in across America both signaled a loss of commitment to the ideals of exploration and innovation.

Summing Up

The modern economies that broke out in much of the Western world had deep consequences for the temper of the times. The birth of the modern in the arts and letters is undoubtedly connected with the spirit of the modern economy in the countries where it sprang up and maintained its force. Yet the connections are two-way. The earliest expressions of the modern, very clearly in music and philosophy, appear to anticipate and perhaps to kindle the spirit without which modern economies would have been impossible;

these precocious breakthroughs in the arts and philosophy are harbingers of the modern economies to come. Nevertheless, the extraordinary waves of artistic innovation in the 19th century and the first half of the 20th are reflections and commentary on the new dimensions of life wrought by the modern economy. In general, the arts, normally critical of society and frequently dark, were positive about the modern life and celebrated the new dimensions of living. (The last two chapters take up the ultimate question of how we might reasonably weigh the positive effects of economic modernity against the costs.)

Readers by now will have gotten a sense of the ports of call ahead and where the ship is bound. Chapter 4, which closes out Part One on the rise of the modern, tackles the question of the evolving institutions, economic and political, and the economic culture that may have given birth to the modern economies hatched in the 19th century. Part Two takes up the 20th-century battles and controversies over the modern economy, some of which led to modifications of the modern system—for better or for worse.

CHAPTER FOUR

How Modern Economies Formed

The Bolsheviks understood that culture [has] a strong influence on people. . . . [They] knew the game was up when the sons
of the Communists themselves wanted to become capitalists and
entrepreneurs.

JOSEPH JANICEK, "Czechs' Velvet Revolution," *New York Times*

T HE EMERGENCE BY THE MID-19TH CENTURY of a pervasively modern
economy in much of the West altered human experience by enlisting
creativity, inviting experimentation, and fostering innovation. It thereby
earned its place as a watershed development in world history. One would
think, then, that historians would have taken up the big questions of its
origin: What was required for economic modernity and how were the
requirements met? What was present here and not there? Present then and
not before?

General historians did not address the questions. What they wrote under
"the rise of the West" are chronicles of the rise of the state and democracy.
Their drama opens with Gutenberg's printing press in 1444, the expansion-
ism of Europe's monarchs in the 1500s, Luther's "95 Theses" of 1517 challenging Rome, and the gradual recognition of the Magna Carta in the 1600s. This
was heady stuff. Yet the era's economies are mainly noted for little but the
growth of long-distance trade from 1350 to 1750.

A few historians, sociologists, and others did write of the rise of several
economies in the West, often under the heading of "the rise of capitalism." In
Jared Diamond's ecological work, abundant crops and animals and the towns
they could support enabled greater specialization of labor in Eurasia than was
possible in sub-Saharan Africa, Australia, and the Americas. That is why Eurasia became richer than the rest. But this thesis does not explain the rise of
innovation and why it arose in Britain, Belgium, France, and Germany but

not in Holland, Portugal, Ireland, Greece, and Spain. Economic institutions and culture are the suspects.[1]

The sociologist Max Weber pointed to a particular cultural shift, believing it was the key to where capitalism flowered. He argued that Calvinism and Lutheranism gave birth to an economic culture of thrift and hard work, which is why capitalism succeeded in the Protestant nations of northern Europe. Though Weber's treatise was well received by the public, critics have noted that some non-Protestant nations, such as Italy, have private saving and net wealth levels that dwarf those of Germany and workweeks that are longer than Germany's as well. What is most telling, however, is that Weber's vocabulary has no room for experimentation, exploration, daring, and unknowability—the hallmarks of indigenous innovation. His thesis may help explain high levels in the aggregate of all investment-type activities reached in several countries. Yet high saving is not necessary for high innovation. (A nation can finance innovative activity by increasing saving or by diverting a part of the unchanged flow of saving to innovation from projects that are relatively uninnovative—houses and conventional business investments. Or it could draw on foreign saving.) And clearly high saving is not sufficient for innovation.[2]

A few scholars did come to grips with Walt Rostow's 19th-century "take-offs into sustained growth." Alexis de Tocqueville, the French political thinker who made penetrating observations on Americans in 1837, thought that the richness of the country's natural resources was the reason Americans were

1. Diamond's book, *Guns, Germs and Steel* (1997), did suggest in passing that European nations became more innovative because, being small, they were forced to innovate or lose population to one another, while the vastness of Asian empires impeded exit. France and Germany were the biggest on the Continent and yet the most innovative.

2. Weber's treatise, known to the English-speaking world in the translation by Talcott Parsons, *The Protestant Ethic and the Spirit of Capitalism,* was first published in German in the 1904/1905 volume of *Archiv für Sozialwissenschaft und Sozialpolitik* (under the title *Die protestantische Ethik und der Geist des Kapitalismus*). It must have been read by every sociologist ever since and by Schumpeter, who is wrongly credited with coining "the entrepreneurial spirit." Yet this treatise was not the high point of Weber's social thought. His big book, 1922's *Wirtschaft und Gesellschaft*, translated in 1978 as *Economy and Society,* offers first drafts on several basic problems in the social sciences: the state, companies, bureaucracy, rationality, legitimacy, and more—topics that went on to enliven social sciences over the century. His most profound insight is his theme that (to paraphrase) an extraterrestrial watching from afar a terrestrial economy would not make sense of what people were doing—unless it was a traditional economy executing the same rhythm every year. (The puzzle would be like the cryptic action in Alfred Hitchcock's *Vertigo* or Michelangelo Antonioni's *Blowup*.) A meaningful analysis requires enough information about the subjects' intents and beliefs to put one's self figuratively in the economy. This is a difficulty physics does not face.

such energetic entrepreneurs. But innovation flowered as much in Britain in the early 1800s as in America. And several countries rich in resources, such as Argentina, became famous for failing to develop any economic dynamism—it was even suspected that natural resources were (or could be) a "curse." Arnold Toynbee, the British historian, took the position opposite to de Tocqueville's. He contended that the British were the first to embrace innovation because, being so poor in climate and natural resources, they had the most to gain if their ship came in. Nothing ventured, nothing gained.[3] But if natural wealth were the drag that Toynbee thought it was, the Americans would have been much less entrepreneurial and less innovative generally, which seems counter to the evidence. Toynbee's idea—*per aspera ad astra*—has some merit: rich kids tend to be short on the focus and hustle necessary for big success. But the exceptions in this case are notable.

The general problem in these four histories is that they never get down to brass tacks. They observe that in some nations more than others labor demand was high (Diamond, de Tocqueville) or supply was high (Weber, Toynbee); then, in a series of leaps, they conclude that high levels of work, saving, wealth, and willingness to take large risks resulted. But even if, where labor increased, great wealth and risk-taking resulted, it does not follow that processes of *innovation* started up. The idea that economic dynamism sprouted from natural and accidental causes implies that countries had no need to devise a set of economic institutions or possess an economic culture favorable to commercial innovation—it implies that the system was already there waiting. Though most if not all peoples, it appears, found self-expression in acting creatively and embracing novelty as far back as prehistoric times, it would be bizarre to exclude the possibility that some countries were more advantaged—politically or culturally—in identifying and building institutions that would enable and facilitate innovation and in fostering attitudes toward experimentation, exploration, and imagination that would inspire

3. De Tocqueville's book, *Democracy in America*, first published in 1835 in France, though it had many observations on economic life, was primarily about America's political life. Toynbee's life work, the 12-volume tome *A Study of History*, published between 1934 and 1961, has the theme that after the rise of wealth out of nothing, accumulation goes on until there is a great fall. His model of decline has a place alongside Gibbon's *Decline and Fall of the Roman Empire*, published in volumes from 1776 to 1789, and Spengler's 1926 prophecy, *The Decline of the West*. In Toynbee's model the difficulty is why Britain should have overexpanded its investments and imperial reach to unsustainable levels. Britain did recoup the huge losses suffered during World War II but never came close to regaining its previous levels of overseas capital and empire. An analogous paradox in every financial crisis is why banks impale themselves on an excess of short-term debt.

and encourage people. A case in point is the Afghan region, now synonymous with backwardness, yet a thousand years ago a place of shining cities and scientific discoveries undreamt of in the rest of the world. This region, to which nature had dealt a good hand, could never develop economic institutions or elements of an economic culture that would open the way to economic modernity—to flourishing business careers and high human fulfillment among all or most of the populace.[4]

If we are to reach an appreciable understanding of the causal forces, conditions, and mechanisms giving birth to a modern sector, pushing out the feudal sector and stealing the show from the mercantile sector, we will have to conceive of the forces and conditions capable of driving the economy's innovative process. We of course recognize that the story we tell can never be error-free, let alone complete. Just as the actors in a modern economy can have only imperfect knowledge of the effects that actions taken in the present are going to have in the future—too much is new and too many actors may be taking novel steps at the same time—theorists of the modern economy can have only imperfect understanding of how, if at all, the beliefs, institutions, and cultures built up over the past enable and encourage the creativity and innovation of the present. In the nations in which modern economies arrived, there were too many developments over previous decades or centuries for us to be able to identify with confidence a set of crucial elixirs. Like canny financiers, we must use judgment and imagination. The competition of ideas has left standing more than one story, or "myth," of the creation of the modern.

These stories are important, of course. Any story a nation tells about its modernization or the lack of it reveals that nation's understanding of the attributes to which it owes its modernization or failure at modernization. Such a story and its retelling are aimed at conveying a conception of things the nation has been right to do and things it was right not to do. Some, if not all, of these stories may therefore be of considerable influence. No doubt the late economist Paul Samuelson had that influence in mind when he said, reflecting on his own story-telling, "I don't care who writes a nation's laws . . . if I can write its economics textbooks." Of course, truth matters, not just influence (which Samuelson never lost sight of). A truer narrative would be a more valuable one—provided it is not so much harder to grasp than the next-truest. Better understanding would help a nation find (or re-find) its

4. See Starr, "Rediscovering Central Asia."

way to a modern economy or to avoid jeopardizing the modern economy it has. Any attempt at a truer narrative will do well to draw on core ideas in the stories already told. Yet the centerpiece of our narrative must be the emergence of the innovation that made some economies modern and even great.

Economic Institutions: Freedom, Property, and Finance

A part of the story of the rise of chronically innovative economies, nascent or mature, is about the creation and evolution of various economic institutions, called in some contexts framework conditions. Some set of economic institutions is necessary to protect and facilitate the activities and arrangements needed for innovation. Not every one of these institutions may be essential by itself—taken alone. Yet, generally speaking, each one makes the economy more able or more disposed to innovate.

It is a commonplace that the range of individual freedoms established relatively early in the West were dear to those who won them. Adam Smith writes of the importance of "dignity" and John Rawls of "self-respect." It is also a commonplace that the emergence of various economic freedoms, such as the freedom to exchange one's goods or services for the goods or services of others, enabled people to realize opportunities for mutual gain. In addition, since many contracts to exchange one thing for another could be violated, people need to see the state protecting economic freedoms by enforcing contracts in order to have the confidence to enter into them. Thus freedoms—to barter or receive income, for example—help weed out economic *inefficiencies*, as Adam Smith saw. But a study of the rise of dynamic economies has to consider the role of individual freedoms in gaining economic *dynamism.*

Economic freedoms were of key importance in enabling processes of innovation. Here, the basic point is that two heads are better than one. We should expect innovation in a nation's economy to be less widespread if large segments of society cannot gain inclusion or, if they could join, would be denied a legal right to share in the fruits of their work. Historians of personal liberty—self-ownership—find that, among traditional societies, those in the East gave a father ownership of his daughters, so they could be worked or sold, while those in the West gave husbands ownership of whatever their wives brought in. In both East and West, blacks could be sold into slavery. In the 19th century, however, the modern societies finally abolished slavery. Somewhat later, they established the legal right of married women to own property. It has been theorized that the evolving nature of work in an innovative economy made it advantageous to society that women have self-ownership, so they would be motivated to adapt and improvise as they see best.[5] Similarly, innovation in a nation's economy will tend to be more widespread if potential providers of inventive ideas are free to open new companies in existing industries. Such free entry permits entrepreneurs to develop and launch new products for testing in the marketplace or to introduce new methods for producing existing products. Also, innovation is more widespread when established firms are freer to offer new products or conduct their businesses in new ways. Thus the rise of such freedoms was to have unanticipated benefits going far beyond exchange—benefits that would ultimately take human development to a new plane.

It is also clear that people are better able and more apt to be involved in departures that may lead to innovation when they have been left free to venture from their homes, regions, and even countries to soak up information on old and new products and new lifestyles. As Weber would have said, people cannot remotely understand the structure and workings of an economy or even a small industry in it—an economy or industry in which future innovations will occur—unless they have considerable experience in it. For innovation to take place, consumers and enterprises, in making decisions as potential end-users, have to be free to adopt a novel product, to judge whether it best meets a need, and to learn how to use it.

The statement that freedoms are good, notably for the expression of creativity and the achievement of innovation, does not imply that freedoms are good in every case—the overstatement for which the libertarian Ayn Rand became famous. Not all freedoms are good for dynamism. A regulation curbing some producers' freedom may allow a consumer to risk trying a new product without having to fear electrocution, poisoning, or the like. A bankruptcy law restraining creditors from seizing what is owed them may allow an entrepreneur to risk attempting an innovative product without having to fear the loss of everything he or she owns (though such laws may dampen the credit made available). On the other hand, some regulations block innovations rather than pave the way for them. (While the libertarians are always contending that virtually all regulation is bad, statists suggest that there is

---

5. Furthermore, parents would see it in their interest to bring up daughters to haul in a good income in business. See the 2002 paper by Geddes and Lueck, "Gains from Self-Ownership and the Expansion of Women's Rights," and the 2011 survey in Edlund, "Big Ideas."

hardly any innovative product that ought not to be submitted for regulatory approval before trial in the market, lest it cause some pioneering users harm.) As the modern economies developed, a welter of regulations by local, regional, and central governments erected barriers to new products and facilities to produce them, thus quite possibly doing more harm than good. In the United States, airport construction has hit a wall not because travelers prefer congestion and delays to the added tax on their air tickets that would be entailed but because every community says NIMBY—"not in my backyard." It is thought that, better than banning some projects, it would be better to require the builder to compensate the community sufficiently to win approval. But that too would have a chilling effect on many innovative projects.

There are good reasons to believe that two more freedoms—the legal right to accumulate the income earned from a new successful product, such as a hit song or movie, and the legal right to invest it in private property, mainly capital—have been of historic importance in boosting dynamism. (We may leave aside for now how much wealth would be enough—whether, for ample dynamism, it might be sufficient for people to be permitted to own an abundance of personal effects, such as clothes and other household durables, a car, a boat, an apartment in the city, and a house in the country.) Here, we are going well beyond the proposition that the legal right to receive money in return is a rudimentary step toward making innovation gainful on a large scale. The proposition at issue is whether it was and is important that people be free to hold wealth in the form of owning firms (proprietorships or partnerships) and, going a step further, owning companies in the form of shareowning—companies privately held and those whose shares are publicly traded. The argument that such freedom is generally helpful to innovation and that some form of company ownership is possibly essential does not hold any surprises at this point. If we want creative ideas springing up from the grassroots and private entrepreneurs and private financiers judging which ones look to be worth gambling on, we will not want to limit the pool of idea-men, financiers, and entrepreneurs to those who would do it for just the usual stipend that the state pays everyone, or for just a chance at earning the annual wage income that workers receive with little or no risk. A nation would not get the right selection of people that way, and those selected would have little incentive to make decisions with the prospect of profit— rather than fun or fame. And there does not appear to be any obvious way of paying the conceiver of an idea, the developer, and the financier except by an arrangement that pays shares to these central actors. There has to be a social device that rewards those doing innovative work according to the fruits of their visions, insights, and judgments—the innovation achieved—not the hours put in. (It is left to the next chapter to take up the socialist argument that society does well to leave most or much of the economy's investment in capital—including economic knowledge—to the state.)

If we agree on the importance of these economic freedoms for innovation, are we then on our way to a freedom-based narrative of the birth of economic dynamism in the 19th century? To be sure, in prehistoric times, when families lived in small groups, a great many family decisions now regularly made with utter freedom must have been submitted to the group for approval. The day-to-day interdependencies could not have allowed much scope for individual initiative. The challenge to a narrative of the eventual flowering of innovation that bases itself on freedom, though, is that most of these valuable freedoms did not arise in Britain or anywhere else until a short gestation period before the modern economy was born—1815 or so. Indeed, recorded history shows that property rights go back more than 3,000 years before the explosion of innovation. In ancient Babylonia, the Code of King Hammurabi, proclaimed around 1760 BC, set out a body of law that assumed individual ownership of property and protected owners against theft, fraud, and violation of contract. Jewish law was established about the same time and came to form the basis for common law, including property rights. In ancient Rome, the civil law was codified and made accessible to citizens, whose property rights were defined and protected against confiscation by the government. The law also supported contractual agreements, and it defined private corporations and their ability to acquire property. These principles were applied throughout the vast Roman Empire.

These ancient freedoms of private ownership did not make it to the 19th century without a setback in the Dark Ages:

> [W]hen the Roman Empire faltered and failed, largely owing to corruptness at its higher levels of government, [t]he weakening of Roman authority diminished the force of Roman law. . . . Distant commercial dealings became more risky and, as a result, the settings for transactions became more localized and compact. . . . Private ownership gave way to collective ownership. Land and other resources, in larger measure than before, became the property of local abbeys, feudal villages and [family-run] peasant farms . . . [which] strove for and secured a large measure

of self-sufficiency. Mutual obligation and collective control of resources substituted for private ownership. . . . The church and feudal institutions were run as cooperatives . . . the peasant farm by the family.[6]

Yet private ownership never disappeared. The cities maintained extensive private ownership of resources. And as the long-distance trade of cities gradually recovered in importance, property law grew in importance. Elements of Roman law survived in the common law that arose in Britain and in the civil law that developed on the European continent. Many principles of Roman law were imported directly into French civil law with the Napoleonic Code of 1804. So, although the economic freedoms involving private ownership began to emerge, albeit fitfully, in ancient times, the gradual spread and codification of these freedoms was ongoing, even in the most modern societies in the West, well into the 19th century. After the middle ages, "[t]he march from status to contract and from collective to private ownership resumed," as Demsetz put it. And, as noted above, the extension of ownership rights to the enslaved and to women occurred only in the middle of that century.

It has to be interjected that a kind of property associated with innovation began to come under legal protections on the eve of the 19th century. Patents, copyrights, and trademarks developed, aimed (with varying success) at protecting *intellectual property.* Laying the groundwork for this shift, Britain in 1623 became the first country to issue patents in a significant volume, granting protection from infringement of "projects of new invention" upon payment of a stiff fee. The Patent Act in the United States offered much cheaper protection, with the result that patent applications soared. (Britain modified its system during the 19th century to make patents as affordable as in America but never reached a comparable volume.) The French patent system was created during the Revolution in 1791. In view of these dates, it might seem plausible that patents were the key—the open sesame—to innovation in the 19th century. Economics gives less support to that notion than may be supposed. In fact, a great deal of intellectual

---

6. Demsetz, "Toward a Theory of Property Rights II" (p. 668; the following quote is also to be found on that page). Harold Demsetz, writing in the shadow of the groundbreaking organization theorist Ronald Coase, sees the latter's work in the middle third of the past century as on the "consequences"—benefits, to be more precise—"of an existing private-ownership system" and sees his own work in the last third of the century as on the causes of private ownership—"why it came into existence."

property stays with the proprietor without benefit of any legal protection whatsoever. Much of a company's chronic improvements in the goods it sells and its methods of making them may simply pass under the radar of competitors, actual or potential. As Hayekian economists would say, much detailed knowledge stays with those "on the spot," who are immersed in it enough to understand it. Even if a company's new method of producing could easily be copied by a rival company, the latter would fear that constructing similar equipment to compete might only wipe out all profit or so much of the profit that it could not cover its cost, so it may not undertake the investment. In films, much of the profits are earned in the first couple of weeks, the rest within the year, so an imitation may succeed but not at the cost of the pioneer. Even when a new book or play is off to a good start, it is rare that another publishing house or theatrical company could imitate or improve on it well enough to overcome the advantages of the pioneering work—its reputation and fame or buzz. Where an innovator is sure it could set its price low enough to keep potential predators at bay and still make a profit, the loss resulting from the appropriability of its innovation might not be large enough to deter it from attempting the innovation.

These gains notwithstanding, demands on the state to provide protection of property rights and other services had the consequence of creating state powers with no counterpart in the middle ages and the mercantile era. And the monarchies and feudal baronies that protected commoners from one another did not protect them against state power. However, in England, Scotland, and colonial America there was a backlash against that power, as commoners began to insist on "rights against the king" as well as rights with respect to one another.

The concept of rights against the king found its first public expression in the Magna Carta Libertatum issued by King John of England in 1215, confirmed in 1297, and repeated in a 1354 statute. Kings were to rule in accordance with law and custom—a concept that sowed the seeds of constitutional government. Yet the great principles were flouted. (They did not stop William II from taxing the politically weak and economically poor farmers, which the outraged Robin Hood sought to redress.) The statute was put into practice only after a struggle in the 1600s between the kings of the House of Stuart and Parliament, culminating in the Glorious Revolution of 1688 and the Bill of Rights in 1689. The latter finally abolished such royal prerogatives as suspending laws, levying taxes without Parliament, and interfering with the courts. The "law of the land" was equated to "due process of law," and due process meant that no one may be deprived of liberty or property without proper adjudication.[7]

This constitutional development has been viewed as having put Britain and later other countries under the rule of law. The protection of businesses as well as households from confiscation by the crown and from new edicts to benefit favorites at the expense of others could have signaled to entrepreneurs and investors that Britain and similar countries had been made safe for enterprise in general and innovation in particular. The contracts clause in the U.S. Constitution of 1787 is seen as in the spirit of the rule of law, applied equally to the powerful and the weak. It became a bulwark against government actions taken in the interests of the politically powerful and at the expense of the politically weak.

But there have been doubts that the activation of the new rights in 1689 could have made the difference between day and night. The sentiment that "law should govern" and authorities should be "the servants of the laws" had been familiar in Aristotle's time in ancient Greece and in Jewish law before that. That it took nearly a century and a half after 1689 for innovation to explode suggests that instituting the constitution was not enough to cause a sharp break in the path of history and, by itself, to open the way to intensive innovation. And the very fuzziness of some elements in the "rule of law" concept—Is every change in tax law unjust? When is a tax a taking from political opponents?—suggests that protections of freedoms from the authorities must be taken with a grain of salt.

Though these freedoms were unquestionably necessary for the transformation from mercantile economies to modern ones, the fact that the explosion of innovation did not take place in the late 1600s or in the 1700s makes it hard to believe that that these freedoms, even taken together, were sufficient for the birth of the modern. We have still not found a spark that could be

---

7. Chapter 39 of the original Magna Carta states:
   No Freeman shall be taken, or imprisoned, or be disseised [dispossessed] of his Freehold, or Liberties, or free Customs, or be outlawed, or exiled, or any otherwise destroyed, nor will we pass upon him, nor condemn him, but by lawful Judgment of his Peers, or by the Law of the Land. We will sell to no man, we will not deny or defer to any man either Justice or Right.
   Sir Edward Coke, Chief Justice in the early 1600s, wrote in a series of opinions that in "the ancient constitution," which the Magna Carta enshrined, law must be based on courts alone, judges must be independent, and neither King nor Church could enter houses without warrants, raise taxes without legislation, and make arrests not according to the law. In the commentary on the Magna Carta in his 1797 *Second Institute* Coke equates the "law of the land" with "due process of law." Due process became the foundation of the common law.

confidently said to have ignited the fire of innovation—the equivalent of Mrs. O'Leary's cow, thought to have triggered the Chicago Fire. Yet we can search for *later* institutions that would plausibly explain the formation of chronically innovative economies, particularly those arising in the second quarter of the 19th century.

In fact there are other economic institutions that began emerging closer to the birth of the modern. Some key institutions had roots in mercantile times or even in ancient times but reached a mature stage only in the mid-1800s. The development of the company is one example. The oldest and still most common form of business organization is the sole proprietorship, which is run by an individual or often by a family. The proprietorship is not expensive to form or maintain, and there are not the moral hazards that owners face in later organizations. For larger operations, the preferred business form was the partnership. Partnerships could conduct businesses having capital requirements out of reach of the typical proprietorship, and they had the advantage that they combined the talents and personal knowledge of persons with managerial and investor backgrounds. From ancient Rome onward, a company was accorded various legal rights. It could, for example, conduct business in its own name. Early in the 19th century, partnerships were surely producing more output than businesses of any other form in Britain and America (with proprietorships, that is, family firms, surely second). And not all partnerships were small. Some grew large by becoming "holding companies" with central headquarters run by some highly senior partner and several subsidiary branches run by other partners. In America, the "investment banks" of the late 19th century were partnerships. Partners risked all their wealth.

The difficulty with many a partnership is that it puts a partner on the horns of a dilemma. If partners had latitude to act alone, a partner could be held liable for the actions, unscrupulous or ill-judged, of another partner. If instead partners were put on a short leash, they would face the nuisance of negotiating an agreement with one another and the risk that in the end no agreement would result. With such a downside, it would not be surprising that partners would not be inclined to take on the complex challenges and uncertainties of venturing on a highly innovative project. Furthermore, expanding a partnership could multiply the hazards hanging over the partners. For these reasons, liability fears must have severely limited the size and scope of most partnerships well into the 19th century—and thus were a drag on undertaking innovative projects when other conditions were making innovation a possibility.

A newer form of business organization eventually developed into a powerful vehicle for risk taking and, at least in that respect, for innovation. This was the joint-stock company—the business corporation, in modern terms. It issued ownership shares and, normally, limited a shareowner's losses to what had been paid to acquire the shares. Owners thus had limited liability. That could be a boon to entrepreneurs, and governments granted it only to companies they chartered. In the 16th and 17th centuries British and Dutch governments chartered several joint-stock companies to carry out public-private projects for trade, exploration, and colonization: the East India Company, Hudson's Bay Company, and the notorious Mississippi Company and South Sea Company. At the zenith of mercantilism about half of Britain's export revenues were produced by chartered companies. In the 18th century Britain began chartering companies in industry, notably in insurance, canals, and hard drink, creating near-monopolies in which owners and the state benefited. But these monopolies were not innovative. The joint-stock company proved unattractive to investors, who were wary of buying shares after the South Sea abuses and later scandals. So the cost of capital may have been too high to permit joint-stock companies to finance a novel expansion or a radical change. And most industrialists—including Boulton & Watt and Eli Wedgwood no less—saw drawbacks in a charter. A charter was costly, the process cumbersome, the profits of a joint-stock company would be taxable on top of applicable income taxes, regulations came with the charter, and the charter could be modified at will. In America, state charters continued to be restricted to "public works"—canals, colleges, and charities.

But radical changes in the joint-stock form came to America and Britain on the eve of the modern economy or hard on its heels. The contract clause of the U.S. Constitution, ratified in 1788, prohibited any state law retroactively impairing contract rights, yet charters did not obviously qualify as "contracts." In 1819, however, dealing with a suit by the Corporation of Dartmouth College, the Supreme Court ruled that all corporations have rights, including the right not to have their charter rewritten by new state laws. The 1830s saw restrictions loosened on business incorporation in one state after another: the Massachusetts legislature dropped its practice of limiting charters to public works, and Connecticut permitted companies to incorporate without a legislative act. In Britain, the Parliament, wearying of chartering a rash of railway lines, passed the Joint Stock Companies Act of 1844, allowing companies to incorporate simply by registering—though without the boon of limited liability, which was under debate. The Joint Stock Companies Act of 1856 granted these corporations limited liability. France followed in 1863, and Germany did much the same in 1870.[8]

A new creature was loose in the Western world—too late to claim paternity for the modern economy born in the 1820s or so, but not too late to contribute mightily to the great innovations in the age of industry—from the 1840s or 1850s to the 1910s or 1930s or 1960s. Adam Smith had criticized the joint-stock company for its poorly designed incentives. He was right about insufficient attention to costs and a weakness for short-term gains. But Smith, with his classical lens, missed the point. A corporation, acting for its hard core of one or a few big-stakes owners, could venture far into the unknown, employ a wide assortment of talent, and absorb a long spell of losses. It thus had some prospect of achieving significant innovations, owing to its ability to find shareowners who, able to diversify, would accept the risk and who, able to hold the stock for years or to sell it to others who could do so, would value profits far in the future. The benefit to investors and to society from the resulting innovations may well transcend the petty objections to corporate waste and managerial problems.

John Stuart Mill may have been saying the same thing when he observed that limited liability reduced an important deterrent to setting up a new business—a particularly daunting deterrent for poor people.[9] This was a splendid point, especially in Mill's time, when limited liability was granted only for 20 or 30 years. (It is a question whether it has a place in companies of an advanced age. The late Peter Martin, a business economist at the *Financial Times,* once suggested that companies be wound up after 20 years.)

---

8. *The Company*, an enjoyable book by Mickelthwait and Wooldridge, surveys the development of the company from ancient to modern times. Among the classics it draws on are Chandler's *Strategy and Structure* and, on Britain and Germany, *Scale and Scope;* DuBois's *The English Business Company after the Bubble Act;* Rosenberg and Birdzell's *How the West Grew Rich;* and Kindleberger's *A Financial History of Western Europe.* An account of the Chinese company is Kirby, "China Unincorporated."

9. Mill's 1851 "The Law of Partnership," reprinted in *Essays on Economics and Society Part II:*
   The liberty of entering into partnerships of limited liability, similar to the *commandite* partnerships of France and other countries, appears to me an important element in the general freedom of commercial transactions, and in many cases a valuable aid to *undertakings* of general usefulness.
   No one, I think, can consistently condemn these partnerships without being prepared to maintain that it is desirable that no one should carry on business with borrowed capital; in other words, that the profits of business should be wholly monopolized by those who have had time to accumulate, or the good fortune to inherit capital: a proposition, in the present state of commerce and industry, evidently absurd.

One of the last of the new institutions to fall into place was bankruptcy. In America, there was widespread imprisonment of persons unable to discharge their debts until 1833, when federal imprisonment was abolished. There are many reasons to celebrate this human advance, but one of them was that people did not have to fear that if they started a business they might land in prison through bad luck or a mistake. Defaults went on of course—they even increased. In an 1836 lithograph depicting Liberty Street in the heart of New York's financial district, four of the nine firms shown were bankrupt within the next five years.[10] The Bankruptcy Acts of 1841, 1867, and 1898 further eased the penalties of default by permitting voluntary bankruptcy and a workout of the debts in federal bankruptcy courts. In Britain, punishments evolved from deportation and death to prison in Victorian times, though debtor's prison was not pleasant. (References to it are recurrent in Dickens, whose father did time at London's Marshalsea Prison.) With the 1856 law, business owners registered for limited liability were saved from the prospect. Then the 1869 Debtors Act abolished imprisonment for debt by allowing proprietorships, partnerships, and all people to file for bankruptcy. This almost surely was good for innovation.

Finally, among economic institutions, there is the rise of financial institutions importantly oriented (whether or not totally dedicated) toward financing business investment projects or financing the early development of new businesses. Credit institutions, along with so very many other institutions, can be found as far back as the inventive Babylonians. Wealthy landowners and temples lent to proprietorships and partnerships for purposes of production or trade, with farmland, houses, slaves, concubines, wives, and children put up as security. In medieval times, some families created banks to which they devoted their careers—most famously the Fuggers in southern Germany and the Medicis of Florence. They were known for their loans to kings and princes in Europe. In the 18th century, there were the Baring family in London and the Rothschild family, whose five sons spread out to Frankfurt, London, Paris, Vienna, and Naples. The former was known for its loans to governments, such as for the Louisiana Purchase, the latter for its loans to Britain for its war with Napoleon. All of them engaged also in merchant banking. Yet it is hard to see in

---

10. See Balleisen, *Navigating Failure.* The author notes the financial panics of 1837 and 1839. Informed estimates, he adds, suggest "among proprietors engaged in market exchange, at least one in three and as many as one in two succumbed to an insupportable load of debt" (p. 3). The casualties in his case studies included many who went on to great success, such as Arthur Tappan (of Tappan Zee bridge), James Watson Webb, and Silas Stilwell. Mark Twain was another.

these merchant banks any new development that could be seen as paving the way for an age of innovation.

Early 19th-century banks in America hold some basic lessons. These banks have been generally viewed as a source of instability and thus a drag on entrepreneurship and economic development, a failure at achieving the "mobility" of capital extolled by neoclassical economic theory, and not the success in driving economic development that the "universal bank" developed in Europe has been seen as. The U.S. system had two kinds of banks. One was the commercial banks, chartered by state governments to accept deposits, issue notes, and finance production and commerce. The other was the private banks, which could neither issue notes nor accept deposits and depended on their own capital. Both sorts of banks thrived. (The latter banks attracted much foreign capital and developed into investment banks, lending to businesses to finance investment projects.) So complex and subtle a system does not lend itself to a quick judgment. Recent thought and scholarship, however, argues that these banks were well suited to serve regional entrepreneurship and development—not perfect, of course, but helping more than hindering. In sticking mostly to the region they knew, they were in the forefront of responses to shifting opportunities. And they practiced the rule of knowing their customers and monitoring their borrowers:

> For economic development to have proceeded, manufacturing enterprises
> needed to arise and grow. . . . For that growth to occur in a timely manner,
> manufacturers needed access to external finance, notably bank credit. . . .
> Bankers—typically being merchants themselves—tended to lend to enter-
> prises and entrepreneurs with whom they were familiar, namely other
> merchants.[11]

In this revisionist view, the absence of universal banks from the American and British contexts was not an impediment, whatever benefits France and Germany may have derived from them.

---

11. Bodenhorn, *A History of Banking in Antebellum America*, p. 24. The author's thesis as it appears on page 12 is that

> a decentralized, federal, Madisonian polity encouraged experimentation and the
> adaptation of institutions to local needs or preferences. Nowhere were the results more
> evident than in banking policy. With the exception of the First and Second Banks of
> the United States, antebellum banks were creatures of the states themselves, reflecting
> the desires, even the whims, of local residents. . . . The decentralized nature of the
> polity allowed for a regional flexibility with the result that banks "grew more and more
> different over time, like the beaks of Darwin's finches."

Political Institutions: Representative Democracy

Political institutions arguably played a significant role in the creation of the modern economy. One of these was representative democracy, which arose rather close to the emergence of economic modernity. The development of modern democracy alongside that of the modern economy is suggestive, to say the least.

In most countries, seats in the national parliaments continued to be held right through the mercantile era by noblemen and landowning aristocrats. With any sense of economic justice centuries away, their lawmaking was mainly animated by narrow self-interest. Yet, in the 18th century, the idea of a representative democracy—a more representative democracy, at any rate—captured popular imagination in both America and Europe, in large part in response to the growing demand of the urban working class and business people for equal representation. America's Declaration of Independence in 1776 proclaimed the right of the people to self-government, free of all kings and aristocracies, although this vision was fully realized only with the abolition of slavery some 90 years later. The French Revolution of 1789 was the rallying cry in Europe for the creation of democracy. The Polish-Lithuanian Constitution of 1791 called for political equality between townsfolk and nobility. Some historians say that the court at Versailles diverted landowners from thinking about better practice, with the consequence that innovation came to France only when the state got out of the way.

This democracy has posed some downside risks for the economy, to be sure. It was more short-termist than hereditary monarchies were inclined to be. It permitted a tyranny of the majority, which constitutions put some limits on. It also put people into government who were so short of money in relation to many of the governed that they were more susceptible to bribery than the aristocratic legislators were. Yet it may very well have been, on balance, rather good for innovation.

The right of the people to govern themselves has long been thought to have had benefits for economic performance in general. And there are reasons to believe it created beneficial conditions for the rise of economic dynamism. For instance, a representative democracy may establish economic institutions and policies that an autocrat would refuse or repress. A democracy would push the public sector to support the interests of the lower and middle classes, thus to protect and nourish individual initiatives, such as serving business activity and encouraging public education. Innovation, which derives so much from inspiration, exploration, and experimentation at the grassroots, could be expected to benefit from this feature of democracy. In contrast, an autocracy would be expected to use the public sector for projects that serve autocratic interests, such as national power or aura. (The other side of the coin is that a democracy may lead to legislative logrolling in the service of a welter of special interest groups that cover all or virtually all the society. The result may be a public sector so swollen that it does more harm to innovation than good. That was unlikely in the 19th century, though, when governments were still so small, except in France.)

Representative democracy may naturally support institutions and a culture for a modern economy that an autocracy would be less apt to do. Where governments have legislated and thus legitimized institutions protecting economic functioning in spite of the uncertainty, change, reversals of fortune, profits and losses, and the rest, the would-be entrepreneur and innovator can be more confident that their company will not be subjected to extortionate holdups by agencies of the government or social partners, to postcontractual threats by creditors or employees, and to mobs allowed to plunder shops and factories without police protection. The argument is that when an institution has been established by a large society of diverse-thinking voters, the probability that the net sum of the changes of mind will be large enough to cause repeal of a previous law is smaller than the probability that an autocratic ruler would have such a change of mind. (This follows from the proposition known in statistical theory as the law of large numbers.)

This thesis bears on the question whether the rule of law can be robust enough to be relied on. As everyone agrees, autocratic rulers heed the rule of law only when it suits them; even a constitution like the Magna Carta does not make it certain that the law will not be circumvented by one device or another. Democratic parliaments can also change laws, though, or circumvent them with added laws. The argument above suggests that the legislature of a large and diverse democracy has difficulty contravening or circumventing an existing law, unlike an autocrat. The "rule of the people" lends credibility to the rule of law.

Another aspect of democracy may also have contributed to innovation. De Tocqueville in his travels through America in 1835 speculated that self-government helped to breed self-reliance and self-expression in business. The fund of experience Americans acquired in governing themselves, from taking part in town meetings to serving as public officials, was constantly useful to them in negotiating contracts, working with employees, and making the contacts needed in setting up a new business. By the same logic, the experience Americans had supporting themselves in the economy provided them with the skills—the self-confidence, easy sociability, and so on—they would need in governing themselves. In the Tocquevillian model, voluntary associations were the "great free school" in America, and they were not much found in Europe.

One more feature of democracy may have been important for the emergence of the modern economy. Representative democracy is a system in which, compared to autocracy, a great many voices are heard and heeded—if only politicians cater to them in hopes of getting their vote. The autocrat is apt to be unaware of many of the needs, particularly new needs. Thus a representative democracy was likely to have been more responsive to the needs for new institutions during the decades of its embryonic modernity.

If it is granted that the governmental mechanisms of a democracy operate in favor of innovation, there remains a historical question: Did the mechanics of representative democracy commence operation in the right places at the right times to have been the *trigger* for the explosion of economic dynamism in each nation to which it came? Did Britain, America, Belgium, France, and Germany develop their modern economies *after* their representative democracies? *Before?* Britain's venerable Houses of Parliament came to represent new wealth and new cities with the revolution of 1688. The Reform Act of 1832 extended the vote in contests for the House of Commons to men without reference to property qualifications and redistributed seats to urban areas. In America, the House of Representatives and Senate created by the U.S. Constitution in 1788 were radically more representative than England's two chambers: voting was open to all men having property qualifications— between a third and a half of the male adult population, citizen or not. (The franchise was soon broadened by steps: to men without property in 1812, to nonwhites in 1870, and to women in 1920.) It appears, though, that both democracy and dynamism were slow to arrive in France. The French Revolution was followed not by democracy but by Napoleon until 1815, the monarchical Restoration until the Revolution of 1830, and the rule of Louis-Philippe until 1848. Democracy in the form of elections with universal male suffrage came with the Revolution of 1848. Likewise, though a modicum of innovation and a resulting degree of prosperity came to France after Napoleon and grew stronger in the reign of Louis-Philippe, it was in only the second half of the century that France, with its productivity take-off, demonstrated relatively high innovation. Belgium is less clear-cut. A long wait for democracy is also found in Belgium, which was ruled by France until Napoleon's fall in

1815 and by the Dutch until 1830, when the Belgian Revolution established a parliamentary democracy. Innovation appears to have gotten ahead of democracy but did even better under democracy than under foreign rule: even before 1830 Belgium saw entrepreneurial advances in mining and steelmaking in the French-speaking Wallonia that gave it a jump over any region in France. In contrast, innovation continued in Belgium after 1830, including notably the creation of the rubber industry, and the country was a world leader in industrialization until 1914. Germany is the exception. It saw little democracy except at local levels throughout the 19th century, while its innovation grew powerful over the last half of that century. That fact leaves open the possibility that Germany would have done far better with democracy, and that most countries were so structured that they did need democracy to support innovation. In any case, the reasonable inference is not that modern democracy caused the modern economy or vice-versa, but that both sprang from the same matrix of values and beliefs—the same culture.

Economic Culture: Differences and Changes

What is a modern economy? From the perspective described above, its distinction is the rewards it offers, pecuniary and experiential, for conception, embodiment, and pioneering of new commercial ideas—thus encouraging the use of resources for attempts at innovation. From the perspective of the present chapter, any society's economy operates on the society's institutions and its cultures. Such a culture is the attitudes and beliefs in the social heritage—though not all members inherit exactly the same culture and a culture does not include the nation's economic policy or any moral philosophy. So we may think of an economy as consisting of its economic institutions and its *economic culture* or cultures. An economic culture is the attitudes and beliefs about business and economic matters. For an economy of one kind or another to work there has to be a supporting culture. But not all behavior is "culture," and much behavior may be effect rather than cause.

Before historians, mostly in the 20th century, sought explanation of the take-offs and prosperity of the modern economies that sprouted in the 19th century, some of the best minds of the 18th century pondered explanations of the rise of notable commercial economies in the 16th and 17th centuries. In Adam Smith's explanation of the rise of commerce in Britain, the end of intrusive and confiscatory government allowed the rise of "truck and barter"—the constant search for better prices. In making people feel it was safe to hold wealth, it allowed thrift to arise. And, in causing wealth to accumulate, trade could be conducted on an ever-larger scale. Thus materialism flowered in the commercial era. Yet Smith saw the desire for material goods as universal and constant through time, not as something unique to the commercial era or to Britain—hence not a prime mover. "The principle which prompts [us] to save," he wrote in *The Wealth of Nations,* "is the desire of bettering our condition, a desire which . . . comes with us from the womb and never leaves us till we go into the grave" (p. 324). (Marx, of course, agreed that the "fetish" of commodities and wealth was not a cause of the commercial economy; he said it was an effect.) The mercantile economies exhibited some other distinctive behavior as well. There was honesty, respect for the laws, keeping promises, trading favors, and all the other commercial virtues known as trustworthiness. Yet David Hume and Adam Smith did not see this bourgeois respectability as behind the mercantile economy either. Hume in his 1740 *Treatise of Human Nature* argues (in a way that would seem conventional to present-day economists) that these commercial practices evolved from merchants' self-interest, including their interest in their reputations. Smith's 1763 *Lectures on Jursiprudence* views a merchant's interest in his commercial reputation as resting on the profit at stake, not his pride in it, and his 1776 classic *Wealth of Nations* views the commercial virtues as effects of the commercial economy, not as preconditions for it.

Our focus is on the emergence of modern economies, not mercantile economies. The essential point to be made is that even if increased effort, thrift, and wealth were the consequences of a cultural shift toward industry, frugality, and bourgeois respectability, as Weber argued, it is hard to see how such a cultural shift could spark the unprecedented feats of the modern economies of the 19th century, since long work weeks, high saving rates, and respecting law and agreements all appear to have been present in the 17th and early 18th centuries, as Smith and Hume imply. (If the work week and saving rate rose to greater heights in nations where a modern economy arrived, there are good reasons to view that as motivated by the fast economic growth and high investment demand that came with the dynamism of the modern economies.) At best, it can be argued that bourgeois respectability was necessary to or supportive of the development of the modern economies just as they were supportive of the commercial economies before them.

There were genuine cultural shifts that can be seen as causes of the emergence of the modern economies, however. It is evident that the Western world came to acquire—much more in some nations than others—an *ethos,* or spirit, that, as the elements of it came together, ultimately provided the impetus for the dynamism that is the essence of the modern economies. This ethos that built up was part of *humanism* (though humanism was broader than this ethos). In countries, regions, and cities where these strands reached a critical mass, they sparked the creation of a modern economy. (It does not matter that the earliest of the elements of the new outlook, or culture, emerged some centuries earlier, as long as other crucial elements were more recent.) This ethos may aptly be called *modernism.*

The meaning of "modern" in the present context is familiar: a modern woman, a modern city, modern life, modern as untraditional, modern as novel, and modern as disruptive or subversive. The modern society creates change within it, and the new ideas of those participating in the modern economy are the main sources of that change. The first modern societies begin in 1815, as argued in Paul Johnson's *Birth of the Modern.* Modern thought, however, begins around 1500, as documented in Jacques Barzun's vast survey of what he calls the "modern era," *From Dawn to Decadence.* Some ideas we reasonably think of as modernist existed in ancient times but were not widespread or they were driven out in the middle ages.

Modern values—attitudes and beliefs—continue to the present day to be prevalent—to significantly differing degrees—in the nations of the West. Modernist values include norms like thinking and working for yourself and self-expression. These values also include attitudes toward others: readiness to accept change caused or desired by others; eagerness to work with others; the desire to test one's self against others, thus to compete; and the willingness to take the initiative, thus to go first. (These cultural elements were not integral to the production, trade, and accumulation in the commercial economies.[12] As noted earlier, complaints were made from Smith to the young Marx that the commercial economies did not enlist these elements of their culture.) Other modernist attitudes are the desire to create, explore, and experiment, the welcoming of hurdles to surmount, the desire to be intellectually engaged, and the desire to have responsibility and to give orders. Behind these desires is a need to exercise one's own judgment, to act on one's

12. Neo-Schumpeterians might protest, arguing that when an external discovery occurs, some entrepreneur does have to take the initiative of undertaking the commercial application of the new possibility if it is to be realized. The general public with some economic background has been led to believe that this is what the entrepreneurial spirit is all about. But Schumpeter himself theorized, especially in his more formal analyses, that it would become clear among the entrepreneurs in the city or town which entrepreneur was best suited to undertake the "obvious" development. None was required to exercise any initiative.

own insights, and to summon up one's own imagination. This spirit does not involve a love of risk—hence enjoying a bet on the toss of a fair coin. It is a spirit that views the prospect of unanticipated consequences that may come with voyaging into the unknown as a valued part of experience and not a drawback. Self-discovery and personal development are major vitalist values.[13]

Modernist beliefs include some distinctive ideas of what is right: the rightness of having to compete with others for positions of higher responsibility, the rightness of greater pay for greater productivity or greater responsibility, the rightness of orders from those in responsible positions and the rightness of holding them accountable, the right of people to offer new ideas, and the right of people to offer new ways of doing things and to offer new things to do. All this stands in contrast to traditionalism with its notions of service, obligation, family, and social harmony.

The first signs of this new spirit appear in the Renaissance. In the middle ages, notions that engaging the world could hold deep rewards (and not just for kings), that not everything is already known and mankind's imagination might uncover more knowledge were undreamt of. The humanist Giovanni Pico della Mirandola (1463–1494), who was in the center of the movement, argued, using the religious constructs he had grown up with, that if human beings were created by God in his image, they must share in some degree God's capacity for creativity. In his funeral oration for Michelangelo, Pico calls man "the sculptor who must chisel out his own form from the material nature has endowed him." Thus Pico depicted an "individualism" in which men and women have to carve out their own development.[14] The influential humanist Desiderius Erasmus (1466–1536) wrote of "the expansion of [a person's] horizon that results from the hope of immortality, the quickening of

13. The value people commonly find in identifying and connecting with others is dubbed "altruism" in Nagel, *The Possibility of Altruism.* The value found in self-discovery and personal growth was dubbed "vitalism" by Jacques Barzun, a towering historian of Western thought at Columbia University. A sizeable discussion appears in his 1962 essay "From the Nineteenth Century to the Twentieth." (By the time he wrote his great 800-page tome *From Dawn to Decadence* in 2001, his many other interests squeezed "vitalism and volunteerism" into a few paragraphs.) Vitalism is also prominent in the writings of the eminent literary critic Harold Bloom, such as 1961's *The Visionary Company* and 1994's *The Western Canon.* The vitalism here is not to be confused with the 18th-century metaphysical craze of that name—the idea that there exists a "spark of life," like a shock of electricity, that brings a creature or organism to life. Luigi Galvini gave electrical shocks to dead frogs in an effort to bring them back to vitality. (The muscles did contract, but they did not get their jump back.)

14. Cassirer, "Giovanni Pico della Mirandola" (p. 333).

new aspirations, the suggestion of endless possibilities," which he attributed to the "spirit of Christianity."[15] The demand by Martin Luther (1483–1546) that members of the Roman church be accorded the "Christian liberty" to read and interpret the bible for themselves was a landmark in the emancipation of people from unproductive or dysfunctional government.

The Age of Discovery was another formative epoch. A profound vitalist spirit swept from Italy through France and Spain and on to Britain in barely 70 years. (Whether vitalism was a response to the heroism of the great navigators or their explorations, another expression of the new vitalism hardly matters.) Born in 1500, Benvenuto Cellini, the great sculptor and subject of the Berlioz opera of the same name, bared himself in his *Autobiography* as a questing, no-holds-barred artist-entrepreneur, the very embodiment of the liberated individualist bent on achievement and success. Born in 1509, John Calvin lauds careers as extending God's work. Born in 1533, Michel de Montaigne, in his collection *Essais,* chronicles an inner life—his own—and the personal growth that he calls "becoming." Born in 1547, Miguel Cervantes in his *Don Quixote* tells of the don and Sancho Panza, stuck in a place without challenges and going so far as to hallucinate them to find the vitality of a fulfilling life. Born in 1564, William Shakespeare in *Hamlet* and *King Lear* portrays the interior struggle and courage of his larger-than-life protagonists.

The wave of investigations between 1550 and 1700, called the Scientific Revolution, was another landmark. It demonstrated that observation and reason could be deployed to discover many of the workings of the natural world, such as William Harvey's model of the circulatory flow of the blood. The lesson to be drawn was that with study and thought it might be possible to figure out how something worked or could be made to work.

The 18th-century Enlightenment represented another step. Looking at the wealth accumulated by venture-merchants in the commercial economy, these philosophers and political economists saw entrepreneurial effort as having individual merit and social value. In France there was a total embrace of the entrepreneur. Nicolas de Condorcet elevates the productivity of business entrepreneurs over the political rent-seekers vying for political favor. Jean-Baptiste Say extols entrepreneurs for constantly reinventing the economy in their quest for higher yields. Voltaire, especially in his 1759 work *Candide,* championed a life of individual initiative and economic independence over conformity with convention and joining with others—*Il faut*

15. Dods, *Erasmus and Other Essays* (p. 300).

cultiver notre jardin.[16] In America, Jefferson likewise advocated an economy filled with participants in "pursuit of happiness" through smallish proprietorships engaging in grassroots entrepreneurial endeavors. Such thinking led to the corollary that such individual enterprise on a wide scale could change the world. This "progress" did not mean that the world would become perfect nor that there would not be missteps, only that societies might whittle away some of their imperfections and advance some of their capabilities. In these respects, humanism and its vitalist subdivision became part of the West's core beliefs.

The Enlightenment also brought the first glimmer of understanding of how creativity comes about. Hume, the first modern philosopher, had the insight that imagination was the key to advances in all kinds of knowledge. In his 1748 *An Enquiry Concerning Human Understanding* he explains that new knowledge does not spring from sheer observations of the world and existing ideas. Our knowledge is never a completely closed system, so originality may break into it. New knowledge starts from imagining how parts of the system not yet studied might work. (Such imaginings may be sparked by new data, but they do not require new data.) It was left for Hayek to point out that nothing will be imagined without considerable familiarity with those observations and ideas.

Something else very important came from the Enlightenment. Few expressed it at all, and no one expressed it more deftly (or succinctly) than Thomas Jefferson. With his imperishable phrase "life, liberty, and the pursuit of happiness" he put two propositions into the minds of contemporary Americans. One is the notion that every person has the moral right to seek his or her fulfillment. This was an idea that had not been widely articulated. It ran contrary to the tradition of the preceding era, which held that lives should be devoted to others—to family, church, and country. (To be sure, there is pleasure in giving, but Jefferson is surely talking about a journey of human development. He saw America as already "flowing with all the necessaries and comforts of life," so he must have meant "pursuits" on a higher plane.) The other notion, later set out by Søren Kierkegaard and by Friedrich Nietzsche, is the existential idea: a real life can come only through one's own endeavors. We may or may not find this "happiness," but we need to pursue it. These two propositions epitomize what we often call modernism. They are inimical to the ideas of traditionalism, which made the individual subservient to the group.

16. See Rothschild, *Economic Sentiments* (p. 33).

No one today can doubt that these revolutionary ideas changed what it was like to be alive. Following the Enlightenment, some European societies were excited and anxious over the Faustian possibility of profound advances in knowledge. Business people—farm and nonfarm—could see themselves as possessing creativity, and their political representatives could advocate the establishment of an economy engaged in exercising creativity and insight in their business. Vitalism became the spark of the modern economies—the elixir of their dynamism. The 19th century saw in the participants in a modern economy a rush of confidence in the power of discovery that they were testing and in the rewards. For the first time in human history there were heady anticipations of new methods, new products, and resulting advances in income. In Britain a growing part of the population was drawn into the new, mainly urban, enterprises, in which people spoke of "getting on." In America they were also getting on. When de Tocqueville journeyed through America in 1831–1832, he noted the self-confidence and the determination. The "American frontier," the borderline of settlements out west, could have been a symbol for the frontier of business methods and products.

Yet de Tocqueville *did* doubt that a new vitalism had come to America— or, if it had, that it was not the same as in France:

> Among ideas that occupy me, two bulk large, the first that this population is one of the happiest in the world, the second that it owes its immense prosperity less to its characteristic virtues, and even less to a form of government intrinsically superior to all the others, than to its peculiar conditions. . . . Everyone works, and the vein is still so rich that all who work it succeed rapidly in gaining the wherewithal to achieve contentment. . . . Restlessness seems to abet the prosperity. Wealth is the common lure. . . . Unless I'm sadly mistaken, man is not different or better on one side of the Atlantic than on the other. He is just differently placed.[17]

Now, nearly two centuries later, de Tocqueville's position looks 180 degrees to the truth. To have laid some of the bustle and drive in the American economy to "peculiar conditions," mainly the opportunities to develop virgin land, made sense in the first half of the 19th century. However, America virtually ran out of virgin land by the century's end, and yet the drive to experiment, explore, and create did not completely stop in the entire 20th century. Had Americans' place as "happiest" hung on an Eden, they would have lost that place by 1920, by which time America was urban.

---

17. De Tocqueville, "Letters from America" (pp. 375–376).

De Tocqueville was also wrongheaded to suppose that economic culture tends to be the same—in the Western world at any rate. Today we have evidence that de Tocqueville did not have. Present-day evidence on attitudes and beliefs shows beyond any doubt that people *are* "different" across oceans and across nations. Survey data in *World Values Surveys* display not only differences in attitudes and beliefs from one individual to another but also differences in mean attitudes and beliefs from one nation to another—differences in the national averages. (Many of the differences can be shown to be systematic, not simply random or the persisting after-effect of a temporary disturbance.) It is hard to see how it could have been otherwise in de Tocqueville's time. If the 19th century, when vitalism was riding high, was different from the 15th century and even the 18th, it would have been unlikely that all nations' average attitudes and beliefs moved in lockstep. Some countries must have been faster to embrace the new values of the Renaissance and Enlightenment than other countries were.

Finally, de Tocqueville seems wrong again when he suggested that some of the "characteristic values" in America (whether or not these values were also the values held in France) contributed "less" than other influences did, such as institutions, to America's greater drive in the 1830s—greater than Europe's and greater than before. Judging by recent studies of contemporary data in the attitudinal surveys, elements of the economic culture do matter for economic performance: for productivity, labor force unemployment rates, and also for reported job satisfaction and reported happiness. Differences in these respects across nations contribute quite a lot to differences in performance, even among nations as alike as the advanced economies of the West, as Chapter 8 shows.[18]

Of the many attitudes toward job and career reported in the household surveys, several can be interpreted as reflecting some aspect of vitalism—the acceptance of new ideas, the importance of work, the desire to have some freedom on the job and some initiative, the willingness to follow, the acceptance of competition, and the desire for achievement. It is noteworthy that about half of these attitudes have significant power in the explanation of inter-country differences in some economic performance indicators. There are so many of them, though, that only the fittest or the luckiest can significantly explain the differences in all the performance indicators. In response, the two recent studies place the various attitudes found in the attitudinal

18. Phelps, "Economic Culture and Economic Performance" (2011); Phelps and Zoega, "Entrepreneurship, Culture and Openness" (2009); Bojilov and Phelps, "Job Satisfaction" (2012).

surveys into a smallish number of affinity groups. Vitalism is the most powerful group in explaining differences across countries in the indicators of economic performance, generally speaking. The next most powerful group can be interpreted as measuring consumerism, or materialism. A traditional group, the one interpretable as a measure of social trust, is also important, as is the group interpretable as measuring self-reliance.

The remaining question is whether differences in economic institutions matter for economic performance to a comparable extent. The two more recent studies suggest that most of a nation's economic institutions, laying aside for the moment its political institutions, do not improve our explanation of how countries rank in economic performance. In accounting for how nations rank, it seems we can get along with cultural data alone, because the economic institutions are merely expressions of the economic culture. A qualification: it appears that one exception is the degree to which institutions offer the "economic freedom" to invest, innovate, compete, and enter.[19]

We have come a long way in a short space, so a summing up may be welcome to reinforce the main points so far: Seeking and acquiring wealth was, in contrast to vitalism, *not* an element of culture that came along at about the right time to launch the modern economy. What one could say was that in the dark ages of feudal times, wealth was regarded as filthy ("filthy lucre"). Wealth seeking and pleasure from the pursuit of or the prospect of acquiring more wealth became acceptable in time for the commercial economy and helped encourage merchants to expand their markets and take on bigger risks. But for the modern economies to emerge, a new sense of the possibilities of life beyond wealth accumulation was required and thus the construction of the required economic and political institutions.

Missing Piece: Population and Cities

This chapter has told the story of how some nations possessed the culture and acquired the institutions that would be important for indigenous innovation. Compelling reasons were found to regard the spread in these nations

---

19. The supremacy of economic culture is found in Bojilov and Phelps, "Job Satisfaction" (2012). Nevertheless, it is unlikely that no institution makes a difference for economic performance once the economic culture is taken fully into account. A composite element, labeled economic freedom, composed of some data on economic institutions as well as economic culture, was found to have some explanatory power in Phelps and Zoega, "Entrepreneurship, Culture and Openness" (2009).

of key economic freedoms, the rise there of vitalism, and the development of democracy as milestones on the way to modern economies. It is plausible that modernity would not have gone so far without the *acceptance* of the corporation—the joint-stock companies with their controversial limited liability; and, more broadly, without myriad institutional arrangements and policies offering people wider economic scope.

Yet something is missing. Why was it that, next to innovation in the 19th century, especially after the first quarter with its wars, innovation was so paltry throughout the 18th? The answer may be that something may have grown to multiply or amplify the faint impulses of innovation—to potentiate the democracy and the vitalism that were already present at relatively high levels by the last quarter of the century. But what might that something be? Economic historians appear not to have identified it. Why did innovation come earlier to Britain, America, and possibly Belgium than to France and Germany? We do not have to share de Tocqueville's impression that culture is everywhere the same to wonder whether differing intensities of the above forces argued to be central—the corporation, democracy, vitalism, and economic freedom—can wholly or largely explain why France and Germany got their dynamism later than the others.

The missing piece, which is obvious once one hits on it, is population density—the number of working-age persons in the country, excluding remote areas. Not many innovations in a country can be encouraged by its culture and promoted by its institutions if there are few minds. (Why, then, are Icelanders, with their small numbers, not backward and therefore poor? The reason is their proficiency in English and Scandinavian languages virtually integrate them into the economies of America and Europe.) Having more persons, all energized by vitalism and encouraged by democratic limits on arbitrary powers, surely increases the total number of new ideas being generated, even if it leaves unchanged the number per generator. Further, if the resulting new products and methods generally lead not to private use by the developers but to adoptions over the country—to diffusion—the end result is an increase in the number of innovations: the new products developed by companies themselves and those developed by other companies, which grew in number with the increased population. Thus, the more people there are in a rather integrated country to inspire, develop, market, and try out new ideas, the greater is its prospective rate of indigenous innovations per capita—provided the necessary institutions and culture are in place. (Why, then, was China, despite a population far greater than that of Britain or America, not generating many innovations in the 19th century? Or earlier? There was a phenomenal abundance of entrepreneurs in China's cities in the 18th century, the Irish economist Richard Cantillon reported in his 1755 study. The reason is China was seriously lacking in the economic institutions or the economic culture or both needed for innovation, indigenous or exogenous. It is far less lacking in the 21st century.) If the economy of the West experiences more innovations per capita now than 100 years ago, it is mainly because there are many more people engaged in innovation in that economy; it does not follow that every (or any) subpopulation of a given size generated more new products and methods.[20]

The benefits of increased population come not only from more creations, most of them available for adoption by others. If new ideas and new products based on them are striking a country, they are likely to spread faster through the economy the more dense the population is—just as heat travels faster when there are more molecules and a disease is apt to spread faster (and farther) through the world the greater the population size. Ideas are communicated very much like diseases. More people, more relays. Also: more people, bigger market. The Beatles could play 1,000 nights in Hamburg, that city being big enough, but not in Liverpool.

A sufficiently large population leads also to a city, simply as a result of various advantages of crowding together—of agglomeration. A still larger population leads to a second city. If land cannot expand proportionally, cities grow larger as well as more numerous as the population increases. It is now understood that cities have some special benefits that go beyond the benefits of more minds or more density over a large space. The urban economist Jane Jacobs, confronting the bulldozers of New York's titan planner Robert Moses, came up with a central insight:

[P]eople gathered in concentrations of city size and density can be considered a positive good . . . and their presence celebrated.

[B]ig cities are natural generators of diversity and prolific incubators of new enterprises and ideas of all kinds. Moreover, big cities are the natural economic homes of immense numbers and ranges of small enterprises. . . . Dependent on a huge variety of other enterprises, they can add further to

20. The first lines of argument began turning up in the 1960s after social commentators had begun to warn that the increase in world population then being projected would cause a general worsening of living standards. One was an 1960 paper by Simon Kuznets, "Population Change and Aggregate Output." The other paper, written in 1968 independently of the first, was Phelps, "Population Increase." The germinal idea is that there is a sort of production function relating the flow of new ideas to the stock of minds. The latter work led to a series of books by Julian Simon.

that diversity. This last is a most important point to remember. City diversity itself permits and stimulates more diversity. . . . Without cities, [these small enterprises] would not exist. The diversity . . . that is generated by cities rests on the fact that in cities so many people are so close together, and among them contain so many different tastes, skills, needs, supplies, and bees in their bonnet.[21]

Samuel Johnson's remark "he who is tired of London is tired of life" evokes the creativity that can be expected only in a city. But Jacobs goes further with her point that only a city can be expected to breed new diversity and originality, thus possibly innovation.

What do the data on historical population changes have to say? Do they support the above thoughts about the effect of population increase on the creation and communication of new ideas? Do they thus help answer the question of why Britain, Belgium, and America could produce so little gross national innovation, so to speak, as late as the last quarter of the 18th century in comparison with the heated innovation they were to produce in the middle decades of the 19th? Data on population size are so spare that we have just three benchmark years to go by. From 1700 to 1820 and on to 1870, population in the Western world (i.e., Western Europe and the "Western offshoots") increased from 83 million to 144 million and on to 208 million. (Growth was far slower between 1600 and 1700.) Britain was helped by a major increase in its population—from 8½ to 21 million and on to 31½ million. America came to have the largest population in the West—rising from 1 million to 10 million and on to 40 million. Belgium's population more than doubled—going from 2 to 3½ million and on to 5 million. Germany's did the same after a slower start—going from 15 to 25 million and on to 39 million. France's population less than doubled—from 21½ to 31 million and on to 38½ million.

---

21. Jacobs, *The Death and Life of Great American Cities.* Jacobs's book was just a salvo in her battle against Moses. She also took to the streets—and ultimately won. See the PBS documentary *The American Experience: New York—The Planning Debate in New York, 1955–1975.* In a later work, which is more of a textbook, Jacobs tries another exposition of her insight:

[I]nnovations were exported from the cities to the countryside, transplanted to the countryside or imitated in the countryside. . . . This is so not because farmers and other rural people are less creative than city dwellers. The difference lies in the contrasting natures of rural and city economies, for it is in cities that new goods and services are first created.

Cities are places where adding new work to older work proceeds vigorously. . . . [Since] cities have more different kinds of divisions of labor than villages, towns and farms do[,] cities contain more kinds of work to which new work can be added than other settlements.

Jacobs, *The Economy of Cities* (pp. 8–9, 50).

Equally impressive is the emergence of cities in the 19th century. Take cities with a population more than 100,000, which were big in their day. The benchmarks are 1800 or thereabout and the period 1846–1851. In this span, Britain went from one to nine such cities. America went from none to six, Belgium from none to two. Prussia went from one to two, and France from three to five.[22]

In societies, the past is not fully determinable. It seems a good bet, though, that even if judgments should sometime shift to the belief that all the attitudes and institutions fueling innovation in the 19th century were present in the 18th after all, contrary to the above sections of this chapter, there were simply not enough minds hatching new ideas to cause innovation to take off until Western populations had reached a critical mass.[23]

Final Comments on Part One

Karl Marx and Max Weber both wrote texts for a *History of the World Part II*. As they saw the Western world after 1600 or so, the wealth accumulation of venture-merchants emerging outside the feudal system of the manor created capitalists, who established standalone factories hiring wage labor in the growing populations of the towns. The manorial lords soon began siphoning for sale to the towns some of the agricultural produce that had been distributed to the serfs. The enclosure movement was another historical force pushing labor from farmlands to towns. This is a story about industrialization, but not much of a causal account. With or without a feudal system dotting the countryside, there would have been towns, cities, stores, and factories springing up along with the massive increase in population that began early in the 18th century.

The story told by Marx and Weber about the *effects* of industrialization is not much better. Their *History* saw this industrialization as the first stage in

---

22. The population data are in Maddison, *The World Economy*. The city data are from Weber, *The Growth of Cities in the Nineteenth Century*.

23. It is worth noting as an aside that demographic influences lead to related points. The steep rise of population in barely more than a century operated in the direction of raising the returns, current and prospective, on capital by lowering wages. At the same time, the opening up to commercial use of new lands and natural resources in the New World, though bringing a mass relocation of labor from Europe to the Americas, was in many ways no different from discovery of new lands and resources in Europe: it too operated to raise the prospective returns on capital. These increases in prospective returns must account for some of the increase in investment activity in the Western world in the 19th century and, through similar mechanisms, some of the increase in innovation activity too. (And the increase in wages brought by the new lands may have brought an increased willingness to sacrifice some income for greater adventure and standing in the community, which could induce an increased interest in engaging in innovative activity.)

a kind of modernization, about which they were ambivalent. Marx claimed there was a tendency for wages to fall, notwithstanding increases in efficiency and in the capital stock. But this claim, once an article of faith in labor movements, had to be quietly retired with the findings that wages had not fallen over the 18th century, had risen strongly over the 19th, and continued rising in the 20th. (Marx himself came to recognize in his and Engels' 1848 *Communist Manifesto* that the modern capitalism he witnessed was "progressive.")

Both Marx and Weber went on to assert that 19th-century modernization brought a dreary rationalization and impersonal bureaucratization to economic life. But it was preposterous to insinuate that the traditional economy of feudal manors provided workers with much "liberating activity." It has never been the prevailing opinion of people who experienced both rural and urban life and labor that rural is better than urban. Migration to the city has been a fixture of demographic history for many centuries.

Present-day versions of their *History* end with the hope that the "knowledge economy," especially the service sector, will bring long-awaited opportunities for work and career that satisfy the "realization of talents." This postindustrial modernization will spread the human development that industrialization never delivered.[24]

The first four chapters of this book take a radically different perspective and tell a different narrative. The modern economies emerging in the 19th century were a stunning success in both nonmaterial and material dimensions: intellectual engagement and personal development as well as sustained economic growth and an inbuilt tendency toward inclusion. This depended on the rise of a new force: economic dynamism. And what sparked this dynamism was a new economic culture. Its necessary nutrients were representative democracy and a cultural revolution originating in Renaissance humanism, Baroque vitalism, and Enlightenment modernism. Representative democracy ensured property rights but also stimulated self-reliance and social engagement. Altruism, vitalism, and modernism caused people to reach out to the world and find meaning through innovative activity. The resulting culture and the economic institutions it led to provided people with the urge and the capabilities to innovate. Adequate numbers of people was the last of the necessary, but not sufficient, conditions.

The series of modern economies, starting with Britain and America, seems to stop arbitrarily—with Germany as the last of the modernizers. Why not

---

24. For example, Inglehart and Welzel, *Modernization, Cultural Change, and Democracy* (2005, p. 1).

Sweden and the rest of Scandinavia? Japan? Italy and Spain? No doubt, indigenous innovation did develop in some industries in those nations. The difficulty is that the economies there were so late in showing what could have been signs of widespread dynamism that those signs could have been in large part the result of those economies' catching up with the new products from the pioneers. The evidence is ambiguous. Similarly there is a continuing debate over how much is indigenous innovation instead of catch-up by imitation and adaption in the economies of Hong Kong, South Korea, Singapore, Taiwan, South Korea, and now China and India. These economies have developed some visible enclaves of innovation, but it is hard to know how extensive and intensive innovation is in these economies—or in any economy for that matter.

Obviously the new kinds of economies, at least the new ones of the 19th century, involved capitalism. Yet these modern economies were a far cry from the mercantile economies, which achieved important expansions of trade and accumulations of wealth though precious little lift to productivity, wages, job satisfaction, and the human spirit—and perhaps little gain in employment too. Of course, all the modern economies emerging in the 19th century represented improvements in the capitalist system of the 16th and 17th centuries—for example, financial institutions became better at selecting and facilitating projects aimed at innovation. Yet these modern economies belonged to modern societies, which made more radical contributions: These societies possessed political institutions and an economic culture that would galvanize their capitalist economies. The result was *modern capitalism*. The world's first modern economies—the first to possess dynamism—were an amalgam of capitalism and the modern.

Although the modern capitalist economies were the first example of a modern economy, it did not follow that they would be the last. In the 20th century the West became a debating platform for discussions of whether a country might build a modern economy—one possessing dynamism, thus given to innovation—that is *not* a *capitalist* economy. The Europeans, who created capitalism, debated whether there might be one or more other systems on which a modern economy could be built—an economy of comparable dynamism. They debated whether economic modernity could be justified in spite of the costs it might be shown to have. And they debated whether economic modernity was even desirable. The question of the justification of capitalism and of modernity itself turned Europe not only into a debating platform but also, at times and places, into a battleground.

PART TWO

AGAINST THE MODERN ECONOMY

Socialism and Corporatism

How much must perish so that something new may arise!

JACOB BURCKHARDT

CHAPTER FIVE

The Lure of Socialism

I am convinced there is only one way to eliminate [the] grave ills [of capitalism], namely through the establishment of a socialist economy. . . . A planned economy, which adjusts production to the needs of the community, would distribute the work . . . and guarantee a livelihood to every man, woman and child.

ALBERT EINSTEIN, *Why Socialism?*

Communism is socialism plus electrification.

V. I. LENIN

You don't understand something until you can build it.

Paraphrase of J. CRAIG VENTER's variation on RICHARD FEYNMAN

THE ECONOMIC INSTITUTIONS AND THE SOCIAL NORMS, or economic culture, on which the world's first modern economies operated were not chosen by the people—by their democratic assemblies or judicial bodies. Legislatures and courts occasionally had to decide for or against this or that piece of the system, but there was never a public choice between one system and another.

Britain and America were the nearest to exceptions. By 1800, so many people had left the traditional economy for a commercial and cosmopolitan life and so many of them were engaged and rewarded in what they were doing that both capitalist institutions and norms—its private property and profit seeking—and the modern economy—its freedom, inquisitive and adventurous spirit, and indeterminacy—had wide support. In America's Constitution and Britain's judicial rulings, capitalism and modernity were implicit. There was hardly an alternative. Few wanted a return to feudalism.

But in the high period of the modern economy, from the mid-19th century well into the 20th, people participating in a quite modern economy were having a highly varied experience with it—much more varied than the experience with the mercantile economy. Even if there were few who did less well than they would have done in mercantile times, it was how well they were doing relative to what they supposed would be *possible* that mattered to them. One who had good luck or advantages could disregard whatever inefficiencies or biases in the system had made the outcome less brilliant than it might have been. But one with bad luck or a disadvantage could be right to blame some of the outcome on the system, pointing to this or that supposed "flaw" while leaving it to scholars to decide whether it was a real flaw and, if so, whether it caused real net harm. The discontent must have been far worse among Russian serfs and eastern European peasants, who worked in conditions untouched by the modern economy. Workers' discontent about inequalities of income and wealth, about unemployment and economic instability, were at the origins of the socialism that emerged in Europe in this period.

Modern Discontents

The evidence does not support popular beliefs of the time that modernization drove down the wages (relative to the median wage in the economy) of the working class—Marx's proletariat—effectively shearing them from the mainstream of society. Neither is there evidence that middle-income earners dwindled as many were pushed into the "proletariat." In fact, from the dawning of the modern economies to the eve of World War 1 in 1913, the working class shrank and the bourgeoisie grew. Nor did wage inequality appear to increase within the set of working class jobs. The term had not been coined yet. Nor is there evidence that labor's share had contracted. (These points were made in Chapter 2.) Yet the modern economy did have a revolutionary effect on the pattern of incomes and wealth levels.

Modern economies opened up opportunities for individuals to make large-stake bets—betting their whole minds and bodies over months, even years—for highly uncertain prospects of reward: from a very large gain to the loss of the whole bet. As a result, enormous differences in economic results could occur—and there is no law that present winnings will sooner or later be offset by future losses. One person might suffer lengthy unemployment, while another not obviously different person might be working overtime. A person might have been led to an industry in decline, while another was led to an industry that was booming. A person's pay might double in a few decades, while another's might quadruple. It is not surprising that those left in the dust by others should take a jaundiced view of the system. Observations by contemporaries and piecemeal historical records all give evidence of an enormous rise in the inequality of income and wealth, though there are not the comprehensive records needed to construct the statistical data we take for granted now. Appreciable numbers of moguls and magnates in the business sector and speculators in the financial markets acquired staggering wealth, some displayed garishly, some tastefully, some hidden from view—especially in the gilded age. Capturing a share of the income from this wealth, if not the wealth itself, through taxation was to become an item high on many socialist agendas. But it was not at the top of the discontents with the modern economy. Great riches were nothing new. It was the democratization of opportunities to get rich that was new. People could take the presence of old wealth among a handful of aristocrats, the origins of which had become shrouded in the mists of time. They could not swallow so easily the "new rich" sprouting up in unexpected places.

Uppermost among the discontents with the modern economy was the precariousness of jobs and wages—the ever-present possibility of the loss of one's job or a major decline of wages in one's line of work. Episodes of high unemployment in the economy as a whole (aggregate unemployment) and sometimes in particular industries were endemic to the modern economy in this period. There had been sharp speculative bubbles and crashes in the era of mercantile capitalism, of course: the bursting of the Dutch tulip mania in 1637 and the bursting in 1720 of both the South Sea bubble in Britain and the Mississippi bubble in France, though these events were not broad enough to drive total employment either high or low. The wars of the period caused booms, often followed by recessions. In 1815, at the cusp of the modern, the end of the Napoleonic Wars sent many countries (but not France) into recession and Britain into a long slump. Though the 19th century was generally peaceful, downswings came with greater frequency and amplitude with the rise of the modern economies: there were the financial panics of 1792 (Wall Street's first crisis), 1796–1797 in Britain and America, 1819 in America, 1825 in Europe except France, 1837 in America, 1846 in all of Europe and, in America, 1857, 1873, and 1893—in addition to minor recessions. Since business was far more tightly tied to the financial sector in the modern economies, employment was far more affected by these financial panics than by earlier ones. Evidence of the time indicates that jobs were on the whole a great deal more precarious than they were in the previous century. (Some of the precariousness in the first half of the century was the result of the financial fragility of companies, especially small firms, and this lessened by degrees over later decades.)[1]

Yet as finance loomed ever larger in the modern economy, the macro-economic fallout of speculative excess and reckless financing grew capable of producing important slumps. In the mid-1840s railroad overbuilding led all Europe into a slump, which triggered the 1848 revolutions that swept over the Continent. Deeper slumps followed—the renamed Long Depression of 1873–1879 (first called the "Great Depression"), when U.S. unemployment exceeded 10 percent for years, and the more severe Depression of 1893–1898, when U.S. unemployment exceeded 12 percent for four straight years. Observers at the time must have wondered why, if these breakdowns were part of the "performance characteristics" of the modern economy, countries should want to continue with such a system. And countries with a less-than-modern economy must have wondered why they should aspire to one.

Not only was industrial life treating people very differently, the people in the cities also represented an ever-increasing variety of backgrounds. Large numbers of Chinese, then Irish, and later Jews from eastern Europe and Italians from the *Mezzogiorno* came streaming into London, New York, and San Francisco. Although the evidence is not quantifiable, it appears that, compared to the yeoman farmers and tradesmen and business owners in 1800 or even 1850, the new populations were more accustomed to communitarian ways—to habits of sharing, equalitarian notions of fairness, and an alienation from capitalist owners, who may have been indistinguishable to the newcomers from the inherited and entrenched owners of property and businesses found in the old country. Many or most of the older populations would have rejected the idea of belonging to a trade union, or crafts union, while many or most in the new populations would have thought it was wrong not to belong.

Talk of socialism arose in these times. The burgeoning diversity of experience and background that gave a boost to commercial innovation—discussed

---

1. Job security in America looks to have improved with the Galbraithian era—the early 1950s to the early 1970s—when Americans were safely employed in big entrenched companies enjoying stable growth and Europeans were steadily engaged in the process of "catching up." It is a question, though, whether jobs were also more secure in the 30-year era from the mid-1970s to the mid-2000s—though that span includes the 20-year Great Moderation dating from the mid-1980s. This era saw the U.S. slump of 1973–1983, the continental European slump of 1978–1988, the global 1987 stock market crash, the 1990 U.S. savings-and-loan crisis, the slump Japan entered in 1990, the East Asian economic crisis in 1997, the collapse of Long Term Capital Management, and the correction of the U.S. tech stocks in 2000–2001. The "Great Moderation" was an egregious misnomer.

in Chapter 1—must have been an impetus to thinking up new elements in the institutions and norms of society. Henri de Saint-Simon was an early socialist.[2] He criticized the economic system that had arisen around him as unscientific and irrational, thus wasteful of resources, and was the first to say that the system was not advantageous to the working poor. The *Communist Manifesto* by Marx and Engels, first published in January 1848 on the eve of the uprisings, was a strong condemnation of the waves of unemployment and its seemingly upward trend in Europe.

The uprisings of 1848 brought expressions of discontent with wages, employment, and working conditions to a new peak, though many of those rebellions were no more than a democratic opposition to the aristocracies, such as the February Revolution in Paris overthrowing the constitutional monarchy of Louis-Philippe and the March Revolution in Berlin and some German states demanding German national unity and a national parliament. Marx was to complain that the workers had no clear objectives or program, so it was not surprising that the workers gained nothing. It was only in the next decades that an extensive socialist agenda was proposed and debated.

The Idea of Socialism

The very idea of socialism was fraught with difficulties. Defining the set of ends that socialism would serve was never completely resolved. Some purposes of socialism in the minds of one might run counter to some purposes in the mind of another.

> Socialism's appeal, when it had one, was to say, at one and the same
> time, that its mission was to transcend capitalism while improving
> it; that everyone was equal but that the proletariat was the leading
> class; that money was the root of all evil but the workers needed more
> of it; that capitalism was doomed but the capitalists' profits were as high
> as ever; that religion was the opium of the people but that Jesus was the
> first socialist; that the family was a bourgeois conspiracy but it needed

2. An early statement of his criticisms is his *Lettres d'un habitant de Genève à ses contemporains* (1803). The "anarchy" of the modern economies was a major theme of Friedrich Engels in Germany and Thomas Carlyle in England. Saint-Simon went on to propose that business people and scientists direct the state and society's use of resources. His last book, *Nouveau Christianisme* (1825), states that the resources ought to be directed for the purpose of improving the conditions of the poorest class. He is believed to have coined the term *socialisme*, first used by Pierre Leroux in an 1834 essay "De l'individualisme et du socialism," that is, "On Individualism and Socialism." (Leroux, an economist and philosopher, was skeptical of both.)

defending from untrammeled industrialization; that individualism was to be deplored but that capitalist alienation reduced people to undifferentiated atoms; that there was more to politics than voting every few years while demanding universal suffrage; that consumerism beguiles the workers but they should all have a color television, a car and go on holidays abroad.[3]

Thus "socialism" was a fuzzy concept, and a variety of conceptions were advocated—Christian socialism, Marxian socialism (called communism), state socialism, market socialism, guild socialism, and Fabian (or evolutionary) socialism.

Declared socialists on the Continent began efforts around 1860 to reach agreement on a core set of values or rights—mostly in meetings of worker associations, intellectual periodicals, and conferences of Germany's Social Democratic Party. Socialist countries were to be guided by a socialist ethic that was an alternative to the spirit of modernity and the capitalist ethic that motivated individuals working in a modern capitalist economy.

In this ethic, access to employment was a right, not only because a job was a worker's livelihood—even in socialism nonparticipants judged of sound mind and body could not claim the wage paid to participants—but also because of its necessity for a person's sense of self-respect. Joblessness was to be combated.

Another part of this ethic had to do with the conditions and opportunities provided to the worker in society's enterprises, private (if any) and public. The right to a job meant the right to a job offering dignity. The abuse of power by the employer was not acceptable, so that dismissal without a hearing or without compensation was not to be permitted. To his credit, Marx brought up the normal need of human beings for a mental life, about which he felt deeply:

> [Adam] Smith has no inkling whatever that this overcoming of obstacles [in work] is in itself a liberating activity . . . hence as self-realization, objectification of the subject, hence real freedom, whose action is, precisely, labor.[4]

---

3. Sassoon, "All Shout Together."

4. Marx, translated from *Grundrisse der Kritik der politischen Ökonomie* (1858, p. 611). Some would say that Smith was better than that. He deplored repetitive tasks, by which he meant unchallenging tasks. (Flying jet planes on the milk routes is repetitive but sometimes severely challenging. "It's hours of sheer boredom," as someone said, but "punctuated by moments of sheer terror.") It could be that Marx's hostility sprang from his anxiety that Smith had thought of the point and others before he did. It could also be that Marx felt impelled to diminish Smith by portraying him as a rightwing zealot.

Similar expressions were to be heard from a range of social thinkers, not all of whom thought of themselves as socialist.

Another socialist value was that wealth and power must not be so disparate in society that some participants are denied the ability to realize their potential. Under socialism, large accumulations of wealth would not be allowed and, upon instituting equal opportunity, "to each according to his contribution" would rule in wage setting.[5] If all auto workers are necessary and interchangeable in producing a car, their wages would be equal; and a farmer would be construed as contributing as much as an auto worker. (Under communism, as *The Communist Manifesto* conceived it, "the free development of each is the condition for the free development of all.")

The socialist ethic saw private business as unattractive—as "money grubbing"—whether it made a profit or a loss. In the capitalist ethic, personal growth is, in part at any rate, a climb up the greasy pole to obtain better terms for oneself in one's career—better pay, higher fees. In the socialist ethic, personal growth comes from the love of one's work and mastering one's craft or profession.

The socialist ethic also condemned amassing and holding great wealth. The aim was to cultivate a "new person" (*Neuer Mensch*) who will be guided by instincts to serve others rather than by the shallow values of an "acquisitive society." In his 1860s cycle of four operas telling the story of the cursed ring of the Niebelungs, Wagner, a passionate socialist, dramatizes movingly the moral that when we choose wealth and power over love, we condemn ourselves to our own destruction. Audiences, especially if they know that Wagner was a dedicated socialist, reasonably interpret the Ring cycle as contrasting the greed of capitalism with the idyll of socialism. (Yet entrepreneurs and investors touched by Wagner's music drama apparently go right back to taking satisfaction from their lives as entrepreneurs and investors.)

Still another socialist value was attached to allocating resources by the principle of where they are most needed rather than by the profit motives of capitalism. Centralized coordination was deemed superior to decentralized

---

5. See Marx's 1875 *Critique of the Gotha Program*. The Gotha Program was a draft statement of socialist goals prepared for the founding conference in May 1875 of Germany's new Socialist Democratic Party in the town of Gotha. In a letter to friends, Marx vented his anger at the program's conception of a socialist state as merely subsidizing "producers associations," and he stated his ideas on the rewards to work in a socialist economy. Marx's *Manifesto, Grundrisse,* and Gotha letter are his basic short works.

competition and individual initiative. "Production for use rather than profit" is shorthand for this principle.

But a functioning economy has to have means to its ends, means in the form of economic institutions and economic culture. These are the norms, rules, institutions, and laws by which it enlists participants; opens them to know-how and experience; inspires them to exercise creativity; and, as neo-classical economics says, allocates land, labor, and capital over enterprises and industries and sets rules for the distribution of income or goods. How, in these terms, did a socialist economy work?

The socialists, though far from united in their ends, instinctively came together on what the means would be—figuring that they could thrash out later the main ends to which the means would be put. A key instrument, both at the communal level and at the national level, would be some mechanism for centralized control over the main directions of investment activity. There would be neither capitalists nor private entrepreneurs to veto investment projects. Another instrument would be the wage paid to workers—miners, nurses, musicians, and so forth. The state would supplement this wage with a "social dividend"—what would be profits under capitalism. The production method and the assignments of workers to jobs in an enterprise would be decided cooperatively with an eye to the workers' satisfactions as well as their productivity; a worker would be motivated by how stimulating the job was, not how long the worker would expect to be in the unemployment pool in the event he or she were fired in favor of a better worker. Finally, the allocation of labor and capital across enterprises and industries would be decided politically, by the workers' representatives, rather than by seeking the lowest cost, highest price, and greatest valuation—the market mechanism.

The various factions within socialism differed in matters of scope. The thoroughgoing, classical socialists, including Marxian socialists, sought centralized control of the capital available and the prices chargeable in all enterprises, large and small, and all industries, from farming to film making. More moderate socialists sought state control only over the "commanding heights" of the economy, including heavy industry. Proponents of *market socialism* wanted state-owned companies, as well as those under private ownership, free to buy and sell their products and intermediate goods in open markets (though prohibitive company taxation was always an option). Britain's Fabian socialists advocated starting small and feeling their way to the right scope over the economy. They wanted some "reforms" of capitalism; for communists, capitalism could not be reformed, only overthrown.

Could a Viable Socialism Be *Built*?

The classic debates of the 1920s and 1930s, the interwar years, were not about what anyone today would suppose they were about, namely the desirability of the socialist values. These new debates were on the feasibility of designing economies that would have the properties sought by socialists. Could the socialists succeed on their own terms? For a pragmatist, the question may have looked entirely empirical: let's wait to see how the socialist experiments turn out. But in the 1920s there was only the experiment starting in Russia and the chance that another one or two might start in Germany or France. So evidence was going to have less weight—and theory, such as it was, more weight—than it would have in an agronomy experiment conducted on several different plots of land. If the socialist economy on Russian soil succeeded in all respects or failed in all respects year after year, that would be no guarantee that the same results would follow experiments in other countries, or even that Russia's results would continue.

Enter Ludwig von Mises, a Viennese economic theorist of fiery temperament who founded the Austrian school of economics with his former student, Friedrich Hayek. Mises, so near to the revolution in Russia and socialist measures in Germany, could be said to have been an eyewitness of the creation of socialism. He immersed himself in the debate from 1920 to the early 1930s.[6] As Mises saw it, trying out socialism was an experiment without a theory. "[I]n the cloud-cuckoo land of their fancy," he wrote, "roast pigeons will in some way fly into the mouths of the comrades, but they omit to show how this miracle is to take place." He went on to argue that a socialist economy is not viable—not just uninnovative but ultimately impossible (*unmöglich*).

Mises's objections to socialism were based on the idea that in the modern economies around him the actors were restlessly trying out departures from normal practice in hope of obtaining higher prices for what they sell or lower prices for what they buy; in that way, new methods were tested and economic gains discovered. While socialists, including Marx, supposed that industrial workers, peasants, and craftsmen would somehow engage in the experiments necessary to achieve high efficiency, Mises argued that a socialist economy, in which nobody really owns anything—even one's own labor—would

---

6. Mises's first publication (in German) was the 1920 landmark, "Die Wirtschaftsrechnung im sozialistischen Gemeinwesen," translated in Mises, "Economic Calculation in the Socialist Commonwealth," where the quote that follows above can be found on page 88 and the next extract on 110. His big work, published two years later, was *Die Gemeinwirtschaft,* translated in Mises, *Socialism* (1936).

not present the incentives and the information needed for the deviations, or experiments, by individuals that ultimately make market prices and wages reflect the costs of products and the value of labor in each use:

> [I]n a socialist state . . . rational conduct might still be possible, but in general it would be impossible to speak of rational [i.e., efficient] production any more. There would be no means of determining what is rational, . . . hence . . . production could never be directed by economic considerations. For a time the remembrance of the experiences gained in a competitive economy . . . may provide a check to the complete collapse of the art of economy . . . [though] . . . the older methods . . . would meanwhile have become irrational, as no longer comporting with the new conditions. . . . [I]n place of the "anarchic" economy, recourse will be had to the senseless output of an absurd apparatus. The wheels will turn, but to no effect. . . . The administration [in a socialist state] may know exactly what goods are urgently needed. But in so doing it has only found what is, in fact, but one of the two necessary prerequisites for economic calculation. . . . It must dispense with the other—the valuation of the means of production. . . . Thus in the socialist commonwealth, every economic change becomes an undertaking whose success can be neither appraised in advance nor retrospectively.

Mises gives as an example the question of whether a new railroad should be built. A market economy, he says, enables an estimate of what the savings in transport costs would be. Mises concedes that the socialist state might have a decent estimate. But if the values of labor, energy, iron, and so forth required for the project's construction are not available in a common unit— in money—it is impossible to calculate whether the savings would cover the cost of the railroad. (In the jargon of economics, a socialist economy does not reveal to the "administration" each input's *opportunity cost*, or *shadow price*, which is equal to the value of its use in production elsewhere; in contrast, a market economy presents to entrepreneurs observable prices, which Mises views as adequate approximations of opportunity costs.)

Mises could have supplied a simpler example. Under a socialist economy in which equality of wages is regimented, no worker would ever try to see whether being more diligent or industrious than the others would be rewarded. Said worker would not receive an increased wage in return, since all wages are equal. And the worker would not save his or her job that way, since their jobs are very secure anyway. No worker has an incentive to exercise greater care and put greater energy into his or her work *no matter how valuable to society.* The system never allows the market to "discover" the correct general level of effort—and the correct general level of wages that corresponds to it—even when everyone is alike and has the same preferences, since no market process of trial moves takes place.[7] The conclusion is that private ownership of the fruits of one's own labor permits and encourages experimentation, without which the pattern of wages and prices in the economy could continue without a tendency toward correction.

The analysis by Mises may have been abstract to most of his readers. History, however, would provide graphic illustrations of Mises's points. The failure of Soviet personnel policy to reward workers taking greater care and to promote workers showing greater talent must have led to a sense of futility, and this helplessness must have been behind the massive alcoholism that plagued Soviet life in its last decades. This was a waste of the natural inclination of people to pitch in, to do a good job, and to try to make something of themselves. An appalling decline in the work ethic resulted, with severe effects on efficiency. There is a story of a foreigner living in Moscow in the 1980s who decided to gather field data by following a large truck as it left a brick-making factory. According to the observer, as the truck bumped along the streets and highways, about as many bricks fell out of the truck as it unloaded on its stops. If workers had had individual earning power and the freedom to make investments that would increase that power, their efforts and wages and self-respect would all have ended up being at far higher levels. For these insights, Mises is regarded as the originator of *property rights theory.*

A second argument by Mises turned on the "profit motive." He hammered away, primarily in *Socialism*, at the theme that enterprises operating as arms of a bureaucracy would not even attempt to operate with efficiency, in contrast to enterprises driven by the profit motive:

> The motive force of the whole process which gives rise to market prices
> for the factors of production is the ceaseless search on the part of capitalists and entrepreneurs to maximize their profits. . . . Without these private

7. The socialist theoreticians could reply that there remains in the socialist system a healthy incentive to perform well: failing to perform up to prevailing standards would likely cost a worker his or her promotion to jobs with greater scope for taking on responsibility. Thus there has to be some inequality, though not wage inequality. But the force of that counterargument would depend on how much more rewarding the jobs higher on the ladder were. Mises could have retorted that if the socialist plan envisioned an essentially stationary economy, in which only the occasional natural disaster interrupted the general tranquility, it is not obvious that there would be any nonpecuniary rewards from moving up the ladder that would be enough to motivate the workforce. And an economy that does not revolve around innovation would not need deep ranks of managerial personnel to begin with.

owners the market loses the mainspring that sets it in motion and keeps it
in operation. (pp. 137–138)

Socialist managers would be lacking in this motive. They would have relatively
little incentive to seize opportunities for increased profit regardless of inconvenience or political cost: If the profit increased, the central government would
not know to what to attribute this increase, so the manager might not get the
credit, and if the profit decreased, it might raise suspicions that the manager was
less competent than others. A manager or worker who knows there is no way to
protect his or her idea from being claimed by others is not apt to think of a new
idea. When nevertheless an enterprise does have a new idea, there is apt to be no
good way by which that enterprise can signal its belief in the benefit of the idea.
Furthermore, the incentives of socialist managers would be mostly undesirable.
They would always do the bureaucratic thing of "following the rules" and attending to appearances. They could compete for promotion up the ladder, but that
incentive would lead them to avoid any risk of failure. For these insights, Mises
could be seen as the originator of *public choice theory*—the decisionmaking of
self-dealing individuals in a bureaucracy, such as a state agency.

Mises's warning led to one of the most famous exchanges in the annals
of economics. Oskar Lange, a brilliant theorist rising into prominence in
the West in the 1930s before returning to his homeland, communist Poland,
challenged Mises's contention that a thoroughly socialist economy must ultimately lead to collapse.[8] Lange argued that a nation wanting a socialist economy without the failings warned of by Mises had open to it a way to put the
right prices on labor, iron, railroad track, and all the fruits of production. It
could use the same markets made use of by capitalist economies. Enterprises
would, in general, be state-owned, as before. These socialist enterprises
would supply each of their products to the market, where other socialist
enterprises and households might convey their demands. Some of these markets might be auction markets, as in capitalism, while others would not be,
just as in capitalism. Thus, the market would determine prices. Wages could
be determined similarly, as enterprises communicated terms and individuals
offered their services. Competition would ensure equal pay for indistinguishable labor working the standard workweek. (When some enterprises offered
a high wage for greater effort, the other enterprises would have to offer the

---

8. The original article appeared in Lange, "On the Economic Theory of Socialism," *Review of
Economic Studies*, October 1936 and February 1937. It is reproduced in Lange, "On the Economic Theory of Socialism" (1938).

same. There could be two or more tiers of workers, differentiated according to their category of effort.) Confident of his triumph, Lange joked that every socialist town in Europe will put up an ironic monument to Mises for having provoked insights showing that socialism was not "impossible" after all. In fact, *market socialism* was tried in Poland and Hungary in the 1980s.

But most of those studying Lange's argument tended to conclude that market socialism would not really work either. It might be an improvement over the more regimented system adopted by the Soviet Union but not an escape from the limits that a thoroughgoing socialism would impose. Mises's profit-motive argument suggests that socialist enterprises will not be driven to supply the socially desirable amount of output in response to any given market price; so where that undersupply is relatively acute, prices will be driven to relatively high levels. Mises scored again in noting that it is one thing to expect the government to motivate socialist managers to "play" at being profit-maximizing producers—some might do a fair job of it. It is another thing to expect the government to delegate to the managers the responsibility for *investment decisions*. No managers would declare it was their duty to let their enterprises shrink in the interest of the economy's "efficiency." The socialists themselves, far from being grateful for the idea of competitive socialism, were all against it—because they wanted to take over the power heretofore residing in the marketplace and/ or because for them the whole point of socialism was to direct the reshaping of the economy—to plan.

The young Hayek, turning his attention to the controversy over socialism, cast a new light on the debate over "socialist calculation."[9] The arguments of Hayek are knowledge-based, while those of Mises were incentive-based. Hayek starts with his idea that the know-how in any complex economy— complex either because it is very modern or highly diversified—is necessarily dispersed over the participants in the business sector. Yet, as he says, any individual or agency desiring to "plan"—from scratch—such an economy's allocation of resources over industries would need all this know-how to set up the most suitable methods of production. Diverting everyone with know-how to advise in planning would be prohibitively costly. Even if all the possessors of know-how could be put in one stadium, the mass of detail would swamp any attempt by the planner to use it all. The planner would not be able to put it all together. Therefore, central planning cannot work satisfactorily.

9. Hayek, "Socialist Calculation" (1935, pp. 201–243), reprinted in Hayek, *Individualism and Economic Order* (1948).

Hayek was fond of a shorter route to the same conclusion. A modern economy, with its institutions and culture and with its production methods and the capital goods it uses, could not have been *built* by one individual or one company or any one body of any kind—the thing is too complex. So a government could not have built one either. Nor build it now.

A socialist state might succeed well enough at first by copying some similar economy abroad, making what socialist changes it could. But inefficiency in resource allocation would grow as the economy took its own path—as product demands rose here and fell there and as older people retired and younger ones entered the workforce. In Hayek's view of the modern capitalist economy, increases in relative prices and wages in some industries or lines of work indicate to participants elsewhere that they might do well to gather know-how in those industries or lines of work. In the socialist economy, people have little incentive to choose an industry or occupation on that basis, and they may be faced with bureaucratic obstacles to moving to the industry or occupation of their choice. An industry in a socialist economy might finally lose the key to how to produce because of its failure to provide individuals with motives to maintain or acquire the needed know-how.

Another Hayekian argument is that a good business decision may often require the input of practitioners whose know-how, born of long experience, offers them insights with which to appraise the difficulty of carrying out some investment project or the difficulty of developing a product that the enterprise had not produced before. This problem appears in a free-enterprise economy as well. How to produce a new thing and how costly it will be are questions to which the answers are not known beforehand. If the state were to decide whether to take an initiative in some industry, the full opportunity costs of the project to all other industries in the economy could not really be known to anyone in the government. Even the experts on the ground would have to make educated guesses. From this Hayekian viewpoint, the private entrepreneur deciding whether to build a new rail line (in consultation with engineers, financiers, and so forth) will usually come to a far better sense of the costs of acquiring the new line, having been in the business for years, than would the administration of a socialist economy, no matter how transparent the prices of things. Here is Hayek in his classic 1935 paper on socialist calculation:

> In a centrally planned society the selection of the most appropriate among the known technical methods will be possible only if all that knowledge can be used in the calculations of the central authority. . . . It is hardly

necessary to emphasize that this is an absurd idea even in so far as that knowledge is concerned which can properly be said to "exist" at any moment of time. But much of the knowledge that is actually utilized is by no means "in existence" in this ready-made form. Most of it consists in a technique of *thought* which enables the individual engineer to find *new* solutions rapidly as soon as he is confronted with new constellations of circumstances.[10]

Over the years, more and more in the general public came to be persuaded by the arguments of Mises and Hayek against the socialist economy—though some needed to see the malfunctions and mounting stagnation of the Soviet economy in the 1980s to feel sure. But what persuaded them was not so much the argument that limitations in a socialist economy would saddle it with growing inefficiencies—an economist's argument. It was the idea, which people read between the lines or simply supposed was a part of the broad critique, that if a relatively well-functioning modern economy went socialist, it would become *less innovative*. It would be saddled with increasingly obsolete products and production methods. People cared more about economic growth, it seems, than they did about dry-as-dust efficiency.

In fact, the socialist economies were fatally lacking in dynamism. The innovatorship of the former state managers was tested when massive privatization began in eastern Europe after the collapse of the Soviet Union. These managers, fearing they would lose their post to a rival or see their enterprise close if they *did not* succeed in innovating, made frenzied efforts to create and market new products. Yet they met with almost total failure. They were willing entrepreneurs, when their backs were to the wall at any rate, but they were not *able* at entrepreneurship. The Darwinian process in the communist economies had not selected managers for that talent, so those managers who had that trait were few and far between.[11]

Mises *seemed* set to make the innovation argument. He implied that those in control of a socialist enterprise, doubting they would win much of the credit for an innovation and fearing they would have much to lose from failure, will be far less willing to attempt an innovation than private owners of such an enterprise would, since the latter can expect to pocket any winning

---

10. Hayek, "Socialist Calculation" (p. 210). The italics have been added.

11. The construction of the survey of managers and the statistical findings are described in Frydman et al., "When Does Privatization Work?" (Mises could have said in defense that his argument about prices being increasingly wrong in a socialist economy clearly implied that innovative effort in that economy would go increasingly awry.)

and, thanks to limited liability, escape much of the loss. Mises also understood that the "ceaseless search" for profit has also the function of tending to weed out the wrong people from various jobs and to put in new people to be tested. Lacking the profit motive, a well-functioning socialist economy—far more than a well-functioning modern economy would—would let into managerial positions people whose talents did not lie in either the conception or the development of ideas for novel commercial products. But Mises did not make the point explicit.

Hayek's conception of the modern economy may have seemed to lead to the innovation argument. In his bottom-up, grassroots theory, the modern market economy, in the process of creating new products, whether goods or methods, draws on the freedom of individuals in that system to exercise their originality and thrives on the individuality of their situation and their know-how. Hayek opened the door to a model of indigenous innovation— innovation indigenous to a country's economy—based on the new and diverse ideas that strike individuals in the economy. In contrast, the socialist economy does not confer on individuals any right to apply for financial support for an innovative project. At best, an individual would be free to suggest an innovative idea to the manager of the socialist enterprise, and a manager would be free to apply to the national bank for a loan to develop such an innovative idea into a new product. From Hayek's perspective, a socialist economy could not realize its potential for innovation, since diverse entrepreneurs are not free to compete with one another for market share through new products and methods, diverse financiers are not free to bet on their private judgments in deciding which new ideas to back, and diverse creative types are not free to compete with one another for an entrepreneur to help develop their new ideas.

The loss of innovation would be particularly clear and pronounced in the case of a knowledge economy. Government takeover of enterprises in which the talents and services of most participants are idiosyncratic, such as architectural firms, soccer teams, comedy clubs, oil drillers, gourmet restaurants, ballet companies, and wine growers, would be unworkable for the Hayekian reasons that the government would have little or no knowledge of the business and of which ones to invest in. Moreover, worker management would typically vote no to moving, to newcomers, and to innovation. Those who had dreamed up new ideas would lack the clear channels they had used before. (In modern economies there are companies called ESOPs in which employees are the shareowners, but they are seldom as successful as their owner-managed competitors.) A socialist state with a knowledge economy would thus be particularly hard-pressed to acquire dynamism.

Why, then, did Mises and Hayek not make these innovation arguments? For one thing, Mises and even Hayek, writing as late as the mid-1930s, were still Schumpeterian in their thinking about innovation. Had they warned of a dearth of indigenous innovation in a nation choosing a socialist economy, acute readers would have commented that a socialist economy is as free as a modern capitalist economy to *import* the magnificent new technological advances wrought by scientists and inventors around the world. The concept of the modern economy—creative and successful at indigenous innovation— had not surfaced in their 1920s and 1930s papers or even in Hayek's famous 1944 tract.[12] For another thing, to argue that the nations like czarist Russia that had gone socialist could realize high dynamism if they just returned to private ownership would have been seen as absurd. (It was nations like America, Germany, Hungary, and France that would lose their dynamism if they switched to socialism—as those that tried soon found out.)

Over the decades most economists, including many on the left, came to declare the Austrian team the winner of the debate. The Austrian school persuaded the economics profession that a socialist economy would cause a decisive deterioration of efficiency. The Austrian side did not have to claim that the modern capitalist economy was free of its own inefficiencies—the misdirections and the waste brought by financial panics hardly needed to be acknowledged. They had only to argue that such an economy, once socialized, would suffer a sickening slide into greater and greater inefficiency.

The Austrians lost another battle, though. They seemed to believe that *every country* that threw out its capitalist economy in favor of a socialist

---

12. In his *The Road to Serfdom* (1944) the terms innovation, creativity, originality, invention, growth, advance, and progress do not appear in the index. Hayek scholars might agree that the first flicker of recognition that—as was virtually pointed to in his own work!—indigenous creativity could occur within a nation's economy, not just its scientific establishment, may have come when Hayek was sent a lecture by Oskar Morgenstern in 1937. Hayek had supposed in influential work in 1927 that the economy has a tendency to home in on some equilibrium path, though errors could cause disequilibrium for some time. Morgenstern's lecture argued that to suppose that was to assume that the actors in the economy possessed perfect foresight, which they could not do in a world of endogenous innovation (nor, for that matter, in scientific research outside economies). Certainly Hayek saw the problem. His recognition of the uncertainty within an economy caused by innovators (and more generally the pluralism of views among participants) became explicit in the 1960s. Hayek's 1961 paper "The Non-Sequitur of the 'Dependence Effect'" teased J. K. Galbraith for supposing that would-be innovators bringing out new products know they will succeed or know the probability of any given level of sales.

economy would soon be worse off owing to growing inefficiencies. But it was one thing to argue that there would be, generally speaking, a decisive loss of efficiency from socializing in its entirety an economy of great complexity and sophistication, which had required a long evolution of institutions and culture to achieve—a modern economy or merely a knowledge economy. It was quite another thing to suggest that *every* economy, no matter how ineffective, would be still worse off by going socialist. And it was yet another to argue that *any* amount of socialism, no matter how moderate and how aimed, would spell worse inefficiency than would otherwise have been experienced. The socialist movement could live! And it did.

Socialism managed to take power in economies that were not advanced and were not rapidly becoming advanced through modernization. It was no use to tell the Russians that their socialism would not be as efficient as well-functioning capitalist economies were, since the Russians had no experience with such an economy. And it would not have been persuasive to tell them that their socialism would not be as innovative as an economy of high dynamism, since they had no experience with that either. In fact, Soviet Russia had an extraordinary run of *Schumpeterian* innovation from the 1920s to the 1960s as electrification and other advances were quickly introduced. No one yearned for the return of the czar.

Socialism also managed to take over limited sectors in some economies—the less-advanced economies, to be sure, but also in some economies that were relatively advanced. The notion grew that socialist ownership and control would work well in the "commanding heights" of the economy—energy, telecommunications, railways, ports, and any heavy industry. The unexpected revival of this thinking in China was confirmed in an address by Prime Minister Wen Jiabao in Beijing in March 2010. "The socialist system's advantages enable us to make decisions efficiently, organize effectively and concentrate resources to accomplish large undertakings."[13]

The socialist discussion, especially in the more advanced economies, shifted from the workability of a socialist economy to the workability of state ownership and control in one or more sectors. It also shifted toward the regulation and taxation of the private sector. The Austrians' perspectives were applicable to this discussion, of course. The power of Hayek's perspective can hardly be overestimated. There was a Hayekian moment in the past decade when Western governments took measures to encourage the

13. As reported on the *International Herald Tribune*'s website, www.iht.com, March 5, 2010.

use of biofuels instead of the conventional fossil fuels, coal and oil, by induc-
ing farmers to switch land from raising the usual crops to producing soy-
beans, which could be used for making soy biodiesel. The reallocation of land
caused a catastrophic rise in the price of various staple foods and thus led to
hundreds of thousands of deaths by starvation. It was also a cause of the further deforestation of the Amazon basin. On top of all that, the soy biodiesel
produced was later found to have virtually no advantage over conventional
fuels in terms of overall greenhouse gas emissions.[14] There was great irony
in the failure of "planning," since the socialists in particular and government
planners in general were always asserting that socialism, by virtue of being
rational, would look to the long term in contrast to the short-termism of capitalism. But it was precisely capitalism, with its huge step forward in introducing shareowning, that solved the problem that the principal owner would
not be expecting to live forever. It was the single proprietorship and, earlier,
the feudal barony that were apt to suffer the problem of no heirs.

In particular, even an incremental move toward social ownership raises
the question of why the government should nationalize to undertake projects that veterans of private industry presumably rejected. Mises's point that
a socialist government does not face the right prices does not apply if the part
of the economy under social ownership and control is too small to change
the configuration of prices in the economy. But in the Hayekian perspective,
the lack of the needed know-how in the socialist government may cause it
to proceed in the wrong direction or to fail when it is moving in the right
direction.

Yet the Austrians overgeneralized, supposing that their theory applies
in every case and must always trump other considerations. It can happen
that business people, not having worked much in government, do not know
everything known by the state. Possibly the state has knowledge about some
industries that would make state ownership and control better on balance
than private ownership. On the issue of nationalization of any particular
kind of production, then, the Hayekian bias in favor of private ownership
may be outweighed. However, Hayek was certainly correct to see the dangers
of totalitarian control of the economy—by the state or by anyone. He was
not the extremist he was taken to be. He never proposed a zero-level of state
activity in production. In his famous wartime tract, *The Road to Serfdom*, he

---

14. Ammous and Phelps, "Climate Change, the Knowledge Problem and the Good Life"
(2009). See also Volpi, "Soya Is Not the Solution to Climate Change" (2006).

proposed a range of roles for the state, including research to increase longevity.[15] Hayek was not an ideologue.

Socialism's Strange Side

It is clear now, from the distance of time, that something was very odd about the socialism debate of the interwar decades. The Austrians made the strange assumption that the goal of the socialists was economic efficiency. But the socialists were not plotting revolutionary changes in the structure of the Western economies for the sake of bringing economic waste under better control. Output per head in Western Europe had quadrupled between 1820 and 1920. So even the most earnest socialists could have afforded to let go whatever loss of output resulted from the occasional panic and the unemployment that accompanied the modern economy.

Most socialists, in fact, held aloft their goals of stability, equality, dignity, and contentment. They had no wish to smash the individual. But to the extent the individual is encouraged to excel in the social sphere, it is through his alignment with the state. The values expressed in this set of goals represented a fundamental shift from the core values of the Western world—some from as far back as ancient Greece. Absent from the socialist terms was the vocabulary of the humanist tradition—terms like exploration, creation, and exhilaration.

---

15. In a 1933 paper, "The Trend of Economic Thinking," Hayek wrote that laissez-faire is not "the ultimate and only conclusion." (p. 134). In *The Road to Serfdom* he speculated that "nothing has done so much harm to the liberal cause as the wooden insistence of some [libertarians] on certain rules of thumb, above all the principle of laissez-faire" (p. 13). That tract brought a range of reactions. A mild one was from Keynes, who in a letter expressed great admiration for the book, then said he differed with it at only one point. He favored a radically different list of activities for the state to do—an agenda as odd from present-day perspectives as from Hayek's. The fury of some of the reactions is incomprehensible to scholars in the present age. On its sixtieth anniversary in 1994, *The Road to Serfdom* won high praise from Amartya Sen, writing in the *Financial Times*. It remains true that Hayek was alarmed as few others were by the loss of individual freedom he expected to result from British economist William Beveridge's plan for a massive system of social insurance and other interventions.

Incidentally, many imagine that *Road* was a broadside against Soviet socialism based on Hayek's previous theoretical work. In fact, it was Hayek's answer to those in Britain who claimed there was no reason to fight a war with Nazi Germany. It was a warning against the state-sponsored corporatism in Germany more than against communism in the Soviet Union, though Hayek often alluded to the latter. Maybe Hayek saw corporatism in Beveridge's extreme welfare state. During the war, Hitler's economists got hold of a draft of the Beveridge blueprints after it was air-dropped over Nazi-occupied Europe. The Nazis apparently exclaimed, "This is what we need here in Germany!" See "Commission on Social Justice: Beveridge's Appeal for an Attack on Five Giant Evils" in *The UK Independent,* October 25, 1994.

The socialist goals were pursued with fanatical zeal. The socialist experiments, dating from Lenin's to Castro's, made a fetish of enforcing rigid equalities, controlling population in the name of "full employment," and forbidding virtually all individual initiatives in the economy. These economies became faceless, suffocating, boring—not just grossly inefficient.

So it was odd that, at first, Mises and Hayek did not criticize these goals. They gave the impression that efficiency was decisive in the choice of an economic system. It seemed they would have been willing to accept socialism—the limitation on wealth, bars against opening a business, workers voting on the conduct of businesses, and so forth—if they could be persuaded that no loss of total output, or economic efficiency, would result. Economists effectively voted to award victory in the debate to the Austrians on the narrow grounds on which the Austrians made their arguments. Had there been, following the debate, a consensus that, all things considered, the socialist economy's avoidance of unemployment and swings in employment would increase output more than new inefficiencies would decrease it, Mises and Hayek would have lost their debate.

Later, in *The Road to Serfdom*, Hayek conveyed his sense of tragedy over the loss of *freedom* suffered in Italy and Germany since the 1930s with the rise of authoritarianism. There could be no longer any doubt about his feeling for humanity. If Sen's reading is right, freedom in Hayek's thinking is a means to other goals. Yet *The Road to Serfdom* did not indicate what goals would be infringed on by a loss of economic freedom at the hands of the authoritarians other than efficiency—except to warn that output, or efficiency, would be diminished if the freedom of businesses is crimped by the authoritarian leaders. (Most of the book is concerned with the importance of political freedom.)

With hindsight we can see that missing in the discussion of socialism was a debate between socialist values and Western humanist values. It has come to be clear that neither the proponents of the modern economy nor its opponents—the advocates of socialism and those of corporatism—could formulate a justification of the system they favored until they could show that it served compelling social values.

The Fear of Socialism

For many of those who feared the coming of socialism, the problem was not that socialism might fail but that it could succeed well enough by its own lights to go on and on. One could not be sure that a robust majority would always be there to stop socialism in one's own country—in Italy, say, where the capitalist economy paled next to those in America, Britain, and Germany. By 1919, little more than a year after the Bolshevik revolution, several countries—Italy, Germany, and America too—were in the grip of the Red Scare.

In Germany and France, an incremental socialism was making some headway. Germany's Social Democratic Party (known as the SPD), which sought a socialist economy, headed the coalition that gained control of the parliament in 1919. The socialists won the establishment of factory councils (*Betriebsrat*) in which workers would have a say in various company matters. An arbitration mechanism was set up for labor disputes. Private capital retained ownership but lost some control. The work day was shortened not to 10 or 9 hours but to 8 hours. Social reforms that ought to have been discussed in the society at large and, if chosen, paid for by taxpayers because they wanted the reforms, were squeezed out of the business sector. The West was started in the direction of regulations, mandates, and fees that were to take a toll on investment and innovation.

As the 1920s dawned on the West, there was a great sense of foreboding about the economic future. A revolution had started, and no one could know whether it was going to spread.

CHAPTER SIX

The Third Way:
Corporatism Right and Left

Corporatism is not an internal reform to satisfy the selfish interests of each of us. . . . [I]t represents the end of civic and economic individualism, the coming of a new social and economic regime, and the revelation of an organized nation made up of mutually supporting bodies.

GEORGES VALOIS, "La Coordination des forces nationales"

W HEREVER THE MODERN ECONOMY ARRIVED, with its institutions and culture, there were preexisting social customs and social values going back centuries. Over the latter half of the 19th century, extensive modernization in parts of continental Europe, including France and Germany, rode roughshod over traditional ways of life. Though socialists went on with their critique of capitalism—the modern capitalist economies not excepted—other social critics arose to deplore other things about the modern economy. By the mid-1920s, these critics had formulated the standard 20th-century indictment of the modern economy. While the unemployment and wages that socialists complained of in capitalism could have been addressed and eventually were, the new indictment struck at the heart and brain of the modern economy.

Corporatism's Indictment of the Modern Economy

The modern economy, as argued earlier, was driven by the altruistic individualism of Renaissance humanism, the vitalism of the Baroque, and the modernism of the Enlightenment. That last current, in adding to (as well as building on) the earlier currents, made the critical mass that fueled the modern economy. At modernism's core was the idea that individuals ought to be free to pursue their own happiness, with some regulations for their own benefit. In arts and letters, the author of a work should be emancipated from service to extrinsic moral and political ideals. Art for art's sake, as Oscar Wilde and E. M. Forster proclaimed. In business, the entrepreneur should—on the same grounds—be freed from service to society. Business for business's sake.[1]

In social life, a "modern woman" felt free to depart from tradition or even break taboos. Ordinary people went from being dependents on mutual protection to adventurers out in the world in quest of career challenges and whatever other chances might lie ahead. Men and women might become heroic figures on a small or large scale, far more so than in the mercantile age that Smith saw as unheroic. In some countries, important political leaders and activists were early champions of such a society, voicing little or no support for the state's pursuing social goals other than the goal of individual prosperity and individual development for all. In *Common Sense*, first published as a pamphlet early in 1776, Thomas Paine's argument for American independence from Britain was built on the proposition that it would boost Americans' prosperity; if Paine recognized another social value, it was not evident. Jefferson, in the second draft of the Declaration of Independence in July 1775, wrote that the institutions of America "opened . . . to the unfortunate & to the enterprising of every country . . . the acquisition & free possession of property," thus suggesting that self-support, a career, and some wealth were markers on the road they took in pursuit of happiness and the reason they came to America. In a 1925 speech after his election, President Calvin Coolidge saw Americans as still on the course that Paine and Jefferson evidently supposed they were on and left little doubt that his government would be oriented accordingly. "After all," he said, "the chief business of the American people is business. They are profoundly concerned with buying, selling, investing and prospering." Even more strikingly, Lincoln's second lecture speaks of Americans' "rage for the new."

Also at the core of modernism was the idea that everyone who enjoys the legal rights of a modern society and pays little for them has obligations of responsibility: to respect the laws and people's rights, so as not to cheat others; and obligations of independence: to bear the consequences of one's mistakes so as not to be a burden on others. Responsibility implies that persons, alliances, and even the state may not violate property rights of persons or companies; extort payments from them; induce the state to block competitors from

1. See Sidorsky's "Modernism and the Emancipation of Literature from Morality" and his "The Uses of the Philosophy of G. E. Moore in the Works of E. M. Forster."

introducing new products; or solicit subsidies, grants, and indemnities from the state. (The modern state may make investments to open up new innovation and enterprise, as the Louisiana Purchase did, and may take actions to prevent external forces from crippling innovation and enterprise—if these are not judged to cost too much. And the state may act to combat what is seen to be economic injustice in the rewards from cooperation. But it is *not* a function of the modern state to block development of innovative products or block new investments to protect competing producers from the new competition or to indemnify them if it is too late to protect them. In a modern society, even a just state is not in the business of comprehensive insurance.)

This modernism that impelled the emergence of modern economies was nothing less than a cultural revolution, and the modern economies it was injecting were a cultural shock, especially in continental Europe. In the last half of the 19th century, whole operas dramatized the costs of modern self-finding and self-expression in societies still heavily traditional: Mascagni's 1890 *Cavalleria Rusticana*, Wagner's 1868 *Die Meistersinger*, and Verdi's 1853 *La Traviata*. ("A subject for our age," Verdi wrote to a friend. To obtain a theater he changed the setting to "Paris and environs, 1700.") Modernism and modernity stimulated counter-currents in those Continental countries where a modern beachhead was substantial but traditions remained strong. The most important counter-current began in late 19th-century Germany— one eventually culminating in an economic system that came to be called *corporatism*. But why was it bound to elicit a backlash? In a classic treatise on the healthiness of traditional life, which became a fount of corporatist ideas for decades, the Prussian sociologist Ferdinand Tönnies points to the trader who, armed with the "contracts" created by Roman law, makes offers that put others out of business. For Tönnies, this trader is the force destroying the traditional community, not the "division of labor" brought by factories, which Marx had emphasized.[2] Much of the corporatist critique of modernity consisted of unfavorable comparisons of city life with community life. More

2. Tönnies witnessed this disruption as a youth in rural Schleswig. He further distanced himself from Marx in arguing that specialization had existed in communities for centuries and had actually strengthened them. Neither was he a fascist. He joined the Socialist Party in 1932 just to spite the Nazis. Tönnies's magnum opus, in German, was first published under the title *Gemeinschaft und Gesellschaft* in Leipzig in 1887, when he was still young. Though *Gesellschaft* often refers to a business, so one might think the title meant "Community and Business," Tönnies used *Gesellschaft* to mean modern civilization, business included. Editions in 1912 and 1920 gained wider attention. A new 2001 translation into English is *Community and Civil Society*.

generally, a large part of the corporatist critique of modernity protested features and properties of the modern economy that broke with traditions.

A corporatist critique of the modern economy developed over the next several decades. One of the corporatist criticisms of the modern economy was that it had no leadership, thus no course, its heading being the net resultant of millions of individuals pulling in myriad directions. In the medieval past, corporatists supposed, attempts to innovate were directed by the economy's communal authority, with results generally along the lines of what the community had hoped. When such communal goals came to be largely crowded out by the unannounced, largely unobserved, and often inscrutable initiatives of a welter of individuals and companies in the business sector, the economy could be said to have been left *rudderless*, which gave rise, understandably enough, to a sense of disorder. And that sense, no doubt, lay behind some of the unease felt across Western Europe in the last years of the 19th century and the early decades of the 20th. The desire for direction (for *dirigisme,* as the French said) was a major strand of corporatist thought.

Many corporatists saw the *uncoordination* in capitalism as another source of disorder. They sought a system of concerted action. At the micro level, a company's owners could act on a proposal only if "stakeholders," such as employees, agreed (codetermination or *mit Spreche*). At the macro level, legislative action needed the consent of the main players, capital and labor (*Concertazione*). Later they spoke of the "social partners."

Conservative corporatists sought not just order but the *old* order. As they saw it, the modern culture with its yen for change was eroding the economic order in traditional communities, where members had a sense that they were working toward the shared goals of their traditional culture. They bewailed the lack of *solidarity*. For Freud, the conflict between modern and traditional was, ultimately, "the struggle between the claim of the individual and the cultural claims of the group."[3] The yearning for the traditional culture is evidenced not just in the writings of corporatist theorists but also in artistic works of a splinter group of classicists who broke away from modernism in the 1920s. A return to the harmony and perfectionism of the classical

---

3. Freud, *Civilization and Its Discontents* (p. 50). He wanted aggressions to be constructive, lest another war broke out. The title of the 1930 German original, *Das Unbehagen in der Kultur,* raised the problem of translating *Unbehagen*. (Freud suggested "discomforts." His 1930 translator Joan Riviere proposed "discontents.") What Freud meant by *Kultur* was the entire acquisition of knowledge, practice, attitudes, and even "tools." Today, tools and even technology are usually kept out of "culture" but included in "civilization."

order was evoked in sculptures such as Aristide Maillol's *Ile-de-France*, paintings such as those from Picasso's period of classical portraits, and film, notably Leni Riefenstahl's documentary film *Olympia*.[4]

Many social critics, most of them in continental Europe, saw failings that had to do with the *materialism* of the societies around them. They charged that the quality of life in society had been debased by what they saw as a spread of money-grubbing. They complained of the economic disparities between those who scurried to make the most of their material advantages and those who lacked them. They also complained of the outbreaks of violence between owners and workers, neither of whom seemed to have limits on the means they would use to achieve material gains. These were the themes of the Roman Catholic Church and the articles of what came to be called Catholic corporatism. For the mitigation of this misery the 1891 papal encyclical of Leo XIII titled *Rerum Novarum* called upon those who hire labor to pay a wage adequate for raising a family. Today this would be called exercising social responsibility. (One wonders why the Church's economists did not look for a way that would not destroy jobs; the public could have paid a tax to finance subsidies for hiring factory workers.) *Rerum* also threw its support behind the establishment of labor unions to negotiate improved conditions. The 1931 papal encyclical of Pius XI, *Quadragesimo Anno,* gave its approval to the corporatist invention of vocational groups and to producer associations. Neither of these encyclicals attacked private property but rather appealed to private owners for a kinder face. By this time, both the Church and many, if not most, intellectuals had turned away from the socialist contention that state ownership would serve any good purpose. Freud wrote in *Civilization and Its Discontents* (p. 60) that "[i]n abolishing private property we deprive the human love of aggression of one of its instruments," such as amassing more wealth than our neighbors, no doubt, "but we have in no way altered the differences in power and influence which are misused by aggressiveness, nor have we altered anything in its nature." The stark inequalities that were fast developing in the Soviet Union bore out this prophecy.

Much animosity toward the modern economy, though, expressed not a desire for order, whatever the new order might be, or even nostalgia for the

---

4. The classic study is the 1925 essay by Franz Roh, reprinted in 1995. Many examples of the period are reproduced in Silver, *Chaos and Classicism*. Silver's earlier book *Esprit de Corps* covers some of this ground.

old order, whatever order that was, so much as the fear and anger of various social classes whose social status and very survival were threatened. The modern economy was dissolving the social hierarchy and the distribution of power. In the societies of medieval Europe, the classes were imbedded in a system of mutual protection: peasants could appeal to authorities, such as the lord of the manor, for protection when the actions of another raised their costs or reduced their revenues. Competition among manufacturers might be forestalled by limiting production to the manufacturer granted a royal charter. Merchants formed merchant guilds, which served to control the sale of staples such as food and cloth, thus exercising a degree of monopoly power. Artisans and craftsmen formed the craft guilds, which sought to regulate standards for, thus entry into, their line of work. There was a sense that the terms demanded by the various producer groups were sanctioned by an unwritten social compact, whether or not the terms were exactly the "just price" conceived by some theologians.

In contrast, modern capitalism did not offer a social contract—it could not and be true to the values for which it stood. Thus the various groups of producers, merchants, artisans, and the rest experienced a newfound *powerlessness*, though some of them were on the rise, so they were not materially suffering. In some countries, the manufacturers in the new infant industries tended to be protected by an import tariff, but few manufacturers, if any, faced the reliable and stable demand that manufacturers enjoyed in the traditional economies, owing to the economy's evolution and advance over time. And few manufacturers enjoyed monopoly power for very long. As a consequence, individual producers and producer groups had no power to set their terms outside a narrow range—they went from price setters to price takers—and they lost some of their power to set standards and maintain prestige. The sense of powerlessness in trades, industries, and professions could have been for many people a gnawing frustration to be set against the satisfactions that they found in their work. If they loved the business they were in and the work they did, that was all the more reason to suffer from their inability to set their own terms in hopes of maintaining their social position. The corporatism of 1920s Europe held out the promise of some defense against the relentless innovation of the modern economy and against the desertion of consumers—defense that they later dubbed "social protection." Farmers could go on producing, even if not all of their produce could be sold in the marketplace. Movie makers could be subsidized even if their former audiences now preferred not to watch them. This broad "social protection," as it became known, was one of the last strands of corporatism to fall into place.

In continental Europe all these intellectual strands and the political forces championing them came into a confluence during the 1920s: the elites in a city like Munich or Rome, many of them nationalists who felt the need for a return to unity and purpose in society; the intellectuals who felt the need for economic order; the peasants, artisans, and other interest groups losing ground to modernization, who wanted protection; the scientists who wanted state support for research and artists who wanted it for the arts; and, not least, the Christian corporatists, who advocated restoration of traditional communities and vocations through curbs on mobile capital and the "trader spirit" in profit-driven businesses.[5] True, the socialists had already decried the scramble for social status, money, and power, most dramatically the socialist-sympathizer Wagner with his opera cycle, *Ring of the Niebelung*. To pick up votes, the corporatists took up that socialist theme and other parts of the socialist agenda, such as some sort of codetermination, without saddling themselves with the socialist baggage of social ownership and without making a fetish of wage equality and full employment.

All these factions hoped for some way of curbing or overriding the various tendencies and impulses of the modern economy with its modernist culture. The result was the corporatist economy. Its core function was to keep the private sector under public control. To what ends? The corporatists' main aims were state-led investment, industrial peace and solidarity, and social responsibility. There was much thinking about economic growth too. Economies on the fringe of modernity were growing so slowly as to leave a widening gap between their productivity and that in America and Germany. Italy and Spain were being passed by others in the league table of productivity.

---

5. There was an ethnic dimension to the politics of protection. The competition from which the Christian Social Party sought to protect the Catholic lower class came from predominantly Jewish businesses. The German nationalist parties wanted government to use its power to protect people of their ethnic background against competition from Slavs and especially from Jews. The socialists were no different. The Social Democratic Party boasted that it, not the corporatist group, was the true opponent of the "Jewish big capitalists," "Jewish exploiters," and "rich Jews." It went out of its way to characterize its targets as Jewish where the targets were disproportionately Jewish. Anti-Semitism was endemic in Europe during this period. See Muller, *The Mind and the Market* (p. 353). It is fair to ask whether the advancing entrepreneurs were opposed because they were Jewish or the advancing Jews were opposed because they were entrepreneurs. The answer would appear to be the former, since Europe had long exhibited a bias against Jews. It was more than that, however. The problem that the corporatists later called the "Jewish question" was not the Jewish identity of so many in Germany but rather that many successful Jews were mostly in the "liberalism" camp, which was integral to the birth of economic modernity, rather than in the corporatist camp. The first solution was to take over their businesses, the "final solution" was the Holocaust.

Some corporatists, Benito Mussolini included, laid Italy's problem to the cautious performance of the small family businesses that dotted Italy. Others, corporatist or socialist, laid the problem to the degree of monopoly and cartelization among the big businesses. The corporatist theoreticians supposed that, with the concerted effort of all society, and in particular its community of scientists, a country could drive scientific advances at a faster pace. And the state might act to steer scientists toward projects that would yield, with the involvement of engineering and other specialities, advances in useful technology—thus possibilities for better methods of production and new kinds of goods. This was the doctrine dubbed *techno-nationalism* by Richard Nelson. It is one manifestation of the more general belief called *scientism*—the belief that scientists, equipped with the tools of their science, more effectively advance the flowering of new products and methods than do the diffuse and poorly directed initiatives taken in a free enterprise economy. (It was under Mussolini in 1923, then prime minister, that Italy founded its national science foundation, the Consiglio Nazionale delle Ricerche, a full 27 years before America's National Science Foundation.)

The corporatist system also aimed to enlist artists. The preservation and promotion of the culture of the nation was a natural outgrowth of the elevation of the society over the individual. And the belief grew up, which could be called *culturalism,* that artistic advances could drive a country's economic progress, just as scientism held that scientific advances could be such a driver. Article 9 in Italy's constitution charges the government with responsibility for maintaining and promulgating the nation's cultural heritage. (This culturalism persists today: When the Milan opera house La Scala saw its budget cut back by the government in 2011, some opera fanatics called the move unconstitutional. Only increases are constitutional, not decreases.)

All this control had to mean putting the private-enterprise economy under political control—not back under propped-up lords of the manor, of course, but under some sort of political governance. If the main direction or directions of the economy were to be determined politically, the corporatists supposed, there would be progress along the lines they ardently wanted. By what means was this control to be achieved? The economy was to be organized into groups of companies and workers, large and small. The impression was that workers and indeed all groups, from taxi drivers to pharmacists, suffered from competition—from others and each other. Some socialist thinkers had argued that workers' wages were depressed by the power of capital to "divide and conquer." A company's workers had to expect to lose some jobs to workers in competing companies or industries to the extent that a wage increase would push their company to raise its price relative to others' prices. If represented by a very broad labor union, best of all a nationwide one, the workers would find themselves with the monopoly power of their dreams. In the thinking of this unionism, it was not imagined that the increase in wages would or could bring a decrease in jobs. Oddly, corporatist thinkers thought that grouping producers into a few large cartels would solve the problem—that, with the formation of cartels, the balance of power between labor and capital would be restored, and jobs would not be lost as a result of either the unions or the cartels. It seems to have escaped notice that enabling an increase in mark-ups by companies constituted a contraction of supply on top of the contraction of supply caused by enabling an upward push on wages. The last argument of the corporatists, however, was that, with labor and capital talking together in their "chamber," a new economy of unity and purpose would arise that would put an end to lockouts and threats of mass dismissals on the part of employers and to shirking, work stoppages, and general strikes on the part of employees. This new industrial peace would improve the efficiency of business operations and thus might end up expanding rather than contracting employment while raising wages and profits too.[6]

Whatever the merit of the corporatists' beliefs, aims, and means, the attraction they held for Europeans would be hard to overestimate. Corporatist doctrine was soon put into practice over a vast swath of Europe and the rest of the world.

Early 20th-Century Corporatism

Italy can be said to be the first country to build an economy along the lines of corporatist thought. Benito Mussolini, born in 1883 (like Schumpeter and Keynes) to a poor family in the province of Forli, became the most forceful champion of a corporatist economy in Italy and eventually its chief operating officer. A school teacher briefly, he became a political journalist, editing the Marxist weekly *Avanti!* Deciding that private ownership of enterprises

---

6. Some scholars define "corporatism" in terms of its structure rather than its aims. In a 1974 paper, "Still the Century of Corporatism?" Philippe Schmitter writes that corporatism could be defined as "a system of interest representation in which the constituent units are organized into a limited number of singular, compulsory, noncompetitive, hierarchically ordered and functionally differentiable categories, created, recognized, or licensed by the state and granted a deliberate monopoly" (p. 97).

could better serve high economic performance than either worker ownership or worker control, he broke with the socialists as World War I approached and founded the daily paper *Il Popolo d'Italia,* which would be his organ. Italy, after its costly combat against Austria in World War I with no rewards to show for it, needed a leader to give them hope for greater importance in the world. A forceful speaker and a shrewd tactician, Mussolini was well suited to take on the role. He was able to enlist to his side most of the corporatists and many of his old socialist allies, becoming the leader of the Fascist Party. Rapidly gaining popular support, he was elected a deputy in the Parliament in 1920, organized the March on Rome in early 1922, and was named prime minister by King Vittorio Emanuele III soon after. In 1925, Mussolini reduced the powers of the parliament, becoming dictator. There was no constitution in Italy, nor elsewhere in Europe at the time, hence no judicial review to put a check on such moves.[7]

In these years, Mussolini's program had been critical of Italy's capitalism. The Fascist Manifesto of 1919 demanded a heavy capital levy, workers' participation in company management, and a minimum-wage law. There was much emphasis on productivity. When the Mussolini government formed, it quickly aimed for a revival of economic growth. Yet the policies that were attempted led to another lurch in his thinking.

The Mussolini government saw Britain and America as having shown the way to a 100 years of growth in the form of 19th-century liberalism. Mussolini moved to repeal much of the socialist legislation of the previous decade: to end the state ownership of the insurance business in 1923 and the telephone network in 1925. Also in 1925, he disempowered the trade unions that had been empowered by the socialists and moved to exempt inward foreign investment from taxation and to make trade agreements. In moves reminiscent of the travails of present-day capitalism in some countries, the government bailed out the banks in 1926 following speculative attacks on the currency. In the end, Italy's experiment with cosmopolitan mercantile capitalism failed to generate appreciable economic growth and failed to protect the population from a sharp recession. Mussolini concluded that laissez-faire, or (classical) liberalism, was a weak reed on which to depend for rapid economic growth.

By then Mussolini's thinking had graduated to a conception of the corporatist economy. What Mussolini was seeking was more than a pickup of the

---

7. Sardinia's Statuto Albertino, which King Charles Albert's son had imported to all of Italy on his ascension to the throne, did not create review.

growth rate. It was a radical modernization of the Italian economy through a fundamental recast of Italian institutions, values, and beliefs. Mussolini took pains to register his dislike of "super-capitalism," with its mass production of homogeneous consumer goods, and his dislike of socialist cartel or monopoly capitalism, with its loss of the innovative spark and increased bureaucratization. His discontentments with capitalism were no doubt real enough, though he was not a philosopher of corporatism—that role fell to Giovanni Gentile, who would later ghostwrite *The Doctrine of Fascism* for him in 1932. Though no corporatist philosopher, Mussolini was nonetheless a builder of a corporatist economy. And the system he built could hardly have differed more from modern capitalism.

The architecture of his corporatist economy is laid out in his own publications.[8] The molecules of the institutional framework are entities called "corporations" (*corporazioni*). In the industrial classification there were finally 22 categories, for example, cereal, textiles, steel, hotels, arts, and credit. Each such *corporazione* was required by the Sindical Laws of 1926 (the "Rocco Laws") to have one employers association (*Associazione*) and one labor union (*Sindicato*):

> The class struggle in the Marxist sense between workers grouped on one side and masters grouped on the other is replaced by debates on matters concerning various categories of producers. Disputes . . . may arise between various categories of workers or between various categories of masters, or even between masters and workers, but they are viewed as one of the inevitable forms of human restlessness, indeed of human life. . . .
>
> The *corporazione* was conceived as an organ where managers and workers might come in touch with one another and establish cooperation. The *corporazione* took definite shape through the Act of February 1934 as an organ for collaboration.[9]

This was a big change from the socialist period before the war. By the early 1910s Italy had a spate of trade unions, some legally recognized by the socialist government only recently. In 1910, a broad employer association, the Italian Confederation of Industry, was founded to work with the unions and to

8. His main speeches in the early 1930s and a sort of handbook of the structure of the corporatist economy were published in the original Italian in Mussolini, *Quattro Discorsi sullo Stato Corporativo* (1935), and in English translation the same year under the title *Four Speeches on the Corporate State*. ("Corporatist" or "corporative" would have avoided a seeming reference to corporations in the English sense.)

9. Mussolini, *Four Speeches on the Corporate State* (pp. 81–82).

serve as a lobbying organization. But conflict arose after the war with the militancy of the working class. The unions led the "factory councils" movement in 1919–1921 for the sharing of company management between capital and labor; the Confederation, relaunched as Confindustria, worked to save owner control. The Fascist regime then acted to marginalize these unions by creating Fascist unions. Historians date the emergence of corporatism in Italy to October 1925, when Confindustria and the new unions concluded a pact at Palazzo Vidoni recognizing each other as the only legitimate representative of capital and labor.[10]

Mussolini's corporatism was not exactly the restoration of the control of private owners, however. Article 43 of the Decree of July 1926 declared that "the *corporazione* is not a civil person but an *organ of the state*." Article 44 adds that "corporative organs are endowed with powers to conciliate disputes that may arise between the affiliated organizations."[11] The Labor Charter of April 1927, while reaffirming rights to private "ownership," asserted the state's right to intervene even in companies' hiring of workers. So the Italian government was free to reject agreements between employers and employees until it got the agreement it wanted and free even to dictate company employment. Mussolini spoke of this power to intervene in his January 1934 speech, explaining that it would be invoked only when the decisions of Italy's patriotic owners and employees suffered from some miscalculation or coordination failure:

> Corporate economy introduces order in the field of economy. . . . In what way should this order be put into practice? Through self-discipline of the various categories concerned. *It is only when various categories fail to come to an agreement, or to establish the proper balance, that the State may intervene, although the State always has the undisputed power to do so, because it represents the other aspect of the phenomenon, which is consumption.*[12]

In this passage, Mussolini was being naïve or cynical, though. Italian corporatism with its *corporazioni* created or aggravated problems that it then called upon the government to solve. Corporatist theoreticians, by perverting capitalist industries into employer "associations" that were larger and had more pricing power than the capitalist cartels, and "syndicates" that were larger and in some cases more powerful than the traditional craft unions, increased the

10. James, *Europe Reborn* (p. 99).
11. *Four Speeches on the Corporate State* (p. 83).
12. *Four Speeches on the Corporate State* (p. 33).

monopoly power of many bodies and coalitions to the point where it would require pervasive and invasive government action to curb. Yet it would be quite a leap to conclude from this bit of analysis alone that corporatist economies were bound to perform worse on the whole than the modern economies or, at any rate, worse than the relatively well-performing among them.

This tripartite system began operating in piecemeal fashion by 1926, and the scaled-up system was operational by 1935. The system was something new in the firmament, and references to it—admiring or envious—were made by Winston Churchill, George Bernard Shaw, and John Maynard Keynes. It hardly needs saying that, in the second half of the decade, Mussolini, done with his economic designs, moved on to pursue his imperial designs on Ethiopia and the Adriatic, and then tainted his government forever by turning the force of the state against homosexuals, Gypsies, and Jews. Yet in the first half of the decade, Italy's construction of a functioning corporatist economy fascinated much of the world and surely played a part in emboldening some other countries to proceed along corporatist lines.

Germany, for one, had already been incubating its own corporatist philosophies before the full realization of Italy's example. In fact, the development of corporatism there started sooner than in Italy. Even before Leo XIII pontificated for social responsibility, Germany had had its early corporatist critics of capitalism: Ferdinand Tönnies, with his thesis in 1887 that communities and guilds were being destroyed, and Émile Durkeim, who argued that capitalism raised conflicts without rules. In the 1920s, German politics gradually gave voice to the elements of corporatist thought that Italy did—the revulsion against individualism, the rejection of laissez-faire economic policy, and disdain for the petit bourgeoisie. Yet some other strains of thought were more salient, and socialism was more embedded in Germany than in Italy, so the rise of an Italian-style corporatist economy was more complicated and took longer.

Adolf Hitler played a pivotal role in much the same way as Mussolini did. A former art student born in Austria and working in Munich for the German military in 1919, Hitler was sent to spy on the leftwing German Workers Party, an upstart rival of the venerable Social Democratic Party, and found that its ideas—German nationalism and anti-Semitism—were like his own. A stirring orator, he gained mounting leverage in the German Workers Party, recruited some of the military to it, and in 1920 proposed it be renamed the National Socialist German Workers Party, known as the NSDAP, and later nicknamed the Nazi Party to underline the nationalism and to retain votes that still lay in socialism.

A theme of the Nazi Party in the 1920s and later was their desire to see a return of the economy to high performance (*Leistung*), much as Mussolini's party harped on *produttività*. In 1920 the party's first program, known as the "25 Points," was as anti-capitalist as the Italian manifesto of 1919. It demanded the abolition of unearned income, the nationalization of trusts, land reform, and the nourishment of a "healthy middle class." And it vented an opposition to self-interest verging on hatred:

> The activities of the individual must not clash with the interests of the whole . . . but must be for the general good. . . . We demand ruthless war upon all those whose activities are injurious to the common interest . . . usurers, . . . other profiteers . . . the Jewish materialist spirit. . . . The Party is convinced that our nation can achieve permanent health from within only on the principle: the common interest before self-interest.[13]

The Nazis gained a plurality in the Reichstag, and Hitler was named chancellor in 1933, a win paved by Germany's 1929 Depression, or "slump," and the Nazi's portrait of the Weimar government as weak on the issue of German reparations (even though it had twice negotiated them down and little had been paid). The National Socialists set out to construct a corporatist system of the tripartite type—capital, labor, and government—in 1933. The 1934 Act for the Organization of National Labor established a number of industrial groups, each with "followers" under a hierarchy of "leaders." In 1935, labor unions were regulated and called on to find noncommercial incentives to raise productivity. Cartels were spread over nearly the entire economy, and joining them was made compulsory. The National Economic Chamber was formed atop all these associations, with power to issue laws and decrees. The system was such that the state could intervene as widely or as little as it wished.

For a time, the government attempted to direct a large part of the economy: conscripting labor to work as desired, telling companies what to produce and how much, and imposing price and wage controls. But by 1937, the government drew back: the Chamber was directed not to engage in any more price and market regulation, and the cartels resumed setting prices and wages. The focus of the Nazi government swung to foreign policy, and companies were largely free to compete for customers in the marketplace and to compete for government contracts. Yet the limitless power of the state ensured that no company would dare go far against the government's

---

13. Quoted in Heinz Lubasz, *Fascism: Three Major Regimes* (p. 78).

manifest desires. Companies might also become arms of the state, vying for government contracts and subsidies. Hayek thought, as he said in his 1944 *Road to Serfdom*, that the German business people were deluded in believing they retained the autonomy from the state they had enjoyed when Germany's economy was relatively modern.

Germany, like Italy, had possessed elements of corporatism long before the interwar years. Mercantile guilds, craft guilds, and guilds of professionals, which were relatively important in German lands as far back as the 1100s, sought to control prices and standards of manufactures and also to exert influence on the provincial—or national, if there was one—ruler and legislature. But the waves of competition brought by capitalism had weakened them, and Napoleon had banned them throughout his empire, so their influence was at least diminished in the modern economies of the 19th century. Germany reached a turning point when in 1871 Otto von Bismarck completed the unification of the German states under Kaiser Wilhelm's Prussia, the states having lost their unification under the Austrian Empire in 1866. The historian Ulrich Nocken dates German corporatism from 1871, while Werner Abelshauser puts 1879 as "the birth-point of the modern system of corporatist interest mediation."[14] Germany's emerging modern economy went corporatist to some extent. Employer associations, called "chambers" of commerce and of industry, arose, which served to lobby, set wage norms, and agree on prices. Industrial unions, mostly small, arose too, though they were weak (especially from the enactment of anti-socialist laws in 1879 until their repeal in 1890) compared to the German unions in World War I and post-World War II. The employer confederations and to a small degree the unions were players in the "wheeling and dealing" with the government that characterized the Wilhelmine economy. Bismarck, the Reich's chancellor from 1871 to 1890, failed in his efforts to set up a National Economic Council that could both veto and propose legislation in the parliament (Reichstag) like the Prussian Economic Council he set up to curb the Prussian Diet. But though he had to share power over economic matters with the Reichstag (unlike Hitler), the Iron Chancellor exerted great influence and later wielded his power to pave the way for financing the iron and steel industry in the 1880s and 1890s. Thus, the German Empire could be said to have developed a version of what historians have variously called a voluntary or consensual corporatism

---

14. See Nocken, "Corporatism and Pluralism in Modern German History"; Abelshauser, "The First Post-Liberal Nation" (p. 287).

in the late 19th century, in contrast to the mandatory and generally comprehensive corporatism of the 1930s. Germany's voluntary corporatism went on to embrace labor unions in the early Weimar years from 1919 to 1924, when the employer associations, caving in to the stronger labor unions of the war years, agreed to sit down with them as equals at the bargaining table.

Interwar corporatism's popular appeal is evident in the mass rallies and wide support it inspired, as well as in the direct reports of contemporary observers and the indirect responses of artists to the era's shifting mood. There was in many quarters a sense of a new path with new discoveries along the way. The impetus, all or most of it, behind the corporatist project is easily seen. It was the public's mounting rejection of both capitalism and socialism. Corporatism was the *third way* (*la terza via*). It was "neither right nor left," in the telling phrase of the historian Zeev Sternhell— neither the old right nor the old left, at any rate. (One could say—getting ahead of the story—that, well into the postwar period, a new corporatism was to become the medium of both a new right and a new left.) Thus corporatism could capture both the interest groups that felt ill-used by capitalism as well as the interest groups that feared socialism. The former grasped at corporatism as an escape from all the ills that modernism and the modern economy brought or threatened to bring: the perils from market competition, the instability of jobs, and the rudderlessness of industry. The latter saw corporatism as an alternative to the arbitrariness and dreariness of a socialist economy: the loss of their savings and the loss of their fun—the bars to building companies, and the difficulties of building careers. Corporatist politicians could argue that the corporatist structure would resolve the capitalist conflict between workers and owners and dissolve the socialist conflict between the proletariat and the rest by reengineering men and women to pursue the common good—the state would take care of their vestigial needs for pedestrian private goods. That the politicians could not first build a prototype corporatist economy for the populace to test under laboratory conditions against their actual capitalist economy gave them an excuse to scrap much of the capitalist structure and put in its place the new corporatist economy. Ridding the country of the capitalist economy was their primary objective; fine tuning the corporatist economy for best results was secondary. That the world economy was in crisis in 1929, with the Great Depression looming ahead, made it all the easier to portray the existing capitalist economies as systems to be jettisoned as quickly as possible. Finally, the politicians could boast that they were taking action, which the legislatures, in a stalemate between those who would remake their capitalism and those who would step up their socialism, were unable to do. The politicians, once in power, could be seen as *doing* something—not simply standing idly by with the sole justification that they were not making things worse. In a string of countries with elements of corporatism, the populace was thrilled at the prospect of a new start.

Corporatism did not stop at Italy and Germany. With the 1936 coup, General Francisco Franco ended the socialism of the Spanish Republic, although corporatist thought in Spain never became as pervasive and the corporatist superstructure never as vast as in Italy. Portugal's Antonio Salazar, a professor of economic sciences at Coimbra and an admirer of the author Charles Maurras and Leo XIII, drew on corporatist ideas in his presidency between 1932 and 1968. (The experiment was of great interest in France.) Austria was next in 1934 when Engelbert Dolfuss, on becoming chancellor, adopted some of the corporatist doctrine of Monsignor Ignaz Seipel. Corporatism came to Ireland in 1937, where it was championed by anti-capitalist parties such as Sinn Féin and supported by the Church.

What of France? Early in the century the salons of Paris were full of militant intellectuals with visions of a fusion of socialism that would end individualism and democracy—Maurice Barres, Georges Sorel, and Charles Maurras among them. Yet France did not adopt in the interwar years the Italo-German corporatist apparatus introduced by Mussolini and Hitler. But when German soldiers marched into Paris in 1940, the Vichy regime they installed in the summer of 1941 quickly established a system of economic planning in the corporatist spirit. Less than half a decade later, Vichy was out, but General Charles de Gaulle's 1944–1946 government introduced the *plan indicatif* in 1946, and the Fourth Republic of 1946–1958 adopted Five-Year Plans, taking a leaf from the Four-Year Plans in 1930s Italy and Germany. In this way the government tried to point French industry in the directions in which they wanted it to go.

In South America, elements of corporatism came to Brazil during the regime of Getúlio Vargas, especially the dictatorship of 1937–1945. The labor law was taken verbatim from Italy's law, cartels were set up to control key products, and the government sought to steer industrialization. (Yet the mild-mannered Vargas, like Salazar, suppressed the Fascist and Nazi parties. He was also the undoing of Plínio Salgado's radical Catholic party Acao

Integralista Brasileira.[15]) Corporatism of another color came to Argentina in the first presidency of Juan Perón, 1943–1955. Industrial labor unions became the backbone of the Peronist party in its sweeping interventions in industry and agriculture.

In Asia, Japan's large vertical monopolies, called *zaibatsu*, typically controlled by a single extended family, became so prominent after World War I (even though they emerged in the Meiji period in the last decades of the 19th century) that they were necessarily in close contact with the central government. A corporatist arrangement resulted, as the imperial government did not keep them at arm's length or break them up. Korea fell into a corporatist structure with the end of Japan's rule in 1945, when the government awarded Japanese plants and other favors to a handful of Korean businesses in return for kickbacks.

As for the Anglo-Saxon countries, it would be an immense distortion to say that they too installed in the interwar years a corporatist system like that introduced by Italy and Germany. During the 1920s and 1930s, labor unions grew in power and size in America and Britain while they were being hobbled in Italy and Germany. The Americans continued the opposition begun by the Progressives while the Continent was busily creating cartels. The question is whether the American and British economies possessed a corporatist character more or less equivalent to that in Italy and Germany. America saw widespread governmental intervention in the economy after its horrendous slide from 1929 until 1933 into the Depression. Franklin Roosevelt was swept into the presidency, taking office in 1933, and a spate of New Deal legislation soon followed. In 1933 the National Recovery Act established the National Recovery Administration (NRA) to organize a team of leaders in each industry to set codes for prices and wages aimed at arresting their downward spiral, which Roosevelt believed had greatly amplified the downswing of employment. Joining was not compulsory, but reserving a Blue Eagle seal of approval to every company that complied with the code must have exerted social pressure on companies. (TV viewers can still see the seal in the first frame of the Marx Brothers movie *Duck Soup*.) Many commentators, including some

---

15. Salgado and his *Integralistas* wanted to abolish self-interest and put in its place pity, charity, and sympathy. Vargas needed them for a crackdown on the communists and the success of his 1937 coup establishing a single-party state, the Estado Novo. Once in power, however, he had no more use for them. The *Integralistas*, in a midnight attack on the presidential palace, attempted a takeover, called the Pajama Putsch. The army arrived barely in time to put down the assault, and the *Integralistas* were finished.

widely considered to be thoughtful, viewed the NRA as a worrisome step toward the "collectivism" of a corporatist economy:

> The vital essence of the whole conception was that each codified industry would enjoy an approximate monopoly of the American market, and that its monopoly profits would enable it to pay high wages. But in order to protect the monopoly, competitors had to be excluded. Thus, in the more "advanced" codes, barriers were raised against new enterprises and new processes, and the whole establishment was then protected . . . by the power to lay an absolute embargo against any imports.[16]

To most observers, though, the New Deal interventionism did not match that on the corporatist Continent, where intervention was unbridled—where no legislation was required, legislatures were disempowered and no court had powers of judicial review. As it turned out, the NRA was ruled unconstitutional in a unanimous decision by the Supreme Court in *Schechter v. United States* in 1935. Roosevelt soon after enlarged the Court, making it more to his liking. The NRA was not resurrected, however, and the Court's reputation seemed to improve, not to decline.

With the New Deal, social thought in America—if not always social action—radically distanced itself from 19th-century liberal thought. A statement by the NRA's head, Donald Richberg, is arresting:

> There is no . . . return to the gold-plated anarchy that masqueraded as "rugged individualism." Unless industry is sufficiently socialized by its private owners and managers so that great essential industries are operated under public obligation appropriate to the public interest in them, the advance of political control over private industry is inevitable.[17]

Yet the bark was more fearsome than the bite. A range of unfamiliar initiatives, some verging on the radical, were taken by the government in the Depression years, which created new classes of jobs. For instance, the Civilian Conservation Corps employed photographers and documentarists to record the look and sound of rural America before it became nearly extinct. The Works Projects Administration undertook major construction initiatives at a time when the federal government had previously lent money for the railroads and state governments had built canals, but the massive federal dams, such as Hoover Dam, were not a familiar sight. These novel initiatives resembled some of

---

16. Walter Lippmann, *The Good Society* (p. 139). Lippmann, whose newspaper columns made him a household name, was immortalized (along with Schopenhauer) in the burlesque number "Zip" in Rodgers and Hart's *Pal Joey*. Hart clearly drew on his courses at Columbia.

17. Quoted in Schlesinger, *The Coming of the New Deal* (p. 115).

those undertaken in Germany. Yet these new frontiers could be regarded by the public as temporary measures rather than a shift from the capitalist culture to the corporatist culture. "Things have to change," Prince Don Fabrizio Salina says in Visconti's *The Leopard*, "so that they can stay the same."

The New Deal also wrought a range of changes supposed to be permanent. In response to the abuses and failures to disclose conflicts of interest in the banking industry and the securities business, as uncovered by the Pecora Commission, Congress enacted the Glass-Steagall Banking Act of 1933 to separate commercial from investment banking; the Securities Act of 1933 on filing false information in stock offerings; and the Securities Exchange Act of 1934, which created the Securities and Exchange Commission to regulate the stock exchanges. The National Labor Relations Board was created in 1935 to prevent and remedy "unfair labor practices by private sector employers and unions." Yet these measures too were hardly daggers at the heart of modern capitalism. The protections they provided potential investors and potential employees brought a considerable renewal of confidence in markets.

A big step in the corporatist direction was the establishment of rights of employees to organize or to join an already organized labor union in the National Labor Relations Act of 1935, the Wagner Act. Congress argued that "unequal bargaining power" between employees and employers leads to "economic instability" and that the refusal of companies to negotiate leads to strikes, both of which impede the flow of commerce. This was new: previous governments did not boost organized labor; they only broke up organized business—cartels and sprawling monopolies. The progressive movement, led by Theodore Roosevelt in the 1910s, was aimed at busting the monopolies. So was Woodrow Wilson. ("I am for big business, and I am against the trusts.") After the Teapot Dome scandal of 1923, a case of bribery of federal officials, the government tried harder to keep businesses at arm's length and not to award them increased legal protections. Relations between business and Washington were distant in the 1930s.

These changes and others did not make Americans feel there had been an abandonment of what they held to be the traditional social values of the country. One may view Franklin Roosevelt as having made accommodations to corporatism that served to preserve modern capitalism from wholesale replacement by corporatism. It is arguable that corporatism began to make deep inroads that threatened to kill modern capitalism only long after Roosevelt was gone.

What was the performance of the newly corporatist economies of continental Europe, particularly Italy and Germany, compared with the economies that remained in the category of modern capitalism, such as America and Britain? Italy's corporatist economy was operational only by the late 1920s, Hitler's by 1933, and World War II was breaking out by the end of the 1930s. So the time span offers few "natural experiments" from which to learn. One of these "experiments" was the onset of severe slump—Britain's in 1926 and the others' in 1929. Both Hitler and Roosevelt came to power in early 1933.

It is widely believed that Hitler wielded corporatist tools so as to pull Germany out of its slump in short order, while Roosevelt, burdened by the laissez-faire thinking in most of the country, was compelled to look on while the slump lengthened into a depression that would go on for the next eight years.[18] But the national output numbers in Germany and America tell a quite different story:

> By [1936] German GDP in real terms had recovered to roughly the same level it had stood at in [1929]. This was no doubt a rapid recovery. But it was not superior to the recovery achieved [over the same span] in the United States under a very different policy mix. Nor, in terms of the rate of growth, was it superior to the rebound from the Weimar Republic's first severe recession over the winter of 1926–27, when the twelve-month growth rate was higher than at any time during the Third Reich. It is possible therefore to imagine a similarly rapid recovery taking place even under a very different policy regime. In this strict counterfactual sense, Nazi economic policy cannot claim to have "caused" the German economic recovery.[19]

Moreover, had Roosevelt and his predecessor, Herbert Hoover, expanded the building of capital facilities, that would not have made the economy fundamentally corporatist (or closer to being fundamentally corporatist) and it might have made the American economy recover faster—faster than the Germany economy recovered. ("Might have" because a government action intended to boost aggregate employment does not work with the classical certainty of a lever and fulcrum lifting a heavy weight.) A look at all four of

18. One historian of the period writes, "Three years after [Hitler's] accession to power the German economy was booming. Unemployment was reduced so drastically that labour shortages became a problem." See Nicholls, "Hitler's Success and Weimar's Failure" (p. 156).

19. Adam Tooze, *The Wages of Destruction* (2007, p. 65). Tooze referred to 1928 and 1935 rather than the bracketed dates 1929 and 1936, but both versions are true, and it is the recovery from 1929, not 1928, in which we are interested.

the large economies recovering from a deep slump—Britain's in 1926 and the others' in 1929—shows that national output in all of them gradually began recovering within a half-dozen years or so.[20]

More striking, productivity—as measured by national output per man-hour or more sophisticated measures—leapt ahead in America at a record-breaking speed from 1930 to 1941, a speed even faster than in the previous decade, while productivity growth in Italy and Germany was far slower than America's in the 1930s and gained only moderately in the 1930s over the 1920s rate. According to one explanation, America achieved a surge of innovation over the 1920s, much of which involved the development of many new products and processes sparked by electrification. But the innovation had not completely diffused through much of the economy by the decade's end. As a result, the ground was laid for further diffusion of the new products and processes in the 1930s. This latter diffusion caused an immense number of workers to lose their jobs—a situation made worse by the over-valuation of the dollar and the resistance of overseas nations to increased American exports.

The growing disparity in productivity was at first no more than a thorn in Hitler's side. In his "table talk," he complained that German automakers in the 1930s had barely reduced the number of workers required to produce one car while Ford Motor Company had reduced the labor requirement to a small fraction of its former level. As historians later noted, this extraordinary productivity in America made it possible to produce the many thousands of tanks, trucks, and fighter planes that ultimately defeated Germany in World War II—not so much the bombing of cities. The surge of productivity that threatened America's modern capitalism for awhile in the 1930s eventually saved that modern capitalism from the threat of takeover by corporatist thought.[21]

The defeat of the Axis powers in World War II toppled the national governments and prepared a return of the old democratic political systems in Italy and Germany as well as in the nations they had occupied. In 1947, Italy produced its first constitution, which made provision for judicial review of policies carried out by the executive branch and laws enacted by the

20. To a varying degree, employment rose slower than output did, owing in part to productivity growth.
21. Hitler likely had in mind the years 1935–1941 when U.S. output rose at a torrid pace, punctuated by the 1937–1938 recession, while Germany hit a soft patch after the door was closed to trade in 1938. Hayek may have had that in mind when he wrote in *Road* that German producers would suffer from corporatism.

parliament. Germany followed in 1949 with a constitution that was closer in spirit to the Weimar constitution's goals of social democracy than to Bismarck's imperial constitution of 1871.

Some political parties of the radical right survived, and new ones emerged after the war. They echoed several fascist themes: "fears of decadence and decline, assertion of national and cultural identity, a threat by unassimilable foreigners to national identity, and the need for greater authority to deal with these problems."[22] But to gain enough votes to be represented significantly or at all, most of these parties had to espouse programs of the moderate right and to drape themselves in the obscure term "postfascist," whatever that meant. And not even the far right parties attacked democracy and the rule of law.

These gains on the *political* side presented Germany and Italy with an opportunity to reexamine the character and effectiveness of the national economies that had developed over the interwar years. Did these reappraisals lead European nations to retrench in their corporatism, in its institutions, policies, and thinking? Or did the subsequent decades see a growth of corporatism on the whole? What precepts of corporatism have been sloughed off and what new ones, if any, have been added?

Evolution of Corporatism after the War

In the popular mind, the influence of corporatist ideas waned after the war because the strength with which these ideas were held has since diminished. And the strength with which these ideas were held has diminished because the social tensions wrought by the interwar catastrophes—the wreckage caused by the Great War, the Great Inflation, and the Great Depression—have passed. It is also suggested that popular democracy is now so strong that people can obtain the protection at the ballot box that they once needed unions, lobbies, and a strong state to obtain. But social democracy and a corporatist economy are not contradictory ideas, so it is not obvious that they could not coexist. A small number of serious economists in Europe argued in the 1960s or 1970s that their countries did not understand the continuing damage they suffered from a failure to keep enterprise relatively free— Herbert Giersch in Germany, Raymond Barre in France, and in Italy, Luigi Einaudi and Paolo Sylos-Labini. Yet there was little systematic research into corporatism in the second half of the 20th century.

22. Robert Paxton, *The Anatomy of Fascism* (p. 186).

Did Germany and Italy in the decades after World War II show evidence by any of the measures suggested here of shedding their corporatism and developing further modern institutions, policies, and cultures? Or evidence of keeping or renewing or even intensifying their corporatism? And what about Britain and France? And America? These questions have received little study.

The Western European continent in general and Germany in particular made in the early years after the war a number of economic reforms in the direction of laissez-faire, or neo-liberalism—quite a change from interwar corporatist policy. Continental economies became vastly more open to foreign trade (first, bilateral trade, or barter, then multilateral trade). Later they opened themselves to capital outflows, thus denying their governments the power to imprison private capital within their borders. And finally they permitted financial companies and businesses to compete across borders and move headquarters. (Much of the organization of all this took place at the European Economic Commission, established when West Germany, France, Italy, and the Benelux countries founded the European Union.)

In Germany, a sharp turn in policy was prophesied with the announced Economic Reform of 1948 under Economics Minister Ludwig Erhard. It declared that neo-liberal principles opposite to those of the corporatist model were to be embodied in the "social market economy" of the Federal Republic created in 1949. In his 1957 book *Wohlstand für Alle,* titled *Prosperity through Competition* in the English translation, Erhard credits the near-doubling of West Germany's national product between 1949 and 1956 to the rebirth of competition in the economy and the restoration of confidence that inflation would not rob lenders of their gains. Erhard believed that the nation gained by rejecting the corporatist tendency to dispense with individual incentives and rejecting also the socialist tendency to think of the distribution of wealth more than of the level to which productivity might bring it.

Erhard's analysis suggests, cleverly or unconsciously, that when in 1949 German output regained its last fully-peacetime level of 1936, there was no more damaged capital left to restore, so all of the subsequent doubling of output is to be attributed to increased competition and greater confidence than existed in the Hitler years—and the new investments and productivity gains that resulted. Never mind the obvious omission that in fact there may have been capital structures, such as rail lines and factories, still needing repairs, so that huge output gains were a certainty for more years to come—increased competition or not. The more important omission deluded all of Europe into believing they had stumbled onto a road taking them to Rostow's "sustained growth" forever. It was not understood that productivity on the Continent was shooting up in large part because companies could cheaply boost productivity and profits by identifying, adapting, and adopting the new goods and methods of production that had been developed and embraced in America and to a lesser extent Britain and a handful of other non-Continental nations in the 1920s and 1930s but which had not been adopted on the Continent owing to its upheavals and the lurch under corporatism toward closed economies. For this brilliant "catch-up" growth, neo-liberal competition and confidence were not sufficient: there had to be bountiful low-hanging fruit across the Atlantic for the taking.[23]

Was corporatism put back in place after the bricks and railway ties were restored? After 1949? If, at this point, we were playing statisticians seeking to measure the degree of corporatism's return, we would need a checklist of measures, yearly or decadal, of the force of corporatism, such as its effects on policies. These measures include state interventions in *production*: the volume of regulation (statutes and rulings), bureaucratic "red tape" (permits, etc.), limits on entry in industries and professions, "industrial policy," and tax collection. (Socialism, it may be noted, cares more about how things are made than what things are made.) Another set of measures capture the diversion or control of *income*: subsidized social insurance, "coordination" of wage determination by industries and unions, the depression of share prices viewed as evidence of the state's overriding of shareowners' property rights, and the prevalence of zombie companies impeded from selling or scrapping. High employment in the public sector is another measure, since intervention in the private sector requires personnel to conduct it. There are quantifiable measures of the strength of *values*—desires and beliefs—allied with or opposed to corporatist thought. (Several of these measures of corporatism's force are used to test the claims made on behalf of corporatism in the next two chapters.)

We are playing historians in this chapter, though, so we focus on significant events: the high points—or low points. Two developments suggest that

---

23. The German results do not prove that competition is necessary either. Spain provides an intriguing case. Though notorious for an economic system and economic policies that were considered disadvantageous by a range of economic opinion, Spain nevertheless posted phenomenally rapid growth both in real domestic product per person employed and in real hourly earning in manufacturing consistently over the period 1960 to 1980—much faster than the German growth.

corporatism did not have to wait very long for its comeback. Amid a crisis precipitated by the "Korea boom" in Germany, Abelshauser writes, "influential sections of German industry [began] reformation of [the] state corporatist system of the interwar period" (ibid., p. 308). The cooperation between various employer associations that reemerged in the early 1950s reminded one scholar of the "well-proven German tradition . . . which survived the end of the Nazi economy and the . . . Reform of 1948 virtually unbroken."[24]

The other development was the shift of power between capital and labor within the corporatist framework. From one perspective, corporatism results in a merger of government with the business sector, so that much of business activity is decided through negotiation with the government rather than through the market, though much of that activity is nevertheless influenced by the market. But that leaves open how much of a connection to the government organized labor would have. By the end of the 1960s Europe had greatly increased the voice of labor—making the "tripartism" of the classic corporatist doctrine into a reality replacing the earlier "bipartism."

One aspect of labor's new power was its seats on the supervisory board of directors of the large companies. This was not considered of any great moment in Germany, where the socialist hostility to big business had never completely died out. It went further, however, in the 1990s, when the labor unions managed to get a seat on the investment committee. This time, Germans blanched. There were fears that this change might block profitable investments or block efforts of companies to make reforms in order to survive—and some jobs to survive with them. But the economists need not have worried. It was disclosed in 2005 that Volkswagen, the German auto maker, had been paying bribes to union officials for over a decade.

The Economics Ministry in 1967 made tripartism explicit, undertaking a program of Concerted Action that brought labor, capital, and the government to the bargaining table. Although this formal tripartism lasted only 10 years, *informal* trilateralism has continued with the cooperation of "liberal" corporatists on both the union and the employer side. In these same years Italy was developing its own trilateral structures. It was at this time that the term *Tavola di concertazione* came into use in Italy to refer to the practice of formal consultation among labor, capital, and government. But was this postwar trilateralism on the Continent all "sound and fury," or did it have influence?

---

24. H. Adamsen, quoted in the useful survey by Berghahn, "Corporatism in Germany in Historical Perspective" (p. 117).

Trilateralism has had its good moments. The Wassenaar Agreement, reached in 1982 by organized labor and employer organizations amidst the European slump of that time, inaugurated a new era of wage moderation and appeared to create some jobs in the Netherlands. But it is not clear that either result has been lasting. The Organisation for Economic Co-operation and Development (OECD) tabulates national data for the member countries. Those data show that, two decades later, in 2004, the Dutch unemployment rate was in the middle of those for the OECD nations—between the British and the American rates—and hours worked per employee near the bottom. Thus a permanent influence on the labor market is not discernible with the naked eye. On the other hand, under the coaxing of Chancellor Gerhard Schröder of the Social Democratic Party, Germany negotiated a series of measures in 2003, called Agenda 2010, to cut wage costs and increase the "flexibility" of the nation's labor market. The reduction of labor costs in the business sector has lasted the decade and is credited with much of the German export boom of recent years. Yet, today, the labor market statistics in Germany are not seen as outstanding. The German unemployment rate in recent years has been typical of European rates if the high rates in crisis-torn Italy and Spain are set aside, and hours worked per employee is only a little higher than in Holland and Norway. (Unemployment may nevertheless be lower than it otherwise would be.) However, the influence of corporatism, embodied formally or informally, could reach far beyond wage setting, as the discussion above has tried to make clear.

It might be guessed that the graduation to tripartism and, more broadly, the idea that nothing important may be done without the "social partners" on board, were harbingers of a new springtime for corporatism in Germany and Italy—and perhaps in much or all of continental Europe too. What, then, do some of the corporatist statistics proposed in the previous pages show? There are data on the rise of the public sector in several countries over the course of the postwar decades. And there are census data from interwar Germany. The public sector in Germany employed 9 percent of all employees in 1933, and the number rose to 12 percent in 1938, owing to an increase in the armed forces. In 1960, this statistic stood at 8 percent. But it grew to virtually 15 percent in 1980–1981 (OECD 1983, table 2.13). It may be significant that the size of the public sector grew to be even larger than in the peacetime years of the 1930s corporatist economy. Another striking corporatist statistic is the rise of total government outlays—for consumption-type goods and services and for purchases of capital (plant, equipment, etc.)—over the same span from 32½ percent of the gross domestic product (GDP) to 49 percent in 1981 (OECD 1983, table 6.5). Italy's public sector employment statistic went from 9 percent to the German level of 15 percent; and the total government outlays statistic went from 30 percent to 51 percent.[25] The German figures were very nearly peaks. In 2006, before the onset of the huge downswing, Germany's public sector employment statistic was at 12 percent, and its total government outlays stood at 45½ percent. In Italy, the size of the government by either measure reached new peaks in the early 1990s. By 2006, though, the public sector employment statistic was again around 15 percent, and the government outlays statistic was back at 49 percent. In the Western world, at any rate, these measures indicate unprecedented levels of government involvement and lend weight to the hypothesis that corporatism on the Continent, far from fading, actually grew more influential. We are curious, though, whether these countries grew to be more corporatist than some comparator countries.

France's corporatism dates back in some respects to the time of Jean-Baptiste Colbert, finance minister of Louis XIV. Yet in the present era, judged by how they score on various measures of corporatism, France is not easily distinguished from Italy (and some other European nations). France's public sector employment also grew—from a jumping-off point of 13 percent—and reached 16 percent in 1981, and an astonishing 22 percent in 2006. France's total government outlay statistic also started higher, reaching Italy's 49 percent level in 1980 and going ahead to 52½ percent in 2006.

How do these three countries compare by another measure of corporatism, bureaucratic "red tape"? In this respect, France tied Italy in exceeding all the others according to a 1999 survey. Germany had less red tape but markedly more than Britain and the United States.[26]

French and Italian labor relations continue to look conflictual to foreign observers, while the unions complain that they do not have the power that the public imagines. A spate of "boss-napping" broke out in France during

25. Over that same span, Germany's government *consumption*-type expenditure, that is, purchases of good and services, rose from about 13½ percent of GDP to about 20½ percent. And social security outlays (benefits under old-age, sickness, and family allowance programs, plus social assistance) rose from 12½ percent to 17 percent (OECD 1983, tables 6.2 and 6.3). Italy's employment statistic started higher, at 9 percent, and its government expenditure statistic started lower, at 10 percent, but both statistics ended precisely at Germany's levels in 1981.

26. The red tape estimates were published in *The Economist*, July 1999. The scores were United Kingdom, 0.5; United States, 1.3; Netherlands, 1.4; Sweden, 1.8; Spain, 1.8; Germany, 2.1; Belgium, 2.6; France, 2.7; and Italy, 2.7.

2008–2009, and general strikes in France and to a lesser degree Italy—the awesome "manifestations"—sometimes paralyze the economy. Certainly in its outspoken rhetoric there was no country in Europe more hostile than France to "market society" and more alienated from business life.

Looking back at the history of these three countries since the war, the most influential development in corporatism appears to be the rise of labor unions to positions of political power verging on equality with business interests. Labor power did not substitute for company, or "corporate," power. (In product markets, it effectively added to the total amount of monopoly.) The concept gained strength that workers and investors could exert myriad and profound influence on the behavior and direction of the economy—generally to protect their vested interests—by mobilizing labor unions, companies, and business federations to exert influence through nonmarket channels. A huge increase in the activity of the public sector and a thicket of regulations has resulted. The question at this point is the extent to which and the ways by which this new system and accompanying culture, in narrowing the possibilities of change, of innovation, has choked off the possibility of the deeper rewards of business life in return for stability and the status quo.

In Britain, the experience with corporatism was comparable to that of France until a turnaround in the early 1980s. The share of total jobs located in the public sector by 1960—at about 15 percent—was already the highest in Europe and skyrocketed to the extraordinary level of about 23 percent by 1981. Britain's total government outlays statistic was at the Italian and German level in 1960 and rose to a level, 47 percent, just below the level in those two countries. But by 2005 it had fallen to 45 percent, well below Italy's 48 percent and still under Germany's 47 percent. What happened in the 1980s is becoming better known in recent years. The debate about the economy that polarized Britain for a decade was not over its "socialism." There cannot have been any other advanced economy with as small a share of enterprise output produced by state-owned enterprises (SOEs), which hardly budged from 1.3 percent from the early postwar years to the present. The debate was over corporatism, a debate that began in 1979 when Margaret Thatcher became prime minister.

> It is hard to recall now what a shock Mrs Thatcher's election in 1979
> brought to employers as well as to trade unions. Her bracing dose of free
> markets and deregulation [led to] the most tumultuous period in Britain's
> postwar history. . . .

The Confederation of British Industry was marginalized by the Thatcher government and many of its members reacted with horror as high interest rates and a strong pound deepened the early 1980s recession and drove many manufacturing businesses to the wall. But as the economic medicine and tough trade union laws began to work, attitudes softened. Sir James Cleminson, who got on well with Mrs Thatcher, did much to dispel the CBI's reputation as a bunch of "moaning Minnies" always seeking government help. "Business is now recognizing that four-fifths of the things it wants done it can do for itself; it is saying that all we can expect government to do is clear the path," he said in 1985. That attitude largely survives today.[27]

After this period, Britain slowly turned the corner in the corporatist standings, leaving France in top place followed by Italy. Among countries in the G7, Britain was estimated in 1999 to have by far the lowest amount of red tape impeding business.

Last, we come to the corporatist influence in America. By 1960, despite the postwar cutbacks in the standing army, public sector *employment* as a share of the labor force was already higher than Britain's at that time—thus the highest in the G7. By 1980 the American level continued to exceed that in Germany, Italy, and France, though passed by Britain. In contrast, America's total government *outlays* as a share of GDP, which was in the middle of the pack, at 27.5 percent, in 1960, was the lowest in the group by 1980, standing at 35.5 percent. And, measured by red tape in 1999, the United States was well below the levels in Italy, Germany, and France.

The corporatist influence in the decade past must be judged to have increased. The Federal Register of Regulations has continued to rise steeply. Some of the new regulations, such as the Sarbanes-Oxley law, which holds chief executives legally responsible for the way in which the accounting of their corporations is presented, could be argued to have reduced the willingness of corporations to embark on novel projects shrouded in uncertainty.

The state's intrusion into resource allocation was most remarkable in the individual income tax code. The so-called Reagan tax cut legislation of 1981 abolished myriad tax "loopholes," thus bringing in billions of dollars of additional revenue, in return for cuts in the structure of tax rates—the marginal

---

27. Groom, "War Hero Who Became Captain of British Industry" (p. 7). The second sentence is from Groom, "Gloom and Boom" (p. 16). "Jimmy" Cleminson was an industrialist and later president of CBI from 1984 to 1986. Incidentally, fame came to him as a parachute captain at the battle of Arnhem. His exploits are a part of Richard Attenborough's 1977 film *A Bridge Too Far.*

tax rates in the tax brackets from lowest to highest. But loopholes and even rulings individualized to benefit particular persons or companies have mushroomed. The U.S. tax code runs to 16,000 pages. In contrast, the French have a tax code with only 1,900 pages.

A no less stunning development in America is the spectacular rise of litigation and the consequent fear of lawsuits. While Americans may not have as many unions to protect and defend them as they did in the 1930s, they now have access to rich legal resources and a vast court system with which to protect and defend themselves from being set back by others in the to-and-fro of society's pursuit of change and advance. The fear of being sued has noticeable consequences for individual initiative and judgment, and thus on efforts at innovation:

> [W]e have created a society paralyzed by legal fear. Doctors are paranoid. . . . Principals [are] paralyzed. Teachers don't even have authority to maintain order in the classroom. With no one in charge, the safe course is to avoid any possible risk. . . . A huge monument to the unknown plaintiff looms high above America, casting a dark shadow across our daily choices.[28]

It would be hard to argue, therefore, that corporatist influences in the American economy abated after World War II. It is easier to make the case that corporatist influences have intensified.

The conclusion to which this evidence points is that, generally speaking, corporatism gained or at least consolidated its influence in Europe over the decades, taken as a whole, since World War II. The drift in America may not be obvious to some, but there is evidence it has grown there too. Britain is an exception in having registered a decline of corporatism after a long rise until 1980. The major evolution in corporatism over the postwar decades was surely the rise of the labor unions to positions of power comparable to or at times exceeding that of business interests in some countries.

The concept that the market was never to be presumed right, that the voices of capital, labor, the professions, and other key groups could exert their influence through nonmarket channels such as lobbies, was a profound change. The big question not resolved in the 1930s was whether corporatism, in narrowing the market, removed or impaired the dynamism required for the pursuit of indigenous innovation.

---

28. The classic indictment is Howard, *The Death of Common Sense*. The quotation is from Howard's *The Collapse of the Common Good* (2001).

The New Corporatism

As seen above, the classic corporatism of the interwar years can be said to have survived to a degree in several countries in the past half-century. Although corporatism sooner or later allowed organized labor to become a social partner on a par with organized business in most economies, it was still *classic corporatism*: Classic corporatism widens government powers (relative to that under 18th-century liberalism) in order to forge a *state-led* economy. This corporatism, it will be recalled, refers to a set of aims: *directedness* rather than disorder, *solidarity* rather than individualism, and *social responsibility* rather than anti-social behavior. After the war this basic corporatism added to the agenda *codetermination* instead of owner-control and *stakeholderism* instead of companies maximizing the income to be divided between owners and workers. These ideas radically widened what the state may grant to interest groups—and where it may take the economy—in the name of the national interest. Now, time has added new dimensions to corporatism.

A new kind of corporatism has developed in recent decades. What we may call the *new corporatism* either reverses the flow of power or provides a two-way flow. The state is less a guide choosing the heading than a pilot paid by the passengers to take them where they ask. Some of the power has shifted to large-wealth owners and holders of powerful positions in business. (Even if all of them were mere atoms, the government might heed what the bond market and other markets have to say.) The state may retain some of the scope found in classic corporatism, though. It still takes it upon itself to act when society or a large part of it is in difficulty or faces the prospect of it.

The new corporatism also goes beyond the groups of classical corporatism—the groups that may bargain collectively and the groups yoked together in "concerted action"—by embracing the idea of a social compact: every person in a society is a signatory to an implicit contract with the others—its terms understood by all—and, according to this contract, no person may be harmed by others without receiving compensation.[29] This populist corporatism had vast consequences. Where in the past a group of lawyers,

29. Something like this emerged in economics during the 1970s when it became fashionable to suppose that the entire workforce of the country was in a lifetime implicit contract with existing employers. In every community the employers were seen as providing insurance to their employees in the event of poor business prospects warranting layoffs, and banks in the community provided employers insurance when conditions warranted some rationing of credit. This new wave of theorizing made it seem as though the feudal economy, with its lifetime employment and "relational banking" was the economic optimum after all, not laissez-faire with all its rigors—its cold showers and thin gruel.

pharmacists, or garment workers might have been granted the status of a *corporazione* with which to exert monopoly power, now all sorts of groups can demand a voice, request powers to protect themselves, or seek to be protected by the state. This new element of corporatism goes beyond the classic demand for state control that improves the conditions of society—national growth through state direction and industrial peace through "concertation" and co-determination—to the demand that the course of development at no time set back some while propelling the rest. The new thinking sees the state as undertaking to protect everyone from everyone else—or as close to it as is practicable. Social protection for all is the motto of the new corporatism.

A panoply of new roles has been given to the state. The state may compensate those hit domestically by a range of developments, from foreign competition to storm damage. Government grants of unlimited scope may be made to regions and cities, even if their latent function (in Robert Merton's term) is to dispense patronage in return for support, political or financial. Lobbyists are welcome to submit requests for legislation, regulations, and interpretative rulings, especially if they come with bribes. Regulations of industries are instituted, aimed at shielding companies or workforces from competition. Bans spare influential communities from new airports, landfills, and the rest. Shakedowns of companies by communities, nonprofits, or governments extract donations or other accommodations. Class action suits add to the diversion of income from earners to those receiving compensation or indemnification. (Other features of the new corporatism are mentioned in Chapter 10.) The result was not necessarily an extremely large government, but it was in important ways unlimited government.

The new corporatist economy, then, is pervaded by fears of holdups by the government, by stakeholders, by organized labor, and by an ocean of persons and companies ready to litigate. It is a familiar point that in economies where labor and capital are protected from having to compete, thus frozen indefinitely in companies producing the same old products, investment activity is generally meager. It is also familiar that the powers in a corporatist society to threaten existing companies can weigh heavily on the prospects for profit at affected companies and thus on their share prices, and thus depress the economy's investment activity and employment levels.[30] It needs to be

---

30. That high share prices usually lead to high investment activity and thus high employment—they induce the investment or they reflect impulses to invest inside the companies—is shown in Phelps, "Behind This Structural Boom" (1999).

added that if would-be innovators fear to embark on novel undertakings for fear of a feeding frenzy of pressure groups demanding a cut of any potential resultant innovation and profit, it becomes impossible for ordinary people to thrive and flourish. Indeed, the whole economy may gradually become obsolete and fall into a mounting depression.

Corporatism's Dark Side

The next two chapters undertake some economic research to test the central claims made on behalf of corporatist economies. But some of the false claims of corporatism can be detected with no economics at all, only a little common knowledge.

The corporatist system was idealized as having dispensed with individualism and competition, which were demonized as ugly and inhuman. But the system merely transplanted individualism from the market to the state, where individuals would elbow their way to increased power. The system would end competition among producers for the many buyers in the markets. But it replaced that with the insidious competition of producers and professionals for a share of government contracts and a place in government-sponsored enterprises—for a single, all-powerful buyer. The system was idealized as having put an end to the conflict between capital and labor, but in the end the postwar systems simply conferred large monopoly power to unions as well as large employers, thus licensing both of them to contract output. The system was portrayed as restoring the balance between materialism and high culture, but the system then undermined most of the great literature and art because they were individualistic. The system was extolled as scientific in contrast to the chaos of the modern system it replaced. But the system would replace uncertainty about what the myriad would-be innovators were up to with uncertainty about the outcome of the *state's* attempts at innovation. That might create more uncertainty than before. The corporatists demonized the power that the modern economy conferred on the industrial mogul or financial speculator who became rich, portraying their new system as a servant of society as a whole. But their system concentrated far greater power in the hands of *political* moguls and their financial backers.

It is understandable that, under early capitalism, market forces caused participants to feel they are like sheep being driven by snows, floods, and the rest. (The saving grace of the market in this respect is that it drove people to do voluntarily what needed to be done for a better allocation of resources.) The times of mercantile capitalism may not have been very happy for that reason. But with the advent of *modern* societies, participants in the economy were able for the first time on a mass scale to conceive and look for new ways of producing and new products to produce, thus to make new careers. Individual opportunity meant opportunities for mental stimulation, engaging work, and rewarding lives of challenge and personal development. Corporatism suppressed this individual opportunity, forcing participants to gain permissions to enter an industry and possibly to curry favor to enter an industry or win business. Thus it was an oppressive system. The idea of corporatism inspired systems of varying totalitarianism (to use Mussolini's own term) that turned most participants back into sheep.

CHAPTER SEVEN

Weighing the Rivals on Their Terms

The hen is the wisest of all the animal creation because she never cackles until after the egg has been laid.

ABRAHAM LINCOLN

H OW WELL HAVE THE CHALLENGERS to modern capitalism—corporatism and socialism—done? As the above narrative suggests, Bismarck's Germany, which had elements of corporatism, did well, though whether much of that success was owed to corporatism would be hard to say. The corporatist economies of Mussolini and Hitler rebounded from national crises no better than the American and British economies did. But what about the new corporatism or the new socialism of the mid-1960s to the present? We are now poised to study their consequences and influences over the past half century.

This chapter will explore whether the neo-corporatist and neo-socialist economies have performed as claimed. In the chapters that follow, this book will go on to argue in favor of a criterion for judging the performance of an economy that is radically different from corporatist and socialist thought. But first it ought to show how socialist economies failed to achieve socialist goals, and how corporatist economies failed to deliver corporatist benefits.

Socialism—Claims and Evidence

Socialism means many things but at its core is social ownership of a range of enterprises: economies with wider state ownership are generally seen as more socialist than those with markedly narrower state ownership. In the most basic sort of socialism, state-owned enterprises (SOEs in the jargon) are largely confined to health care, education, and some insurance industries, while highly socialist economies extend state ownership more widely.

So we would like data with which to test the socialist belief that state ownership boosts economic performance. Fortunately, evidence on the scale of state enterprise started to be available two decades ago. Estimates of the share of total domestic output (GDP) produced by SOEs were published in a 1995 study by the World Bank, *Bureaucrats in Business*. Among the advanced economies—our focus here—the percentage share of GDP in 1986–1991 produced by the SOEs was 10.0 percent in France, 7.1 percent in Germany, 5.6 percent in Italy, 4.0 percent in Spain, 3.0 percent in the United Kingdom—down from 5.9 percent pre-Thatcher—and 1.0 percent in America. (The data exist for two smaller countries, Austria (13.9 percent) and Portugal (14.2 percent).) A wider coverage of countries was provided by Branko Milanović in a 1989 book *Liberalization and Entrepreneurship*, and some further countries were added by using the SOEs' share of total *employment*, rather than output. In these calculations, covering 1978–1983, France is again at the top, now followed closely by Italy and Austria; next Sweden and Finland; then Germany and the United Kingdom (before Thatcher shrank state ownership in the next decade); next Norway and Canada; then Australia and Denmark; and lastly Spain, Holland, and America. See Table 7.1 for the full data.

Most proponents of a relatively socialist organization of economies—the so-called advanced ones, whether or not the low- or middle-income ones—stress the *availability* and *steadiness* of work they believe it provides. As for the availability of work, they see the socialist enterprise as more willing to hire and retain marginal workers at risk of chronic joblessness than capitalist enterprises are; also more willing to retain workers in the face of downswings, thus shaving off troughs in the employment cycle. Yet these two points, even if valid, are not conclusive, since new enterprise formation in modern capitalism may generate as many new jobs as are lost by established enterprises during slumps.

Belief that the more socialist economies were superior at job creation gained credence in the shining period from the mid-1950s to the mid-1970s. Using the "standardized" unemployment rates calculated by the OECD, we see that the American rate had an average level of 4.4 percent from 1960 to 1973. The rates in the European countries widely considered relatively socialist were at a spectacularly low level in that period: 0.8 percent in Germany, 1.3 percent in Norway, 1.8 percent in France, and 1.9 percent in Sweden. (The European Economic Community as a whole had an average unemployment level of 2.6 percent in that period.) But that impression was dispelled in subsequent decades. By the mid-1980s unemployment rates were markedly higher in the entire West. Europe had largely run out of the remaining new products and processes it could "transfer" from the rest of the world, so labor supply and business investment both retracted. America suffered a milder retraction

TABLE 7.1 Importance of Public Corporations and
State Sector in Some OECD Countries

Country*	In terms of output (%)	In terms of employment (%)
High share (above 15%)		
France (1982)	16.5	14.6
Moderate share (10–15%)		
Austria (1978–1979)	14.5	13.0
Italy (1982)	14.0	15.0
France (1979)	13.0	10.3
New Zealand (1987)	12.0	n.a.
France (1973)	11.7	9.3
Turkey (1985)	11.2	20.0
United Kingdom (1978)	11.1	8.2
West Germany (1982)	10.7	7.8
United Kingdom (1983)	10.7	7.0
West Germany (1977)	10.3	7.9
United Kingdom (1972)	10.2	7.8
Sweden	n.a.	10.5
Finland	n.a.	10.0
Low share (5–10%)		
Portugal (1976)	9.7	n.a.
Australia (1978–1979)	9.4	4.0
Denmark (1974)	6.3	5.0
Greece (1979)	6.1	n.a.
Norway	n.a.	6.0
Canada	n.a.	5.0
Negligible share (below 5%)		
Spain (1979)	4.1	n.a.
Netherlands (1971–1973)	3.6	8.0
United States (1983)	1.3	1.8

Source: Milanović, *Liberalization and Entrepreneurship* (1989).
Notes: Excludes government services proper (i.e., includes only state-owned enterprises in commercial activities). n.a., not available.
*Ordered according to share in output (when available).

from a different cause—a sharp drop of innovation from a high level. (Chapters 9 and 10 tell that story.) By 1995, the lowest unemployment rates among the larger countries were 5.6 percent in America, 6.5 in Holland, 7.0 in the United Kingdom (in 1997), and 8.2 in Germany. The *highest* joblessness was in Spain (22 percent), Italy (11.7), and France (10.3). Here too, the more socialist economies *cannot* be said to have demonstrated a widespread tendency to lower unemployment. And they may very well tend to have higher unemployment but act to contain that tendency through aggressive interventions. Most of the relatively socialist economies—Germany, Finland, France, and Sweden—have huge state programs aimed at reducing unemployment, thus masking to a degree their tendency to high unemployment. In contrast, most of the least socialist countries—namely, the United States, the United Kingdom, Canada, Australia, and Norway—make such interventionist expenditures least often. (See OECD, *Employment Outlook*, 2005.)

Socialism has traditionally stood for high participation in the labor force, not just low unemployment among those participating. Yet labor force participation rates, expressed in percentage of the working-age population, do not show a connection between socialism and participation. In 1995, as estimated in the OECD *Economic Outlook* for June 2000, the participation rates among the "major countries" were 76.9 percent in the United States, 75.8 in Canada, 75.3 in the United Kingdom, 71.2 in Germany, 66.7 in France, and 57.4 in Italy. (Denmark at 80.2 percent and Holland at 77.7 are two other countries low in state ownership and high in participation.) Hence, relatively socialist economies *cannot* be said to show a tendency toward high labor force participation. It appears pretty safe to infer just the opposite. (There are just two anomalies: Austria had a high 76.5 percent participation despite a high state ownership. Spain, which Milanović did not cover, had an abysmally low participation rate of 61.5 percent despite its dislike of state ownership.)

The disappointing performance in both unemployment and participation is a striking failing of European socialism in view of the oft-expressed dedication of most socialists to economic inclusion—the absorption of working-age people into the mainstream economy at terms allowing them the normal sorts of participation in society. Some socialist leaders have complained that they are up against the obstacles posed by "multiculturalism," though the continental European nations ranking high in socialism are not unique in facing cultural, ethnic, and racial diversity—there is surely more diversity in America. The source of this failing may be that the horror of business that fueled the socialist movement also fuels low labor force participation. It may also be that participation is apt to be low—and unemployment high—among countries in which the workplace is very bureaucratic—in which post office jobs at post office wages typify existing work. In such countries, large numbers of working-age people prefer to be occupied at home or in what is known as the informal sector, or underground economy. Rainer Werner Fassbinder's movie *The Marriage of Maria Braun* immortalized a period when German women entered the economy in the last years of World War II and even after, but German socialism could not stop them from going back as soon as they could afford it to *kinder, küche, kirche* (children, kitchen, church).

Another possible explanation for the disappointing performance in unemployment and participation of some economies is that the households in those countries exhibit high levels of household saving in relation to household disposable income. Among the large economies in the OECD in the early 2000s, the standout savers were Belgium, France, Italy, and Spain (*Economic Outlook* 2011); and the ones ranking the lowest in labor force participation were Italy, France, Belgium, and Spain. The lowest savers were the United States, Canada, and the United Kingdom; and highest in participation were Canada, Germany, the United Kingdom, and the United States. The most direct causal link is from high saving to high wealth to high demand for leisure, and late entry and early retirement from the labor force. (Wealth data are available only for the G7 nations.) An indirect link runs from wealth to the wherewithal for a welfare state that weakens incentives to work by offering so many things free of charge. (Mario Draghi, president of the European Central Bank, quotes the late Rudi Dornbusch as saying, "the Europeans are so rich they can afford to pay everybody for not working.")

Socialists' other claim of superiority on the employment front is that work is less precarious in a socialist economy. They could argue that work is steadier because there is less job change owing to less innovation. Most socialists, however, would prefer not to premise their argument for the superiority of socialism on an assumed lid it wisely puts on innovation. (It is imaginable that socialist economies innovate as much but do it better, setting higher hurdles for innovative projects at enterprises while compensating by undertaking projects of a longer term. But most observers of the more socialist economies see weak dynamism.) What admirers of a socialist economy argue is that, by its nature, it has key tools to moderate cyclical swings in employment that a capitalist economy lacks.

America in the 1930s gave the impression that it was lacking in just these kinds of tools. When its economy went into the steep downswing that was followed by the Great Depression, the government's monetary weapons were pinned down supporting the price of gold until the gold standard's demise in 1933. In any case, those weapons would not have been sufficient against structural forces moving labor away from building houses or farms and into making cars and other consumer durables. (The lesson was learned: In the 2008–2009 downswing, the world's monetary authorities did not sell their gold stocks to block a rise of gold prices.) The government had little fiscal weaponry with which to combat the unemployment arising. With no thought of taking over private industry, President Hoover, an engineer by training, resorted to massive construction projects to tame rivers and create dams for hydroelectric power. But some strain of conservatism held back the government from dotting the whole country with dikes and dams. The employment problem was finally thrown back on the modern capitalism on which the economy was built. In contrast, the central government of a socialist economy, when faced with a downswing, can compel SOEs to maintain or boost their investment expenditures—as if money were no object. This was the case with China in the aforementioned global recession, when it induced local governments to turn on the spigot of funds for increased local construction projects.

Yet the experience of recent decades does not bear out belief in the greater resistance of socialist economies to swings. The relatively socialist economies of continental Western Europe suffered an immense swing in employment (and other measures of economic activity) from the late 1970s to 1985—truly a Second Great Depression.[1] Yet the Europeans did not reach far into their arsenal of fiscal weapons, while the United States, faced with a similar downswing, however weaker or stronger it may have been, deployed fiscal weapons unknown in Hoover's time—higher investment tax credits and lower corporate profits tax rates—and fashioned some new ones—revenue-neutral cuts in marginal tax rates and increases in the earned income tax credit. (The monetary weapons at Paul Volcker's Federal Reserve were aimed at putting out the fires of inflation.) In the global downswing of 2008–2009, the more socialist economies were again more restrained in combating the slump. And it would be hard to decide which area suffered the wider downswing: the euro zone, which holds many of the more socialist economies, or the United States.

1. The earliest treatment of this episode is the 1988 monograph by Jean-Paul Fitoussi and Edmund Phelps, *The Slump in Europe.*

If there is a dimension in which the relatively socialist economies are still widely thought to have surpassed the others, it is in the measures taken to reduce *income inequality* and in the apparent effects of such inequality. While classical socialism meant full employment and less unequal wages, latter-day socialism has meant less unequal income. Some relatively socialist countries, namely France, Finland, and Sweden, as well as some not apparently socialist countries, namely Germany, Denmark, and Holland, have achieved reductions in inequality—say, between the bottom 30 percent and the top 30 percent—by instituting services free of user charges for all, thereby narrowing the inequalities in consumption levels.[2] Yet the relative narrowness of wage inequality in these countries has been the result not of redistribution by the state through spending and taxes, but the result of relatively low inequality to begin with: pre-tax incomes differ far less than in the Anglo-Saxon countries, for example. The Scandinavian nations are very homogeneous. Much of the remaining part of the explanation may be that there is less opportunity to innovate, thus to strike it rich. Various moral philosophers, from Immanuel Kant to John Rawls, opposed measures that would reduce inequality at a cost to everyone. But these qualifications miss the crucial point.

A deep decline of economic inclusion, particularly among less-qualified workers, swept over the Western economies in the 1980s—socialist, corporatist, and capitalist alike. Germany, France, Italy, and Sweden reacted strongly. In the first two, the *relative wage* of the *least-educated men* actually increased between the late 1970s and the mid-1990s; in the latter two, the relative wage slipped 1 or 2 percent. Holland, at the other extreme, apparently did not do enough, allowing the relative wage to fall 10.5 percent. In the United Kingdom and the United States the relative wage fell by 8 percent and 6 percent, respectively. It is striking, however, that the countries that pushed up the relative wage in the face of a strong headwind paid a stiff price—a far greater rise of unemployment among less-educated individuals over the 1980s than in the other advanced economies. The countries that settled for resisting most of the relative wage decline, Italy and Sweden and to some extent the United States, paid a much lower price. Holland suffered the smallest increase in the unemployment rate by far. What evidently happened is that France, led by a socialist party, and Germany, which refers to its "social market," used blunt instruments, such as statutes or labor union actions, to

2. The 2011 book by Vito Tanzi, *Government versus Markets,* provides expert discussion and helpful data.

force companies to pay higher wages to the poorly educated; Italy and Sweden, both relatively socialist-minded, used similar methods to resist a significant decline of the relative wage. These crude measures had the side effect of reducing the numbers of the least-educated that companies could afford to employ. The "catch" in the socialist progress on the wage front was a forced retreat on the employment front.[3]

Proponents of socialism widely think of the more socialist economy as more scientific, owing to the better organization of state enterprises and enterprises generally. It is also thought to have an education system that is better at supplying the middle and lower strata of society with the human capital they will need in the economy. If these claims are valid, we should expect the more socialist economies to exhibit higher levels of productivity—output per unit labor and output per basket of labor and capital, called total factor productivity (or multifactor productivity). In fact, some of the more socialist countries in Europe have been rocked by international studies evaluating their educational institutions far more poorly than imagined. But never mind. We may as well let the productivity data speak. What may be the first statistical study of the effects of socialism used cross-national data to estimate the relationship between the growth of output per worker and the share of national output produced by state enterprises.[4] A negative association was found. In short, a high SOE per unit of GDP hampers the rise of GDP. (That does not mean that even the best corporatist economies may never catch up to the leaders. It means that if they do catch up, it will take longer.)

There could be more here than meets the eye. It could be that high state ownership and low growth are both effects of a third influence—a heedlessness toward property rights or an outright antagonism toward private property with resulting fears of expropriation for any wealthy private investor

3. Phelps, "The Importance of Inclusion and the Power of Job Subsidies to Increase It" (2000/2, p. 86). See also figure 1 in that report. The article adds that "in the first half of the 1990s France and Germany again compressed low-end pay and again saw the steep rise in unemployment of low-skilled labor (see Figure 2)." The paper set out the case for an approach to raising low-end wages that is more employment friendly, namely a system of low-wage subsidies to be paid to employers for their ongoing employment of low-wage persons. In presenting this paper at the OECD Secretariat in Paris, I was going into the eye of the storm. Participants applauded the proposal except the U.S. delegation, which saw the proposal as endangering the Earned Income Tax Credit, which was designed primarily to encourage low-income mothers to earn some of their own support.

4. No statistical analysis was done, surprisingly, until the paper by Darius Palia and Edmund Phelps presented at the 1996 Villa Mondragone conference of Rome's Tor Vergata University. The conference volume, Paganetto and Phelps, *Finance, Research, Education and Growth*, came out in 2005.

brave enough to venture his or her capital. In such a country, SOE is better than no enterprise. That does not really alter the implications of the findings. Where a country opposes private ownership of enterprises—where it is socialist minded—it suffers poor economic performance.

Corporatism—Claims and Evidence

Classic corporatism, such as Mussolini's, sought to restructure the capitalist economy so as to speed economic growth—growth of productivity and of various national capabilities—far beyond the puny capacity of Continental capitalism. This meant more initiative in the public sector and more direction of the private sector—thus "ownership without control" for the owners. The quest for greater national growth and national power was to be subject to considerations of solidarity and, in particular, "social protection." That meant "concertation" of the state with the "social partners," and, more broadly, subsidies for regions or industries. In an equivalent view of classic corporatism, the state is free to take whatever measures it chooses in the name of solidarity and protection, constrained only by the need to take steps aimed at restoring growth when growth has slowed too much and too long.

This system, in which, in principle, the state may intervene at its own discretion without any restraints, poses serious moral hazards; and insofar as politicians fall into these hazards, their misconduct becomes part of the workings of the system. A constitutional democracy might be able and willing to curb such intervention but may fail to do so. Even in a democracy, self-interested legislators are apt at times to use their votes, and agency heads their powers to award projects, to win the support of interest groups that can keep them in office. In this political process, "growth" may take a back seat or be altogether neglected—even if it continues to be paid lip service. And, with the politicians focused primarily on their own political support, "social protection" is not really the rule either. Politicians may also be so venal as to dispense patronage to regions, companies, and labor unions in exchange for money under the table—kickbacks. (In 1990s Italy, bribery became so rampant that Italians saw themselves living in *Tangentopoli*—Bribesvilles.)

The hazards of a corporatist system do not stop there. If only *insiders* are well-enough connected to become clients of the politicians, the system may operate to protect insiders *against outsiders*. The clients and cronies of the state have no need for contracts paid with scarce taxpayer money if their enterprises can be awarded monopoly power. The gain of the insiders is the loss of the outsiders, who may be unable to start a business, break into an industry, or have a rewarding career—whether or not "protected" with subsidies for medical care, food, and heat. This is the burden of extreme corporatism: the deprivations of some, few or many—deprivations of basic goods like careers—who are not morally compensated by the spoils of the advantaged, few or many.

To rate how well the more corporatist economies perform their mission we need criteria and evidence with which to judge which countries are relatively corporatist and, preferably, to judge the degree of corporatism. It makes sense to begin looking under a lamppost where there is plenty of light. The directiveness of the state in the economy is widely seen as measured by the sheer size of the government, but not every such measure is helpful. Though a highly corporatist economy would need armies of bureaucrats to direct it, a swollen public sector is not a safe measure of corporatism. In 1960, the United States had, among G7 nations, the highest share of total employment working in the government—15.7 percent. It may have been the most corporatist in capabilities, with all its soldiers and schoolteachers at the ready. But few, if any, would believe it was the most corporatist in spirit. And, in fact, the other countries were fast pulling up their capabilities. By 1980, the United Kingdom and Canada exceeded—and France, Germany, and Italy were near—America's 16.7 percent. Evidently, government employment levels do not differentiate the advanced economies. (See OECD, *Historical Statistics 1960–81*.)

A better measure of the state's reach is government purchases of all kinds (not just labor) plus subsidies encouraging certain things and transfer payments awarded to certain people. Government purchases and subsidies are a standard measure of the extent to which the government guides the use of resources in the economy; transfer payments may in some cases be part of a social bargain to pursue corporatist goals. On this broad measure, the high-income economies had come to differ enormously by 1995. At one end, Sweden stood at 65.2 percent of GDP (55.0 percent in 2005), France at 54.4 (53.3), Italy at 52.5 (48.1), Belgium at 52.3 (52.1), and Holland at 51.5 (44.8). At the other end, America stood at 37.1 percent (36.3 in 2005), Britain at 43.9 percent (44.1), and Spain at 44.4 (38.4). In the middle were Germany at 48.3 percent of GDP (46.8) and Canada at 47.3 (38.0).[5] Among

5. Tanzi, *Government versus Markets.*

the smaller countries, Finland was at 61.5 percent of GDP (50.1), Denmark at 59.3 (52.6), and Switzerland at 34.6 (35.0). But before we declare Sweden the most corporatist nation (and Belgium third-most) we had better widen our investigation.

Among the larger high-income economies, France, Spain, and Italy rank worst in legal barriers to entry in industries; Spain and Italy in barriers to entrepreneurship; Italy, France, and Spain in economy-wide product market regulation; Spain and France in competition law and its enforcement; and Holland, Spain, Sweden, and Germany are seen as the most excessive in their employment protection legislation (EPL). On the whole, Italy, France, and Spain rank worst on these counts, while Britain, America, and Canada rank best—with Sweden, Holland, and Germany in the middle. Among the smaller high-income nations, Switzerland generally ranks in the middle, Ireland ranks high, and Denmark even higher. A broad measure of business interference, derived from OECD data, which *The Economist* in July 1999 dubbed an index of "red tape," differs a little: it puts Italy and France at 2.7, Belgium at 2.6, next come Germany at 2.1 and both Spain and Sweden at 1.8; Britain is best at 0.5, next America at 1.3, and Holland at 1.4. (Canada and Austria were omitted.) All these results are informative, although they are better at detecting levers of control and an obstructiveness that might be economy-wide than at gauging selective meddling and directing.[6]

While the above indicators describe the arms of a corporatist economy, another dimension of corporatist economies is the extent to which wage setting uses a trilateral mechanism connecting the state with labor unions and business confederations. This institution is still at the heart of Italian corporatism—both the rhetoric of Mussolini and the reality after the war. Indexes of "union and employer coordination" constructed by Stephen Nickell show only trace amounts in the United States and Canada, with very little in the United Kingdom (though the CBI still exists). We find the highest levels of coordination in Sweden, Austria, and Germany; next are France,

6. For these data see OECD, *Going for Growth: 2007,* a project led by Jean-Philippe Cotis. It might be suspected that these indexes of hindrances to innovation and to the conduct of business generally purport to measure the unmeasurable. However, the indexes are compounded out of concrete and measurable things, such as the number of days it takes to obtain a license to build a warehouse, which ranges from about 80 days in the United States and Canada to about 170 days in France and Germany and 284 days in Italy. It might also be wondered whether these differences among economies matter at all. However, a nation's investment in information and communications technologies (ICT) exhibits a rather tight relationship to its product market regulation index. Nations' unemployment rates have been shown to have some relationship to their EPL indexes.

Italy, Belgium, and Holland; tied for the lowest levels are the United States, the United Kingdom, and Canada.[7]

Another dimension of corporatism is the hazardous and uneven *playing field* on which private property has to operate. Some markers here are the amount of corruption in the public sector, the risk of expropriation borne by private enterprises, and the risk of government repudiation of contracts. How nations rank in these respects may help us rank nations according to their corporatism. Of course, corporatism does not have a monopoly on these bad traits, but that is not a decisive objection to their use as signs of corporatism. However, measurements of these qualities are generally proprietary information. What is available is an average of these three indicators and two other indicators (namely, law and order and quality of the bureaucracy), which are in turn averaged with an indicator of openness to foreign trade. The advanced economies rank in descending order as follows: Switzerland, the United States, Canada, Germany, Iceland, Denmark, Norway, France, Belgium, Austria, Britain, Japan, Australia, Italy, Spain, Portugal, Ireland, Korea, and New Zealand.[8] Taken at face value, this ranking suggests that, among the nations under examination here, Spain, Italy, Britain, Belgium, and France are relatively corporatist.

The evidence on the differing degrees of corporatism in the advanced economies cannot be entirely satisfying until we have evidence on the scope of *statism* in the advanced economies. We need data on the degree to which the state goes around the capitalist institutions and the competition of the marketplace to exert its influence on industries and the companies—enabling or privileging some activities or players and not others. To that end, we could use data on the extent of lobbying and government contracts. We could use data on informal pressures exerted by the state on businesses—such as offers or denials of positions in the government. (France is thought to be a revolving door of executives who shuttle between jobs in the private and public sector.) We could use data on the presence or absence of a constitution that allows the government only "limited" roles in the economy. Some countries lack constitutions that, with judicial review by the highest court, would restrain the government from playing a directive role in the business sector, while some other countries have constitutions prohibiting the government from

7. The data can be found in Layard and Nickell, *Handbook of Labor Economics.*
8. This last ordering, dubbed the Index of Social Infrastructure, can be pulled off figure II in Hall and Jones, "Why Do Some Countries Produce So Much More Output per Worker Than Others?"

interfering with the direction of the business sector.[9] A readily available statistic that may well reflect the privileging of some companies over their competitors is capital's relative share of the income generated in the business sector. (When a company is anointed a national champion in its industry, it can raise its price; its competitors, seeing it has become easier to compete, will up their prices.) Capital's share in national income may also be a clue. In 1995–1996, among large economies, Italy and France ranked highest, with a capital share of 42 percent and 41 percent, respectively. Germany and Belgium were in the middle at 37 percent. In the bottom group were the United States at 34 percent and Britain and Canada at 32 percent.[10] (Among smaller economies, Austria was highest at 41 percent, Spain and Holland were at 40. Switzerland and Sweden were low at 31 and 33 percent, respectively [1996–1997].)

These data all show that in almost no part of the world is the government a silent partner in the business sector. They also suggest that the degree of involvement by the state varies a great deal from one country to another, even among those countries commonly thought to have the same economic organization. The totality of the above evidence suggests that the economies of Italy and France have relatively high degrees of corporatism, America and Canada the lowest, with Britain and Germany between these two poles. Corporatism is also rather high in Spain, Holland, Belgium, and Ireland while rather low in Switzerland, Denmark, and Norway. Sweden, so oft-discussed, is a mixed case: interventionist yet pro-business.

Sensing now which countries had relatively corporatist economies in recent decades, we are ready to answer the main question of this chapter: what was the outcome of the corporatist project in which these countries were engaged between the war's end in the mid-1940s and the last years of the 20th century? Painting with a very broad brush, one could say that in that half-century productivity levels came close to converging. But how close is "close," and what happened after near convergence?

Consider first output per (employed) worker. According to OECD calculations, the GDP per employee of Italy, Ireland, and Belgium came near the U.S. level in 1996. (Italy weighed in at 62,500 dollars, while the United States was at 67,500.) In a lower group was France along with Norway, Canada, and Holland. Below them were Germany alongside Austria, Sweden, and Denmark.

9. Early political philosophy touching on the scope of government is the subject of Andrzej Rapaczynski's 1987 volume, *Nature and Politics*.

10. See *OECD Economic Outlook,* Annex table 24, Capital income shares in the business sector, p. 214.

Real GDP per employee
(1996 PPP $)

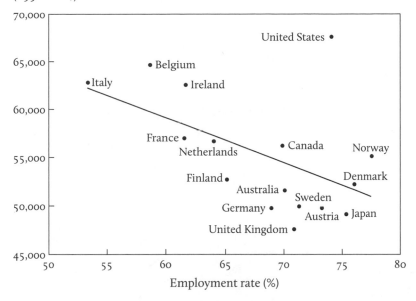

FIGURE 7.1 Real GDP per employee and the employment rate (employment per working-age person). GDP, gross domestic product; PPP, purchasing power parity. (Source: OECD.)

See Figure 7.1. These results do not appear to be a success for the corporatist experiment: after 50 years, only three of the high corporatists beat Canada and not one beat the United States. And there is more that must be said.

The GDP per hour worked has also been calculated by the OECD. See Figure 7.2. By 1996, the U.S. level was reached in Italy, Ireland, and France—more or less. Germany and Canada reached somewhat lower levels, while the United Kingdom and Sweden occupy a still lower notch. But there is less there than meets the eye. For several reasons, these observations have little significance. For one thing, Europe is a continent of many nations, so it should not surprise us that there are a couple of "outliers," such as Holland and Norway, that have higher levels of output per manhour than the United States. If we looked at America's 50 states, we would also see outstanding levels in California and Massachusetts. For another thing, the employed are a rather narrow section of the working-age population in the many corporatist economies with an employment problem. For example, Italy's 1996 GDP per hour, at almost 39 dollars, is so high next to America's, at only 36 dollars, because Italy's economy fills

Labor productivity
(output per person-hour, 1996 PPP $)

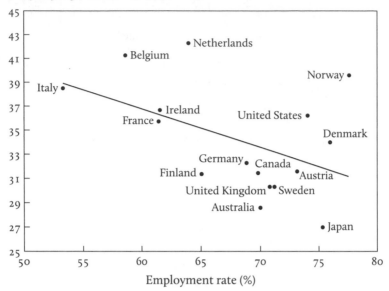

FIGURE 7.2 Labor productivity (real GDP per hours worked) and employment rate (employment per working-age person). (Source: OECD.)

only jobs that are rather productive and it fills them with its most productive workers—low-wage employment is not permitted. Had Italy employed 75 percent of the working-age population, as America, Norway, and Denmark did, its GDP per hour would have been 32 dollars—a great deal less than Norway's 40, Denmark's 34, and America's 36. Differing levels of labor-force participation in Europe and America spoiled productivity comparisons from the mid-1970s to the mid-1990s. Finally, data on total output per total number of hours worked in less-corporatist America, Canada, and Britain are further biased downward by the fact that people there tend to work longer hours, which drives down their output per hour, while the reverse is true in corporatist Italy, France, and Spain, where people tend to work far fewer hours per year.[11]

11. Another point: Whatever the Continental and Anglo-Saxon productivity levels, measured by output per hour of labor, Continental productivity levels would be *decreased* relative to Anglo-Saxon levels if they were all measured by output per basket of labor and capital—the measure called *multifactor productivity* (or total factor productivity)—because Continental economies *raise* their output per labor ratios by investing more capital with which labor can work than Anglo-Saxon economies do. For this extra output, it may be argued, the Continentals must suffer the reduction in consumption levels required to meet the interest payments on the extra capital.

On this evidence, then, it *cannot* be said that the corporatist economies delivered on their claim to be superior in productivity to the remaining modern economies—those in America, Canada, and Britain. Quite the contrary: taking account of the considerations just noted, America's relatively modern economy retained its edge in productivity. And two other relatively modern economies, those of Canada and Britain, gained ground in the past two decades.

A stronger argument can be made using Figure 7.2, where the shortest distance of a country from the sloping line can serve as a makeshift measure of how well it performs in *both* employment, which is the socialist focus, and productivity, which is the corporatist. Among the large economies, the relatively corporatist ones—France, Italy, and Germany (not to mention the smaller Austria and Sweden)—*all* lie some distance *southwest* of the sloping line, while the relatively modern ones, including America, lie some distance *northeast* of the sloping line. Canada, though it is in the southwest, is not as far away as Sweden, Finland, and Australia, which have all come under suspicion of possessing significant corporatism in their economies.

Furthermore, the seeming catch-up of Italy and Germany by 1995 proved ephemeral. From 1995 to 2005, their participation rates recovered, with the predictable result that the added jobs offered diminished productivity. (A Cambridge don of yesteryear, Dennis Robertson, perhaps hoping to make his lecture on the law of diminishing returns more vivid, imagined that the 10th man in a construction crew, though they had no shovel left for him, could go to get the beer.) Over the same period, America saw workers of low productivity or whose jobs offered low productivity leave the labor force, with the result that U.S. output per employee clambered from its former (rising) track onto a higher track. Thus American output per manhour (and per employee) distanced itself further from the Italian and German levels.

This chapter has been focusing on dimensions of economic performance— all highly materialist—to which corporatism and socialism have been dedicated. We could look at other dimensions without straying from the materialist ones. The notable emigration of young people from France over the past two decades could be indicative. That evidence may, to some extent, reflect failures by the Continent's corporatism to deliver economies gleaming with productivity and brimming with jobs. (The fact that the high tide of unemployment since the 2007–2008 international financial crisis has damped that migration is not evidence that the corporatist economies have improved or that the less corporatist ones have worsened. It is too risky to quit in search of greener pastures.) The drawback is that the emigration phenomenon does not identify which deficiencies of corporatism and socialism are at work—only that they have deficiencies. The deficiency may be nonmaterial, such as oppressive companies or a repressive economic culture.

Wage inequality or, more aptly, unjust wage inequality is another dimension of performance on which corporatism might be judged. In view of the data discussed earlier on wage inequality, it is accurate to say that the relatively corporatist nations—Italy and France, and to a lesser degree Spain, Holland, Belgium, and Ireland—have less wage inequality than the exemplars of the modern economy: Canada, America, and Britain.[12] But, as stressed before, this may mean only that Canadians, Americans, and Britons are rolling the dice with greater frequency than the Continentals do. Yet their considerable ethnic and racial diversity may also have some array of effects on unjust wage inequality. However that may be, this chapter has set out to examine whether corporatism achieved its goals, and uprooting wage inequality was never a part of the corporatist manifesto. (Some corporatist countries, for example, have been notorious for leaving substantial minorities unintegrated.) If, as corporatism holds, the accomplishments and initiatives of the nation are what matters—and not personal freedom or individual aspiration and rewards—then the very idea of economic justice ceases to have any possible meaning. And, in fact, among the larger of the relatively corporatist countries, neither Italy nor Spain nor Germany did much to address wage inequality with training programs or employment subsidies. (On the European continent, only Holland and France put appreciable resources into pulling up wages at the low end of the labor market.) The countries that have long developed sophisticated machinery for raising the rewards to low-wage work are Britain and America, neither among the relatively corporatist nations, with their program of wage supplements for the working poor.

A Paucity of Innovation

It is apparent by direct observation that in the past three decades, up to the 2007–2008 crisis, the growth of the Big 4 on the European continent—France,

12. These OECD data are shown in Phelps, "The Importance of Inclusion" (2000/2); see figure 3a, "Trends in Wage Rate Dispersion, 1997." The gauge here is the 50-10 ratio, that is, the ratio of the mean of the wage rates of workers one-tenth of the way up the population of employed persons, thus at the 10th percentile, to the mean wage rate at the 50th percentile. It is also known as the D1/D5 ratio.

Germany, Italy, and Spain—continued to be driven by advances *external* to their economies, mainly (but not exclusively) advances made in the United States. Thus, the *degree* of these economies' catch-up with the American economy was not powered by a great rebirth of the indigenous innovation that was visible in continental Europe from about the 1870s to the 1930s. The corporatist economies must have come close to catching up with the American economy mainly by imitation. If growth relied on outside forces, by the way, the same is true of employment. A total cessation of American innovation would have sent the Continent into a long slump.

But what did the corporatism in some continental European countries *do* to inhibit or fail to promote innovation? One can imagine that the welter of bars put up by the relatively corporatist economies, such as barriers to entry and the OECD's barriers to entrepreneurship, would hinder or block various advances in productivity. However, it would be satisfying to see evidence that this barrier or that deficiency operated to dampen or fail to spur *indigenous innovation.*

A piece of the mechanism has been detected. A country's stock markets offer a clue to the dynamism of its economy. The current inventory of promising yet unexploited commercial ideas is a key kind of capital in the business sector of an innovating economy. The prospective size of this inventory in the near- or medium-term future, following the arrival of additional ideas, is a major determinant of the value of businesses in an enterprise economy: the larger this prospective inventory is, the greater the value of these business enterprises, and the greater, we may suppose, will be the capital market's estimation of that value. That might be the only value of start-up companies in their first day of life, but not of companies in general. The other component of the value of enterprises is the equipment and plant owned by them—the physical capital. Hence the "market capitalization" of a nation's enterprises, which is the value of the shares outstanding plus the bonds outstanding, taken as a *ratio* to the acquisition cost of the physical capital, is an indicator of how good the prospects for unexploited ideas are in relation to the physical capital stock. The same ratio, which came to be known as *Tobin's Q,* was used by James Tobin, who saw it as an index of speculative fever or fear, to predict the ups and downs of a nation's investment activity. For our purposes, taking the nation's annual business output as a crude proxy for the physical capital, we construct the ratio of "market cap" to the size of business output and reinterpret that ratio as an indicator of how significant the prospective new ideas are in relation to the

Market capitalization
(% GDP in logarithms)

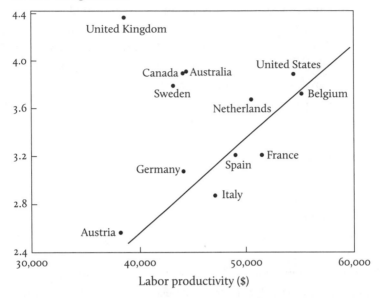

FIGURE 7.3 Market capitalization and labor productivity: business output per employed worker. Market capitalization variable measures the value of shares in the corporate sector in 1988. Labor productivity is calculated as business output per employed worker in U.S. dollars. The employment rate is the ratio of total employment to working-age population. (Sources: Morgan Stanley International; OECD.)

size of the economy or its business sector. Theoretically, this is a very natural indicator of an economy's dynamism. In Figure 7.3, this hypothesis receives considerable support. We see that the market-cap-to-output ratio in a country is a surprisingly good predictor of its labor productivity some years ahead.

This wonderful ratio is an even better predictor of *national employment* a few years ahead, as Figure 7.4 shows.[13] Remarkably, the size of the market-cap-to-output ratio in 1990 would have permitted one to forecast rather accurately the countries that rode the wave of the internet revolution arising in the second half of the 1990s. While it is intuitive that a relatively high rate of idea formation, in leading very probably to a high rate

13. See Phelps, "Reflections on Parts III and IV" (2003, figures 3 and 4).

Market capitalization
(% GDP in logarithms)

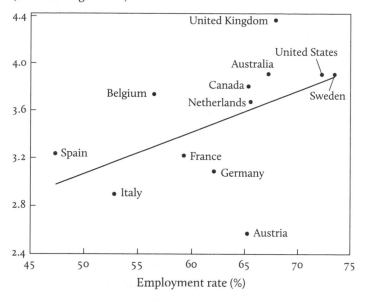

FIGURE 7.4 Market capitalization and employment rate: employment as a share of the working-age population. The market capitalization variable measures the value of shares in the corporate sector in 1988. Labor productivity is calculated as business output per employed worker in U.S. dollars. The employment rate is the ratio of total employment to working-age population. (Sources: Morgan Stanley International; OECD.)

of innovation, tends to result in high productivity, a reader might wonder whether the path from high innovation to high employment is on safe ground. Might innovation destroy more jobs than it creates? It might at any given place and time. It may be that the phenomenal economic advances occurring in the 1930s hindered the climb out of the Great Depression more than they helped. But in the most common (and most studied) case, two positive effects are working. First, innovation in the form of new consumer goods or in the production of existing consumer goods, which tend to be capital intensive, by lowering their prices, lifts up the real value that firms making capital goods place on having added labor, just as it raises the value of the enterprises that make them; and that sparks new hiring. Second, when productivity is streaking ahead, pulling wages in its train, workers' wealth feels smaller to them—it is smaller relative to their improved wages—so they are

Market capitalization
(% GDP in logarithms)

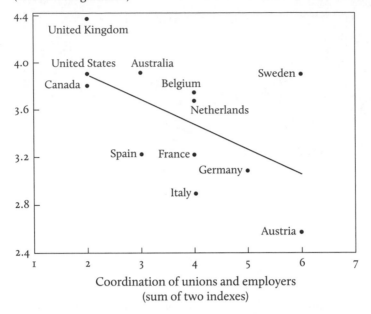

FIGURE 7.5 Coordination and market capitalization. Market capitalization is the value of shares in the corporate sector in 1988. The coordination variable is calculated as the sum of Nickell's indexes of union and employer coordination for the years 1989–1994. (Sources: Morgan Stanley International; Layard and Nickell, *Handbook of Labor Economics* (1999).)

more willing to work, to move, and to take a chance on a different career. An innovation must be very labor-saving to overturn these effects.[14]

Now we ask whether some of the corporatist elements discussed above impact unfavorably on our market-cap-to-output ratio. One such element is the twin institutions so emblematic of corporatist economies—wage setting by labor unions and employer confederations. Figure 7.5 shows that an increase

14. It is often commented that employment will be falling if output is growing slower than productivity: the growth rate of productivity is the "stall speed" of the economy. That may suggest that a decline in productivity growth would have the silver lining of reversing the fall of employment. But little is known about the short-run effect of that on the direction of employment. It is known that there is no long-run, sustained link going from the productivity growth rate to the growth rate of employment; the latter is a matter of demographics. There are long-run connections between the *level* of employment and the productivity growth rate, as pointed out above. (Moreover, a drop in the productivity growth rate certainly would reduce the long-run growth rate of output.)

Market capitalization
(% GDP in logarithms)

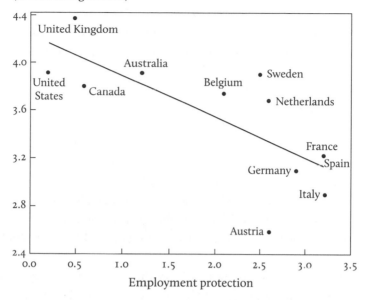

FIGURE 7.6 Employment protection and market capitalization. Market capitalization is the value of shares in the corporate sector in 1988. Employment protection is the number of months of salary that goes in mandatory redundancy payments. (Source: Morgan Stanley International.)

in coordination between unions and employers is associated with a decrease in the market-cap-to-output ratio. Another element of the relatively corporatist economies is the extremism of their EPL. The benefits and harms from EPL have been much studied yet with very little consensus resulting. Figure 7.6, however, is rather persuasive in indicating that, though the beneficiaries of protection may have appreciated it, there is an ill effect on the market-cap ratio, which, as just argued, reflects a decrease in the actual and prospective stock of innovative ideas. There are other elements of corporatism that line up rather nicely with low market capitalization, of course. But there would be little utility in proliferating additional correlations. It is time to sum up.

To the question, how did corporatist elements prevent countries from reaching American levels of productivity and employment, the answer in *this* chapter is that some of the corporatist elements slowed the inflow of new commercial ideas and that constriction of the inflow was a drag on the advance of productivity, which in turn imparted a drag on hiring, thus causing relatively low levels of employment as well. Thus, the relatively corporatist economies failed to deliver because they lacked something needed to enable, stimulate, and spur experimenting, exploring, and trying things out. Therefore their economies were missing the ingredients required for operating at the productivity frontier and thus for having high mean levels of employment.

Postscript: There is a puzzle outstanding. How did the Big 3 of continental Europe—France, Germany, and Italy—come as close as they did to catching up with the American economy in terms of productivity and in terms of employment (in Germany and Italy) if, as has been observed here and elsewhere, they suffered such a paucity of endogenous, indigenous innovation? One would think that if the growth of the Continent's productivity was founded on its being behind the leader from whom all innovations flow, its growth would stop if somehow it caught up, just as greyhounds in a race would stop running if they were no longer behind the rabbit. (Greyhounds do not run for the fun of it.)

That is what happened. In the mid-1970s the American economy stopped running like a rabbit. Output growth had fluctuated around 4 percent annually from the mid-1950s to the mid-1970s—of which 3 percent was productivity growth and 1 percent employment growth. Then the Great Productivity Slowdown came in the mid-1970s. From 1975 to 2005, output grew at rates around 3 percent per year—relatively fast in the 1990s and relatively slow in the 2000s. With its growth engine having lost power, America was a sitting duck for catch-up by the rest of the world. A tendency to convergence arises as the leaders slow.

With America no longer producing the greater part of the world's innovation, which it had done in the 1920s and 1930s, then again from the mid-1950s to the mid-1970s, Europe, devoid of indigenous innovation, had little choice but to slow likewise. Further, once operating at reduced speeds, Europe became more vulnerable. It felt the rise of competition from the nations emerging into the global economy far more keenly than it would have in its "30 Glorious Years"—the 26 years stretching from 1955 to 1980. Also, upon resorting to fiscal deficits to make up for slow growth, Europe became increasingly tangled up in public debt.

By the late 2000s the entire West saw its economic growth reduced to slow motion and its employment levels depressed as the boom, stimulated by massive tax cuts, new entitlements, and new subsidies, fizzled out, as it had to do.

CHAPTER EIGHT

The Satisfaction of Nations

[The] big thing that's missing is a technocratic understanding of the facts, where things are working and where they're not working.

BILL GATES, quoted in the *New York Times*

T HE PREVIOUS CHAPTER, weighing the rivals on their own materialist terms, sought the effects of corporatism (and socialism) on the material economy—mainly on employment and productivity. Yet there is a *nonmaterial* dimension in a modern economy, as in modern life in general. Much of what is most valued about participating in a relatively modern economy is the challenge and experience it usually offers, and the intuitions and ideas it excites, rather than the material goods and services produced. As emphasized from the start, the modern economy is a vast imaginarium, a virtual laboratory in which to dream up and try out ideas. The modern revolution in arts and letters mirrored the new experience sought and widely found in modern working life. Household surveys have provided evidence for the nonmaterial rewards of work in the more modern economies, and their respondents often say that they look for kinds of compensation beyond the material reward of the paycheck.

The question here is whether, as this book has been arguing, the relatively modern-capitalist economies are *more* rewarding in nonmaterial terms than the relatively corporatist or socialist economies. To approach that directly would require neatly decomposing each country—"this one 1 part modern capitalism, 3 parts corporatism," "that one 2 parts modern capitalism, 1 part socialism," and so forth. That would be highly subjective. Our approach will necessarily be indirect. Some features found in economies are thought to be most pronounced or more common in corporatist (or socialist) economies, other features most pronounced in modern-capitalist economies. We will investigate some signature features of corporatist, socialist, and modern-capitalist economies to see whether they are conducive or inimical to nonmaterial rewards—features such as corporatism's high "employment protection," extensive welfarism, short regulation work week, and collective bargaining; socialism's gigantic public sectors; the bureaucratic "red tape" found in both of the latter systems; and capitalism's individual freedoms. Not knowing exactly how to measure the degree of, say, modern capitalism in each country, we use data measuring the size of the "modern" organs— the organs understood to function in the generation of dynamism and thus inclusion—to see how they correlate with nonmaterial rewards.

Yet, as important as institutions and policies may be, we must recognize that every economy is a *culture* or mix of cultures, not just policies, laws, and institutions. The *economic* culture of a nation consists of prevailing attitudes, norms, and assumptions about business, work, and other aspects of the economy. These cultural forces may affect the generation of nonmaterial rewards indirectly through their influence on the evolution of institutions and policies, but also very directly through their impact on participants' motives and expectations. An economy may owe its vibrancy—its readiness to apply newly discovered technologies and adopt newly proven products— to one or more components of its economic culture; an economy may owe its dynamism—its success at using the creativity of people to achieve indigenous innovation—to some other components in its cultural repertoire. A *political* culture may also suit a nation for innovation under some conditions, at any rate. To the extent that cultural differences are important, inter-country differences in nonmaterial rewards are to be explained not by crude labels—modern capitalism, corporatism, and socialism—and not only by the size and settings of a few institutions or policies, each characteristic of one kind of system or another, but also by measurements of some elements in the culture, each thought to be a key force in modern capitalism or corporatism or socialism.

In the economics that has been standard from David Ricardo and John Stuart Mill to the present day, the concept of a culture does not come up, as if there were just one culture in Western civilization—despite the dissents of Thorstein Veblen and Max Weber. Outside standard economics, however, anthropologists recognized that not all societies' cultures are alike and the differences matter. Claude Lévi-Strauss argued that every society's culture deserved respect, having arisen to meet its own special needs, and Ruth Benedict maintained that some societies had cultures that were not the best for them. The psychiatrist Erich Fromm said that some cultures were extremely bad, arguing that fascism took over where the culture did not value individual freedom.

In the past decade, though, culture has been making its way into economics. It is increasingly hypothesized that culture is the glue or "missing link" that loosely ties a country's economic performance in the present to that in even the distant past. "The apple does not fall far from the tree," good tree or bad.[1] Many observers have remarked at how effortlessly some countries, after being down and out, climbed back to a high place in the league tables: most European countries climbed back more or less to the position they had before their interwar traumas.[2] However, there can be no doubt that new experience and new ideas can change a country's culture. Nazi opposition in the 1930s to women working had a long-lasting effect, but over the past decade Germany's female participation rate has rebounded. Margaret Thatcher's campaign in the 1980s to sweep away British companies' aversion to competition has left a mark in the view of most observers, but there are now calls in Britain to return to "industrial policy." Historians of China are suggesting that China's economic reformation in 1978 under Deng Xiaoping succeeded thanks to a deeply seated culture that could be traced back to 1500. The West's modern era brought new thinking and, to varying degrees, new ways of behaving, as this book has argued at several places.

Disparities in Job Satisfaction

It is widely assumed that the "economically advanced" countries do not differ significantly in their *nonmaterial* rewards. Since they are about equally productive, the reasoning is, they must produce things the same way, and so the *work experience* must be the same too. (Standard economics supposes that the robotized economies of their theoretical models have no culture.) But that is a profound and serious misconception.

In fact, there are striking differences in job satisfaction within the West. That became clear with the publication of a wave of survey data gathered in

---

1. This theory sees the culture as a slow-moving causal force that may ultimately trigger an abrupt change of institutions—as shifting tectonic plates finally provoke an earthquake. See Roland, "Understanding Institutional Change" (2004). (There the culture is another institution—the slow-moving one. This book breaks out culture from institutions.) The hypothesis here allows new ideas to drive institutions and possibly culture too. Things would change even if culture never did.

2. A Spanish economist, chatting with me at a 1993 meeting in London, observed that in the early 1920s Spain's GDP per person put it in 8th place in the league tables, Western division—trailing America, Germany, France, Belgium, Holland, Britain, and Italy. After all that Spain had been through since then, from the Spanish civil war to Franco's reign and the post-Franco decades, Spain was again in 8th place.

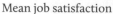

Mean job satisfaction

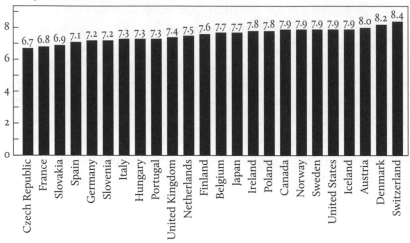

FIGURE 8.1 Mean job satisfaction, 1990–1991. (Source: World Values Surveys.)

1991–1993 for World Values Surveys (WVS)—a mine of data on individuals' satisfactions as well as "values," that is, attitudes, norms, and beliefs. The bar chart in Figure 8.1 gives graphic evidence of differing levels of mean job satisfaction among Western countries.

Understandably, doubts are raised. Is job satisfaction another term for wages or wealth? Empirically, ranking high in national wealth and wages is not a predictor of a high rank in job satisfaction. David Blanchflower and Andrew Oswald comment that job satisfaction was very high in one of the poorest countries in their 1990s sample, Ireland, and low in Mediterranean nations. It may be wondered whether the disparities in job satisfaction are merely transitory differences. Happily, the 1999–2000 job satisfaction data gathered by WVS in its subsequent survey, which unaccountably omitted the United States, do not rank the countries much differently from the first survey, as Figure 8.2 shows.

It is sometimes asked why it is useful to study *job* satisfaction. Why not go directly to the overall measure called *life satisfaction*? The answer is that we come to understand better what determines life satisfaction by studying job satisfaction on the way. It would be neglectful to study life satisfaction without studying the components: satisfaction with jobs, with family, and with economic situation ("financial satisfaction"). When we can study the sort of

Mean job satisfaction

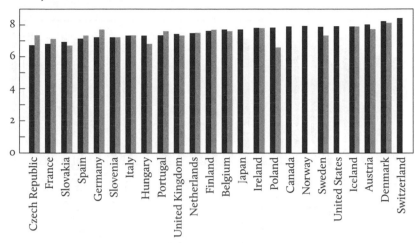

FIGURE 8.2 Mean job satisfaction, 1990–1991 (black) and 1999–2000 (gray). (Source: World Values Surveys.)

satisfaction that is specific to jobs and the effects that economic institutions and cultures have on it, we should prefer to start there for the sake of clarity.

One issue is urgent, however. Conventional opinion holds that if a society's economy is geared to create jobs that offer significant challenge and reward, it pays a steep price in the form of reduced *family satisfaction:* harried couples and neglected kids. That traditionalist perspective views it as an open question whether a modern economy makes a net positive contribution to *life* satisfaction. Observation is all on the side of the modernist perspective, however. Children clearly benefit from parents engaged in their jobs and having interesting things to talk about at the dinner table. So while intensive involvement in work and career detracts from the time available for the family, it has benefits for the value of the family time that remains. In a survey a decade ago, kids expressly said that they wanted their parents not to sacrifice more of their careers for the sake of children but rather to solve their problems and get on with their lives.[3] The WVS adds its support for the modernist view. Its data show that the countries lowest in job satisfaction are *lowest*

3. One authority setting out the family tensions thesis is Anne Marie Slaughter. Lucy Kellaway, with evident relish, set out in the *Financial Times* the counter-thesis.

Mean job satisfaction (black),
Mean life satisfaction (white)

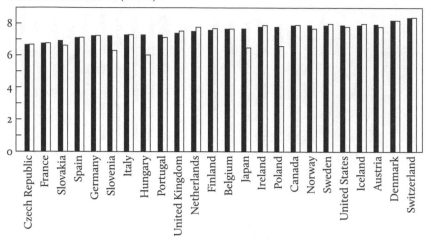

FIGURE 8.3 Mean job satisfaction, 1990–1991 (black) and mean life satisfaction, 1990–1991 (white). (Source: World Values Surveys.)

in family satisfaction, and the ones highest in job satisfaction rank—such as Denmark, Canada, America, and Ireland—are *high* in family satisfaction. All of this telegraphs the punch line in Figure 8.3: *life* satisfaction is positively correlated with job satisfaction and strongly so. Case closed.[4]

The waves of data on reported job satisfaction that have washed up in recent decades have led to misuses and misinterpretation. Some observers, pointing to Sweden's high score in job satisfaction, take this to be evidence that the Swedish economic system—a unique mixture of capitalism and welfarism with little dynamism—is the "best system." Others, pointing out that Denmark scored even higher, conclude that the Danish system—with its Flexicurity or some other attraction—is the best. That way of using the data is absurd. It is a schoolboy error in Statistics 101 to draw inferences from "outliers" rather than from the data as a whole. "Well, yes," one might say, "but it is fair to conclude that the United States does not have one of the best systems!" That too is a methodological error. A country's finishing on

4. The tight relationship between job satisfaction and life satisfaction, also known as total satisfaction, is shown in Bojilov and Phelps, "Job Satisfaction" (2012). In a paper given at a conference some five years earlier, Phelps and Zoega, "Entrepreneurship, Culture and Openness," the authors treat life and job satisfaction as interchangeable.

top in some test may be the effect of some purely *temporary* boost either from an extraneous force or from an unsustainable improvement of its system. When the best tennis player is put up against many contenders, one of them may win the tournament, but we know enough not to infer the winner is the best player. If there are many contenders, the best player may have only a small chance of being the winner. In fact, after all the hoopla over Denmark, the 2002 *International Social Survey Programme* delivered a sharp downgrade to Denmark's job satisfaction. The second wave of WVS data, from 2000 to 2002, shows a similar drop in Sweden.[5]

A common misinterpretation is to suppose that reported job satisfaction mainly reflects the job's pay, not the nonpecuniary satisfactions that household surveys were intended to measure. First, if wages among the countries in the West differ little, we cannot attribute differences in reported job satisfaction to differences in wages. Second, if pay were the main source of reported job satisfaction, one would wonder why the United Kingdom, with very low wages relative to their wealth, reports a pretty decent level of job satisfaction and why Germany, with its fairly high wages relative to wealth, reports a middling level of job satisfaction—like Italy and Austria. Third, what slender association there is between high reported job satisfaction and high income is significantly explained by the tendency of high-income job holders to have attitudes and beliefs conducive to high nonpecuniary satisfactions.

The plausibility of the reported job satisfaction levels receives a big boost from the reported satisfactions from work of particular kinds—pride in one's work and the importance to one of one's job. See Table 8.1. The rankings of countries by these two reported satisfactions, Pride and Importance, are very similar to their ranking by reported job satisfaction. Among the G7, one of the top countries in mean job satisfaction, the United States, scored highest in both Pride and Importance. (It scored above Sweden and tied Denmark in these respects.) The country at the bottom in mean job satisfaction, France, was at the bottom in Pride and Importance. (Perhaps the importance that the Scandinavians place on their jobs, the pride they take in them, and even their job satisfaction owe more to the Lutheran attitude of seriousness and

5. A quite different problem is that, when we ask whether some causal force raises or lowers performance of economies on the whole, the effect in each small country—Finland, Sweden, Luxemburg, Denmark, and Iceland—receives the same weight given to the effect in the entire United States. It might be better to start with a sample in which California, Oregon, Massachusetts, Illinois, and other U.S. states receive the same weight as each of the European countries.

TABLE 8.1 Indicators of Mean Nonmaterial Reward in the G10 + 2

Country	Mean job satisfaction	Pride in your job	Importance to you of your job	Net migration* (%)	Immigrants per 100 persons (%)	Participation rates of males 55–64 (%)	Participation rates of females 55–64 (%)
Canada	7.89	2.70	0.15	2.6	19.5	58.31	36.22
France	6.76	1.74	0.04	1.0	10.6	36.08	27.12
Germany	6.98	1.79	0.11	4.6	12.9	53.92	31.06
Italy	7.26	2.03	0.08	1.4	05.2	46.50	14.07
Japan	7.66	2.20	n.a.	-0.1	01.6	84.83	48.54
United Kingdom	7.42	2.80	0.07	0.4	09.7	62.46	40.76
United States	7.84	2.87	0.17	2.8	13.0	65.99	49.23
Spain	7.02	2.31	0.05	0.0	10.7	55.39	19.78
Holland	7.48	2.16	0.07	1.8	10.6	42.26	18.60
Sweden	7.93	2.63	0.11	2.0	12.3	70.92	63.91
Austria	8.03	2.03	0.18	1.5	14.0	44.71	19.07
Switzerland	8.40	n.a.	n.a.	3.9	22.3	82.56	46.77

Sources: Data are from Inglehart et al., *Human Beliefs and Values* (1997); Stock of Immigrants per Person (2005); United Nations Development Program, *Human Development Report on Mobility* (2009).

Notes: Job satisfaction responses are numbers between 1 and 10 (c033 in the World Values Surveys codes). Responses to "Do you take pride in your job?" (c031) are between 1 and 3. Responses to "Is your job the most important thing in your life?" (c046) are between 0 and 1. The table shows the mean of the responses. These data are from the wave of surveys taken during 1990–1993. n.a, not available.

*Net migration is for 1981–1990 as a percentage of the 1981 population.

the Calvinist significance of work than to a humanist delight in challenge and testing one's ingenuity and one's vision.) So it appears likely that the scores on job satisfaction *are* based on respondents' consideration of various non-pecuniary, or nonmaterial, rewards from work.

A contrarian interpretation argues that a country's low score on reported job satisfaction may be more about how demanding the respondents are than how unstimulating their jobs are. They may suffer low job satisfaction because, as in Italy and France, they are spoiled by their wealth. But America and Canada did not lack for wealth, especially in 2001, coming after the dot.com boom, and they have continued to rank high in job satisfaction. And Figure 8.2 reminds us that when Ireland went from poor to rich in a decade, it remained near the top in job satisfaction. Furthermore, if high levels of reported high job satisfaction are not genuine, one would be left with no explanation of why foreign populations flock to the countries with the highest reported levels—namely, Canada, the United States, and Sweden plus Germany. (Immigration into Germany may be laid in part to its proximity to the outflows of people from Eastern Europe.)

Institutional Causes of the Disparities

Comparative studies in recent decades of various dimensions of economic performance in the economies of Western continental Europe have implicitly assumed that the basic economic system in these nations—a corporatist system that lets big business, big labor, and big government (plus any smaller special interests that can win influence) have a veto over market outcomes—were about as effective as the modern-capitalist system in meeting a variety of goals. What the authors argued was that the European countries tripped up by injecting one or more impediments and hindrances in the market, apparently on the belief that their cost was negligible or modest enough to be worth paying. Some economists hypothesized that EPL helped explain the relatively low economic performance found in several of the 18–22 advanced economies of the West.[6] Some others hypothesized that the high unemployment

6. Lazear, Elmeskov, and Nickell are among the leading investigators into the matter. An interesting paper by Bentolila and Bertola, "Firing Costs and Labour Demand," built a hypothetical model of the representative firm in which theoretically the adverse impact of EPL on the rate of hiring is more than offset by the negative effect on the rate of firing, which pointed to the conclusion that, on balance, EPL reduces unemployment. That analysis, however, overlooked a "systems effect"—that the insiders, entrenched by the job protection, drive employers to raise wages and thus trim jobs throughout the economy.

insurance benefits financed by a payroll tax that are pronounced in some of these countries led to their inferior performance.[7] Other studies suggested that the combination of big unions and big industrial confederations bargaining over wages (and many other things) is significantly damaging.[8] The rate of the value-added tax and the average tax rate on labor income were also suspect—either as a measure of after-tax wage reduction or a measure of the scale of the social insurance benefits that the "social charges" on wages were paying for.[9] Also suspected were the short work week or work year,[10] so beloved on the Continent, and the protectionist interferences with imports.[11] A clever hypothesis was that the drag on the Continental countries was not the corporatism of their economies but the Roman law they stayed with in preference to the Common Law in the Anglo-Saxon countries.[12] The trouble is there is no end to such hypotheses, and many of the supportive findings would likely be spurious—correlations that are just happenstance, not causal. Our interest is in differences in economic dynamism between corporatist and modern-capitalist economies and any resulting effects on job satisfaction, which EPL, unemployment insurance benefits, and value-added tax might have little to do with in the larger scheme of things.

It is a theme of this book that the Continental countries in adopting EPL and the rest were not starting with a system as good as (or better than) the relatively modern-capitalist economies. Differences in the deep institutional structure as well as deep differences in economic culture between the relatively corporatist and the modern-capitalist economies are mainly responsible for the disparity in their dynamism and thus in their job satisfaction: corporatist economies underperform in job satisfaction mainly because they fail to develop fully modern-capitalist institutions and a modern culture that meet the requirements for high economic dynamism. That contrasts sharply

7. Jackman et al. (1991); Phelps and Zoega (2004).

8. See for example the 2001 paper by Nickell, and the 2004 paper by Phelps and Zoega titled "The Search for Routes to Better Economic Performance in Continental Europe: The European Labour Markets." Lars Calmfors argues that the ill-effect of this bargaining, organized in the corporatist way, disappears if a single union represents all the economy's workers, for in that case the union will see any wage increase as costing more jobs than it would if it knew the industry could raise its price relative to other industries so as to pass along the cost increase.

9. Phelps and Zoega (2004).

10. Phelps, "Economic Culture and Economic Performance."

11. Phelps and Zoega, "Entrepreneurship, Culture and Openness" (2009). After discussing job satisfaction as well as life satisfaction, the study focused on life satisfaction.

12. Balas et al. "The Divergence of Legal Procedures."

with the view, implicit in most economic investigations, that some countries, which happen to be corporatist, in injecting EPL, unemployment insurance benefits, high value-added tax, and the rest, threw a monkey wrench into the works of their otherwise perfectly fine economic systems. This latter view, pronounced by academic economists from Chicago to MIT, is a tenet of neo-liberalism, which holds that a country has only to prohibit governments and market actors alike from overturning competitive, or free-market, prices and wages, to have successful economic performance. It is conceivable and maybe plausible that the elimination and avoidance of interferences with competition would be sufficient for satisfactory performance, as a line of economists descending from Adam Smith maintained with qualifications, in an age when performance—even the best-possible performance—was only a matter of productivity and jobs. But in the modern era, those neo-liberal institutions are insufficient. Ever since the modern era finally began planting the ideas that blossomed into the first modern economies—economies with a demonstrated aptitude and capacity for indigenous innovation—a country cannot have *high* economic performance without high economic dynamism. And it cannot have much dynamism without institutions and an economic culture that potentiate conceivers of new commercial ideas, facilitate entrepreneurs to develop these new ideas, allow employees to contract to work long and hard, and protect against fraud financiers willing to invest in or lend to enterprises and consumers (or other end-users) willing to try products found in the market. Many of the institutions performing those functions—a virtual infrastructure of legal rights and procedures—arose in the formation of commercial capitalism over the 17th and 18th centuries, but they helped to support innovation as well.

In this thesis, the *modern* capitalism arriving here and there in the 19th century boasted new institutions aimed expressly at potentiating or facilitating innovation, such as a well-designed system for patents and copyrights, and some other institutions aimed at encouraging participants to bear the heightened uncertainty that attends ventures into the unknown, such as limited liability, protection of creditors and owners in the event a company fails, and protection of the manager against shareowner suits. Similarly, some elements of modern economies' economic culture originated in earlier eras, such as the notion of the good life originating in ancient Greece, while modern morals germinated only at the dawning of Barzun's "modern era." That is the theory. Does it to a degree explain differences in job satisfaction? Differences in dynamism?

A wide-ranging study in 2012 by Gylfi Zoega and the present author explores the parts played by *capitalist institutions* in determining mean job satisfaction in the OECD countries studied.[13] Note first of all that countries differ in the strength and breadth of several categories of institutions. Some legal institutions of the capitalist type appear to be strongly developed in Ireland, Canada, Britain, and America and weakly developed in the others. For example, the Fraser Institute since the mid-1990s has been ranking a large number of countries by their score in a category labeled Legal Structure and Security of Property Rights. (A country's score is the value of an index, or average, of the numerical measures of its institutions under that category.) In 1995, Ireland and Canada ranked 8th and 11th, respectively, and the United Kingdom and the United States were 14th and 15th. On the low side were Belgium in 24th place, France 25th, Spain 26th, and Italy 108th. The highest-ranking nations tended to be northern: Finland 1st, Norway 2nd, Germany 5th, and Holland 6th.[14] But property rights are just one institution that may help account for differences in job satisfaction.

Three categories of financial institutions are at the core of capitalism. One is represented by the capital access index, which is compiled by the Milken Institute from its measures of the "breadth, depth, and vitality of capital markets." Another is the number of companies choosing to list their shares for public trading on an organized stock exchange, expressed as a percentage of the number of firms in the economy. The third is the market value of the shares traded on the exchange, called stock market capitalization, expressed as a percentage of the GDP. The worth of these institutions for innovation might be questioned in view of the problems with so-called corporate governance in recent years. (The next chapter sets out some serious defects of the present-day system.) However, even a highly *imperfect* institution, if it helps both new and established firms to obtain capital through an initial public offering or a flotation of additional stock, may well be superior

13. Phelps and Zoega, "Job Satisfaction: The Effect of Modern-Capitalist and Corporatist Institutions."
14. These data are in Gwartney et al., *Economic Freedom of the World* (country data tables). Another Fraser category bearing on innovation is Freedom to Trade Internationally. (Clearly it is a boost to dynamism if aspiring innovators can expect adoption overseas, not just at home.) Here, Ireland ranked 4th, Britain 10th, America 18th, and Canada 31st, while Spain ranked 19th, Italy 24th, and France 32nd. Here, though, Belgium ranked 5th and Germany 9th. (The Nordics do not stand out here.) So the Continentals do not score badly at all in the institutions affecting foreign trade. But America is large enough to trade mostly with itself, so it suffers less from its failings in the free trade department than would a small country.

to a system without public capital markets. New companies, being small at first, have some key advantages in developing radical new ideas; while ever-small companies, generally family owned, that are able to hang on by reinvesting their profits or by borrowing and then seeking bankruptcy protection are holding on to resources that could have been used in innovative enterprises. So what do the data show? The statistical study in the aforementioned working paper by Phelps and Zoega finds that underdevelopment (or atrophy) in these two time-honored capitalist institutions—access to capital and public stock exchanges—help explain deficiencies in job satisfaction. A society benefits from a Jeffersonian freedom to *start* small companies, but it also benefits from institutions enabling them to *grow* to larger ones.

Are differences in the spread or well-functioning of *modern* institutions, such as those at the birth of *modern* capitalism, not also significant in accounting for differences in job satisfaction? Yes, of course, though the measurement of many of those institutions—the measure of a well-designed patent law, for example—is somewhat challenging. Since generally speaking, radically new ideas are best developed in new firms, the dismantling of feudal and mercantile barriers to the entry of new firms and the formation of new industries, which America accomplished when it gained independence from the tight rein of King George III, is one of the key institutional steps for the functioning of modern capitalism. In concept, then, institutions that remove red tape, if we had measures of such institutions, would help to explain high job satisfaction in modern-capitalist economies. But the granularity and idiosyncratic nature of many institutions in this area make it hard to represent them with numerical measures. So a couple of telling anecdotes might not be out of place: the founder of eBay, the Frenchman Pierre Omidyar, told an audience at Aix-en-Provence in 2005 that he would not have been able to found eBay in France, but he did not articulate why; perhaps he could not easily do it. Another prominent entrepreneur told Britain's Prime Minister David Cameron recently that he could not have started his business there owing to Britain's lack of some key institutions.

An institution that is basic to the operation of modern capitalism is company law: bankruptcy protection of companies from creditors, protection of companies from self-dealing by managers, protection of companies from employees who do not perform, limits on what companies may ask employees to do, and so forth—a concept articulated to a degree by Heritage under the rubric of business freedom. Under the proto-capitalism of pre-modern times, a landowner might contract labor to harvest the crop.

Under modern capitalism, companies and individuals come together, each party investing time or money in the relationship, without being able to foresee the tasks, some of them emergencies, which may arise in the future. It is impossible for an employee and employer to write a contract that would take account of all possible contingencies. Law is needed to set limits on the resolution of conflicts when the contract does not cover the state that the company is in. Without such legal support, an entrepreneur or an investor might hesitate to embark on the creation of an untried product if it would be problematic to hire or fire as necessitated by unforeseeable developments, or to replace an ineffective manager with a better one. Creation does not always cause destruction, but destruction-prevention makes it harder to obtain resources for creation.

Finally, the *economic policy* in a country is an institution that may significantly induce or thwart entrepreneurship aimed at innovation. Relying on scant data and an overly specific theory, Conservatives leap to the conclusion that every element of economic policy providing a role for the government has a cost exceeding the benefit—with few exceptions. But while there may have been a presumption that this or that intervention by the state in the activities of the business sector—more corn or less cloth—would be harmful in the pastoral economies of mercantile capitalism, there is no presumption that, say, more money for education or less money for education would disturb innovation from its optimum equilibrium—or disturb innovation at all. We do not know whether this or that concrete governmental activity would be constructive or detrimental for the dynamism of the economy and thus for job satisfaction. Yet research on such a question is often possible and may turn up results that force rethinking. For example, the evidence of the working paper cited above does not corroborate the supposition that subsidies to low-income workers, such as America's Earned Income Tax Credits, intended to draw the disadvantaged into employment and greater self-support reduce job satisfaction. It could be that integrating marginalized people into the business world has served to enlist the creativity of a whole section of society whose talents would not otherwise have had an outlet.

The welfare state offers another example. The same working paper by Phelps and Zoega finds that countries with high levels of state spending for social insurance, that is, medical care, and retirement benefits, let alone education, do not tend to have depressed levels of job satisfaction, though that finding may be driven by the data from some very peculiar nations, such as

Norway, with its oil, and Austria, with its waltzes.[15] Jean-Baptiste Say, the great French economist of the late 18th and early 19th century, identified a problem with big government in his 1803 treatise *Traité d'économie politique*. To paraphrase Say:

> Where the government's purchases are spread thick over the whole economy, the thoughts of entrepreneurs, which would have been occupied with a better method or a better product that caused incomes to grow, inevitably turn to how to exercise influence in order to beat out competitors for the government's new contract. So a high level of government consumption costs an economy some of its dynamism and thus, in turn, some job satisfaction.

In contrast, the working paper does not find that all that corporatist intervention for the "protection" of employees and industries *raises* job satisfaction either. The corporatist belief that core elements of human fulfillment would be lifted by making people more secure appears to be an illusion.

Regulatory institutions appear to be a significant depressant on job satisfaction, particularly credit market regulations (such as interest rate controls) and goods market regulations. The institutions of collective bargaining and regulations on hiring and firing are also estimated to depress mean job satisfaction. *Some* corporatist institutions, such as a willingness to run large export surpluses to finance interest and dividend payments to foreign creditors and investors, may have helped these nations attract foreign investment and transfer foreign technologies and foreign capital. However, if the evidence does not mislead, corporatist institutions nevertheless led to reduced job satisfaction.

Cultural Causes of the Disparities

An economy, it will be recalled, consists of an economic culture as well as a set of institutions; and that is especially true of a modern economy. (Schumpeter says in his 1942 book *Capitalism, Socialism and Democracy* that a capitalist economy is essentially a culture, but he meant that it develops habits and standards.) The hypothesis here is that a basic element of the culture, namely

---

15. It is interesting and not hugely surprising that there is no such baleful effect of government investment expenditure. Perhaps capital projects, from the federal highways to NASA and NIH, raise the job satisfaction of the engineers, technicians, and scientists engaged in them—just as innovation and investment in the private sector lift the satisfaction of the people participating in them.

prevailing attitudes and beliefs, has consequences for one's efforts at work and for the effectiveness with which one can collaborate with others; in both ways, one's job satisfaction is affected. These attitudes and beliefs are often called values. (The economic culture also includes attitudes such as those developed in companies, so that we often speak of the company culture at outstanding firms like Google.)

What values spark economies capable of offering high satisfaction with economic life? We will draw on the data gathered on attitudes, norms, and beliefs by anthropologists, ethnologists, and sociologists to see whether inter-country differences in the prevalence or intensity of these cultural values help account for inter-country differences in job satisfaction. (The analysis leaves aside the question of whether the influence of values held by employees, managers, and customers on satisfaction are indirect, in that they lead to a change of institutions, or direct, in that no change in institutions results unless the institutions adjust accordingly.)

The mention of economic culture brings immediately to the mind of many social scientists the characteristic called *trust*. It would seem that, very generally, a society works better if people are brought up to be law-abiding and respectful. The idea burst forth around 1970 with *The Gift Relationship* by the sociologist Richard Titmuss and, slightly later, *The Possibility of Altruism* by the philosopher Thomas Nagel. The issues were aired in a conference and ensuing volume organized by the present author.[16] But trust is left aside in the argument at hand for two reasons. One is that it might seem rather confusing to mix altruism with culture for the same reason that we keep morality separate from ethics. (Morality is about what ought to be done universally for the common good—such as, be altruistic—and ethics is about what an individual person is wise to do for her own good.)

---

16. Phelps, *Altruism, Morality and Economic Theory* (1975). At a 1974 meeting of the Law and Economics Seminar at the University of Chicago I set out the reasoning behind the belief of those at the conference that a dose of altruism contributes to an economy's efficiency. (I had not begun to think about economic dynamism at that time.) George Stigler, the lion of the seminar, demanded an example. I replied that people will be more willing to pay their full income tax if they are glad to make a small contribution to the work of the government or if they feel that other income earners will be paying their full tax too. Gary Becker, then a flaming neoclassical, said, "We'll give you that one but can you give us one more?" I suggested that people would be afraid to venture out into the street or use a car if they were not confident that others want to obey the traffic laws in order not to do harm. Professor Stigler rejected that, arguing that people observe the traffic laws only to avoid their own inconvenience. Warming to his theme, he said, "People don't want to have to stop to peel off the flesh on the windshield."

The recent literature on the effects of economic culture appears to have put altruism aside. The more powerful reason trust is omitted here is that there is no clear presumption that economic dynamism would be helped (or would be hindered) by more altruism, and, even if there were, there is no strong presumption that altruism is the preserve of modern-capitalist nations and not corporatist ones (or vice versa). So altruism is best left aside in this study.

The French businessman Philippe Bourguignon, whose working life has been divided about evenly between America and Europe, has portrayed the two regions as having quite distinct cultures.[17] In his analysis, the differences originate in the very different upbringings of children. French mothers, he observed, watch their children closely in the playground; they are attentive and warn them to be careful. American mothers, on the other hand, pay little attention and do not teach caution. As a result, Americans grow up taking failures in stride and moving on, so they are relatively undaunted by high rates of failure.

Another observer found a deep divide between the vocabulary of values on which business life is viewed in continental Western Europe and the normative concepts deployed in America, Canada, Britain, and Ireland. Investigative reporting by the journalist Stefan Theil found that France and Germany view private enterprise and market outcomes through radically different ethical lenses:

> The three-volume history book used in French high schools, *Histoire du XXe siècle*, . . . describes capitalism at various points in the text as "brutal" and "savage." "Start-ups," it tells its students, are "audacious enterprises" with "ill-defined prospects." German high schools . . . teach a similar narrative with the focus on instilling the corporatist and collectivist traditions. Nearly all teach through the lens of workplace conflict between . . . capital and labor, employer and employee, boss and worker. . . . Bosses and company owners show up in caricatures and illustrations as idle, cigar-smoking plutocrats, sometimes linked to child labor, Internet fraud, cell-phone addiction, alcoholism and undeserved layoffs. One might expect Europeans to view

17. Bourguignon, "Deux éducations, deux cultures." The notion of "two cultures" will remind many readers of a famous lecture *Two Cultures* by C. P. Snow, who as a novelist and a scientist deplored that artists are ignorant of science and its remarkable culture. He could have added in the spirit of Bourguignon that the culture of scientists, like the culture of innovators, accepts failure: it is an integral part of the game. A game in which there was a certainty of success would be incredibly boring. It is true, though, that the scientific research and the entrepreneurial development we do tends to express who we are, so it hurts to fail.

the world through a slightly left-of-center, social-democratic lens. The surprise is the intensity and depth of the bias being taught in Europe's schools.[18] Theil's investigation suggests that the lenses through which people look at their world are quite different from country to country—more different than the worlds being viewed are. It also suggests that such differences result from some marked differences in the values that people have or in the way they rank some shared values, such as safety and security, invoked by Bourguignon.

The WVS, which this book has drawn on previously, produce large sets of survey data on values around the world. These surveys show that the prevalence of almost every value—precept or attitude or worldview—differs considerably from country to country. Statistical analysis of the individual responses to questions about values shows that little of the inter-country differences can be ascribed to the chance variations that result from the random sampling of individuals possessing a degree of uniqueness; the inter-differences far exceed what might be forecast from the observed differences. As could be expected, some values in these surveys are markedly stronger in the relatively modern-capitalist economies than in the corporatist economies, some other values markedly stronger in the corporatist countries.

It is a central proposition of this book's thesis that several values play a part in a country's generation of high economic performance—a proposition that, up to now, has been a hypothesis in search of confirmation. Some of these values affect the capacity and desire to conceive novel ideas, to develop these ideas into new products, and to try out the new products. Other values may affect economic conditions that support or damage the commercial prospects for innovation. In these ways, many values in the West—whether associated with modern capitalism or with corporatism—can be presumed to affect job satisfaction. They could affect job satisfaction through their *direct* effects on the stimuli and challenges of the workplace or through *indirect* effects by opening possibilities for new institutions that served to make the economy more challenging and rewarding. The moment has come to confront this hypothesis with the available survey data.

A research program at Columbia's Center on Capitalism and Society has been testing the influence on economic performance—ultimately, the effect on job satisfaction—of the West's culture of problem-solving, curiosity, experiment, exploration, and novelty and change. The first results were announced in a paper given at the 2006 conference in Venice on what ails

18. Theil, "Europe's Philosophy of Failure."

the Continental economies.[19] The paper injected the values of the economic culture into the discourse. It selected nine workplace attitudes from WVS to study their possible effects on economic performance. Several of these values were significantly associated with high economic performance in one or more dimensions. How the survey respondents in a country valued the "interestingness of a job" (c020 in the WVS classification) was significantly related to how well the country scored in several dimensions of economic performance. The acceptance of new ideas (e046) was also a good predictor of performance. The desire to have some initiative (c016) was also a good sign. A low willingness to follow (c061)—to take orders, which is conspicuous in some European nations—exacts a significant toll on a country's economic performance. A readiness to accept change (e047) and a willingness to accept competition (e039) are quite helpful. A desire to achieve (c018) matters little: it is the experience—the life—that people want, not some object.

It appears that the hypothesized influence of the various cultural elements is borne out rather generally. It appears also that the WVS values that are so successful are modern-capitalist values; they are values in which the countries suspected of being corporatist—France, Italy, Holland, Belgium, and so forth—are lacking relative to the usual comparators—America, Canada, and Britain—and small seafaring nations, such as Denmark, Ireland, and Iceland. But the paper did not test for effects on the performance indicator that is the focus of the present chapter: job satisfaction. It would be feasible to return to those data to check that the attitudes found to affect significantly the time-honored measures of economic performance—labor force participation, relative productivity, and unemployment—also significantly affect job satisfaction. There is no doubt about the results, though. And a more structured approach is more interesting.

The history told in this book suggests another way to test the importance of economic culture for job satisfaction (and, more widely, for economic satisfaction in general). The history speaks of the modern ethic—a desire for self-expression through the exercise of imagination and creativity—and the modern morality—the right of individuals to pursue this search unchained from traditionalism: obligations to family, community, country, and religion. The history of the world, Part Two, is all about this seesaw battle between modernism and

---

19. Phelps, "Economic Culture and Economic Performance," given at the Center's 2006 conference and republished in the 2011 volume *Perspectives on Performance of the Continental Economies.*

traditionalism—the great, endless struggle in the West from the early 1800s to the present. Where modernism gained the upper hand, traditionalism losing ground, a modern economy developed and society flowered, as in Britain and America. Although France, with its fraternity and equality, differed somewhat, as did Germany, where traditionalism (and socialism) remained a force, these nations also fashioned relatively modern economies. But with the revivals of traditionalism over much of Europe in the 1900s, national economies there drew back from the modern end of the spectrum.

If that is a fair history, we should expect to find a more impressive flowering and very likely a wider one, thus a higher level of mean job satisfaction, in a society where the cultural values of modernism are strong. And although elements of traditionalism might have their uses, we should not be surprised if job satisfaction is also higher where the values of traditionalism are weak.

A 2012 working paper by Raicho Bojilov and the present author tests whether modernist values in a country contribute to mean job satisfaction. It measures in each nation under study the attachment to some values found in the WVS that are a sign of a modernist culture or a lack of it.[20] The measures were calculated from the responses to the following yes-or-no questions: Do you think that it is fair to pay more to the more productive workers? (c059). Do you think that the management of firms should be under the control of their owners? (c060). Do you agree that competition is good? (e039). It also asks questions that call for a response on a scale from 1 to 10: Should one be cautious about major changes in life? (e045). Are you worried about new ideas? Do you believe ideas that have stood the test of time are generally better or may new ideas be worth developing and testing? (e046). Do you worry about difficulties that change may present or do you welcome whatever possibilities something new may present? (e047). By quantifying the responses in a country to these questions, we calculate the mean strength of that value in the country. By taking an average of these six quantitative measures, we obtain an index of modernism.

An index of traditionalism is constructed in a somewhat similar way. Survey questions were selected that would presumably pick up a strong concern for obligations to family and community, a concern strong enough that economic developments that would draw children away from the family or the community would not be well received. Some traditional values are captured by four of the WVS questions: Do you feel that service to others is important in life? (a007). Do you think that children should have respect and love for

20. Bojilov and Phelps, "Job Satisfaction: The Effects of Two Economic Cultures" (2012).

Mean job satisfaction

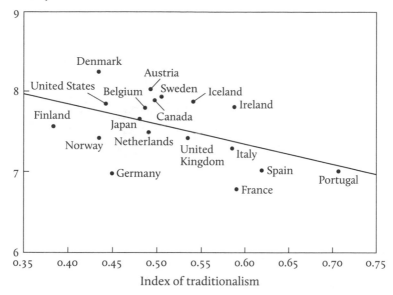

FIGURE 8.4 Traditionalism and job satisfaction, 1991.

their parents? (a025). Do you think that parents have responsibilities to their children? (a026). Do you agree that unselfishness is an important quality for your children to have? (a041). It is not being suggested here that it's a terrific aid to innovation to have economic actors who are monsters toward their parents or neighbors, only that innovation could be suffocated by a fixation on family and community to the exclusion of the individual.

What are the results? It might be thought that the traditional values are a precious glue holding society together and thus indirectly raising job satisfaction and other rewards from participation in the economy. It might also be thought that a little bit of modernism goes a long way; that important amounts of modernism weaken coordination, causing angst and a loss of the deep job satisfaction known to craftsmen in olden times. Continental politicians pay tribute to these cherished beliefs in every speech. The findings from the study, however, strongly suggest that neither one of these prejudices is true.

The results are shown in graphic terms in Figures 8.4 and 8.5, which draw on the indexes of modernism and traditionalism tabulated in Table 8.2. In the first of these figures, traditionalism appears to be an impediment to high job satisfaction. There are three countries, Finland, Denmark, and America,

Mean job satisfaction

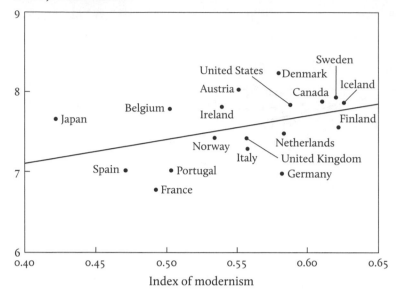

FIGURE 8.5 Modernism and job satisfaction, 1991.

that score conspicuously low in traditionalism and quite high in mean job satisfaction—countries often cited for their high dynamism too. And there are three countries, Portugal, Spain, and France, that score conspicuously high in traditionalism and very low in mean job satisfaction. Furthermore, the (negative) statistical correlation in the sample as a whole is highly significant. Sweden, Canada, Ireland, and Denmark have higher satisfaction than their modest or low traditionalism explains, but they have something that most of the others do not—as the next figure shows.

Figure 8.5 shows that modernism gives a strong boost to the level of job satisfaction. The countries scoring high on modernism scored high on job satisfaction. The nations with the most modern cultures—Iceland, Finland, Sweden, Canada, and America—did very well in job satisfaction. (In 2001, though, Sweden's job satisfaction fell considerably.)

The two figures together show that Italy's mediocre satisfaction is well explained by its high traditionalism, which its above-average modernism could not offset. France's low satisfaction is explained by the above-average traditionalism and below-average modernism. Germany's depressed workers and Austria's delighted ones are a puzzle. Evidently, values are not everything.

TABLE 8.2 Indexes of Modernism and Traditionalism

Country/region	Index of modernism	Index of traditionalism
Austria	0.55	0.49
Belgium	0.50	0.49
Canada	0.61	0.50
Denmark	0.58	0.44
Finland	0.62	0.38
France	0.49	0.59
Germany	0.58	0.45
Iceland	0.63	0.54
Ireland	0.54	0.59
Italy	0.56	0.58
Japan	0.42	0.48
Netherlands	0.58	0.49
Norway	0.53	0.44
Portugal	0.50	0.71
Spain	0.47	0.62
Sweden	0.62	0.51
United Kingdom	0.56	0.54
United States	0.59	0.44
Average	0.58	0.51

It may be surprising that so many countries ranked higher in modernism than America did in the last available measurement—the country that most embodied it in the 19th century and much of the 20th. Could something have happened over time? Significant changes in a country's culture are rare in 10 years' time, as we saw in Figure 8.2, but not so rare in the space of several decades. Whether the American economy has suffered a loss of dynamism in recent decades and whether, behind that, is a decline of modernism or a rise of traditionalism are questions for the next chapter.

PART THREE

DECAY AND REFOUNDING

How Some Dynamism Has Been Lost and
Why It Is Right to Try to Regain It

It is only in the shadows when some fresh wave, truly original, truly creative, breaks upon the shore, that there will be a rediscovery of the West.

JACQUES BARZUN

CHAPTER NINE

Markers of Post-1960s Decline

I called Silberman collect one morning . . . crazed on acid. . . . So
what came up was this "Death of the American Dream" thing, and I
thought, well, the best way to do that is to take a look at politics.

HUNTER S. THOMPSON, *Songs of the Doomed*

T HE AMERICAN ECONOMY IS NOW QUITE DIFFERENT from the modern economy that was so scintillating over most of the 19th and 20th centuries.
The central dimensions of performance—job satisfaction, unemployment,
and relative productivity—make this very clear. Data show deterioration setting in on all three fronts as early as the mid-1970s, with only a temporary
uptick in job satisfaction in the last giddy years of the internet boom. A similar deterioration came sooner or later to the rest of the West: to Germany
in the 1980s and to both Italy and France in the late 1990s. These nations, so
lacking in indigenous innovation, could not prosper any longer on the back
of the American economy when it was similarly lacking.

The secular deterioration of the American economy was at first a mystery. The torrent of women and young people entering the labor force from
the late 1960s to the late 1980s caused some rise of unemployment and somewhat reduced wages, but the effects of such demographic shocks on productivity growth were surely transient. That the deterioration has been lasting
suggests that the economy was undergoing a shift of its tectonic plates—a
systemic, qualitative change.

Early Data on Diminished Performance

Although evidence of a serious slowdown of productivity in the American
economy became unmistakable by the early 1970s, it had actually begun several years earlier, only to be masked by booming employment. In the fall of
1962, John F. Kennedy campaigned for the presidency with the slogan "Get

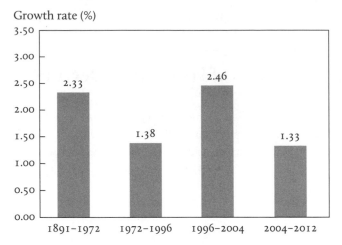

Growth rate (%)

FIGURE 9.1 Average growth rates of U.S. labor productivity over selected intervals, 1891–2012. (Source: Robert J. Gordon.)

America Moving Again." Ironically, present-day data show that a discernible slowdown of productivity began around 1964 and gained force—off and on—until the mid-1970s. Productivity growth remained very slow until 1993, and after recovering nicely during the build-out of the internet, fell back to the snail's pace set in the 1970s.

The anatomy of the productivity slowdown helps us understand it. There are two types of productivity. The more familiar is the relation between output and hours worked, called labor productivity. The growth rate of labor productivity is charted in Figure 9.1.[1] For a great many decades, the growth rate of labor productivity averaged 2.33 percent per year until 1972. Since then it has averaged 1.57 percent. For a time, it could have been supposed that the rapid growth of hours worked from the early 1970s to the early 1980s had brought diminishing returns to labor. However, the underlying slowdown was marked by an even greater reduction of the growth rate of output *per unit of capital*, which could hardly be laid to larger labor inputs. We may as well cut to an amalgamated measure of the two: the growth rate of so-called total factor productivity or multifactor productivity, as previously defined in

1. The calculations in Figure 9.1, based on standard data from the U.S. Commerce Department, and the very effective organization of the chart were set out by Robert J. Gordon. Figure 9.1 is Figure 4 in Gordon, "Is U.S. Economic Growth Over?" (p. 13). He kindly provided to me for use here the further calculations, based on the same data set, shown in Figure 9.2.

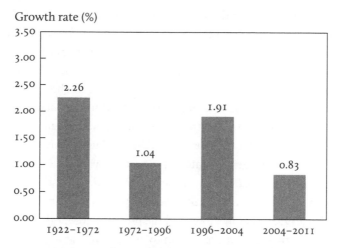

Growth rate (%)

FIGURE 9.2 Average growth rate of multifactor productivity over selected intervals, 1922–2011. (Source: Robert J. Gordon.)

Chapter 7: roughly output per basket of capital and labor inputs. The growth rate of productivity is charted in Figure 9.2. The data show the growth rate of total factor productivity to have run around 2.26 percent before 1972 and then around 1.17 percent after 1972. The slowdown of total factor productivity is more severe. As Figures 9.1 and 9.2 suggest, the slowdown was put in doubt by the productivity speedup during the years of the build-out of the internet, but since then the growth rate has been even worse than before the internet years.

By 1973, when the fall of the growth rates was already pronounced (and on its way to becoming even more so), a towering rise of the unemployment rate began—from lows of 3.4 percent over much of 1968 and 1969 to a high-water mark of 9.0 reached in May 1975. The rate averaged 6.6 percent in 1972–1981 after two decades when the average was 4.6 and the non-war years from 1900 to 1929 when it was 4.95. The urban unrest in this period was extraordinary. Sharp rises in oil prices in 1973 and 1979 added fuel to the fire, but they proved transitory (in inflation-adjusted terms). In the next three decades the unemployment rate averaged 6.3 percent: 7.0 in 1982–1991, 5.4 in 1992–2001, and 6.5 in 2002–2011. The increases in unemployment in European nations during this era were comparable. Throughout the West, heightened joblessness was as emblematic of the era as slower growth of productivity.

Are the fall in growth and the rise of unemployment cause and effect? Two decades of observing a variety of economies, some still quite modern and some no longer modern if they ever were, suggest a systematic connection from the slowdown to the joblessness. Starting from levels *below* the American level, the unemployment rate in the United Kingdom climbed above the American level in the early 1980s; the rate in France climbed further above the American level later in the 1980s; and the rate in Germany climbed further still by the mid-1990s, as *The OECD Jobs Study* (OECD 1994) records. Correspondingly, the decline in the growth rate of productivity was greater in the United Kingdom than in America, still greater in France, and greatest in Germany. So slower growth was systematically followed by increased unemployment, a fact uncovered in a 1997 paper by Hoon and the present author.[2] (It was so clear in the minds of journalists that they began to use "growth" as a *synonym* for high employment. It took the "jobless recovery" of 2010–2011 to break the habit.) It is noteworthy that the growth connection was very tight despite the fact that the slower growth in Europe had origins different from those in the United States. Still, the 1930s saw blistering productivity growth in America alongside a depression of employment—the Great Depression. (And economists remind us that high innovation is liable to create some frictional unemployment.) But that mass unemployment cannot plausibly be laid to rapid productivity growth; other monetary and nonmonetary forces pushed up unemployment. Unemployment might have been worse without that productivity growth—without men laying electric cable across the land.

Three mechanisms connect employment to the rate of innovation. One of these is direct. A firm raises prices and lowers employment if it expects a reduced threat of new products or new methods to come from new or old competitors.

The second mechanism connects a firm's employment to its own innovation prospects. If it expects its productivity to be growing at a reduced rate, it will place a reduced value on each additional employee it hires. (The fall in the growth rate is like a rise in the interest rate.) That will lead the firm to cut back its hiring.

The third mechanism works through wages and wealth. The simplest setting is an economy in which output is produced by labor without any physical capital; its capital is the investment companies have made in transforming new recruits into production-ready employees, as in the Hoon and

---

2. A simple analysis measured a nation's slowdown by the decrease of the growth rate from 1950–1970 to 1970–1990. See Hoon and Phelps, "Growth, Wealth and the Natural Rate" (1997).

Phelps paper. Here an increase in the productivity of labor would raise labor demand—that is, it would raise the wage that employers are willing to pay a given work force—and that, taken alone, would pull up employment and the going market wage. What if, after a long period without any change, the technology is suddenly *improving*, so that output per man is suddenly on a rising trend? The *wage* will then likewise start rising, and employment will be pulled up at least for a while. But how far? What matters for employment is the wage relative to *wealth*—the value of households' shareholdings. As levels of productivity and hence income go higher, saving per year will be correspondingly higher, so wealth will be rising. And the increase in household wealth will contract labor supply: it raises the wage required by workers so that it pulls employment down and pushes the wage up. Yet wealth is *not* going to grow large enough to bring employment back down as long as wealth has not caught up with the wage. And if productivity and the wage go on increasing steadily, wealth will never catch up to wage. (There is a phase, then, in which wealth, while rising, will be falling relative to the wage; that phase ends when the wage-wealth ratio is so elevated that wealth, though reduced as a ratio to the wage, is at last growing at the same rate as the wage.)[3]

Hence, a *decline* in productivity *growth* in the American economy and in some others can be seen as having two *deleterious* effects on employment and unemployment. First, when the pace of productivity growth slowed, saving did not drop, so wealth did not slow at first: as a result, the *ratio* of wage to wealth, which had reached a postwar high of .38 by 1968, fell over the 1970s to .32 in 1980 and to .29 by 1990. Disgruntled with their wages, many demanded higher wages—else they would retire or look elsewhere. (The corresponding swelling

3. This argument is along the lines of Hoon and Phelps, "Growth, Wealth and the Natural Rate." Households will be enjoying rising profits alongside the rising wage, but that does not alter the conclusion: saving does not jump, so wealth falls behind the wage. The implications are clouded if households extrapolate the observed income growth into the future: Then consumption would jump, saving would drop, and the drag on wealth adds to the rise of the wage-wealth ratio. Yet the sense of future riches—of increased "expected wealth"—operates, considered by itself, to boost "expected wealth" and thereby to encourage increased consumption and decreased work. However, the analysis in the text could still carry the day.

Once the argument is broadened to economies using physical capital for production as well as labor, real complications arise. Declining labor requirements and declining capital requirements have different results. Falling labor requirements in producing capital goods would exert a downward push on the relative price of the capital goods, which would reduce the wage that these industries would be able to pay but also reduce the wage that households would require. Falling capital requirements in producing consumer goods would raise relative prices received in capital goods industries, thus boosting the real wage in the latter labor-intensive industries while also raising wealth.

of the wealth-to-wage ratio boosted consumption relative to income as well as wage demands: consumption rose from about 62 percent as a percentage of domestic output in 1970 to about 69 percent in 2001.) See Figures 10.2a,b. Second, as the lowered expectations for growth of profitability lowered valuations of business assets—employees and customers included—share prices turned down sharply in 1968; as poor results reinforced the lowered expectations, shares did not level off until 1974. Reduced employment resulted. Workers in consumer goods industries, finding themselves devalued as a business investment by employers, would have had to accept a much reduced real wage to salvage their jobs, and many of these workers would not have accepted lower real wages, since their real wealth had largely held up or had not so dramatically fallen. Similarly, workers in capital goods industries, finding that the market value of their output was depressed, would have had to accept a steep real wage cut if they were to hold on to their jobs. Yet some degree of gradual recovery is normal as wealth falls, though a full recovery of wages and employment from a such structural shift cannot be expected.[4] Share prices ultimately regained their 1968 level in 1992. But the opportunities of the labor required to produce additions to the capital stock had improved by 1992—thus the opportunity cost of labor in producing capital goods was greater by then—and 1992 workers had much greater wealth than they had in 1968, so many had to be paid more to stay on.

Does all this imply the paradox that saving is bad? No. Acts of saving are necessary to finance investing and projects aimed at innovation. Current stocks of capital and hard-won knowledge are proud monuments to people's savings. Yet this wealth makes additional investing and innovating harder by reducing people's need to save and work in the future. Normally, productivity

4. In some conventional representations of the economy, all products are produced with the same method or recipe, capital goods and consumer goods alike. A fall in the valuations put on capital goods—plant and equipment—in some use does not cause *total employment* or the real wage to be depressed in the *long run*: The idled quantities of capital and labor finally regain their use and regain their rental and wages in parts of the sector where relative prices did not dip. But in fact consumer goods production is, generally speaking, relatively capital intensive, unlike capital goods, not to mention the capital firms have invested in employees. In *two-sector* economies, for example, the relative, or real, prices might fall over a great range of the capital goods sector, owing to a slowdown of the productivity in the consumer goods sector or a slowdown (or possibly a speedup) of the productivity of labor in the capital goods sector. Then workers in the capital goods sector will face the problem that most of the consumer goods producing sector is relatively capital intensive, much of it dramatically so—as Hitchcock impressively illustrated in *North by Northwest,* where on the vast cornfield there is no labor in sight, only the Cary Grant character looking out of place. So labor can find work only at a wage so reduced that some workers with high wealth levels may not accept it. In Phelps, *Structural Slumps* (1994), this model, the customer market model, and the trained-employee model offer escapes from the conventional model.

growth brought by saving helps an economy to "grow out" of the wealth that saving brings. But when innovation is nil or weak, saving brings less and less productivity growth, so the economy cannot go on growing out of the wealth that saving has brought.[5] The cause of the slump and the accompanying malaise, then, was the sustained and still prevailing slowdown of total factor productivity—known also as multi-factor productivity. And this slowdown can only be laid to a contraction of indigenous innovation, since grassroots innovation—not scientific advance—was the main source of innovation in America from the 1830s to the 1960s.

A concomitant effect of the decline of innovation was a reversal of the gains in *inclusion* that innovation had brought. When prosperity comes to a region, it is the marginal workers and the marginal properties that see the largest gains—even going from a zero level to a positive level. Likewise, depression visits the worst damage in percentage terms on the marginalized in society—not the advantaged or the wealthy. This development was to become an increasing part of the discussion in subsequent years.

In summary, investment activity of all kinds—investing in new machines, new employees, and the like—and the innovation that underpins investment provide the force essential for high employment as well as growth of labor productivity. The waning of innovation was largely behind the increased joblessness and downward pressure on wages that have been endemic to the post-1972 period.

Policy reactions and other feedback. The policy reactions to the decline of growth and the rise of unemployment—and the subsequent failure of

---

5. The question of which did the worst damage, the slowdown of labor productivity or the rare fall of capital productivity, would be difficult to answer. Some observers have made that discussion all the more difficult in claiming that there was a speed-up of innovation in new information and communication technologies (ICT), which *raised* labor productivity in making transistors, semiconductor chips, and other capital goods used in making consumer goods; and this productivity increase pulled up real wages and thus employment. Of course, no employment boom is apparent in the aggregate data. Yet such a spurt of labor's physical productivity in producing capital may very well have occurred. However, a speed-up in the productivity of labor in making capital goods, if it occurred, might *not* have been a force in the direction of raising "total output" and real wages at all: productivity advances in the production of semiconductor chips and other capital goods could have driven down the prices of the capital goods produced by enough to be a force for lower real wages and employment. So productivity gains in capital goods industries may have contributed to the *reduction* of real wages and increase in unemployment (relative to trend)! But aggregate technical progress almost stopped between 1968 and 1978, so it would be odd to blame such progress for the slumping economy. (A related paper that explores some of these insights in its beginning pages is Hoon and Phelps, "Effects of Technological Improvement in the ICT-Producing Sector on Business Activity.")

those policies—are a major part of ensuing events. It was apparent by the 1980s that productivity growth was still slow, with no hint of when, if at all, fast growth would resume. Businessmen stopped banking on the fast productivity growth of previous times. (An employee today would not be a super-employee in the future.) Economists and politicians understood that to engineer a sustained lift of total factor productivity growth by as much as it had fallen would require moving mountains, but no one knew which ones to move. However, they could consider steps that would offer prospects of symptomatic relief: medicine for swollen unemployment and for the disproportionate privations among the less advantaged.

In 1981, Ronald Reagan, just elected president and keen on the prescriptions of supply-side economics, wanted cuts in income tax rates across the board, believing they would boost employment by raising people's incentives to join the labor force and to work hard in hope of better pay. He also proposed tax credits to business for their investment outlays. (More investment in plants and equipment, while not raising total factor productivity, would increase growth of output per unit of labor.) In those times, fiscal responsibility in the Congress was not as elastic as it had become by the 2000s. Kennedy's tax cut bill had been enacted by the grieving Congress after his assassination. Rather similarly, Reagan won passage of the tax cut bill after he was shot in an assassination attempt. (Tax loopholes were closed with the hope of bringing in nearly as much revenue as the rate cuts would lose—thus achieving so-called tax neutrality.) With the Reagan cuts, the unemployment rate rose some more, peaking at 10.4 percent in 1982, before falling to 5.4 at the end of 1989.

In 1989, George H. W. Bush, just elected and suspicious of supply-side economics—he once called it "voodoo economics"—wanted to address the lingering fiscal deficits. When in 1990 Democrats refused to agree to expenditure cuts, the Congress voted and Bush signed into law a 1990s bill increasing tax rates. The unemployment rate began rising in mid-year, reaching 7.5 in 1992, then shrank to 6.1 in 1994. When in 1993 Bill Clinton took office, thinking changed: his advisers argued that budgetary *surpluses* would create more jobs within a few years than they would destroy in the meantime. In any case, the second half of the 1990s saw the internet revolution and the dot.com boom. Then, in 2001, with joblessness heading up again, the newly elected George W. Bush, subscribing to the supply-side model, pushed through income tax cuts in 2002, then the invasion of Iraq and the expansions of entitlements in 2003, and finally measures to heat up the housing boom. Yet the boom did not last, and unemployment grew higher than before. (That massive numbers of baby boomers were absorbed into the economy—upping the employment-population ratio from 58 percent to 60 in the 1970s, 60 to 63 in the 1980s, and almost 64 in the 1990s—is evidence of effective labor market institutions.)[6]

Evidently, even in those years of initially low public debt, Keynesian stimulants to consumer demand and supply-sider fillips to the supply of labor could not push back the tide of slow growth and enlarged unemployment. This is not to say that every effort was futile, only that the action taken could bring temporary relief but little lasting benefit—and less benefit over cost, if any.

Fallout: Inclusion, Inequality, Job Satisfaction

A setback of another kind started toward the end of the 1970s and grew until the early 1990s: a decline of economic inclusion. This "inclusion" generally refers to the relative unemployment rates and the relative wages among the disadvantaged. A rule of thumb has long been that the unemployment rate of disadvantaged groups is nearly twice that of the rest. A setback in relative unemployment rates was not evident over this period. However, there was a widening gap between the lower reaches of the labor force and the middle strata of the labor force in terms of *wages*—the magnitude of which is captured by the 10-50 ratio: the size of the wage earned by workers found 10 percent of the way up the distribution as a ratio to the wage of workers found 50 percent of the way up (better known as the median wage). The decline in the position of low-wage *men* was particularly deep. In the 1940s, the position of low earners relative to median wage earners improved strikingly—men included. Yet this era of improved wages for workers at the low end of the spectrum sputtered out in the last quarter of the 20th century. Low-wage men in fulltime jobs fell farther behind the median earners by 9 percent in the 1970s and by another 10 percent in the 1980s. They lost ground at about the same rate in the early 1990s and stabilized in 1995. As a result, the relative wage of low-wage men by the mid-1990s was about 20 percent below its 1975 level.

---

6. These fiscal experiments have inspired a basic proposition in public finance: when an income tax cut increases the after-tax wage, which makes work more attractive in the normal case, saving goes up (not just consumption); so wealth rises faster until it catches up to the after-tax wage, after which work no longer looks more attractive. Leaving aside the effect of whatever uses the government would have put the lost revenue to, across-the-board tax cuts have no long-lasting effect on unemployment—only a lasting effect on the fiscal deficit. See Hoon and Phelps, "Payroll Taxes and VAT in a Labor-Turnover Model of the 'Natural Rate.'"

Since the wage gap was rising markedly by the late 1970s, a few scant years after the slowdown took hold, it is natural to suspect that the productivity slowdown was behind the widening of the gap. The links from the former to the latter are still rather speculative, though not improbable. Much has been made in this book of the point that innovative activity itself, quite apart from its stimulating higher valuations of capital goods and thus driving productivity, wages, and employment onto a steeper path, generates jobs *directly,* since product development, marketing, and evaluation are apt to be quite labor intensive. But the phenomenon for discussion here is the decline in the wage going to low-wage workers relative to the median wage. The answer *could* be that the emergence of high-tech systems—ICT systems— raised the skill requirements for most business innovating. Steve Jobs had to acquire an understanding of these technologies to be able to judge well whether some new product would be feasible. The new high-tech systems also required more highly skilled workers for their operation. In short, rapid innovation has been the problem. But the data on the productivity slowdown suggest that, in the economy as a whole, the rate of innovation sagged from the mid-1960s onward and recovered only partially in the sub-period 1996– 2007. Imagine the misery if innovating had kept to its rapid pace! A more realistic hypothesis is that companies innovating or adopting innovations are constantly driving down the costs of what they make, and when the innovation stops, their prices stop falling—at a cost to disadvantaged workers and most of the working class.[7]

The U.S. government made efforts, starting in the 1970s, to roll back or contain this increase in inequality. Prophetically, Rawls's *Theory of Justice* opened the decade. He argued for a conception of economic justice that would require the state to intervene with subsidies or other tools to raise the lowest wage rates as high as it could raise them. A few years later, Wilbur Mills in the House of Representatives led the way to passage of the Earned

---

7. Another possibility is that productivity slowed down in the consumer goods industries, which slowed the *decline* of consumer goods prices relative to capital goods prices, while productivity in the capital goods industries actually increased, which slowed the *rise* (or caused a fall) of *capital goods* prices relative to consumer goods prices. Both developments would lower the path of prices—relative to the past trend—for the goods that low-wage labor had the greater stake in, namely, capital goods. Similarly, it is shown in a recent paper that a technical improvement in the ICT-producing industry, in lowering the real price of ICT equipment, reduces the "demand wage" employers will pay, thus lowering employment as well as the real wage. See Hoon and Phelps, "Effects of Technological Improvement in the ICT-Producing Sector on Business Activity."

Income Tax Credit (EITC) in 1975. Those with low wage earnings for the year could take a credit against future taxes owed. Seven hundred dollars might turn into a thousand. This measure was just in time, as the wages earned by the bottom tenth slipped in the late 1970s and continued to do so until the early 1990s. The 1985 Reagan Tax Act amended the EITC, making it more biased toward working families with dependent children than it was at the outset, and therefore it became more of a child raising subsidy than a work subsidy. In any case, the annual expenditure never approached even 1 percent of GDP.

The efforts to address inequality were mainly directed not at raising earnings and thus stirring people to help themselves by continuing to work—Smith's "self-help." They were directed at providing economic support of low-income persons *whether or not* they were employed. The modest flow of income from the EITC was a drop in the bucket next to the sums a low-income person was provided in food stamps, Medicaid, low-income housing projects, aid to mothers of dependent children, disability bene-fits, and many smaller programs, all of which added up to a massive flow of income compared to the wage they could earn. OECD data record that "social transfers" in the United States grew from 7.26 percent of the GDP in 1960 to 10.21 in 1970. But in the 1970s these transfers grew to 15.03 percent, thus almost matching the United Kingdom, then grew to 21.36 percent in the 1980s, far outstripping the United Kingdom. As the slowdown remained, so did the trend in social benefits. Data from the U.S. Census Bureau record that the percentage of the population living in a household receiving some government benefits climbed in a virtually straight line from 29 percent in 1983 to 48 percent in 2011. Hence the income from not working skyrocketed as low-end pay for work stagnated:

> The entire bottom decile earned only $15 billion in 1990, which is about $1,200 per person. (This compares with economy-wide earnings per mem-ber of the labor force that year of about $25,000. . . .) How could 12 million workers have survived on so little? In large part the answer lies in the scale of welfare payments, particularly [but not only] those for which active and potential workers are eligible. . . . Total public spending for Medicaid, food stamps, housing benefits, and supplementary security income, all of bene-fit to the employed, came to about $150 billion that year. Thus the income received under current entitlement programs dwarfs the wage income of those in the bottom decile. We have here a measure of their dependency:

they earn only a small fraction of the total income (cash and in-kind income) they receive. But removing the support of the welfare system would not make them independent. . . . [T]hey would still be dependent, their dependency shifting to relatives and charities.[8]

Thus work was seriously devalued. No wonder fewer low-wage people found it convenient to work in a fulltime job or any job.

Another response of the policymakers in recent decades was the near-abolition of taxation in the lowest 40 percent—essentially the lower half of the population. Those who did choose to work, mostly people farther up the wage ladder, were taxed at rates that are lower than almost any other country in the Western world: very nominal tax rates on income, no tax on the ownership of residential property, no federal value-added tax, and so on. By running a huge budgetary deficit on the lower half, the government had very nearly scaled after-tax wages, wealth, and consumption back to the size they would have had in the absence of the decline in their relative wages. Yet this policy did nothing to restore the lower half's integration in society and their sense of self-support through the earnings from their contribution. The country's lower half went from running their careers but having no share in running or monetarily supporting the government to having no careers but a say in the running of government without sharing in the cost of it.

But all these efforts of the state to redress the damage where it could be seen and treated to a degree were superficial. The economy had fundamentally changed. Furthermore, even if the tax credits, the social expenditures, and the tax cuts had been enduringly effective in reducing unemployment and inequality back to their initial levels, there would have been a problem. If the economy was weighed down by diminished innovation, the satisfactions of economic life would likely have been depressed too. The policy measures were not of a nature to treat the effects of the slowdown on the *texture* and *experience* of economic life.

The losses in job satisfaction and the issue of job security. Job satisfaction did in fact suffer a significant decline in the new era of slowdown. In theory, with new products and methods coming up much less rapidly after the early 1970s, especially new methods and products that were the fruit of indigenous grassroots imagination, we would expect that work in the business sector

---

8. Phelps, *Rewarding Work* (1997, p. 23). The book discusses how the devaluation of work might be reversed.

soon became much less rewarding than previously; so data on the trend of job satisfaction provide a test of the thesis of important economic deterioration. It should not be surprising that, among all the many questions about job satisfaction asked by the several household survey organizations, *some* of the responses show no downward trend after the early 1970s. But overwhelmingly, the surveys found a marked decline. Surveys by Gallup and Ipsos-Reid asked, "Do you enjoy your work so much that you have a hard time putting it aside?" The percentage that said "yes" was 51 in 1955, 33 in 1988, and 23 in 2001. Roper asked, "Is work the most important thing and the purpose of leisure to recharge batteries . . . or is it leisure?" The percentage saying "work" was 48 in 1975, 46 in 1985, 37 in 1995, and 34 in 2000. Finally, Gallup asks whether you are "satisfied or dissatisfied with your job/the work you do." The percentage saying "satisfied" averaged 86 around 1966, was 77 in 1973, 70 in 1984, 73 in 1995, and 70 in 2001.[9]

The analysis of job satisfaction data from General Social Surveys by David Blanchflower and Andrew Oswald, pioneering economists in investigating job satisfaction data, likewise confirms "a small but systematic" downward trend across the period. Blanchflower and Oswald point out that this is a startling result precisely because physical working conditions steadily improved over the decades in question. The trends are not very different between men and women.[10]

One might wonder whether the downward trend in job satisfaction reflects only some ill effects on morale or on the worker-employer match resulting from the shift to higher unemployment rates following the great slowdown. After all, the unemployment rate shot up to 10.8 percent in November and December 1982—the worst months in the campaign to slay the dragon of inflation. However, the decline is barely less steep when we

9. See the valuable compilation of several survey results in AEI Public Opinion Studies, *The State of the American Worker 2009: Attitudes about Work in America,* updated August 21, 2009. http://www.aei.org/publicopinion17. Of the half-dozen surveys, two recorded no decline of job satisfaction between the early 1970s and the early 1990s. The National Opinion Research Center asked whether "work gives a feeling of accomplishment." The percentage saying "yes" showed *no trend* between the mid-1970s and the early 1990s, then a drop-off in the 2000s. Asked by Harris Interactive "how satisfied are you with your job—very satisfied, somewhat satisfied . . .," the percentage saying "very satisfied" was 59 in 1974 and the *same* in 1984 (after dipping to 45 in 1978). The later percentages were lower: 46 in 1994 and 49 in 2002.

10. Blanchflower and Oswald, "Well-Being, Insecurity and the Decline of American Job Satisfaction." The authors comment that the last finding "might be viewed as unexpected because of a presumption that gender discrimination has dropped over the last few decades."

Job satisfaction
(% very satisfied)

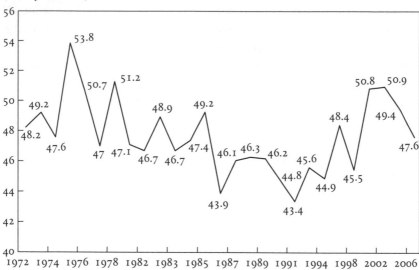

FIGURE 9.3 Job satisfaction in the United States, 1972–2006. (Source: David Blanchflower and Andrew Oswald.)

restrict our attention to the (increasingly rare) years when the unemployment rate was as low as that in the early 1970s.[11]

Declining job satisfaction was not confined to America. Although internally generated innovation in Western Europe, which had been a large source of job satisfaction there, had paused in the 1940s and finally died in the late 1950s, the flow of designs for new products and blueprints for new methods coming into Europe from overseas, largely from America, had been filling the gap with little let-up from the late 1950s to the late 1970s, thus providing jobholders with a modicum of job satisfaction in those years. But America's slowdown in the 1970s and the Continent's running low on overseas ideas in the 1980s sharply reduced opportunities for job satisfaction in Continental workplaces—just as

11. Of those over age 30, asked by General Social Surveys, "How satisfied are you with the work you do?," the percentage replying "very satisfied" was 54 in 1972 (when the yearly unemployment rate was 5.6 percent), 51 in 1988 (the year when the unemployment rate recovered to 5.5 percent), and 47 in 1996 (a year with a 5.4 percent unemployment rate—the new normal of that era). Blanchflower and Oswald, "Well-Being, Insecurity and the Decline of American Job Satisfaction" (table 1B). This development is presented in Figure 9.3.

it reduced available jobs. So we should be prepared to find that Europe experienced a moderate decline in job satisfaction in the 1980s—a lesser decline since it had less to lose. In fact, drawing on the earliest and smallest wave of data collected by WVS in 1980, we see that Britain suffered a serious decrease of job satisfaction from 1980 to 1991 and an equal decrease from 1991 to 2001. Italy suffered a decrease from 1980 to 1991, and Germany a smaller one. Ultimately, Europe's own productivity had to slow down. Italy went into a sharp productivity slowdown around 1997 and France in 1998. (France enjoyed an upswing of job satisfaction between 1991 and 2001 but a decline in the 2000s.) Germany has had recurrent periods of slow growth since 1984.

Many suppose the loss in reported job satisfaction reflects a loss of job security. Those who only think of security would suppose that. So do some who take a broader view: Several experts in household surveying suggest that job security is a part of job satisfaction. Their thinking seems to be that if you draw immense satisfaction from "the work you do" and something makes you fear you will lose it, you will say you are dissatisfied with your *job*! (But wouldn't it then be more accurate to say that your *economy* is dissatisfying?) At least one survey directs respondents to include their feeling of job security in their reported job satisfaction by presenting it to them as one of three or four components of what the survey defines as job satisfaction. Do we see a statistical correlation between job satisfaction and job security? One can be seen if enough underbrush is cleared away. But that statistical relationship may not be causal, running from security to satisfaction. Low job satisfaction and low job security may be a feature of economies with large numbers of *low-level* jobs. Job security is not sufficient for job satisfaction: Hungarians report great job security but miserable job satisfaction. In any case, the historical data of the era of diminished performance do not show significant downward trends in job insecurity—in the perception of precariousness. Gallup reports that the percentage of U.S. jobholders "completely satisfied" with the "job security aspect of your job" went from 45 percent in 1989, the first year of the survey, to 55 in 2002 and again in 2006. (These data, drawn from the AEI compilation of job satisfaction data, do not go back further.) The General Social Survey reports that the percentage who felt it "not at all likely" or "not too likely" they would lose their jobs or be laid off in the next 12 months fell insignificantly: from 91 percent in 1977–1978 (the earliest data available) only to 89.5 in both 1990–1991 and 1994–1996. The percentage who felt it was "very easy" or "somewhat easy" to find another job with the same remuneration went from 59 percent in 1977–1978 *up* to 60 percent in 1990–1991, then down to 57 percent in 1994–1996.[12] It appears that the lost dynamism caused little insecurity.

In fact, there was little basis for supposing that the loss of dynamism would cause increased insecurity. With productivity growing more slowly, one would suppose that Schumpeterian "job destruction" *fell* along with "job creation." And the evidence confirms the prediction. In 1989, 8 percent of jobs were measured as destroyed, while the percentage destroyed fell to the 7s in 1992–2000 and to the 6s in 2002–2007.[13] This may seem improbable, but it is not. Job insecurity *is* heightened in recessions. But the two long stretches in the 1990s and the 2000s each came *after* a recession. In recoveries and even in flat times, jobs are not particularly prey to destruction—even if the previous recession has left employment depressed—since the storm and its destruction have passed: the loss of dynamism and the wave of dismissals, while not reversed, are over for the foreseeable future.

A new development in the era of diminished performance was the onset in the 1990s of a *structural shift* from manufacturing to services and to finance. Employment in heavy industry—in durable goods manufacturing—started and finished the decade at 11.5 million persons. The number employed in *non-durable* goods manufacturing, though, fell from around 7.2 million to 6.7 million by 2000. Since manufacturing is worker intensive, especially intensive in workers without a college education, the shift of expenditure to the other sectors did not create enough new labor demand to absorb the loss of old labor demand. A full recovery of employment would have required a much greater level of total output. The insufficiency of the output rise for a full recovery of employment came to be known as a "jobless recovery." The decline of manufacturing steepened in the next decade—the 2000s—as a result, in part, at any rate, of increased imports from China. For awhile, however, the boom in construction soon took up the slack and more. (Resources for a rise in domestic investment—in construction expenditure—were made available by a shift from buying domestic products to products imported from China, with no change in domestic saving. When the latter decreased and the boom increased, all that

---

12. Blanchflower and Oswald, "Well-Being, Insecurity and the Decline of American Job Satisfaction" (1999, table A1, *a* and *b*). It is only the most secure who felt a noticeable loss of security. The percentage who felt it "not at all likely" they would lose their jobs or be laid off in the next 12 months went from 68.5 percent in 1977–1978 to 64.5 percent in 1990–1991 and on to 62 in 1994–1996.

13. These data were reported in *Business Dynamics Statistics,* a product of the U.S. Census Bureau that measures business openings and closings, startups, job creation, and job destruction by firm size, age, industrial sector, and state.

was necessary were counterbalancing increases in the import surplus—fewer exports or still more imports from China.)

Last, but not least, in the era of reduced performance is the greater *fluctuation* of employment. The tendency toward elevated unemployment has been noted, but job separations and the resulting dislocation are another dimension of economic performance. The era produced five downswings in little more than three decades: the recession of 1975 (when the monthly unemployment rate brushed 9.0 percent), 1982 (when the rate hit 10.8), 1992 (when the rate hit 7.8), 2002–2003 (when the rate hit 6.3), and the Great Recession of 2008–2009 (when the rate touched 10.1). It is fair to infer that the post-1972 economy became more recession prone. A familiar explanation draws an analogy to the bicyclist who is more likely to go off course when forced to go at a slow speed. While a slowdown of innovation is apt to be the cause of a slowdown of productivity and hiring, a recent paper makes the point that companies are apt to draw back from an innovative venture when, on top of the possibility that the new product may fail because it is rejected in favor of other products, there is the strong possibility that the demand will be critically weak because of another recession.[14]

The violent slide of 2008–2009 is in a special category not because it is the deepest of these, which it is not, but because it became the prelude to the protracted slump from which the economy is emerging only haltingly. (In contrast, the 1933–1937 recovery from the Great Depression set a speed record for rate of recovery. But deep troughs often reflect overshooting, not fundamentals, and thus are followed by a period of high-speed recovery.) Yet *all* the recoveries from the aforementioned recession were unusually protracted. The bicycle explanation argues that a rapidly growing economy is more robust to recessions, just as a bicyclist going at high speed is quicker to get back on track. In the 1949 recession, at a time when the American economy was gaining back the rapid growth of old, the unemployment rate, after peaking at 7.9 percent (up from 3.7 a year earlier), was back to 4.2 in just a year. In the 1975 recession, after peaking at 9.0 percent (up from 5.1 a year earlier), the unemployment rate took 3 years to fall back to 6.0. It is fair to infer that in the post-1972 era America's recoveries from downswings were much more protracted than they were in the

14. Aghion and Kharroubi, "Stabilization Policies and Economic Growth" (2013). If it is expected the economy is heading down, the cost of innovation is still high, but the future benefit, if the effort achieves an innovation, will be reduced. Symmetrically, if the economy is thought to be on the uptick, the cost of innovating is still low and the benefit contingent on success will be high.

golden years 1950–1972. Even in the high-growth period 1920–1941, the American economy was not *highly* recession prone or *chronically* in great flux: it suffered its steep downswing following the speculative excesses of the late 1920s, a downswing exacerbated by policy errors.

The set of actions that caused the 2008–2009 collapse to be so powerful are widely known: government actions aimed mainly at widening home ownership, unsophisticated efforts to make a profit on the naïve speculation that housing prices could only go higher (long enough to sell), fraudulent practices of mortgage originators, big banks greatly leveraging their capital by borrowing huge sums with which to bundle mortgages into packages to be sold to banks overseas—"originate and distribute"—and other practices.[15]

Yet the 1975 and 2008–2009 downswings and many of the other stresses of the era we are examining show the influence of many households stretching thin their income by drastic cuts in saving, the national economy stretching its national wealth by borrowing heavily from overseas, and, not least, the government stretching thin its revenues by borrowing heavily and deploying one ingenious measure after another to pump up investment, output, and employment in ways that would prove unsustainable and thus disappoint expectations. Through it all there has been a dogged denial of the era of slowdown and thus refusal to make a sober reckoning of the domestic consumption that the future would make possible. The result was a sick society, an electorate to whom political leaders did not dare to speak the truth. This state of affairs need not have followed the Great Slowdown. One could not have predicted that the slowdown would send society into a manic mode leading inevitably to speculative excess. (It could have sent the society into a mode of depression and paralysis.) In any case, it is important that we understand why the slowdown took place and what best we can do to end it.

15. The epilogue is a vehicle to take up the degradation of the financial sector that developed in the past decade and the new policies needed from the perspective of this book. The body of the book focuses on the questions raised by a well-functioning modern-capitalist economy—questions about stability, economic inclusion, and especially unemployment, and kinds of inequality; the questions raised by diminished economic dynamism, which even an economic system free of malfunctions can suffer; and the question of whether modern capitalism is politically sustainable and morally justifiable.

CHAPTER TEN

Understanding the Post-1960s Decline

[Life] used to be about trying to do something. Now it's about trying to be someone.

MARGARET THATCHER, quoted in *The Iron Lady*

I N ONE OF THE STORIES TOLD ABOUT THE AMERICAN DECLINE, the postwar decades had been a golden age: The federal government supplied social security to working people—old age and disability insurance—while state governments supplied unemployment compensation. Regulations provided safety for workers and consumers and protected people's savings from bank failure and their investments from fraud. Big, diversified corporations provided de facto tenure for employees, giving them more reason to remain loyal. Unions fought against layoffs and for seniority rights. In addition to widespread economic security, unemployment was low and stable, and growth was fine.

Then, in this narrative, the golden age passed. Businesses shed the mantle of paternalism that was their redeeming feature and became models of efficient managerial capitalism: putting shareowners ahead of employees, corporations were Machiavellian in their efforts to push up share prices. Underperforming managements became targets for corporate raids and private equity buyouts; jobs were axed so that other jobs might live. Governments, caught up in the new spirit, cut tax rates to enhance corporate incentives and, if government revenue was squeezed, they cut back programs. Unions decamped from the private sector. As a result, unemployment rose, workers felt insecure, firms felt uncertain, and investors saw nothing attractive to invest in.

The moral of this story—security lost, efficiency gained—is that America would do well to return to the postwar corporatism. Some who accept the narrative differ about the moral, saying that the paraphernalia of protection arising in the "golden age" were sustainable only as long as the wind was at America's back.

On the left, there is a persistent suggestion that . . . the midcentury model could have been sustained, that the private equity "vultures" could have been held at bay, and that what worked for the United States when Europe was in ruins and half the world was Marxist-Leninist could have worked in the age of globalization as well.[1]

However, most economists would say that even if that corporatist-communitarian model had been propped up, it would not have staved off wage stagnation brought on by external and internal forces, such as global competition, domestic demographics, and rising social charges on employment—not to mention slower innovation.

There are basic faults with this populist narrative. For one thing, the postwar era was not exactly a golden age. Its growth rate was a far cry from that in the interwar years, and both its unemployment and its participation rates were not outstanding next to the 1920s and earlier. The anomie of the 1950s workplace became the subject of David Riesman's *The Lonely Crowd*. For another, though globalization caused collateral damage, any standard analysis would see important benefits amid the costs: The expansion of the market to global proportions—increasingly perceived in the 1980s and 1990s—could only have stimulated American innovation; and the low interest rates at which China would lend might have been a stimulus to innovation too—or would have been had U.S. economic policy not redirected the stimulus to residential investment by speculators and sub-prime borrowers. Lastly, although the drive to increase profits through increased efficiency cost some jobs and cost unions some of their power, trimming jobs served to save the remaining ones, and the new freedom from unions can only have helped open up new jobs. There are no good grounds for believing that the corporatist spirit in postwar American business assured dynamism or created jobs; and no good grounds for believing that the neo-conservative swing to putting business first and restoring owner control cost the business sector its dynamism or job growth.

In another story of the decline, a longer and different golden age had started decades earlier and lasted into the 1960s. Free enterprise received strong support from both the public and government. Regulations were few and manageable. Most tax rates were still comparatively low in America. College attendance was the highest in the world. The medical and education industries saw new private colleges and new private hospitals enter,

---

1. Ross Douthat, "The Benefits of Bain Capitalism," *New York Times,* January 15, 2012.

expecting to be profitable. Even big corporations like DuPont and IBM were innovative. As prejudices waned, ethnic minorities broke into the professions and business. Growth was good and, the 1930s aside, unemployment low. It was the age of enterprise.

In this story too, the golden age passed away. Mushrooming regulation increasingly narrowed investment opportunities. Dysfunctional public schools and family environments deprived companies of people equipped for recent technologies. (People who can staff the phones are hard to find, it is said, and companies pay for BAs to run errands.) Taxes on savings and investments became comparatively stiff. Even small firms generally felt compelled to obtain limited liability. Only 65 percent of business income is left after corporate taxes and just 55 percent after the tax rate of 15 percent on dividends and capital gains. Growth slowed and unemployment rose.

The moral drawn by conservatives is that America would do well to return to textbook capitalism: The economy needs fewer and simpler regulations and sharply lower corporate rates to restore employment and growth. Some observers friendly to capitalism question whether America's social setting would make that any longer possible:

> Most of the Republican candidates talk as if all that is needed is . . .
> lighter regulation and lower taxes. . . . But [those steps] won't, on their
> own, help the . . . 40 percent born out of wedlock and [lacking] commu-
> nity support—get the skills they need to compete. . . . To ensure there is
> skilled labor . . . Obama would have to champion different policies.[2]

An economist would comment, however, that even if social institutions and "community support" had sustained the necessary skills, it is doubtful that market forces exerting a drag on wages—notably forces choking off innovation—would have been overcome.

The basic fault in the moral drawn is that although low taxes and stiff competition may be necessary conditions for very low unemployment and high efficiency,[3] those precepts of sound economic management are not sufficient conditions for the high dynamism that low unemployment and high job satisfaction require. The argument has appeared before in this book: Rolling back the government expenditures and the taxes on wage income and employer wage bills to pay for them would raise private saving and ultimately

---

2. David Brooks, "Free-Market Socialism," *New York Times,* January 24, 2012, p. A19.

3. Some observers say that the experience of Sweden and Norway proves that they are *not* necessary conditions.

private wealth, so paychecks would no longer look elevated. On this count, employment would no longer be higher than where it would have been without the reforms.

In a third story, a detachment from the ethos of business and individual responsibility in the postwar decades has been breeding a dysfunctional culture among disadvantaged communities and families, fueling social problems and threatening society's ability to support free enterprise or to sustain itself. The moral here is neither left nor right. In my 1997 book, *Rewarding Work*, I argued for a system of graduated subsidies to corporations to employ low-wage workers. This would immediately build inclusion by increasing employment and paychecks. Now many argue for improving education, upbringing, and community support in ways aimed at significantly reducing those disadvantaged in the next generation. It is clear that subsidies to improve the terms offered to less-fortunate workers and investments to improve their preparation could not be enough to restore their rates of employment and participation to the pre-decline levels of the 1960s. The reason is that returning to the self-support, education, upbringing, and social norms of old would not greatly lift the economy's overall dynamism and thus restore low general unemployment rates and fast growth of productivity and wages.

This book's narrative of the modern economy differs from these popular stories. The narrative points to a *deterioration* in the *core functioning* of the (surviving) modern economies that must have caused a significant loss of economic dynamism and, with it, a loss of economic inclusion. It does not fault the decrease of human capital (years of schooling, etc.) faced by companies nor the modest rise of taxes. It sees evidence to suggest that the handful of modern-capitalist economies *have been weakened by flaws in their institutional-cultural operating system and further weakened by political reactions.*

The moral of this narrative is not a call for more spending and regulation by the state or more libertarianism or even more intervention in education and business hiring, however welcome some measures of this sort might be. It is a call to rehabilitate *modern capitalism* by clearing away blocks to its dynamism both in society's values and in its institutions.

Sources of the Decline

What flaws account for the apparent weakening of the dynamism of America's modern-capitalist economy—its desire and capabilities for indigenous innovation? The progressive era was rife with criticisms of American capitalism, many valid enough to act on—the emergence of monopolies, for example. But the objections were on grounds of static resource allocation: monopoly power was used to constrict output to raise price relative to costs and thus create a monopoly profit. The so-called "natural" monopolies, where maximum economic efficiency is achieved by single-firm production, were turned into public utilities subject to price controls. Progressives also leveled criticism at the crude libertarian dogma that no wage ought to be subsidized and no interest income ought to be taxed. But the flaws we seek to detect in the history of our current situation are those impairing the capacity for innovation, which is the object of this book's study.

Structural Faults in Large Firms, Mutual Funds, and Banks

Worldly students of American business and finance found acute faults as early as the 1930s. Some of these faults have spread, and certain ways of organizing companies, once beneficial from the standpoint of efficient production, must now be reexamined from the standpoint of innovation.

The prominent business historian Alfred Chandler used the buoyant term *managerial revolution* to characterize the rise of a "professional management" able to bring "multiple product lines" under the control of a "hierarchy" of middle and top managers.

> By the middle of the twentieth century these enterprises employed hundreds and even thousands of middle and top managers who supervised the work of dozens and often hundreds of operating units employing tens and often hundreds of thousands of workers. . . . Rarely in the history of the world has an institution grown to be so important and so pervasive in so short a period of time.[4]

The new management methods were credited with finding "least-cost" methods of production—achieving economic efficiency. And the new methods were themselves significant innovations that changed managerial practice across the world. Moreover, the vast scale of these new big businesses made it possible to self-finance radically novel projects that smaller companies could not have funded. Yet other impediments to innovation arose: In a company of traditional size, even the lowest-paid employee, if he had an idea for doing

---

4. Chandler, *The Visible Hand* (pp. 3–4). Dupont impressed Schumpeter in the 1940s, though not enough to cause him to believe that capitalism had much time left. General Motors was Chandler's greatest fascination.

something new or different, could expect a chance to get the ear of someone well up the ladder, if not at the top. So employees of the company were alert to new ideas crossing their minds and were, for that reason, more likely to have new ideas. There is no such prospect in giant companies larded with managerial hierarchies.

One might wonder why owners would not intervene to limit company size and improve communication. Large companies, even those spectacularly successful in breaking into, or even creating, an industry, are vulnerable to the same self-dealing that befalls most large bureaucracies—even if the chief executive is also the largest owner and chairman of the board. That is what reportedly happened at Microsoft.

> Early in my tenure, our group of very clever graphics experts invented a
> way to display text on screen called ClearType. . . . Although we built it to
> help sell e-books, it gave Microsoft a huge potential advantage for every
> device with a screen. But it also annoyed other Microsoft groups that
> felt threatened by our success. Engineers in the Windows group falsely
> claimed it made the display go haywire when certain colors were used.
> Then the head of Office products said it gave him headaches. The vice
> president for pocket devices was blunter: he'd support ClearType and use
> it but only if I transferred the program and the programmers to his con
> trol. As a result, even though it received much public praise, internal pro
> motion and patents, a decade passed before a fully operational version of
> ClearType finally made it into Windows.
>
> Internal competition is common at great companies. It can be wisely
> encouraged to force ideas to compete. The problem comes when the
> competition is uncontrolled and destructive. At Microsoft, it has created
> a dysfunctional corporate culture in which the big established groups
> are allowed to prey upon emerging teams, belittle their efforts, com
> pete unfairly against them for resources, and over time hector them out
> of existence. . . . It's an open question whether Microsoft has much of a
> future.[5]

These problems arise even when the chief executive has the extra power that comes with also being the chairman of the board or even the founder of the company—as Bill Gates was during the ClearType controversy. Founders often lack the talent and the time to run a complex organization.

---

5. Dick Brass, "Microsoft's Creative Destruction" (p. A27). Mr. Brass was a vice president at Microsoft from 1997 to 2004.

At Facebook the visionary founder, Mark Zuckerberg, was canny enough to hire a chief operating officer, Sheryl Sandberg. Nevertheless, difficulties mount as an organization becomes complex and depends on decentralization of self-interested middle managers. These various problems have not been enough to stop innovation, but they have reduced it.

While large companies can be mismanaged by even the most motivated leader, they are apt to fare worse in the hands of a manager who is not a founder and not a controlling shareowner—in short, a professional manager, or hired gun. It came to be argued, not long after they appeared, that corporate governance of large companies run by professional managers was deeply flawed: the critique by Adolf Berle and Gardiner Means in their 1932 book *The Modern Corporation and Private Property* is the classic account. The device of share owning brilliantly enabled companies to reward present stockholders with immediate capital gains from undertaking projects expected to pay off only when many stockholders have since died—a masterstroke promising a long-termism that socialism could not match. Yet the manager of a large corporation is presented with an incentive—whether or not he or she acts on it—to sell the shareowners out: to pursue projects offering prospects of short-term gains—gains within his prospective tenure at the helm—to the disadvantage of projects with superior prospects over the long term. To deter such practices, directors on the board setting the manager's compensation have understood that they might reward the manager with a bonus when the stock goes up and, in some cases, even a negative "bonus" when the stock goes down. But managers, especially those with dependents, would then need a larger fixed salary to cushion negative bonuses; and that would present the manager with an undesirable incentive to avoid all projects that could put her job at risk, namely, long-term projects of high cost. Long-termism remains difficult to encourage. The governance problem is sometimes solved by aggressive shareowners with a large stake, although it can be aggravated by institutional shareholders whose interest is just as short term as that of the managers.

The short-termism at large corporations has been exacerbated in recent years by the rise of mutual funds—a theme of Louis Lowenstein and his son Roger Lowenstein's work. Hedge fund profits depend heavily on investors who remain with the fund rather than move about. Thus the fund is extremely averse to any appreciable risk that the stock of any company in which it holds shares might suffer a substantial drop in price. This leads to harsh pressure from mutual funds to announce the company's earnings "target" for the next quarter and to be intent on hitting it. As a result, the manager of a company with shares traded on a public exchange will spend much of his time setting and aiming at quarterly earnings targets rather than formulating strategies for long-term investment and innovation.

Mutual funds create the further flaw that their capacity for vast diversification reduces the incentive of wealth owners to use their specialized Hayekian knowledge of particular companies, industries, and technologies in favor of simply turning over their wealth for management by one or more funds. Scientific portfolio diversification, which seemed a wonderful gain in economic welfare to the fundamentally neoclassical economist Paul Samuelson, was actually a huge step backward for modern capitalism, as Amar Bhidé pointed out in "The Hidden Costs of Stock Market Liquidity" in 1993. What is most significant in the present context is that companies may see little rise or fall in their share price despite local knowledge about their shifting opportunities, owing to the determination of mutual funds to maintain the relative weight they give to each category of company. Thus investing and innovating for the future is delayed. Moreover, people who leave their investments to professionals will have less incentive to acquire local or specialized knowledge.

Most seriously, multiple flaws in the modern economy arose inside the large investment banks. Imperfections in many financial markets were whittled away, and assets became highly liquid. Large investment banks came to devote much of their borrowing capacity—and divert much of the expertise in the financial sector—to speculation on currencies and government bonds rather than to evaluating companies and industries and judging the merits of new directions. Furthermore, these banks greatly stepped up the amounts they had at risk. To do that, the banks, which had always been partnerships, wherein the partners had most of their fortunes at stake, changed into corporations listed on public exchanges where the shareowners had little control. If things went wrong, the shareowners suffered the losses, while the manager, no longer a partner, was free from personal liability for any investment decisions, no matter how egregious. (In one respect, it is not *casino* banking, since a casino takes virtually *no* risk. But, ironically, it *is* banking that pretends it can depend on the law of large numbers to manage its risk scientifically and precisely.)

Speculation by banks also puts the economy at risk of wider asset-price swings and bigger crashes. Banks love to borrow short term when the rates are low and lend long when, as usual, long rates have not fallen as far; it looks like easy money. But while the odds may continue to be rather favorable, it is uncomfortably close to a game of "gambler's ruin." If an unexpected revival of short rates occurs, pushing up rates on long bonds, their prices fall—just as the prices of houses fell after the long speculative boom in housing—and the banks incur huge losses on their borrowings. Most nations with capitalist economies have long failed to require that investment banks must borrow long to lend long—so that the banks have a chance of recovering before the bonds come due. Another social effect of this unbridled financial speculation is to push nations toward capital controls and other populist restrictions that harm innovation by making it easier for marginal incumbents already possessing capital to hang on, while making it harder for start-ups to raise capital and be confident they can get through their project before the next crisis strikes. (None of this means there ought to be a blanket prohibition against all speculation by persons, businesses, or even banks.)

In many respects, America's commercial banks—banks where households and companies keep their bank deposits—were reined in by the Glass-Steagall Act of 1933, after the crash of 1929 caused a fifth of all commercial banks to fail. Ferdinand Pecora, a former prosecutor, gave evidence to Congress that the banks had played a role in the speculative excess. The new law prohibited commercial banks from engaging in the underwriting business of handling new issues of securities, in the brokerage business of buying and selling stocks and bonds for customers, and in trading them on its own account. In 1999, though, the law was repealed. In the next several years these banks, like Citibank and JPMorgan Chase, built or acquired investment banks, leveraging their capital through massive short-term borrowing.

A severe flaw in the banking industry and a similar one in the airline industry arose from what came to be called ruinous competition—until the very concept fell out of use. An airline plunges into more routes and a bank goes on a lending spree on the calculation that overhead costs can be spread over more routes or more assets, so that profits are increased. But as all airlines do it, they ruin one another's chances of any profit. The loan frenzy of originate-and-distribute in 2005 and 2006 was based on the calculation that losses might be in store if additional assets were not acquired. What was not taken into account was that the competitors were simultaneously making the same calculation, with the result that the industry overexpanded. Consequently, the recurrent crises in these industries have cost the industry jobs and profits and have been costly for the rest of the economy as well.

The banking industry betrayed the very concept of a modern economy by betting on enormous piles of assets without exercising the vision and judgment essential to the well functioning of the modern economy.

The "Money Culture," Self-Importance, Doing, and Thinking

In an interview with RTL radio shortly before she died, Danielle Mitterrand, whose husband, François Mitterrand, was president of France in the 1980s, railed against French economic culture. "Everybody knows that the foundation of the system today is money. Money is the guru, money decides everything." In this statement is the thinly veiled suggestion not simply that there is a stronger orientation toward money than there was in past times but that capitalism operates on money while the corporatism of Mitterrand or Pétain or Colbert did not. But such systems of rent seeking or patronage are as much about money as the systems of capitalism are—pre-modern and modern. In modern capitalism, unlike corporatism, the economy is largely driven by people who, while attending to the bottom line, want to make a difference—to contribute to society or build monuments to themselves or connect with exciting ventures—not just make money.

Even in America, money lures all too many in both public life and private life. It is impressive how intent the top 1 percent of income earners are on keeping their taxes down and—if the discussion in the press is accurate— how keen the bottom 99 percent are on putting the nation's hands on top incomes. The question here, in our search for sources of reduced dynamism, is whether money "decides things" *more* than it did in the 1960s or the 1920s. A renowned philosopher, John Dewey, was a thoughtful observer of the role of money in 1920s America. (Thinking that almost all those engaged in a company play no imaginative, intellectual, or emotional part in its activities—only the manager does—he sought employee cooperatives to nurture a "new individualism." Yet he was important for having put the imaginative, the intellectual, and the emotional into public discussion. Process is important: Desired ends may not justify the means.) In 1929 Dewey wrote:

> [W]e are living in a money culture. . . . Worth is measured by ability to
> hold one's own or to get ahead in a competitive pecuniary race. . . . [T]he
> chief ambition of parents in the [working] class [is] that their children
> should climb into the business (and professional) class. . . . [T]he personal

habits most prized [are] clear-sighted vision of personal advantage and resolute ambition to secure it at any human cost.[6]

Dewey went on to suggest how the new "money culture" could have come about:

Industry and business conducted for money profit are nothing new . . . they come to us from a long past. But the invention of the machine has given them a power and scope they never had in the past from which they derive. . . . [W]e depend on a novel combination of the machine and money, and the result is the pecuniary culture characteristic of our civilization. . . . There is a perversion of the whole idea of individualism to conform to the practices of a pecuniary culture.

Dewey's argument can be taken in other directions. Just as the size of markets, measured by revenue, heightened the desire to make a top salary by driving up the salaries of those in top positions, so the Reagan cuts of the high-end tax rates faced by top managers, bankers, and investors fueled a craze for money in the 1990s—a craze refueled by the Bush tax cuts in the 2000s.[7] On the Deweyan view, the "pecuniary culture" must have received another boost around the world—from Shanghai to Munich to Silicon Valley—with the globalization of the 1970s and 1980s and the information and communications revolution of the 1990s. The sight of companies going global and people making billions naturally excited the imagination of many more firms and people. The big gains won in the stock market in the 1960s, the fortunes made in corporate raids by private equity firms in the 1980s, and the speculative fever of the dot.com years of the 1990s suggested the possibility of endless and enormous gains.

The question in this chapter is not whether "greed is good." What the good *is* belongs to the next chapter. The question here is whether the heightened aspirations for money or wealth help account for the economic decline that was clearly underway in America by the early 1970s: the slower growth, higher unemployment, and lower job satisfaction, as well as for the massive fiscal stimuli, dereliction of regulators, and the speculative manias. The answer is yes. Wealth seeking competes with innovation seeking, so many turned away

---

6. Dewey, "The House Divided against Itself," republished in Dewey, *Individualism Old and New*. This extract appears on p. 6 of that volume; the following extract appears on p. 9.

7. These tax cuts may have been unintended consequences of technical papers by Phelps in 1973 and Efraim Sadka in 1976 arguing that if the marginal tax rate in the highest bracket is a positive number, the rates cannot be tax-efficient: cutting rates at the top could coax income earners to step up their income and so pay a larger tax while doing so taxes unchanged incomes at the old rates.

from innovating. Also, investors and managers became more interested in the quick buck. The financial sector thus leveraged its equity to make huge bets in the areas it had long known—home lending and trading in government securities and foreign currencies—and to step into areas about which there was no empirical knowledge—asset-backed securities and credit default swaps. Business expansion and business investment were squeezed. Given the monetary rewards, more and more able and talented young people chose to go into the financial sector, rather than into the business sector. Significant amounts of capital, too, were redirected from the business sector to the financial sector. Since this development was global, not all financing could come from foreign saving: some domestic business investment was necessarily displaced.

The nearly obsessive focus on money no doubt lies behind the much-commented rise in the litigiousness of American society. Those who envy the talent of others know that little can be done about it, but people who envy the wealth of others can seize opportunities—or manufacture them, if necessary—to sue other people. The lawsuit culture undoubtedly costs an innovative economy some of its dynamism. People devoting their time and energies to suing one another have less time and energy left for innovation. A Silicon Valley entrepreneur commented that today a start-up company would need as many lawyers as engineers.

Several observers have spoken of other sources of a change in the prevailing culture of contemporary societies, however. Mrs. Thatcher's observation that people used to aspire to do something, not to reach some social station, strikes a chord. In the culture of social standing or celebrity, people struggle to get ahead of others, to rise in rank—to climb the greasy pole, but not to produce anything. Substantive achievement is not recognized. This culture depreciates the moral qualities that high-achieving people generally have—determination, judgment, and care—and puts a harsh light on the ways in which they are ordinary or worse—their everyday habits and their peccadilloes. In many recent biographies of some great figures, the pattern is to dwell on the subject's failings and transgressions. Biographies of Edwin Hubble, Edward Hopper, and Alfred Hitchcock are examples. More evidence of this can be seen in recent biographies of Thomas Jefferson that paint him as going along with slavery when in fact his hatred of slavery was a salient feature of his public life. Some reviewers devoted more space to the accusations than to the achievements for which their subjects had become recognized and admired. Ironically, reviews of the recent film biography of Mrs. Thatcher, *Iron Lady,* saw the film as about the "pathos of her personal life," not noticing that the film traced her entire career and was rich in scenes, speeches, and remarks on politics, political economy, and the society around her—including her withering remark about the desire to "do something."

The ethos of American society has declined to even lower lows, however. Recent decades saw the development of a *culture of self-importance* or *entitlement.* Many academics, once researchers endlessly testing ideas, now rate themselves so highly that they pontificate with no research at all. Cold callers and bulk emailers intrude as if their exigencies justified the disruption. Teenage girls have babies as pets to reinforce their importance. The growing sense of entitlement helps explain the ever-rising outlays for the safety net, which, in artificially raising economic independence beyond what people's private wealth would provide, makes it harder to obtain employee loyalty and employee engagement. The attitude of entitlement can only make it harder for a start-up firm to obtain employees who take initiative, give a hand to others, and lend the concentration and judgment on which success importantly depends. The culture of self-importance is another contributor to the litigiousness touched on above.

Many observers of America have commented on the rise of what is called an adolescent culture. What is being observed is not a lessened willingness to make bets. Adolescents are often drawn to taking a risk, and many of today's financial firms have been "betting the ranch," or the company. A lessened willingness to save *is* observed, but high saving in a nation is not an absolutely necessary condition for high innovation: some other nation may do the saving, or the effort required may come out of other investment activity. Yet developing creative, innovative products does require entrepreneurs with the willingness to dedicate themselves to a process that, whatever its fascinations, would be jeopardized if they paid themselves cash that the project may need. And, unfortunately, the willingness to accept austerity for a year or two or more in the quest for an achievement, which grown-ups routinely did in the 19th century, does appear to have dwindled. Peter Thiel, a venture capitalist in social media, noticed in his interviews of fledgling start-up CEOs that the young entrepreneurs were paying themselves more than 100,000 dollars a year (until he met Mark Zuckerberg at Facebook, who paid himself very little). Furthermore, originality requires being willing and able to intensely concentrate on a regular basis for a long period of time. And this ability seems also to have waned in recent decades. An educator told Elie Wiesel that Shakespeare's *Julius Caesar* could not be taught any longer in New York State high schools because students lacked the attention span to read it.

As has been widely noted, today's young people have, on average, less experience with solitude than those in previous generations. A large proportion of persons entering the labor force from the late 1940s to the mid-1960s were only children, so they learned when growing up to fantasize and think by themselves. Since then, only children have become more rare. Furthermore, people by themselves with some time to think are now offered the distractions of the social media—"the economy of internet self-gratification." The young generation today needs to be continually in contact through blogs, email, and Twitter. That leads to a decline in thinking, which reinforces conformism. More and more people accept the positions taken by their political party or religion or friends rather than working out their own positions. It would be surprising if this conformity did not weigh on innovation in the business economy.

With the rise of the group in the American economy, one might think that the support of the group has bolstered the sense of security, so that a person would feel safe enough to venture to innovate. However, the group may have operated instead to potentiate the importance of not losing position in the group, as measured by income and employment status.

Besides all these new values, there has appeared a resurgence of traditional values that has encroached on dynamism in another way. The movement for a new attention to family values has put pressure on companies to allow employees to work at home, as many, both men and women, are doing. The detachment of an appreciable part of a company's workforce from the company offices is bound to reduce the frequency of interaction among employees and thus reduce the innovativeness not only of the remote workers but also the innovativeness of the employees still in the office. This is not sheer speculation. A front page newspaper story describes the rise of home-workers to alarming proportions in recent years and the courageous move of one corporation, Yahoo and its new head, Marissa Mayer, in the past year to bring home-workers back to the office.[8]

In summary, modern values may well remain intact—that these nutrients of a life of richness and personal growth are not extinct is basic to this book's thesis that grassroots dynamism and the resulting indigenous innovation must be a goal of every nation that can reach it! And traditional values are not all bad—not all of them. Yet a society may allow some of its traditional values lying alongside its modern values to get in the way of its dynamism.

8. See "Yahoo Orders Home Workers Back to the Office," *New York Times,* February 25, 2013.

A Broader Nexus between the State and the Economy

Critics of the role played by the state on both the left and the right have pointed to ways in which governments have gone well beyond the classical role of stepping in to repair market failures and redress economic injustice. Politicians use their governmental power to dispense patronage in hope of electoral support, and political parties solicit or accept contributions from companies, unions, political funds, and wealthy individuals in return for support of their special interests. In the competition for votes and campaign funds, some economic inefficiencies and injustices are lost in the shuffle. It has not been considered, however, that the politicization of government costs a *modern* economy some of its *dynamism*—even if static inefficiency and injustice have not worsened.

There has always been some degree of corporatism of one variety or another—interrelations between the state on the one hand and capital and labor on the other. By now, though, there has been a considerable broadening of the nexus between the state and the business economy, much of it in the past decade. Chapter 6 recounted America's corporatist developments in the 1930s, when unions gained huge power. (Unions shrank in the private sector over the postwar decades with the Chandlerian transformation of companies into upper and middle managers and their assistants, but union coverage has since expanded into the public sector.) The chapter also recounted fresh corporatist developments that began in the 1950s when powerful companies exerted enormous influence on the government. This development in America was clear to Dwight Eisenhower, who referred to the "military-industrial complex" in his presidential valedictory in 1963.

Recently, a *congressional-banking* complex has developed far beyond what existed before. One would think that the government would be in an adversarial relationship to the banks in view of its duty to police their observance of regulatory restrictions and requirements. Yet banks and political interests have entered into new arrangements for their mutual benefit. One such relationship regards banks' holdings of U.S. government debt. A bank is generally required to hold equity against its holdings of assets, so it does not become insolvent at the slightest fall in their prices, and government debt is not exceptionally safe—governments can default without a bankruptcy court to look after the bondholders. But U.S. banks have been exempted from equity requirements on their holdings of U.S. sovereign debt (and multilateral agreements at the Bank for International Settlements exempt all banks from equity requirements on all sovereign debt). The benefit to the banks is that they are spared the capital cost of the equity. The benefit to the government is that it obtains higher prices on its bond offerings—thus lower interest rates—to the extent that the banks seize upon the decreased cost of holding government debt to acquire more government debt. The government in turn may seize upon the reduction in its interest cost to sell more public debt with which to finance larger or more prolonged budgetary deficits. The gain to the political parties from being able to borrow more cheaply and thus borrow more is obvious: The bailouts that a group of nations sent to Greece in its 2011/2012 fiscal crisis went straight to the banks that held Greek debt, to protect the banks' willingness and capacity to hold huge levels of sovereign debt. Yet society does not gain by privileging the debt of the state, since that makes it harder for businesses to finance capital expenditures and innovative projects.[9] And interventions to discourage or prevent governments from defaulting shuts down the credit market's function of curbing credit to nations that borrow so much as to destabilize their economies and those of commercial and financial partners, thus making the global economy more unstable, which is a deterrent to attempts at innovation, which are already quite risky.

Another such relationship regards residential mortgages. In 1970, two government-sponsored enterprises went into the banking business when Congress authorized the existing Federal National Mortgage Association, known as Fannie Mae, to purchase private mortgages not insured by other agencies and created the Federal Home Loan Mortgage Corporation, known as Freddie Mac, to compete with Fannie Mae. Legislation signed by George H. W. Bush in 1992 directed that these government sponsored enterprises (GSEs) extend their financing to "affordable housing" for "low- and moderate-income families." The Clinton administration in 1999 pushed Fannie Mae into subprime mortgages and into easing credit requirements on subprime borrowers. Congress in that year charged both GSEs with buying 30 percent of the mortgages on new dwellings in their respective markets, and banks were pressured to step up their purchases from the GSEs of mortgage-backed securities. By 2006, Fannie Mae and Freddie Mac had acquired mortgages costing 2 trillion dollars—one-seventh of the annual GDP. The role the government played here is not sufficient to explain the breadth of the speculative boom in housing that occurred: High-priced houses defaulted

9. See Amar Bhidé and Edmund Phelps, "More Harm Than Good: How the IMF's Business Model Sabotages Properly Functioning Capitalism."

with the same likelihood in 2008 as low-priced houses. Neither is that role sufficient to explain how housing prices rose 60 percent before falling to earth: There had to be a speculative fever, since stepping up homebuilding by 30 percent would not seem to require a 60 percent increase in prices.

These financial relationships are the tip of an iceberg—a corporatist *complex* between the government and the private sector. The pervasiveness was suggested by the inexorable accumulation of regulations cited in Chapters 7 and 9. Data from Unified Agenda report that from 1997 to 2006 there were about 80 new "significant" rules a year (each costing at least 100 million dollars annually).[10] Significant new rules per year went into an even steeper climb in 2007—reaching 150 a year in 2011. That is not only an ominous trend. The cumulative addition of new rules since 1996 may already be having perceptible effects on investment and on interest in innovation. Start-up firms may need more and more lawyers to navigate their way through an ever-larger thicket of regulation.

A parallel development concerns patents and copyrights. In 1704, when commissions of literary works by princes and the aristocracy could no longer slake the literate public's thirst for reading, Daniel Defoe, the novelist, economist, and foremost advocate of intellectual property of his day, complained that literary works were copied so fast that no one made a living from writing—a clear market failure. England introduced the first copyright protection with the 1709 Statute of Anne in the reign of Queen Anne. Parliament had already enacted patent protection with the 1623 Statute of Monopolies in the reign of James I. In that early time, patent protection almost certainly encouraged creating new methods or new products more than it discouraged creating them through fear of royalties owed others and the legal costs of disputing royalty claims. (For the first patent owner there was nothing but blue skies.) But now the economy is clogged with patents. In the high-tech industries, there is such a dark thicket of patents in force that a creator of a new method might well require as many lawyers as engineers to proceed. In the pharmaceutical industry, excessive patent protection is causing litigation and

10. The data are compiled semi-annually by the Regulatory Information Service Center at Unified Agenda. Note that the cumulative mounts up to non-negligible levels. If those costs are undiminished, the total cost per year of just those post-1996 rules must have mounted to *at least* 80 billion dollars a year by 2006; and if 80 such new rules continue to be written, the cost will mount to at least 160 billion by 2016 and 240 billion by 2026. The latter cost is 2 percent of a 10 trillion dollar GDP and 1.5 percent of a 15 trillion GDP. Very possibly each new significant rule will be subject to "increasing costs," as lawmakers run out of rules that meet little resistance.

the rise in pharmaceutical prices.[11] Copyright protection has only recently seen controversy. The industries producing literary and artistic products do not seem so clogged with copyright protection as to have driven away many working writers, artists, and designers. But it is important to recall that an innovation is greater, the wider its use. The passage by Congress in 1998 of the Sonny Bono Act lengthening copyright protection by 20 years—to author's life plus 70 years—prevents wider use of Walt Disney's creations and prevents wider use of performances copyrighted by the record companies. The length of the copyright term may also be deterring new innovations that would have had to draw on products at Disney and EMI. Members of Congress have a private interest in lengthening copyright and patent protections, since they can expect to share in the big gains of the few without paying for the small costs borne by the rest of society.

Industries in which the government has been an important regulator or protector are particularly liable, in view of their close contact, to become industries that seek more extensive government aid. As Luigi Zingales wrote, businesses took advantage of "a new opportunity: using political influence not just to reduce government influence but to mold it to companies' advantage."[12] That nicely sums up one of the important ways by which corporatism metastasized into a densely interconnected system of mutually beneficial relationships between private and public—a system that is virtually a parallel economy. It is a system its advocates call industrial policy; its critics, corporate welfare.

A subsidy is not inherently bad. But subsidies to industries (including the farm industry)—grants, loans, guarantees, and tax breaks—often masquerade as changes in the direction of the market economy when their real function is to benefit supporters and cronies of legislators. And not with small potatoes: the outlay for corporate welfare reached 92 billion dollars in fiscal year 2006. As could have been expected, a number of prominent subsidized programs became notorious for their disastrous losses: the Supersonic Transport and the Synthetic Fuels Corporation in the 1970s, the ethanol subsidy of the 1990s, and Fannie Mae and Freddie Mac in the past five years. Of

---

11. The pharmaceutical industry lays the diminished flow of new drugs to the longer time required for drug approval by the regulatory body and suggests that lengthening patent protection of new drugs would be a natural remedy. But the long time it takes the regulatory authority to license new drugs operates to reduce their number and to stretch out their expected lifetime, and the lengthy patent protection merely ensures that competing producers will not drive down the prices, causing the innovators to lose their monopoly rents.

12. Zingales, *A Capitalism for the People*.

course, many companies, notably Hollywood studios, have had their disasters too. The problem is that subsidies redirect the economy's innovation toward politicians, who lack deep specialized knowledge, and away from the private sphere, where judgments are made by idea men, entrepreneurs, financiers, and market people who consider whether there are not better initiatives to think about or develop.

The nexus between private and public, while pervasive, is far more invasive in a few targeted industries. The control of the government over the education and healthcare industries has attracted attention of late. It can no longer be described in terms of enumerated regulations, protections, and subsidies: it is organic and granular. A recent paper by Arnold Kling and Nick Schulz describes this government control:

> [H]ealth care and education are increasingly government-dominated
> industries. And this domination produces two ill effects that exacerbate
> the changes these sectors are already undergoing: Government influence
> artificially increases the demand for both health care and education (by
> significantly subsidizing both) and it makes both sectors even less efficient
> than they would be otherwise (by shielding them from market forces).[13]

Efficiency is not the only thing adversely affected. Some pathways of innovation have been blocked as well. There is little room now for entry into the industry of private schools and colleges or of private hospitals, which had spearheaded the 20th-century advances in American education and medicine; and little room for doctors to deviate from standard procedures and teachers to try out new courses and teaching methods.

It is easy to find a downside in virtually everything done by politicians—a "latent function" masquerading as benevolence. We forget that most regulations, protections, and effective nationalizations have benefits as well as costs, else it would have been hard to make a case for them. So one wonders: How large a toll does the corporatist trend take on dynamism? Fortunately, the spread of such corporatist relationships across the economy, if it is as deep and pervasive as suggested above, can be expected to leave evidence of various kinds. We know that corporatist governments find it more convenient to deal with an industry populated by a few giant corporations than one with a great many small enterprises: The government has the phone numbers of the corporate giants. And there is evidence of a huge rise in industrial concentration in the American economy over the past six decades. In the financial

13. Kling and Schulz, "The New Commanding Heights," p. 10.

sector, the big banks have become behemoths, while the small banks have shrunk. In the non-financial sector too, economic activity has moved dramatically away from small and medium-sized enterprises (on which innovation largely depends) to large corporations, as shown in official data compiled in 2011 by John Foster, Robert McChesney, and Jamil Jonna.[14] Gross profits of the 200 largest corporations as a percentage of gross profits in the economy went from about 15 percent in the early 1950s to 26 percent by the mid-1960s, a level around which it fluctuated until 1966; then it rose steeply to about 30 percent in the period 2004–2008. (About the same is true of the revenue.) The market share of the four largest firms in selected retail industries has— very roughly—doubled between 1992 and 2007, reaching astonishing levels, such as 71 percent in book stores and 73 percent in both computer/software stores and general merchandise stores. As a consequence of government regulations and union work rules, there are often routine delays in starting and completing urban office buildings—delays so long that some new ideas have to be passed up.

Furthermore, if the large companies that have spread in the past couple of decades are relatively secure, their exciting and unpredicted growth behind them, we should expect to find evidence that more and more of the economy, companies or industries, are zones of stability—zones not firing many and not hiring many either—and, nestled among such zones, fewer and fewer zones of development (these are the start-ups) or growth (these are the successful ones) or shrinkage (the ones that are failing). It is no surprise, therefore, to find in Figure 10.1 a downhill trend in *job destruction* from 1989 to 2007, as more and more workers are safe in the cocoons of the large established companies. The economy seems to be moving to a frozen state! Over the same span, a downward trend in *job creation* is visible too, as fewer and fewer of the working-age population are entering or leaving the start-ups, the growth companies, and the failing companies.[15] In short, the economy gives

14. Foster et al., "Monopoly and Competition in Twenty-First Century Capitalism."

15. It must be added that, since the former, relatively stable, zones, taken together, are the preponderant part of the economy, they are capable of providing a significant amount of creative, intellectual work in the aggregate while a small amount per worker; the other zones provide a disproportional amount of creative work, but they are a small part of the economy. When in the autumn of 2009 the large companies took fright at the fall-off in prices and sales, they terminated many of the forward-looking projects—projects building "organizational capital," in recent terminology—and terminated the employees who were at work on them. (The national statistics recorded the subsequent rise in output per employee, and most commentators called it a rise of "productivity," though no advance in methods of production or improvement in prices had occurred.)

Fewer new businesses are being started . . .

Business births (thousands)

2006   550   2009   400

. . . but start-ups play a crucial role in job creation . . .

Net job creation by type of company (millions)

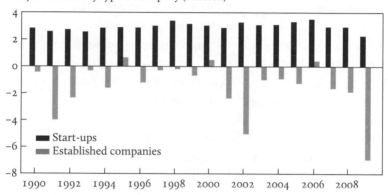

- Start-ups
- Established companies

1990 1992 1994 1996 1998 2000 2002 2004 2006 2008

. . . which remains weak

U.S. private sector job creation and destruction (% of employment)

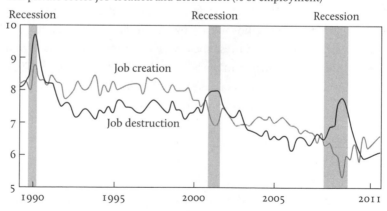

Recession   Recession   Recession

Job creation

Job destruction

1990   1995   2000   2005   2011

FIGURE 10.1 Start-ups in the United States, 1990–2009. (Source: *Financial Times*. © The Financial Times Limited 2013. All Rights Reserved.)

evidence of a relentless decline in *turnover,* which is one of the rather reliable signs of a decline in economic vitality and the fruit that can grow from it if properly tended: economic dynamism.

The abovementioned activities of government represent a corruption of the role of the state, once seen as advancing people's prosperity and achievement. From 1830 to 1930, federal government initiative and intervention were animated by a classical concern for *resources* and *productivity:* the canals, the Louisiana Purchase, the transcontinental railroad, public schools, and so forth; attention later widened to abuses in business, such as protection for workers, creditors, and investors. There was no initiative and intervention aimed at the direction and stability of consumption, such as social insurance programs that supplemented available private insurance. With the reemergence in Bismarck's time of the corporatist idea of government, that began to change. By the end of the 1940s, entitlements in the category of *social insurance* had been established in America, Britain, and elsewhere: insurance for the aged and the disabled (Social Security in the United States) and medical insurance (Medicare in the United States) as well as smaller programs, such as unemployment insurance. By the end of the 1960s, entitlements in the category of *social assistance* were widespread: help with medical needs of the poor (Medicaid in the United States), nutritional needs (Food Stamps), and housing needs. What Europe terms its "social model" socialized the provision of medical care with state-owned hospitals and state-employed doctors, while America's model totally corporatized medical care with programs that regulated services, set prices, and reimbursed the services of private doctors and private hospitals. Now all this is overgrown and bungled.

Few grasp the scale of these social welfare programs. It is true that America fell far behind Europe in social spending in the 1980s: By 1990 social expenditure by governments in the 21 nations of the European Union stood at 20.5 percent of GDP; the figure in the United States was 13.5 percent. But, slowly, the United States has been catching up to the Continent, while Germany and Sweden retrenched from 2003 to 2007: By 2000, the EU spending stood at 21.5 percent, the United States was at 14.5. By 2007 the European Union was at 22.0, while the United States reached 16.2. (All the 2012 figures are up, at 24.1 and 19.5, respectively, owing to unemployment relief.) That spending level in America is now large enough to be quite important. It approaches one-quarter of disposable income. That is in the neighborhood of the share of nonwage income in disposable income—dividends, interest income, proprietorship profits, and land rents. Thus the income of

Americans coming from what may be called *social wealth* is comparable to the income deriving from their private wealth. Moreover, few benefits of social wealth are taxed, while the income from private wealth is all taxable.

In America, as in France and, to a lesser extent, one or two other nations, social welfare outlays will soon have a mountain to climb. A mass of baby boomers working their way through the system will be adding hugely to the annual claims on Social Security and Medicare as they reach retirement. And the baby boomers will not be followed by a mass of replacements entering the labor force. So, sooner or later, additional tax revenues must be raised on both counts (to the extent that "discretionary" spending cannot or will not be cut). Hence, disposable income will be cut. Thus the world of entitlement will nearly swamp the world of work. A calculation by a New York financial economist, Mary Meeker, finds that the *present discounted value* of Americans' entitlements added up to 66 trillion dollars at the end of 2010—a sum that is 569 percent of Americans' disposable income; this dwarfs the U.S. public debt of about 10 trillion. That level of social wealth exceeds Americans' private wealth. (Official data put household net wealth at only 60 trillion dollars in mid-year 2011, or 517 percent of disposable income: assets were 74 trillion and liabilities 14 trillion.) Thus the system of social welfare in America, while commonly thought to be a pale reflection of what is offered by Europe's social model, is in fact quite a colossus.

In one theory of this surge, legislators enacted entitlements on this scale on the assumption that the economy would "grow out" of these entitlements before their deficit financing became onerous, which, as the Great Slowdown went on and on, could finally be seen to be a huge mistake. As Richard Ravitch, a warrior of political reform in both city and state governments, said:

> Politics in America has always been a matter of people running for office
> on the promises that they are going to confer more benefits. But all of a
> sudden, we can no longer afford to . . . pay for all the benefits we've . . .
> obligated ourselves to pay.[16]

But most of the entitlements created were calculated. Even in the past 10 years, new benefits have been enacted where their cost could start later or start small so that little or no tax increase was required. It helped that expansion of the colossus had bipartisan support from Nixon to Bush. The 2003 law signed by President Bush extending Medicare from hospital bills to

16. Quoted in Jacob Gershman, "Gotham's Savior, Beaten by Albany," *Wall Street Journal*, December 11–12, 2010, p. A13.

medicines, which added several trillion dollars to the present value of entitlements at a stroke, had the support of Democrats and Republicans alike. Many Republican legislators, finding that the working class had joined the party in the Reagan years, swallowed their distaste for entitlements. The Democratic party, finding in its midst middle class people who wanted to adopt Europe's social model as much as possible, presented no opposition.

Traditional values have had a more radical influence on the policymaking of Republicans as well as Democrats. Republicans are well known for their unwillingness to use the government's powers of taxation to redistribute—from nationals to foreigners, from profits to wages, and even from high-wage earners to low-wage earners. In their doctrine, revenues are to be reserved for the general interest. Yet, since the 1970s, Republicans from Richard Nixon to George W. Bush have interpreted various government benefit, from social insurance programs to subsidized access to mortgage credit and education loans to the middle class, as being in the general interest.

In another theory of the surge, growth of public benefits follows naturally with the growth of people's incomes—Wagner's Law. But income growth was slower from 1973 to 2007 than it had been in previous postwar decades. A quite different theory of the surge views the rise of the superstructure of entitlements—much like the rise of giant corporations—as a normal phenomenon in the development of organizations. They seek resources with which to achieve their goals and then to grow large enough to be able to survive as long as they can. Once traditional limits on government were withdrawn, the growth of the public agencies was inexorable.

This colossus has had important consequences—and not just the obvious sidelining of alternative government programs, such as addressing the nation's crumbling infrastructure or jobs and wages of the working poor. An effect of consumption entitlements (and public consumption in general) on the population's participation in the economy has long been identified in the classical economics of public finance. The familiar argument is that the higher tax rate imposed on income to pay for the benefit discourages work. (One's savings from the state's providing things free just pays one's tax, but by working a little less one can reduce the tax owed without affecting the benefits.)

Two other links between entitlements to employment, however, operate independently of tax rates. Recall that increased wealth has a "wealth effect," diminishing participation in the economy—the supply of labor—and thus contracting employment; of course, an increase in the after-tax *wage* (or "net wage") that employers offer would have the opposite effect, drawing people into participating in the economy and thus expanding employment. The *ratio* of the net wage to wealth is what matters (in many models), so equal percentage increases in wages and wealth offset one another. That ratio soared from the early 1950s to 1965–1975 with the resumption of fast productivity growth in the 1950s and 1960s, which largely explains the peak levels of employment reached in the 1960s. (See Figure 10.2.) The ratio subsided after the Great Productivity Slowdown brought about slower growth of wages, which partially explains the relatively low employment prevailing from 1979 to 2008. (The years of normal employment in 1995–1996 fit nicely with the normal level of the wage-wealth ratio. The sharp fluctuations of the late 1990s and mid-2000s are explained by the internet boom and the construction boom.) But if we add *social* wealth to the "wealth" in the wage-wealth ratio, fattening the denominator, we explain about half the difference between the high postboom, post-crisis employment rates in 2011–2012 and the level in 1995–1996.

The other link operates through the demand for labor. If the government finances the future explosion of entitlement outlays mostly by an outpouring of government debt, raising taxes later to service that debt (the way governments finance wars), the effect is the prospect of increased interest rates in the future and thus even in the present, and perhaps increased tax rates on businesses at some point. Even today when savers are willing to lend at cheap interest rates, since they no longer are expecting bonanzas of future consumption, these prospects must weigh on share prices and the values placed on the business assets that companies require to produce—plants, employees, and overseas customers.[17]

These employment effects from new entitlements hinge on what might be called the Greek disease but could just as well be called the American disease. The "sound" response of fiscal policy would announce a period of revenue increases leading to a reduction of the public debt that would *decrease* people's *private* wealth by the amount that the new entitlement *increases* their

17. Edmund Phelps and Gylfi Zoega in "Portents of a Darkening Outlook: Falling Equities and a Weaker Dollar Herald Economic Slowdown," *Financial Times*, July 31, 2002, say that "the driving forces behind big swings in a nation's economic activity . . . are non-monetary fundamentals" and high up on the list of those are "workers' wealth and entitlements." The focus was narrowed to future entitlement outlays in Phelps, "The Way We Live Now," *Wall Street Journal*, December 28, 2004. It took readers through the consequences of a demographic time bomb when 15 to 20 years later the bond market will be flooded with public debt to cover the swelling size of Social Security and Medicare outlays. Both essays emphasized that expected future entitlement outlays contract present employment by weighing down share prices and the real exchange rate.

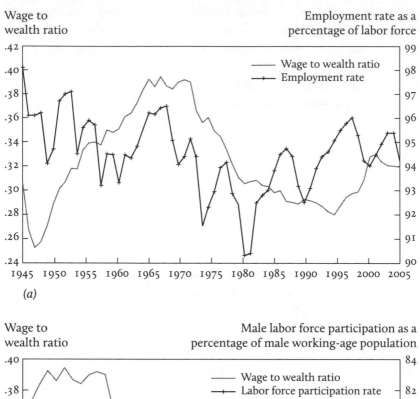

(a)

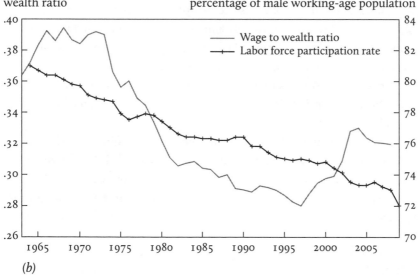

(b)

FIGURE 10.2 (a) Wage to wealth ratio and the employment rate. (b) Wage to wealth ratio and the labor force participation rate (males only). (Source: Gylfi Zoega.)

social wealth. In this way, the government would "neutralize" the wealth effect on employment and saving of the new government program, as first proposed in Phelps, *Fiscal Neutrality toward Economic Growth* (1965). Yet, under President George W. Bush, the government went the other way with the 2001 and 2003 tax reductions. In a February 2001 op-ed, "The Unproven Case for Tax Cuts," the present author protested:

> The tax cut would impose a burden on the future either in reduced public services or else a public debt much increased. This burden . . . makes the tax cut vulnerable to several objections. [One] is that, while the burden of the Bush tax cut would go on forever, its effectiveness [in providing a fillip to labor supply] would not. With time, the incentive effects would progressively weaken and the structural lift to employment would disappear, as workers and managers grew wealthier in response to their higher after-tax wages. . . . If public services are not to be cut back, tax rates must sooner or later go higher than they otherwise would have done in order to deal with the increased public debt. [And] for all we know, the future is as likely to get worse as to get better. . . . Bush's economic policy turns its back on Americans' traditional desire to leave the country better than they found it. In [the 1950s and] 1990s this ameliorist spirit was expressed in the policy of setting tax rates high enough to pay down the government's debts and to emerge with . . . the possibility of falling tax rates in the future. In Washington's lurch toward large tax cuts, and even large spending increases, there is a profound—indeed, disquieting—shift in economic philosophy.

It is not puzzling that legislators let taxes lag behind the entitlements they create, of course. If they had to raise taxes very visibly when enacting a new entitlement, the entitlement might fail to gather enough votes to pass. By cutting taxes they convey the impression that experts have advised that future tax increases are far from necessary: one explanation for under-taxation.

Here innovation finally comes in. We have seen that the welfare colossus shrinks the role of the market by reducing people's incentives to earn; it does that either by causing higher tax rates (with no increase in wealth) or causing higher wealth (with little or no tax increase). That in turn reduces the incentive of market enterprises to engage in innovative activity. The scale of innovation, as Smith would have put it, is limited by the *size of the market.* If, for example, everyone works 30 hours a week instead of 40, the stock of innovations will grow more slowly, as will the stock of capital.

A by-product of the sizeable increase in the scope and size of government in America has been a need for higher taxes. A political pact appears to have been reached in which the upper half of income earners propose to the poor, "we will take on your share of the taxes if you agree that we decide what you will receive in the form of education, public projects, and so on." The result is a bias against state expenditure for education and infrastructure: why would a taxpaying family want music classes for children if the taxpayers had to pay for their own two children plus the children of a nonpaying family? In effect, the lower half accepts a starved public sector in return for a reduction of take-home inequality—a somewhat illusory reduction at that.

It is no wonder, in view of the adverse developments in institutions, values, and economic policies, that America gives signs of a serious decline in economic dynamism and thus—most of the time—in resulting innovation. While the rate of innovation fluctuates, it has been subdued most of the time over most of the business sector since the early 1970s. It is also no wonder, in view of the rise of anti-modern values and policies, that the lower segments of the working population, whose modern values were relatively fragile and their disadvantages daunting to begin with, have suffered a costly decline in their rewards relative to others and in their upward mobility.

The Second Transformation

At this point, which is the end of the narrative and the climax of the book, it may be useful to recapitulate the main observations made and the inferences drawn.

The changes from the 1970s to the 2000s in the way America's economy works—most of which came earlier to the other great avatars of modern capitalism, Britain, France, and Germany—are momentous. The new reworking of the American economy constitutes a Second Transformation—a transformation a century and a half after the Great Transformation, 1820–1930, brought modern capitalism. That first incarnation of modern capitalism did not entail zero government. It could and did operate alongside activist governments that decided whether to purchase new lands, whether to provide infrastructure capital with or without user charges, and where taxation would best raise the revenue needed to function. That modern version of capitalism could have instituted low-wage work subsidies to companies to widen inclusion, without weakening its modern spirit. But while the government, of necessity, was making basic judgments in the political sphere, there was a private sphere in which individuals made the final decisions. Wealth owners—capitalists—got to judge how best to invest their wealth, drawing on the new ideas of imaginative business people and the zeal of resourceful entrepreneurs. This modern capitalism became a worldbeater when, in the 1800s, it acquired endemic, impressive capabilities for indigenous innovation. Those few societies willing and able to adopt it enjoyed unrivaled prosperity, widespread job satisfaction, productivity that was the marvel of the world, and the end of mass privation for the first time in human history.

The second transformation has injected a tacit and finely articulated form of corporatism into the American economy. Modern capitalism has been cordoned off (health and education are to some extent restricted areas) and constrained where it is still in place. The system is less primitive or blatant than that of Bismarck or Mussolini. But its political nature is similar: it draws no line between the state and the market, thus it creates a parallel economy that competes with the market economy and is another source of risk, scaring off innovations. Corporatism's managerial state has assumed responsibility for looking after everything from the incomes of the middle class to the profitability of large corporations to industrial advances. Corporatists, like the communists before them, assumed that all their wishful goals were possible without cost.

The economic performance of the economies that had so recently been exemplars of modern capitalism has recently been disastrous. Yet the fault lies not with the inevitable shortcomings of a well-maintained modern capitalism or even a "reckless" one allowed to operate with a "lack of regulation." It lies with the new corporatism:

> The new corporatism chokes off the dynamism that makes for engaging work, faster economic growth, and greater opportunity and inclusion. [It] does that by maintaining lethargic, wasteful, unproductive and well-connected firms at the expense of dynamic newcomers and outsiders; and by pursuing goals such as consumption, social insurance, and rescue of companies and industries over nourishing lives of engagement, creating, and exploring. Today, airlines, auto manufacturers, agricultural companies, media, investment banks, and much more have at some point been deemed too important to weather the free market on their own, receiving a helping hand in the name of the "public good."
>
> The costs of corporatism are all around us: dysfunctional corporations that survive despite their gross inability to serve their customers; sclerotic economies with slow output growth; a dearth of engaging work; scant opportunities for young people; governments bankrupted by their efforts to palliate these problems; and increasing concentration of wealth in the

hands of those connected enough to be on the right side of the corporatist deal.[18]

Tragically, this system in parts of the world, notably north Africa, is commonly called "capitalism" because the capital there is largely under private ownership, no matter that it is a system ruled by political power—by an alliance of leaders in the state and leaders in the state-backed corporations, generally coming from the same elite—not by private capital in the sense of faceless and friendless capitalists in a brutal competition to find profits before someone else does—"capital" in the sense of Marx. And, cynically, in America, Britain, and continental Western Europe, the corporatist system's apologists and beneficiaries have the temerity to blame all the recent failures on "recklessness," and "lack of regulation" and to suggest that "the future of capitalism" hangs on more oversight and regulation, which in reality means more corporatism.

In all the numerical data on the broadened nexus between government and society—between the state and the individual—there is no clear evidence on the degree to which corporations, banks, and individuals are the drivers of the new system and the extent to which politicians supply the impetus. A 2012 documentary film, *Heist: Who Stole the American Dream?* sees corporations and banks as the sole instigators:

> In 1978, Supreme Court Justice Lewis Powell . . . urged American corporations to take a stronger role in influencing politics and law. . . . While on the Supreme Court, he successfully argued for the right of corporations to make political contributions. . . . Starting in 1994, the North American Free Trade Agreement [NAFTA], which encouraged the outsourcing of cheap labor; the 1999 repeal of parts of the Glass-Steagall Act, which had separated commercial and investment banking; and the Commodity Futures Modernization Act of 2000, which deregulated over-the-counter derivatives, allowed financial institutions to run wild. Both major parties promoted deregulation fever.[19]

These charges are not contextualized. There is no mention that the Court was extending to corporations what it had granted in the spirit of corporatism to labor unions long ago—and with little complaint. NAFTA was a step toward free trade, which is much valued by a great portion of American and

18. Ammous and Phelps, "Blaming Capitalism for the Ills of Corporatism," *Project Syndicate,* January 31, 2012.

19. The summary is in the movie review by Stephen Holden, "Tracing the Great Recession to a Memo 40 Years Ago," *New York Times,* March 1, 2012.

European society. Neither is it mentioned that in legalizing over-the-counter derivatives, America was catching up to the structured financial products invented in Italy and analyzed by French mathematicians. Nor is it mentioned that it was the U.S. government that rigged the banking industry for sub-prime housing instead of focusing on innovation and financing government deficits; it was the government that enticed people into levels of consumption and leisure they could not afford.

But it hardly matters. Even if shareowners, lenders, and wealth owners generally have more political power now than in the Galbraithian 1950s and 1960s era—Galbraith thought that big business in those times ran the show, but the silver lining was its pro-social acts that Congress would not or could not legislate—the explosion of corporate welfare, self-serving regulations and deregulations, and a sea of social insurance have all depended upon a willingness or eagerness on the part of government officials and legislators to protect vested interest and to cater to special interests in return for electoral support and financial support. It is a *system* of interlocking parts: a corporatist system fluctuating between tripartism—government, organized business, and organized labor—and bipartism, in which labor is less well connected. What propels the system is ultimately the economic and political culture of self-importance and self-dealing. Sometimes labor is up and business down, and sometimes it is the other way around.

The success of the modern economy from the middle 1800s to the early 1970s raised human spirits as nothing had done in the millennia before. It was a triumph of modern morality and a vitalist spirit, mixed with a dose of ancient materialism. Yet, with the passage of time, it has suffered the predations of the political sector, the decay of its culture, and the betrayals by its managers. Though the world is "ruled by ideas," as Keynes said, modern capitalism was a new idea still not widely understood: Its ethical basis and moral foundation had not yet been developed. Corporatism was an old idea with which many were more comfortable. So the competition of ideas is not necessarily going to play out in the present century as it did in the past. We should have known that, after a spectacular run of more than 100 years, modern capitalism might be weakened and imperiled.

If we are to embark on reform we will need this time to expound our values and aims: to explain what sort of careers and economic life are most rewarding, what kind of economy would promote a good life, and how it can offer justice toward all.

CHAPTER ELEVEN

The Good Life:
Aristotle and the Moderns

It is undeniable that the exercise of a creative power, that a free
creative activity, is the true function of man. It is proved to be so by
man's finding in it his true happiness. But it is undeniable, also, that
men may have the sense of exercising this free creative activity in
other ways than in producing great works of literature or art; if it
were not so, all but a very few men would be shut out from the true
happiness of all men.

MATTHEW ARNOLD, "The Function of Criticism"

[S]omeday, not too long from now, you will gradually become old
and be cleared away. . . . Your time is limited, so don't waste it living
someone else's life. Don't be trapped by dogma, which is living with
the results of other people's thinking. Don't let the noise of others'
opinions drown out your own inner voice, heart and intuition. They
somehow already know what you truly want to become.

STEVE JOBS, Stanford University commencement

CHAMPIONS OF CORPORATISM AND THE NEW CORPORATISM have all
thought in materialist terms—in terms of inefficiencies in production,
wasteful unemployment, and costly fluctuations. Conventional champions
of capitalism did too. The corporatists argued that the corporatist system was
superior in these terms to the modern-capitalist system. They said the system
would generally deliver higher productivity, less waste from unemployment,
and, thanks to job protection, greater stability in individuals' wealth, wages,
and employment. In fact, the performances in these terms of the relatively
well-functioning corporatist economies has proved at best roughly comparable to that of the relatively well-functioning modern capitalist economies in
the last decades of the 20th century. To choose between the two systems we
have to move on from the materialist perspective of classical political economy.

The many words of praise here for modern capitalism tend to emphasize nonmaterial rewards: the stir of challenges, the satisfactions of testing and exploring, and the thrill of success. Exemplars of a well-functioning modern capitalism are seen as offering participants opportunity to find lives of sufficient richness, self-expression, and personal development. Corporatism is seen as a chilling doctrine that, in protecting people from each other, would stifle creativity, block initiative, and penalize nonconformism.

It is the strong dynamism of a well-functioning modern economy that accounts for its distinctive rewards. The engagement in its processes is its own reward—the experience of mental stimulation, the challenge of new problems to solve, the chance to try the new, and the excitement of venturing into the unknown. Of course, there are by-products—the transience of the work, the precariousness of the profit, the likelihood of failed attempts and even ultimate failure; also, the possibility of being defrauded or conned. These rewards and hazards are the pluses and minuses of the modern economy.

Present-day corporatists can reply that their system also brings good feelings and experiences—solidarity, security, and industrial peace. They constantly suggest that these are basic to a good society. Hence, the human *significance* of the rewards and the hazards of the modern economy have to be understood and appreciated to have a sense of the desirability or appeal of the modern economy—relative to a corporatist economy or any other sort. (Some say—many Marxists, though not Marx himself—that the nonmaterial matters little, if at all.) There can be no justification of a well-functioning modern capitalism if people do not want what it is good at offering. So there are *fundamental* questions that are logically prior to questions of what could be done and would be worth doing in America to reverse the decline of dynamism, to which the decline of job satisfaction and other recent malfunctions are arguably linked—questions that must take precedence to matters of fine-tuning, such as banking reform and the income tax schedule.

This chapter takes up the question: Which of the two sorts of economic systems would a person want for himself or herself: the concerted system for solidarity and the rest or the individualist system for exploration and all that? The system for protection or the system for dynamism? Have people long wanted the modern life, since even the dawn of modernity, and before it? (Other fundamental questions having to do with diversity and equity are the subject of the next chapter.) Are there higher dimensions of performance— dimensions of a *good life*—in which an economy must perform well to be deemed a *good economy*?

Questions of the "good economy" and the "good life" it serves are not familiar ground in political economy. As others have complained, socialist thought—the left—does not convey a conception of the desirable economic life—a life that socialists believed their preferred system would be best suited to serve. It sees every economy as a sausage machine, simply linking the hours the workers put in to the sausage that comes out—with close attention paid to how the output is divided among the workers. Corporatist thought has no truck with the good life of the individual either, focusing instead on *national* output and *social* harmony through "concertation," social insurance for spreading wealth, and a cultivated spirit of solidarity.

The trouble with those latter perspectives on economic systems is that they overlook or deny the importance of the *means* to the ostensible ends—the processes and character of the economic system by which each day products are produced and jobs created. The means have consequences beyond the materialist results. Choosing one of the relatively modern economies spells differing pathways and resulting experiences, thus a string of modern rewards and hazards.

It may be asked what hope there is of arriving at a well-considered and widely agreed conception of the good life in view of the differences in what nations and generations chose. Nineteenth-century America drew boatloads of people with hopes of "making it" in new ventures and enterprises, while others chose to remain in Europe. By the end of the century the boatloads seemed more interested in corporatist and socialist practices, such as unionizing and raiding the profits. By the second half of the 20th century, people everywhere spoke of marshaling resources to solve the "real problems" of society. But changing choices do not necessarily signify changing values. It may be that the seemingly new wants are, in most cases, the creature of new conditions or a new capacity, as with those resulting from increased wealth or greater democracy. In recent decades, more and more people say they wish for a level of economic security not dreamt of a century ago. But these wishes have not taken into account a society's adopting a system that, intentionally or not, slows down change. In judging the rival economic systems in the "economically advanced" countries of the 21st century, the right criteria are people's fundamental, well-considered aspirations.

The humanities—especially philosophy and literature, but more recently psychology too—have things to say about the deepest desires and rewards. Over the millennia, humanists have thought about the ways of life that give the deepest, most lasting satisfaction, and they have accumulated several arresting insights. Their insights into the good life help us understand how an enterprising and innovative kind of economy began to sprout up once countries could afford it. (Just pointing to the falling away of restraints is not sufficient.) These insights take us a long way toward a justification for a society's support of an entrepreneurial, innovative economy. If political economy does not learn what the humanities have to teach, it will be the poorer for that: It will continue to be unequipped to deliver the winning argument in the re-emerging debate over the modern economy.

The Humanist Concept of a Good Life

The *concept* of the good life—the idea of such a thing—starts with Aristotle.[1] It means the sort of life that people, on reflection, would choose to the extent feasible—after non-elective goods such as food and shelter are obtained. In his book *Nicomachean Ethics,* which has a large readership to this day, he contrasts ways of life that are just *means* to an end with the *good life,* which is not a means to some end but rather an end in itself—lived for its own sake.[2] To paraphrase his argument: people need food (by producing it or trading domestic products to get foreign food) as a means to energy, need energy as a means to build shelter and sheds, need those as a means to protect oneself and one's produce against wet and cold, and so forth. Every *final* good—gourmet cuisine, haute couture, bel canto opera—is the end-point of a program or activity. Aristotle is interested in the *ranking* of the various "activities," each culminating in some kind of final good. Aristotle credits to thoughtful people a sense of what the "highest good" is. His aim is to explain, or interpret, the ranking—at least the ranking that thoughtful, serious people exhibit with the life choices they make.

Aristotle recognizes that a certain amount of "moneymaking" is "forced" on society (1096a). This recognition might suggest he believes the good life is affordable only to an elite. He implies that, in his time, it was not within the reach of the less fortunate. But he never says—nor is there any reason to believe—that the good life will never be accessible at the bottom rungs of

---

1. The next four sections grew out of a public lecture at Columbia in 2007. They were later the basis of my paper for the Festschrift collection *Arguments for a Better World: Essays in Honor of Amartya Sen*, K. Basu and R. Kanbur (eds.), Oxford: Oxford University Press, 2009. This chapter is a different development of the lecture, with departures, corrections, and deletions.

2. Following convention, page numbers refer to Immanuel Bekker's classic edition of Aristotle (1831). A helpful edition is Aristotle, *Nicomachean Ethics* (1999).

society. Aristotle also notes that slaves generally had slavery forced on them—his own teacher, Plato, might have been sold into slavery—so there is no basis for inferring that they lacked an innate desire or capacity for the highest good.

Aristotle implies that pursuit of the "good" by a person making his entire life on a deserted island, even a rich island, would not compare, generally speaking, to pursuit of the good "in cities"—in a society, in other words. Thus he recognizes the many interactions and complementarities *at the level of ideas* among people in a society. As a consequence, a society needs to decide what the good life consists of in choosing the economic institutions to support and the culture to transmit in school. Thus, "we should try to grasp, in outline at any rate, what the good is" (1094b). This insight exposes a weakness in the competing libertarian idea that the good life is one of freedom. There could be societies in which there is total freedom but a culture of crime, promiscuity, or drugs makes most if not all people unhappy.

Some of Aristotle's finest passages are about what the good life is *not*. It is *not* doing the politically correct thing. That may be the objective of politicians, he says, but "it appears to be too superficial to be what we are seeking, for it seems to depend more on those who honor than on the one honored, whereas we intuitively believe that the good is something of our own and hard to take from us." Next he argues that the good does not consist of virtues either. We require some virtues to pursue the good life successfully, but virtue is not sufficient in itself: you could be miserable being virtuous if you had no sense of the right track to be on—the one toward your happiness.

There is a way to live that is good for people, then. Whatever the particular conception of the good that a nation or people might have, the good life always means the inner condition, or state of mind and feeling, that people seek in the way they live their lives. (When referring to this state Aristotle uses the Greek word *eudaimonia* (1095b), the precise meaning of which comes up below.) This idea of the good life conveys a humanist spirit. This is *not* the idea of a godly life, such as the idea in some religions that men and women have the function of utilizing resources to survive and reproduce themselves in order that another generation might survive and reproduce, and so on over an indefinite future. The difference between the two concepts is the difference between a life of duty to god and a life of value to oneself. In this respect, Aristotle, writing in the 4th century BC, took a position very different from that of the Judaic scholars of the 1300s BC and later clerics.

Lest he be taken for a hedonist, Aristotle hastens to explain that, although the good life is something that humans strive for and find gratifying, a good life is *not* one of "amusement": "It would be absurd," he writes, "if [our] end were amusement and our lifelong efforts and sufferings aimed at amusing ourselves. . . . We amuse ourselves to relax . . . so that we can go back to do something serious" (1176b). Perhaps Aristotle is having a bit of fun with his student-age listeners. Surely we do not have to be slaves of the good life. We ought to allow ourselves a night at the opera or the movie house, even when it will not advance our life projects. Besides, you never know. As the work unfolds we may be struck with some insight for use in an as-yet-unknown future.

We see that Aristotle's subject is the nature of the paths that are *right* for people. He does *not* hold that the good life is a life of freedom, as if it does not matter what people do with that freedom. Neither does he constrain the good path to one of the paths that society has already left open to individuals, as if it did not matter to him whether freedom was narrow or wide. (Perhaps Aristotle would have approved every increase in freedom that can be shared by all—every increase that does not constrict anyone else's freedom. In any case, it was left to Rawls to write that book.)

Aristotle's Conception of the Good Life

What is Aristotle's own *conception* of the good life? In substantive terms, he characterizes it as the *pursuit of knowledge*. In his words, "[t]he best [thing] is understanding. . . . This activity is supreme, since understanding is the supreme element in us" (1177a). "*Eudaimonia*," he writes, "[derives] from some sort of study." Study is the "highest good," he argues, largely because it requires "reason," and reason is the main faculty that separates human beings from the other animals. He adds that this conception fits with his observation that *eudaimonia* is not felt by the other animals.[3]

The thrust of Aristotle's argument, animals aside, is that, with increases in the ability to understand and the wealth with which to afford it, a person reaches increasingly the more elevated kinds of satisfactions rather than just enjoying more and more of the old ones. The satisfactions from the knowledge accumulated and from the pursuit of knowledge are at the top of the hierarchy of final goods. The higher the income level, the larger is the

---

3. That last part could be questioned. Suppose that dogs, dolphins, or others *did* possess reason, as imagined in Gustav Mahler's *Songs of a Wayfarer*. That would not refute the proposition that knowledge is the "best [good]" and pursuit of it the "supreme activity." The claim that *eudaimonia* is felt only by humans is not obviously necessary to Aristotle's argument, though he appeared to think so.

proportion of expenditure on these elevated pursuits. In this sense, they are the highest good.

The narrowness of the knowledge that Aristotle appears to regard as the "highest good" and whose pursuit is the "supreme activity" is out of tune with modern values. He appears to envision that the knowledge sought by people is solely an end, as distinct from a means, and that the pursuit of knowledge is an ascetic activity, practiced in a cloistered setting, perhaps stimulated by the occasional study group or conversation with a friend—the sort of activity carried on by mathematicians, theoretical physicists, and scholars, such as philosophers and historians. No doubt these narrow views of Aristotle's derive from the narrowness of his background, having been confined to a world oriented around classical knowledge rather than practical knowledge, and around the classical way of acquiring it—by study.

There is another problem with the thesis in its original form. If the highest good is exclusively knowledge that is not used for anything, a society, as it becomes more and more productive or rich, will devote more and more time to the leisure activity of pursuing such knowledge, which has no commercial value in the marketplace. So the theory predicts that as hourly productivity increases in a country, we will observe at some point little or no further increases in the production and sale of goods—only steady further increases in leisure activity in the pursuit of knowledge. This is precisely the prediction made in the essay by John Maynard Keynes, "Economic Possibilities for Our Grandchildren" (1963)—an essay adorable to some and appalling to others. But we do not observe that outcome.[4] The puzzle is obviously resolved, though, once we take a broader view of knowledge, and the one or two other things people seek alongside it.

Here we must move on to subsequent thinkers, though Aristotle is never far away.

The Pragmatists and the Good Life

Succeeding philosophers and writers, with no sense of being out of tune with the Aristotelian perspective, have focused on other kinds of knowledge and other kinds of activities in pursuit of such knowledge while bearing in mind

---

4. Aristotle could not have been pleased with the finding of recent happiness researchers that, *after a point*, further increases in productivity do not add to reported happiness, a paradox I have discussed elsewhere. See, for example, Layard, *Happiness* (2007).

Aristotle's fundamental insights about the hierarchy of desires: the desire for knowledge and the place of knowledge as the most desirable good yet the last to be affordable.

Humanist writers and philosophers after Aristotle have introduced *practical* knowledge, a good that is definitely *not* valued just for itself—much of it *informal* knowledge, which does not make its way into documents. These humanists have also introduced the quite different kinds of activities that are carried on in gaining such knowledge and the worldly contexts in which such knowledge is pursued.

In one group there are the pragmatists—so named because they call attention to the ways that ends are pursued and the value that some ways may have and others may lack. (They are far from "pragmatic" about the pursuit of ends.) The pragmatists focus on knowledge acquired and used for the purposes of producing or acting in some way. People start their working life with a stock of knowledge, of course, and gain much new knowledge in solving the problems that typically arise. To succeed in their work or their business they have to be able to meet its technical demands: problem solving is a factor in one's success. The considerable knowledge acquired in the process is generally gratifying, no matter that it was not sought for its own sake. It provides a sense of mastery and of standing on one's own feet.

An early figure in this group is the poet Virgil, who was born of peasant stock in the Po Valley in 70 BC (some 300 years after Aristotle's birth) and settled in Rome in the age of the emperor Augustus. Virgil's well-known poem *Georgics* somehow came to be viewed as a primer on agriculture until fairly recently; but at a deeper level it is an ode to humanity and Roman culture.[5] It speaks at length and admiringly of the vast knowledge the farmer acquires and draws upon in plowing, planting trees, tending cattle, and keeping bees. It expresses the farmer's engagement in this work and his satisfaction at a successful harvest. This poem contains one of Virgil's immortal lines: *Felix qui potuit rerum cognoscere causas.* (Happy is he who knows the causes of things.)

Voltaire fits well in this group. Writing in late 18th-century France, when the feudal manors were shrinking and opportunities for careers in business were opening up, he conveys the importance of a life of action—of work. As he dramatizes in his apparently imperishable book *Candide,* the action need not be for social causes or to right wrongs; Voltaire advises us to forget all that. Instead,

---

5. The change of interpretation is credited to Roger Mynors. See his *Georgics by Virgil* (1990). The quote is from verse 490 in book 2 of the *Georgics.*

he suggests that business life could be meaningful and amply rewarding. The stirring and touching finale for sextet and chorus of the musical *Candide*, composed by Leonard Bernstein with words taken from Voltaire by Stephen Sondheim, manages to condense much of Voltaire's thought to four lines:

We're neither pure nor wise nor good.

We'll do the best we know.

We'll build our house, and chop our wood.

And make our garden grow.

Society, Voltaire is suggesting, lacks the wisdom, expertise, and benevolence to design, operate, and preserve the best of all possible economies. But although we know little about many important things, we can embark on careers, society permitting. All of us can have good lives building our own careers and businesses—and can thus end up with an economy that is good enough. Voltaire urges us to grasp that the knowledge and experiences we draw upon and the knowledge and experiences we gain along the way are likely to make such a life interesting and rewarding. (It is not surprising, then, that French economists were first to see a key role for the *entrepreneur*.)

In the middle decades of the 20th century closer attention was paid to the nature of the satisfactions deriving from the workplace and to the part played by the individual's *acquisition* and *use* of *private knowledge* in those satisfactions. A pioneer is John Dewey, the American pragmatist philosopher and one of the lions of Columbia for decades. Dewey, anticipating Hayek, understands that ordinary workers possess considerable specialized knowledge of use in the course of their work. He emphasizes the human need to exercise this knowledge in problem-solving activity.[6] Even the worker of ordinary education can be engaged in and can gain intellectual development from the formation of skills—a type of knowledge—arising from problems that are put to him or her in the workplace—or could be put to him or her if the workplace were desirably organized. Furthermore, Dewey seems also to grasp that each worker is apt to know things the others do not, so that there is a role for the workers sitting around a table working out for themselves the best solution to the problem of the day.[7]

---

6. His writings in this area run from his *Human Nature and Conduct* (1922) to *Experience and Education* (1938).

7. Dewey disapproved of Fordian mass production and hoped the workplace would be reformed again to provide the intellectual satisfactions of which it was capable. Of course, market forces have by now pretty much eliminated the assembly line—or, in many cases, moved it to Guangdong province.

The psychologist Abraham Maslow in a much-read 1943 paper drew up a hierarchy of human needs, starting with the most basic.[8] In this hierarchy, he gives a place to the need to acquire "mastery" of a trade or skill—typically after some apprenticeship. This need comes immediately after the physiological needs at the base and, next up the ladder, security needs. Maslow also recognizes the need for an ongoing *process* of problem-solving, a process of "self-actualization."

John Rawls, toward the end of his magisterial work on economic justice, sets out with great clarity the main theme of this literature on the good life— the "Aristotelian perspective," as he dubbed it.[9] One acquires knowledge over a career through the development of one's "talents," or "capacities," which is the essence of one's *self-realization*. And this self-realization, or as much of it as we obtain, is the central drive that every one of us has. Rawls's forcefulness and clarity are on full display in his exposition:

> [H]uman beings enjoy the exercise of their realized capacities (their innate or trained abilities) and this enjoyment increases the more the capacity is realized or the greater its complexity. . . . [It] is a principle of motivation. It accounts for many of our major desires . . . Moreover, it expresses a psychological law governing changes in the pattern of our desires. [It] implies that as a person's capacities increase over time . . . and as he trains these capacities and learns how to exercise them, he will in due course come to prefer the more complex activities he can now engage in which call upon his newly realized abilities. The simpler things he enjoyed before are no long sufficiently interesting or attractive. . . . Now accepting the Aristotelian Principle, it will generally be rational, in view of the other assumptions, to realize and train mature capacities. . . . A rational plan . . . allows a person to flourish, so far as circumstances permit, and to exercise his realized abilities as much as he can.[10]

A relatively recent contribution to this topic is that by Amartya Sen in his 1992 and 1999 books.[11] There is something fundamentally missing, Sen suggests, in present-day thinking about the good life in the sense of Aristotle. Neoclassical economic theory, which is still taught (whether or not exclusively), takes "utility," or happiness, to be a function of the bundle of

---

8. Maslow, "A Theory of Motivation."
9. Rawls, *A Theory of Justice* (1971, pp. 424–433).
10. Rawls, *A Theory of Justice* (1971, pp. 428 429).
11. Sen, *Inequality Reexamined* and *Commodities and Capabilities*.

consumer goods and leisure chosen, and this happiness could be seen as *indirectly* a function of the resources possessed. It is as if the economy's actors all participate in a comprehensive once-and-for-all auction in which they will contract their entire future. Sen objects. In his "capabilities approach," any fulfillment from one's life will require one to acquire "capabilities"— capabilities "to do things." And *choosing* which capabilities to try to acquire is part of the satisfaction. Thus he gives content to Marshall and Myrdal's suggestion (cited in Chapter 3) that the jobs absorb the mind:

> [Besides the *indirect* one there is a] connection between capability and well-being . . . making . . . well-being . . . depend [*directly*] on the *capability* to function. *Choosing* may itself be a valuable part of living, and a genuine choice with serious options may be seen to be—for that reason—richer. . . . [A]t least some types of capabilities contribute *directly* to well-being, making one's life richer with the opportunity of reflective choice.[12]

Sen is not imagining some joy of choosing. He is pointing to the deeper satisfaction from being competent at selecting a new route if conditions change. ("Having won the lottery, I'm going to make the smart decision to quit the mine and take voice lessons.")

There is another point, which may have been in the back of Sen's mind. Rawls tacitly postulates a neoclassical world. There may be random events, but their probabilities are known. They do not get in the way of the fact that the *prospect* of "self-realization" has a clear meaning: it is how far you, he, or she would expect to get in your development—how far on the average, with repeated rolls of the known dice. But in a modern economy, some basic change in the shape of the economy is almost certain to have occurred within a generation, but we have no foreknowledge of what it will be. In that sort of economy, the sort of "self" a person develops in one scenario, or evolution, may differ considerably from that developed in another scenario. What is "realized" as one goes through life is not only the distance of one's development but also the direction of one's development. In this world, the "self" is neither fixed nor subject to fixed laws of motion, so the concept of the self is of no explanatory value. In *Henry V,* Prince Hal gives voice to the intense fluctuations possible in personal development, when, two years after his coronation and girding for his great battle with the French, he remarks, "I have turned away my former self."

---

12. Sen, *Inequality Reexamined* (1992, p. 41), italics added. Sen cites Marx and Hayek among several precursors who placed a value on freedom independently of outcomes.

The Vitalists on the Good Life

The post-Aristotelian literature of the pragmatists stops short of saying some of the most important things about a good life. This literature is almost arid in portraying life at its best as one long series of pragmatic exercises in problem solving, which serve to keep us engaged and yield the satisfactions of mastery. This conception of the good life, though it has merits, makes no room for the thrill of imagining new possibilities and new conquests and the satisfactions that result if the "dreams" are realized—and the (lesser) satisfactions if they are not. Life lived to the full has always been richer than the pragmatist description. But it was odd that so narrow a version of Aristotle's good life was being advanced at a time—from 1920 to 1970—when unprecedented numbers were having a much more colorful life. In the modern economies of that time, it hardly needs repeating, individuals were exercising their creativity in conceiving a new product and their imagination in forecasting its benefits to end-users; and teams were taking on the risks of attempting its development and its adoption.[13] Is there, then, some other perspective on the good life that conveys what it feels like to be an actor in such a world and expresses the value that the actors in the modern economy place on participating in its processes?

A quite different conception of the good life was growing up from ancient times in parallel with the pragmatist version. It is the conception to which Columbia's Jacques Barzun and Yale's Harold Bloom gave the name *vitalism.* Some key figures and ideas were touched on in Chapter 4, but a fuller account is called for here. Until not long ago, students in European high schools and American colleges were introduced in the core curriculum to the vitalist literature of the Western canon. The earliest vitalist may be Homer, the Greek poet of the 12th century BC and author of the *Iliad* and the *Odyssey.* These epic poems tell of ancient Greek heroes—their determination, courage, and patience.

Another early vitalist is the sculptor Benvenuto Cellini, a larger-than-life figure of the Renaissance (and the protagonist of the Berlioz opera named after him). In his *Autobiography* he frankly relishes his creativity and revels in

---

13. The transition from mercantile to modern is made by one man—Robinson Crusoe—in Defoe's 1719 novel. Jean-Jacques Rousseau in his 1762 book *Émile* views Crusoe as having allowed only "necessity" to determine what he tackled. But once Crusoe secured food supplies and shelter, he did not simply solve the problems he met on a predetermined path: he succeeded in making pottery and adopted a parrot, neither a necessity, using his creativity and imagination.

making it. Even today, a young reader could be taken aback by such powerful ambition.

In a slightly later period, Cervantes and Shakespeare dramatize the individual's quest. The message of Cervantes' novel *Don Quixote*—the "Man of La Mancha" with the "Impossible Dream"—is that a life of challenge and adventure is necessary for human fulfillment; and if the barren economy of the Spanish desert does not supply such challenges, one must somehow create them by one's self—*imagining* them, if necessary. In Shakespeare's *Hamlet*, the prince concludes he must act against the king if he is to be someone, aware that he may fail and may pay with his life. The play suggests an initial uncertainty over the king's responsibility. (As the columnist David Brooks remarked, it is rare now that anyone will show he knows that what he is saying may not be true.) It suggests too Hamlet's initial ambivalence about taking an action that would risk everything he has—his position and Ophelia. Bloom in his *Shakespeare: The Invention of the Human* lionizes Shakespeare as the complete vitalist—a "spacious mirror" in which we can all see ourselves.

In the 18th-century Enlightenment, such a view is reflected by some, though not all, of the key figures. David Hume, disputing the *rationalism* of the French, gives a crucial place to the "passions" in decision-making and to "imagination" in the growth of society's knowledge. (Hume may be the first modern philosopher.) As already mentioned, Voltaire urged people to look for satisfaction in individual pursuits, to "grow your own garden." Jefferson wrote of the "pursuit of happiness" and commented that people came to America "to make their fortune." The term "pursue" conveys that seeking a fortune is more valuable than *having* one. The journey is the end.

At the dawn of the first modern societies, the Romantics were wild about exploration and celebrated discovery as well as the determination and perseverance it often takes. We all recall the line of John Keats on the moment when Hernán Cortés "stared at the Pacific . . . silent upon a peak in Darien" and that fierce stanza in William Earnest Henley's *Invictus:* "It matters not how strait the gate/How charged with punishments the scroll/I am the master of my fate/I am the captain of my soul."

Next there were the philosophers of modernity. No American philosopher wrote of vitalism with more energy than William James did. He saw great vitality with his own eyes. Born in New York City in 1842, he was witness throughout his life to the transformation of the American economy from relatively slow paced to explosively innovative. In his ethic, the excitement of fresh problems and new experiences are at the heart of the good life.[14] If Walt Whitman is the poet of the American ethos, James is its philosopher.

At the turn of the century, the notion quietly arises that there is indeed a fixed self, but one does not start one's adult life knowing very well what the needs of that self are. The thesis is that the journey of life is not simply advances, one after the other, in self-realization. Rather it is a journey of *self-discovery.* Through a series of trials and experiences we discover "who we are," which may differ quite a lot from who we thought we were when we started. This approach to the good life is set out quite precisely by a successful singer-songwriter of our day:

> This new album [*Born This Way*] is about rebirth in every sense. . . . It's
> about being able to be reborn, over and over again throughout your
> life. . . . until you find the identity inside yourself that defines best who
> you are and that makes you most feel like a champion of life.[15]

The discovery of oneself (before one's career is over) does not mark an end of one's personal development. Maslow's self-actualization and Rawls's self-realization may well continue but will be better directed for having discovered oneself. That suggests that there is no need to postulate that the self remains fixed throughout all this discovery.

A raft of new ideas from Friedrich Nietzsche, the upstart German psychologist and philosopher, changed the way we think about motivation, even life itself. In a hundred aphorisms, he speaks of venturing into the unknown, overcoming obstacles, failing to overcome obstacles, and learning to persevere through adversity, and "what doesn't kill us makes us stronger." In particular, he crystallized the weakness of the pragmatist approach to the good life. We are not really sacrificing for a future gain when we diet before going on our next film shoot or when we tighten our belts to help finance our entrepreneurial project. We are happy to be in a project that offers us so much, no matter that it demands much from us. As Nietzsche sees it, our work on such

14. William James wrote somewhere, "My *flux*-philosophy may well have to do with my extremely impatient temperament. I am a motor, need change, and get very quickly bored." (Cited in Barzun, *A Stroll with William James*, 1983, p. 265.) By "motor" he did not mean anything like a mechanical device, as Barzun remarks.

15. Lady Gaga, interviewed in Fry, "Lady Gaga Takes Tea with Mr Fry" (2011, p. 12). The actor Alan Alda is also eloquent on this theme in his oft-quoted address at his daughter's commencement: "Be brave enough to live creatively. . . . You have to leave the city of your comfort and go into the wilderness of your intuition. . . . What you'll discover will be wonderful. What you'll discover will be yourself." Quoted in his autobiography, *Things I Overheard While Talking to Myself* (2007, p. 21).

projects meets an inner need, not a need for some cash. He explains that the hurdles encountered in our projects are not costs on the way to materialist payoffs. Instead, overcoming obstacles is itself the source of the satisfaction. The projects are their own reward—the highest reward.[16]

The French philosopher Henri Bergson, a friend of James and likewise a witness to the high modernity of the 19th century, was another champion of vitalism.[17] Picking up Nietzsche's notion of people's need for challenges, Bergson conceives of people energized by a current of life (*élan vital*) and organizing themselves for "creative evolution"—the title of his 1907 book. The theme with which he is now associated is that intense involvement in challenging projects transforms people, so that they are repeatedly in the process of *becoming*. The book *Creative Evolution* elevates this "becoming" far above mere "being." There are almost always precursors, though: not only Nietzsche but also Montaigne, Henrik Ibsen, and Søren Kierkegaard, who held that to exist we must create ourselves.

There is little on personal creativity in philosophy. Nietzsche wrote of a person as carving out his or her own values—the lines between good and evil. But he does not speak of the great satisfactions of creating a symphony or a book or any other product (though Nietzsche, a lover of Wagner's operas, was an amateur composer). Bergson clearly understands that creativity would no longer exist if we had reached a world of *determinism*. However, Bergson does not describe a creative life or show any appreciation of its interior rewards.

Some literary critics and biographers have seen creativity as a central subject of literary criticism. Lionel Trilling wrote of literature as the human activity "that takes the fullest and most precise account of variousness, possibility, complexity and difficulty." Matthew Arnold, quoted at the start of the chapter, spoke of "the sense of exercising . . . free creative activity in other

16. In Nietzsche's view, each day's advance with the project "must appear justified at every moment—or incapable of being evaluated, which amounts to the same thing." (This appears in his posthumous notebook *The Will to Power* (1883–1888), which is not about power over other people but is analogous to the will to win the ball game. See the illuminating treatment of Nietzsche in Richard Robb's 2009 paper, "Nietzsche and the Economics of Becoming."

17. Bergson rose to fame with his 1907 book published in Paris and wider fame with the 1911 English edition, *Creative Evolution*. He was appointed to the College de France and won the Nobel Prize in Literature in 1927. (Incidentally, Henrik Ibsen's dramatic poem *Peer Gynt* (1876) anticipates Bergson's theme when the Button Moulder says, "To be yourself is to slay yourself./But on you, that answer's sure to fail;/So let's say: To make your life evolve/From the Master's meaning to the last detail." The quote is from the 1980 English translation by Rolf Fjelde, p. 195.)

ways than in producing great works of literature or art."[18] Several writers have described the creative life and to varying degrees gotten inside the creators who were their subjects. It was a frequent subject of Arthur Koestler's books, such as *The Act of Creation* (1964) and *The Sleepwalkers* (1968) on the making of modern physics. Irving Stone's *Lust for Life* (1937) and Joyce Cary's *The Horse's Mouth* (1944) might be mentioned, both turned into films. Michael Leigh's screenplay *Topsy-Turvy* explored the lives of Gilbert and Sullivan.

Yet we often turn to writers of fiction in hopes of finding an insight into the forces driving individuals—especially when there is a sense of new forces at work or old forces newly empowered. The interwar decades were a turbulent time, full of tectonic shifts and upheavals. Far from showing any slowing down after the historic triumphs from 1870 to the eve of World War 1 in 1913, America resumed its stunning innovation in the 1920s. In the 1930s, undeterred by the Great Depression, it posted a record-breaking rate of innovation. A few writers sought to reflect the exhilaration and intoxication felt in the process of such creation and discovery. An over-the-top novelist of the time made the attempt to express the mystery and thrill of exploration:

> At length, sick with longing for those glittering sunset streets and cryptical hill lanes among ancient tiled roofs, nor able sleeping or waking to drive them from his mind, Carter resolved to go with bold entreaty whither no man had gone before, and dare the icy deserts through the dark to where unknown Kadath, veiled in cloud and crowned with unimagined stars, holds secret and nocturnal the onyx castle of the Great Ones.[19]

Three decades later the expression "to boldly go," thought to derive from this passage, became the mantra of NASA in the early years of the project to go to the moon.

The difference between the pragmatist take on the good life and the vitalist take is striking. The term "hurdle" is in the lexicon of both schools, but hurdles come up in contrasting ways. In the vitalist view, people are *looking for* hurdles to overcome, problems to solve: if you do not happen to meet any, you change your life so that you start meeting them. In the pragmatist view, people *encounter* hurdles in the course of being pragmatic—of working in an industry or profession that seems to offer the best prospects of success.

18. Respectively, Trilling, *The Liberal Imagination* (1950, p. xxi), and Arnold in his 1865 "The Function of Criticism at the Present Time," reprinted in Arnold, *The Function of Criticism* (1895, p. 9).

19. Lovecraft, *The Dream-Quest of Unknown Kadath* (1964, p. 291), written in 1927.

The pragmatists do not specify what humankind wants to succeed at. They only say that, whatever a person's career is aimed at, the person—unless very unlucky—will meet innumerable problems and solve a great many of them. Their *engagement* in problem solving is an intellectual side of the good life. The resulting mastery is another part of the good life: the part called *achievement.* The value of engagement and mastery could be seen as part of what Aristotle had in mind—just as Nietzschean overcoming and Bergsonian becoming could also be seen as having roots going back to Aristotle.

Vitalism—the doctrine of vitalism, regardless of the strength of vitalism in recently modern economies—is enjoying a revival, after decades of pragmatism. Early English translations of Aristotle's *Ethics* rendered *eudaimonia* as "happiness." That seemed right, since one would suppose that persons engaging in "study," as Aristotle recommended, would take pleasure in gaining more of the world's knowledge and feel delighted at knowing so much. And it diminished the human project to suggest that it was the way to "fun and laughter"—even if, in fact, it does cause jokes and smiles. However, some later scholars such as John Cooper have decided that a better rendering of the word is "flourishing," a suggestion later seconded by Thomas Nagel, although subsequent translators have gone on using "happiness." If we adopt that translation of *eudaimonia* as "flourishing," the *Nicomachean Ethics* is arguing that the good life is one of flourishing, while wryly recognizing that it is a fuzzy concept:

> What is the highest good in all matters of action? As to the name, there
> is almost complete agreement, for uneducated and educated alike call it
> flourishing, and make flourishing identical with the good life and success-
> ful living. They disagree, however, about the meaning of flourishing.[20]

If we translate *eudaimonia* as "flourishing," it broadens considerably what Aristotle meant by "study." He must have thought that people would feel excitement at reading the fierce debates and experience a frisson of suspense at uncovering new evidence for or against controversial ideas. He must also have thought that a life of questing for knowledge is deeply fulfilling. (The sober Thomas Jefferson must have thought the same thing when declaring that people had a right to "the pursuit of happiness.") So Aristotle must be reinterpreted. He is not so much an advocate of studying the physical world as he is a champion of searching, exploring, investigating, and experimenting in all areas—to the extent those things were possible in the 4th century BC. He emerges as the seminal thinker on mankind's desire to flourish.

20. *Nicomachean Ethics,* 1.4 1095a14–20.

Some of the vitalist literature conjures up climbers and explorers interested in testing or proving things to a large public. Of course, a successful innovation is also a public thing. (A hermit's invention is not an innovation.) But there are other vitalist models. Sen's emphasis on "doing things" sounds a vitalist note. Another emphasis is found in recent work by the American sociologist Richard Sennett. He finds evidence in his interviews that many Americans want to feel embarked on a mission to "make a difference." He gives the example of a nurse who preferred the front line in the emergency room of the big city hospital to more lucrative work as a temporary nurse. Sennett suggests these people have a deep need for a "sense of agency"—"vocation" was an earlier way to put it.[21]

The latest book on the subject is *Flourish* by Martin Seligman.[22] He posits that mankind seeks "well-being." But well-being, like freedom, is constructed of several elements, and, like freedom, it cannot be measured—only the elements can. (Seligman comments that the *life satisfaction* reported in household surveys captures our current mood but barely reflects "how much meaning" there is in our lives and "how engaged we are in our work.") For Seligman, the elements are: satisfaction with life, engagement, personal relationships, meaningfulness, and an achieving life (that is, achievement for its own sake). Each element, he argues, contributes to well-being, is pursued for its own sake, and can be measured. This wide-ranging inventory of the ingredients of the good life is evidently the product of careful thought. However, it is missing the contribution of vitalism to "well-being" or whatever it is that humans want. Though Seligman enthusiastically uses the term flourishing, he does not recognize the high-level flourishing—testing, creating, exploring—that we associate with vitalism.

Is vitalism in fact a part of the prevailing ethic in the present age? Inferences based on people we know would not be reliable. The World Values Survey produced by the ethnographers Ronald Inglehardt and colleagues at the University of Michigan surveyed household attitudes and compiled the results in many countries during the years 1991–1993. "When you look for a job," they asked, "do you look for opportunities for initiative?" Fifty-two percent of the total respondents said yes in the United States and 54 percent in

21. Sennett, *The Culture of the New Capitalism* (2006, p. 36). His main thesis is that the unfortunate mutations in modern capitalism over the past two decades have caused these people to lose their sense of dedication and direction.

22. Seligman, *Flourish* (2011). Another entrant in the vitalist literature is Jamison, *Exuberance* (2004).

Canada. "Opportunities for taking responsibility?" Sixty-one percent in the United States and 65 percent in Canada said yes. (In France 38 percent said yes to initiative, 59 percent to interestingness, and 58 percent to responsibility.) The pragmatist version of the Aristotelian ethic is also found in those surveyed. "Opportunities for interesting work?" Sixty-nine percent said yes in the United States, 72 percent in Canada.

Such large nations may be different. Are small countries more communal, less success-driven, than the large countries? Asked in the mid-1990s what the attitude of the public toward Iceland's new entrepreneurs was, the economist Gylfi Zoega said, "They don't feel bad about it. They are thinking only about how to achieve their own success." So it is a live hypothesis that vitalism captures a crucial drive and its motivations importantly shape our experience and our resulting fulfillment in our society.

Aristotle, as noted, thought that the ethic named after him was a universal of human nature. Is the Aristotelian ethic—the vitalist and pragmatist versions included—predominant? It has never lacked rivals. Referring apparently to his country, the Italian economist Pasquale Lucio Scandizzo remarked that a life of contemplation also enjoys a following. There have always been people motivated by a desire to be of service to a group or to society, such as Doctors without Borders, or by a desire to express devotion, such as Bach with his cantatas. There are also lives of social entrepreneurship, such as the career of Florence Nightingale, and lives of sexual exploration or conquest, such as the Marquis de Sade and Casanova; but those lives are not counterexamples to vitalism's power, only distinctive directions of it. In the minds of most, however, the materialist conception of the good life is a serious contender against the Aristotelian perspective and may in some countries be more prevalent.

In the materialist perspective, most people are driven by the desire to earn or profit in order to accumulate wealth or power. Wealth is accumulated until it can sustain a high level of consumption or a high level of leisure or both. China's pivotal reformer, Deng Xiaoping, declared that "it is glorious to be rich." In Calvin's doctrine, earning wealth has God's blessing, and a person's attainment of wealth is a sign of God's favor—the more the wealth, the greater is the favor. In America, major wealth accumulation is widely thought to be motivated by the pro-social uses to which it can be put. Yet two of the most common examples invite the Aristotelian interpretation that they were driven by a desire for knowledge. After creating his fortune at Microsoft, Bill Gates founded a colossal philanthropy aimed at trying out new tools to advance economic development in poverty-stricken nations. The German businessman Heinrich Schliemann drove himself to earn a vast fortune expressly to fund his subsequent search for the ancient city of Troy. The fortune made by many an entrepreneur could be seen as a mere by-product of an obsession to test a quirky idea, such as Ray Kroc's McDonalds empire, in which each franchise was to have no scope for initiative—the antithesis of Hayek's idea of the benefit from openness to on-the-ground judgment and the stress here on grassroots creativity. (Kroc's successors backed away from the bee in Kroc's bonnet.) The careers of George Soros and Warren Buffett are perhaps driven by desires to show that their understanding of asset markets and business investment is superior. Yet most people's wealth accumulations, including outsize accumulations, may be aimed at un-Aristotelian goals: security, comfort, beauty, pride, respect, and the rest. In Freudian psychology there is the suggestion that careers of almost demonic intensity and huge ambition are a sign of some wound that the victim hopes to heal through achievement. Far worse off are those who, having made a great fortune, have no idea of how to use it in a rewarding way. The high suicide rate among present-day China's new multimillionaires may be an example.[23]

However one comes out of the tangled motivations of earning and learning, creating and accumulating, few would deny that lives of earning and wealth accumulation do not offer the gratification and pride that lives of creation and innovation offer. The particular conception of the "highest good" we find celebrated in Aristotle, Virgil, Cellini, Nietzsche, James, and Bergson—the experience of flourishing—better captures the sort of life we admire and aspire to than does the ethic of Weber and the subsequent economists who extolled economic progress.

The ethic of flourishing is alive even today in the West, the materialist ethic and other ethics notwithstanding. It flowered with the scientific revolution that began around 1675; England's Bill of Rights in 1689, which expanded rights against the king; and the Enlightenment inspired by Hume, Jefferson, and Voltaire in the mid-1700s. The prevalence of the Aristotelian ethic was necessary for the birth of the modern economies of the 19th century, whether or not it was the trigger or a further trigger. (The continuation of some modern economies could also be necessary for the survival of the Aristotelian ethic in other parts of the world.)

This chapter must not be read as implicitly suggesting that the arrival of a desire for flourishing lay behind the appearances of the modern economy

23. "Suicide: Wealth Leaves Many Unhappy," *China Daily News*, September 11, 2011, p. 1.

in the 19th century or that the ebbing of this ethic lies behind the decline of the modern economy—of economic dynamism—in one nation after another in the 20th century. Aristotle firmly held that the desire for flourishing was a universal of human nature, though the opportunity was not necessarily there for everyone or every country. Chapters 9 and 10 entertained the possibility that elements of the economic culture have weakened over recent decades. But those chapters *do not* propose that there has been somehow a loss in desire to have a life of flourishing. At most they prepare us for the possibility of an erosion of the workplace attitudes requisite or helpful to economic dynamism. These chapters *do* adduce evidence of a resurgence of competing values, such as a communitarian or corporatist ethic and family values, not a loss of the modern desires.

The prevailing culture(s) and the prevailing ethic(s) are not the same things. People may lose—perhaps out of social pressure—some of the right attitudes required for meeting "good" wants of theirs that remain intact.

Implications for a Good Economy

We may suppose, as Rawls supposed, that a society seeks and builds an economy to provide mutual benefits for its citizens. So, as a life in pursuit of the highest good, or benefit, is termed by Aristotle the "good life," an economy enabling people's mutual pursuit of the highest good may be termed a *good economy.* An economy is good if and only if it permits and fosters the good life.

Where flourishing is a prevalent conception of the good life, the economy, to be good, must serve people's urge to imagine and create the new, their quest to "act on the world," in Hegel's image, thus to seek to innovate, and their desire to pioneer new practice.

An economy that is good in this sense may be rife with injustices, of course. Many commentators and academics have recently suggested, though, that such a "good" economy is bound to create inequalities and cause deprivations for others preferring another sort of life. So this "good" economy is unjust. The next chapter sorts out and takes a position on the issues.

CHAPTER TWELVE

The Good and the Just

Ius est ars boni et aequi.
[Law is the art of the good and the equitable.]

PUBLIUS IUVENTIUS CELSUS

A society is a cooperative venture for mutual advantage. . . . There is an identity of interests, since social cooperation makes possible a better life for all than any would have if each were to live solely by his own efforts. There is a conflict of interests, since persons are not indifferent as to how the greater benefits produced by their collaboration are distributed, for in order to pursue their ends they each prefer a larger to a lesser share. A set of principles is required for choosing among the various social arrangements which determine this division of advantages and for underwriting an agreement on the proper distributive shares. These . . . are the principles of social justice.

JOHN RAWLS, A Theory of Justice

T HE CLASSIC DEFENDERS OF CAPITALISM from mercantile days onward have sought an economy having fewer "interferences" with what they see to be the good in capitalism—the "freedoms" and the "growth"—without a thought for what a *just* economy is. In the premise of some of these classic defenders, each participant receives in pay the value of his or her contribution to national product, exactly as if each worked in isolation, so it is difficult if not impossible to see what moral claim one sort of participant might have to the pay of other sorts. But this premise is untenable. Seeing high earners (and their capital) working with low earners, we understand there is a *mutual* gain from the exchange of services. The Progressives of the early 1900s spoke of a "social surplus" from people's collaborative participation in a nation's economy: The productivity gains from exchange of heterogeneous inputs—labor, land, and capital—add to the pecuniary reward of virtually every kind of talent, every kind of soil, and every kind of capital employed in a market economy. In a modern economy, moreover, innovations result more frequently, and their

289

average payoff is far greater when separate populations merge into an integrated national economy of large scale and variety. Bill Gates's new products could not have made him 50 billion dollars without millions of end-users. Thus high earners benefit from cooperating with others and could subsidize the others without going into the red. Yet it does not follow from this idea of a social surplus that, as egalitarian socialists concluded, everyone ought to be paid the same hourly wage. Equal wage rates would not be workable. (Is a would-be innovator to be paid for the hours spent in the garage?) Even if this equalitarian precept were workable, it would remove the pecuniary dividend that many potential innovators would need to induce them to quit their safe positions and make the extreme effort required for innovation.

Some others among the classic defenders, while conceding that the low earners benefit the high earners, jump to say that the high earners, through their capital investment and innovation, greatly benefit the low earners—pulling up their wages and employment. They see no reason why the high earners should dig into their pockets to pay subsidies aimed at further benefiting the low earners. But this view of a market economy is as mistaken as the previous one. The free market sets wages that send signals and present incentives serving *efficiency*—in some rough and ready way, at any rate—*not* any ideas of *equity*. There may be social or economic considerations that would call for modifying the market mechanism through subsidies and taxes to move some market wages and employment in the desired directions. The problem arising in recent decades is that there are so many considerations and so many conceptions of society's interests, from Jeremy Bentham's utilitarianism—the "greatest good"—to the socialist idea of a social dividend financed by the state's wealth or confiscations to corporatist subsidies for anything that special interests can induce lawmakers to legislate.

A breakthrough came with the 1971 treatise *A Theory of Justice* by John Rawls. A moral philosopher by training, he was responding to the absence of any known notion of what "just" means that is not either unclear or badly flawed. Writing in the turbulent 1960s, when university campuses in America were being torn apart by protests, he could not have missed the acute need for an understanding of justice that a consensus might build around.[1]

1. I shared with Rawls some of the turmoil. We had adjoining offices in 1969–1970 at the Center for Advanced Study in the Behavioral Sciences in Palo Alto, California. One winter day, looking down at the Stanford campus, we could see smoke rising from Encina Hall. Radicals had occupied it and set it on fire. Later they attacked the Center, burning the bank of offices where we worked. Rawls's manuscript survived, as did mine, though a nearby one was a total loss.

Obviously the context of Rawls's work in the 1960s—particularly the protests of black activists—has some parallels to the context in which the present book was written—particularly the Occupy Wall Street protests. Both protest groups had only the vaguest of visions and had little or no idea of how to translate it into an operational solution. Rawls supplied a clear vision of distributive justice and said enough to indicate that it could be realized. (It could be said that both the black activists and Rawls showed influences of American thought on work, earning, and opportunity going back to Lincoln and to Paine. Neither the voices of black pride nor Rawls were talking about handouts.)

Rawls starts by sketching general principles of justice based on the idea of a "social contract" in Locke, Rousseau, and Kant and reformulating it "so that it is no longer open to the more obvious objections." To decide what is just, a society's citizens, shedding their vested interests, imagine an *original position* in which they are to deliberate, with no one knowing whose shoes he will be in when their society and its economy begin operations; not even how many shoes there are of this size and that. In this way Rawls was breaking with Jeremy Bentham, whose idea of the "greatest good" had much influence, especially among economists. In the magisterial opening page Rawls writes:

> Each person possesses an inviolability founded on justice that even the
> welfare of society as a whole cannot override. For this reason justice
> denies that the loss of freedom of some is made right by a greater good
> shared by others. It does not allow that the sacrifices imposed on a few are
> outweighed by the larger sum of advantages enjoyed by many. . . . In a just
> society the rights secured by justice are not subject to political bargaining
> or to the calculus of social interests. (p. 3)

This theory, Rawls argues, leads to a precise conception of justice in the distribution of the rewards from work—an element of *economic justice* in the terminology here—*not* to a justification of the entitlements of the welfare state, about which he was silent. In this conception, economic justice demands the avoidance, where practicable, of economic inefficiency. So some sort of market economy is necessary for justice because other types of economy would cause serious inefficiencies—everyone's wages would be unnecessarily depressed. Furthermore, in a world of differing talents and backgrounds, some wage inequalities are necessary because a system of wage equality would be so inefficient as to lower all pay rates, not just high pay rates. (It would cause employers to be stuck with their round pegs in square holes and cause workers to work less or take less productive jobs they had spurned in favor of high-paying jobs, thus a loss of tax revenue out of which wage subsidies could be paid.) Then comes the famous conclusion in Rawls's argument: *inequality* in after-tax, after-subsidy wages is *just* to the extent it *serves* the working poor—the "least advantaged" working in the economy. The just amount of wage inequality—of the wage gap—is precisely wide enough to deliver the *maximum* remuneration of the lowest earners.

The new vision and new concepts in Rawls's book were electrifying and quickly altered the discourse in economics as well as moral philosophy, though the book was scorned by the right for supposedly neglecting freedom, notwithstanding that Rawls had stressed freedom as essential to justice, and criticized by the left, for whom inequality was worse than poverty. Rawls's attention to the wage may look soulless, compared to cries from the heart against exclusion and violence, but he sees a decent wage as the gateway to a person's "self-respect" and "self-realization." He writes poignantly that a higher wage may make it possible to take a son to the ballgame or to participate in school and town meetings, and thus to gain greater social inclusion. The present author's 1997 book *Rewarding Work* supplemented Rawls's argument for redistribution to the lowest-paid: Subsidizing companies' employment of low-wage workers, by increasing their employment in business, would widen their involvement in society's central project and open up a sense of the world of work in poor families and neighborhoods. The message applies as much to India as to America.[2]

Yet Rawls's book did not hold answers to some fundamental questions about the *modern* economy that we would like to address to him were he still among us. Though he refers often to "prospects" and "expectations," his market economy has no dynamism, and the future it brings is always foreseen. In this austere setting, the book has to adopt a view of the "good" that is—in his own words—so "thin" as to exclude the rich facets of the good life from the ancients to the moderns: Instead, the degree of good available to a person is reducible to the traditional things that his or her wage can buy. As a

2. A recent opinion column by Bharat Jhunjhunwala in *Tehelka: India's Independent Weekly Magazine* on May 7, 2012, condemns the unemployment compensation scheme proposed by Akhilesh Yadav, chief minister of Uttar Pradesh, and advocates employment subsidies instead:

> Phelps has suggested the government must give employment subsidy to the employed. . . . People could benefit from the subsidy only by engaging in productive work . . . That is precisely what Gandhi had said in *Young India* of 13 October 1921: "I must refuse to insult the naked by giving them clothes they do not need instead of work which they sorely need." Yadav should listen to Professor Phelps and Mahatma Gandhi. He should devise schemes that create demand for workers and provide relief to the poor through productive work.

consequence, Rawls did not think through the distinctive issues about economic justice that arise in a modern economy. And his theoretical framework did not help with the justification of that economy—of *modern* capitalism.

Justice in a Modern Economy

What if in a society everyone had a passion for the good life of Aristotle, Montaigne, and Nietzsche, and every young person hoped for a career in an economy structured for dynamism—thus the fullest opportunity to conceive new ideas and to develop, launch, and pioneer the new products they envision or inspire? For such a society, any good economy would have to be a well-functioning *modern* economy of some sort. Any economy *not* offering these would-be participants such opportunity, thus frustrating their aspirations for a good life, would be unjust in the sense of Rawls and many others. What, though, would a modern economy have to look like to be *just*?

To arrive at answers to questions of Rawlsian economic justice in this economy, a citizen could ask herself how she would decide a question from the viewpoint of the Rawlsian original position: she knows she would pursue the good life but does not know her chances of being gifted in imaginative powers, curiosity, intuition, pioneering spirit, and other capacities of value in that pursuit. In that original position, the argument goes, she would favor the broadest opportunity to start a business, the broadest access to capital from the financial sector, and the broadest access to legal protections. In short, she would favor equal opportunity: if it were unequal, *she* could be one of those shut out. (She would also favor affirmative action in anticipation she could be one of those not receiving as much access as some others.)

What in a modern economy would justice in income distribution involve? A modern economy is striking for the *extraordinary income*—oversize profits and capital gains in anticipation of profits—that accrues to those whose new idea or whose entrepreneurial development or marketing of a new idea led to a successful adoption in the marketplace. Since those working under the direction of an entrepreneur are paid wages in anticipation of the chance of commercial success, there are also losses and capital losses to deal with. Varying parts of these incomes would be spent or accumulated to pay for the use of others' new products and for helping to finance one's next innovative venture or finance someone else's new project. Thus there is a so-called circular flow. In this way, income and wealth would come to be highly valued, even if tangible capital is not going to be very important. A citizen who puts himself in Rawls's original position might, at first, be against taxing the winnings of the winners to cushion the losses of the losers. With more reflection, however, he might see that such redistribution would *encourage* risk taking by the private sector: the government, as a partner sharing in the gains and losses, is reducing the risk of the private parties. On still further thought, though, the citizen in the original position might wonder why society should encourage risk taking. Why would I want to see the state encouraging more high-risk investing and pure gambling when what I want is to participate in an economy of dynamism? And I might like the frisson of excitement that comes from a leap of faith, a voyage into the unknown. So a citizen, knowing what the good life is but not knowing his endowments, would not be interested in the government's taking a share of the profits to mitigate losses—and certainly not to mitigate losses on failed investments that had nothing to do with innovation.

Taxing profits is widely thought to be necessary to do justice to workers, not to finance cushions for failed innovators. While Rawls's book is about just wages, its focus is on the redistribution of *ordinary income*—in particular, the redistribution of *wage* income from high-wage to low-wage earners.[3] There is no profit income in the non-modern, even classical, economy that is the setting for Rawls's book and for the basic public finance literature—aside from profits arising from monopoly, which would be a distraction here. The subject of economic justice in an economy of *dynamism*, though, raises the question of taxing the *profits from innovation* to subsidize labor. (Note that any resulting increase in after-tax, after-subsidy wage income in the economy would in turn make feasible a higher general tax on labor from which to finance a higher employment subsidy to the disadvantaged.) But this pot of gold is chimerical. It is not established as an empirical matter that taxation of profits garners increased revenue for use in boosting pay of low-wage workers. It is theoretically possible that taxing profits ultimately lowers wages by dragging down future levels of productivity more than it raises wages by collecting more revenue at any given level of national product and national income. So we cannot conclude that

---

3. In the 1970s, the book prompted a spate of papers in academic journals that, building on analytics developed by James Mirrlees in 1971, created theoretical models of the effects of the structure of taxation on wage incomes and identified the structure that was theoretically optimal on Rawls's criterion of maximizing the lowest wage, known as the "maximin" criterion. One of these was Phelps, "Taxation of Wage Income for Economic Justice" (1973). Another paper studied whether Rawlsian justice required the taxation of interest income to subsidize labor.

just taxation, even from the Rawlsian perspective on wage rates, would call for taxing the profits of innovation.

Of more fundamental importance, it is not clear in the present setting, in which all persons aspire to the Aristotelian good life, that all tax revenues must be allocated to boosting through employment subsidies the *wage* of the least advantaged participants. It is possible that even they would rather see tax revenues used to lift the dynamism of the economy than to subsidize their employment. Even if the least advantaged care only about their wage, there may exist government projects that do more—dollar for dollar—to raise low-wage employment and thus pull up the lowest wage rates than employment subsidies would do. These would include government projects that would remove large blockages to efficiency or to dynamism. It is unfortunate, though, that the least-advantaged are seen to be part of what Marx dubbed the *lumpenproletariat,* in whom he evinced little interest, rather than humans in the normal range who are to a degree engaged in what they do and welcome the problems and opportunities that it may present. That view has led economic policymakers of a Rawlsian complexion to assume that for the least advantaged only the wage can be appreciated. That workers, even the least-paid among them, have *interests besides their pay* suggests that workers might not choose—in the original position or in the voting booth—to have the government spend all its tax revenues on their subsidization. They might take an interest in a national project that seizes their imagination. It is a little too narrow to view Rawlsian justice as fully met if there is an annual budget that clears away all the obstacles to efficiency and to dynamism that have arisen over the past year, then allots to employment subsidies what, if any, remains of the budget.

There are other topics of economic justice besides intervention through fiscal means in the life prospects of persons after their talents and capacities are already formed. A classic topic is early intervention in the education of children disadvantaged by their social circumstances—a subject of the economist James Heckman. It can be argued that justice in a modern economy requires the state to take action to address in the early schooling years the disadvantages among people that would impair their ability to compete on a level playing field against others engaged in attempting innovation. (It would be anomalous for the state to spend, say, 5 percent of national income on raising wages of the disadvantaged and not a penny on raising the potential wage of people with poor wage prospects.) Although most citizens already know that their children are normal or better than normal, they can mentally insert themselves into Rawls's original position to consider in an unbiased way what would be a just level to bring the least-advantaged children up to.[4]

Justice amidst Multiple Human Natures

A Theory of Justice gained simplicity in its treatment of the good by supposing that *all* members of the society seek the "primary goods" and they *all* understand that one's wage is the means to them. The section above on the modern economy, in its treatment of the good, gained simplicity by supposing that *all* members of society seek the good life as Aristotle and his humanist successors conceived it, and they *all* understand that having work that is interesting, challenging, and adventurous is necessary to that life. That premise was not as fantastic as might be assumed. In America from the 1870s to the 1960s— the high years of modern capitalism—humanities courses invited students in elite schools to sense and identify with the human condition and the set of values and beliefs that run through Western history. At Columbia College in the presidency of Nicholas Murray Butler, the required course Contemporary Civilization, a course in history and philosophy, was started by John Erskine in 1919, and the required Humanities A, or HumLit, in 1937 by Jacques Barzun and Lionel Trilling. At the University of Chicago, the Great Books program, developed by Mortimer Adler and instituted by president Robert Hutchens, started in 1942. At Amherst College, a humanities course from 1947 to 1968 led all freshmen through a pantheon of epic leaders, truth seekers, humanists, individualists, vitalists, and pragmatists—all to prepare them for former president Alexander Micklejohn's "life worth living." Anthony Kronman, a teacher of humanities and law at Yale, writes of the humanities course in America from Charles Eliot's rise to the presidency of Harvard in 1869 to the "watershed year" 1968:

---

4. If it is agreed by citizens in the original position that justice requires the greatest feasible prospects for the less advantaged, the citizens will also quickly agree that the state must raise its expenditure level on disadvantaged children to the point where the benefit of an additional billion would be less than the benefit of simply putting the billion into employment subsidies or into activities that raise dynamism, which would indirectly raise the prospects of the least advantaged. Rawls would have added that, as the principles of justice do not allow the wages of the more advantaged to be hammered down to the wage level of the less advantaged, so the same principles do not allow the state to slow the pace of education in the schools so that more of the less advantaged can keep up with more of the others. In any well-functioning economy, modern or not, the talents of the most-able people and the capacities of average people are a resource to be drawn on for mutual gain. If choked off, the working poor would be in a desperate plight.

There are patterns of life that have had a perennial attraction for human beings. . . . The humanities acquaint us with the core commitments of these patterns. . . . Understanding [them] can never eliminate [our] demand . . . to live a life that recognizes, honors and expresses our own uniqueness . . . [n]or can it ever by itself answer the question of what living is for. . . . But the humanities can give us guidance. . . . [The humanities course] . . . invited each student to see himself as a participant in a "great conversation" . . . to think of previous participants—poets, philosophers, novelists, historians and artists—as addressing each other in a long, unbroken conversation about the most important matters in life. . . . Shaped by its belief in the validity of the idea of human nature and by a confidence in the perennial significance of a limited number of exemplary types of human fulfillment, [the humanities] formed, for many years, the core of a program [on] the meaning of life.[5]

It appears that these humanities, while welcoming the diversity of talents and career preferences in any human society and recognizing the variety in the "forms" of human fulfillment that result, discern a "human nature," a nature that is universal from the time when humans used caves for flute concerts. This common nature includes—at the highest level—a desire to express creativity, a relish for challenge, an enjoyment of problem solving, a delight in novelty, and the restless need to explore and to tinker. The pursuit and experience of these "highest goods" is the way to human fulfillment—and to "becoming," which is a large part of it. This human nature and this human fulfillment is displayed by artists and scientists, for example, and by a wide range of less unusual people, including business people, engineers, physicians, and lawmakers. These people are often called "modern" because this way of life—this dealing in new ideas—and this human fulfillment became endemic only after the ideas of the late Renaissance, the Scientific Revolution, and the Enlightenment ushered in the modern societies with modern economies that arose in the 19th century. But the potential for this life and this fulfillment was always there, witness some of the impressive figures in the pre-modern societies, such as the incessantly questioning Socrates, the clever Cleopatra, the venturesome Leif Ericson, and the visionary Catherine the Great.

Yet there has always been another view. In the present day, there are dissenters to the humanities who suppose that there is not simply a variety of

5. Kronman, *Education's End* (2007, pp. 78–87).

"forms" of human fulfillment: There exists another *kind* of human fulfillment, which many are still finding. This movement points to those people,
even in today's relatively modern societies, who flock to callings that do not
promise human fulfillment as the humanities know it. In some of the more
traditional societies, such as southern Italy, the occupation of women is pre-
ponderantly in the home, where they take care of their children and their
husbands. In very traditional societies, the occupation of many men is often
in the church, where they serve as priests, ministers, rabbis, or imams. In all
societies, some men and women take up employment as caregivers in a nurs-
ing home or a hospice; some others prefer positions in nonprofit organizations aimed at a cause, such as the environment, to work in an organization
where the individual's own benefit is not the objective. In these lines of work,
there is relatively little prospect, if any, of experiencing exploration or creation. There is no one here like Cellini or Chanel.

The orientation of many people, even in the most modern economies,
toward family or community or country or religion—or, these days, the earth—
harks back to the traditions in Western societies until the modern revolution.
Today's traditionalism—a harkening back to the pre-modern traditions—
presents an opposition to modernism like the opposition between Platonic
"being" and the "becoming" of Montaigne, Nietzsche, and Bergson. Montaigne
associates the former with the transcendental and the divine. The preference
of some people for a traditional vocation such as caregiving in spite of its relatively static character may reflect a love of God or love of community that is
greater than their self-love, thus greater than any stirring to seek human fulfillment as Aristotle or Montaigne or Nietzsche or Bergson conceived it. (To speak
of that sort of satisfaction from such a traditional occupation as "human fulfillment," or "flourishing," would be to deny those terms their accustomed meaning. If fulfillment were so broadened, what activity by a free, healthy, and sane
adult would not be said to be a way to fulfillment?)

The question here is what we should understand Rawlsian justice to
entail in an economy in which people of a *different* human nature, thus apt to
pursue an *alternative* life if the terms are not prohibitive, coexist with people
having the nature portrayed in the humanities—the "human nature" that
Aristotle and the moderns had in mind when speaking of the good life. Certainly the freedom of people to act on their own human nature, no matter if
it deviates from the human nature central to the humanities, is basic to Rawlsian justice. But the just treatment of persons engaged in their very different
pursuits is less obvious.

Late in his career, Rawls finally underlined something that was implicit earlier in his book: His distributive justice, by its very definition, applies to those whose work contributes to the income generated by society's cooperative venture, its economy, not to hermits and others who stand outside it. Rawls stated bluntly, lest there be misunderstanding, that those who "surf all day" are not in his category of the least-advantaged contributors. "Surfers must somehow support themselves" without benefit of surfing subsidies.[6]

The activity of people in the home—managing the household or raising children—is essential to society as we know it. (A recent OECD study reports that the time spent by Australian men in cooking, cleaning, and childcare has risen to 3 hours a day and is still much higher among women.) And we are sensitive to the fact that, for some, this is a "lesser life," in Sylvia Ann Hewlett's striking characterization.[7] Yet this activity is also not to share in the Rawlsian redistributions of *income*. The redistributions in Rawls's theory are made from the economic surplus created by the contributions of paid labor, and it is redistributed to paid labor. Mothers, for example, have no claim to this surplus, since they have no hand in producing it; what they produce they produce for love. (Our intuition suggests there ought to be redistribution of the nonpecuniary benefits within the home, though that may be difficult.)

By this logic, it appears that those who, out of a sense of service or devotion, find an occupation in a *volunteer sector* where there are no receipts from which to pay them an income—volunteers at nonprofits caring for the environment, caregivers tending to the penniless, priests ministering to the faithful for only a bed and a meal, and so forth—would likewise have no just claim to receive a Rawlsian subsidy, since there is no income generated that could be redistributed, and nothing is left for them from the "social surplus" after it has all gone to the lower-paid among those who produced. If this sector *does* have receipts per worker from which to pay these workers a wage, say, the wage rate of the lowest paid in the economy, that would not alter the fact that they have no just claim against the social surplus produced by those pursuing the good life in the economy. That may seem counterintuitive. Wouldn't a citizen meditating in the original position and recognizing the possibility that *she* might be one of those persons of another nature, thus devoted to another life, decide that justice requires paying the Rawlsian subsidy to those

---

6. Rawls, *Justice as Fairness* (p. 179). Rawls then appears to suggest in further comments that one could not safely infer that the surfers are as badly off as the worst-paid workers, since the surfers rejected work and do so even after a subsidy pulls up the net wage of lowest earners.

7. Hewlett, *A Lesser Life* (1986).

whose *calling* is the cause of low wages just as much as to those whose *productivity* is the cause? But the Rawlsian subsidy is paid out of a calculation of equity, not need or deserts. To be eligible for the prizes one has to play the game. Not some other game.

There is also the issue of the thrust of the state beyond its responsibility for distributive justice and efficiency. What would Rawlsian justice allow? The section above observed that the state may take opportunities to repair dysfunctions in the economy that are a drain on its dynamism, just as it may take opportunities to address inefficiencies. Such activities are not unjust from a Rawlsian perspective if the benefits compensate the low-wage workers. But now we are acknowledging that some working-age members of society are active in pursuit of a radically different kind of life. The citizen in the original position might think it is in his self-interest to temper the state's promotion of dynamism in service of the good life and reallocate it in the service of the other kinds of life, since he must anticipate that *he* may turn out to be one of those who march to a different drummer. But he ought to think again: The state's programs and agencies in service of dynamism, while benefiting the working poor among others, come out of the pockets of the working poor. The unknown risk of being drawn to a different life is not a coherent justification for siphoning some of the rewards of the least advantaged in the economy to those who exit from the economy for another life, as if the latter were disadvantaged collaborators. They are not disadvantaged, just different, and they are not collaborators in the production of a redistributable social surplus.

A Liberating System Not Shown to Be Unjust

The discussion above has been about adjustments and extensions that a modern economy would require to be not simply well-functioning, meaning without major malfunctions, but functioning *justly*. That discussion leads to the final question: Whether the modern economy, when well and justly-functioning, would be a just system. Rawls's principle was that a just economy is one with a structure that would make the prospects of the least advantaged higher than they would be in any other system. In his elaborations toward the end of his book, Rawls, whose descriptions of market economies, capital and socialist, were basically classical, was unable to say which one was just: a pre-modern capitalism or a pre-modern socialism; the differences separating them were not decisive in his eyes. But a thoroughly *modern* society, in which modern values are broadly held, would see the modern-capitalist economy and the standard alternatives, such as market socialism and corporatism, as being worlds apart.

The present book, after comparing the main alternatives, sees reasons to believe that a modern economy, when functioning well and justly, is tailor-made to produce the flourishing and personal growth that are at the core of the good life. The book then finds a range of evidence that a modern-capitalist economy is outstanding in the prospects it offers ordinary people for the good life: The economies relatively strong in modern values and with relatively muted traditional values generally perform better in all the metrics of the good life—job satisfaction, unemployment, and wage level. With that evidence in hand, a member of a thoroughly modern society, placed in Rawls's original position and assuming that he might be among the least advantaged, would have good reason to decide that the modern-capitalist economy, if justly-functioning and well-functioning, was the right choice to make. (A member expecting to be the most advantaged might prefer a planned economy in hopes of being the czar.) It would offer the least advantaged better prospects for a good life than socialism's bureaucracies would or corporatism's cronies and clientele. (In a short while, however, a case of pluralism of values will be taken up.)

Of course, anyone making that defense or any other defense of the modern-capitalist economy must be conscious of the deep antipathy that many people have expressed for capitalism, modern or pre-modern. The antipathy for the great mounds of wealth in private hands and for the acquiring of great wealth is particularly strong. In some reflections following his exposition Rawls writes:

> What men want is meaningful work in free association with others, these associations regulating their relations to one another within a framework of just basic institutions. To achieve this state of things great wealth is not necessary. In fact, it is more likely to be a positive hindrance, a meaningless distraction at best if not a temptation to indulgence and emptiness.[8]

It is true that exaggerated estimations of one's wealth lead to excessive demands for leisure and consumption, thus to reduced employment as well as reduced investment and innovation. Trying to justify modern capitalism as a machine for accumulating wealth could not be more crass. Yet, despite its ill effects, people's wealth is bound to soar in the event the product or method they work on turns out to be a highly profitable innovation. And, as remarked

8. *A Theory of Justice* (p. 257).

before, a chance of extraordinary pecuniary benefits helps motivate people to work on projects that may prove lucrative. So it is not inherently unjust that large inequalities of wealth emerge in modern capitalism; it is in traditional societies that the large wealth inequalities are apt to be neither inherent nor just. Furthermore, wealth has a positive side. It is unnecessary to say that if a person's wealth increases and others' wealth does not, that person will be able to live better in every way. But even if everyone's wealth is increased (by the same amount or in equal proportion), people will then be better able to afford to pursue their interests and express their personalities and their values.

Yet many a social critic speaks of an "injustice"—some inherent flaw that some other sort of system does not have—that renders a modern economy—even one outfitted for economic justice, such as economic inclusion—"unjust." There are at least three broad dimensions in which the modern economy might conceivably fall short. Some other sort of economy, perhaps only a variant of the modern economy, might offer *greater* prospects of the good life or offer those prospects to *more* participants than the modern-capitalist economy offered, or offer a *better life* than the good life in its various classic descriptions. And in the universe of potential alternative economies there must be some as yet unknown star that burns brighter than the modern one. It would not be feasible to sift through the whole litany of objections raised. But the claims that a modern economy is unjust, no matter how well-functioning and justly-functioning, has to be discussed.

Critics of modern capitalism, however, tend to argue that the modern-capitalist economies—and maybe all other economies—are unjust relative to some economic system that they *envision* but that is *not built*. Famously, socialists of the 19th century, before there was a socialist economy, supposed that it would offer wider prospects for employment and higher wages than the modern-capitalist economies could. Once built, however, the socialist economies were seen to offer poorer wages and lower employment than the modern-capitalist economies had—those that were left standing after the onslaught of socialism and corporatism.

The corporatists of the 20th century envisioned a state-led economy that served well the aspirations of a largely *traditional* society. Once corporatist France and Italy had a track record, however, it could be seen that state power had not generated the promised dynamism, so they could not sustain rapid productivity growth and low unemployment beyond the 1990s.

By 1970 social critics in the West envisioned a new sort of economy that would pay a lower price for the good life. The new economy was supposed to offer the prospect of substantial economic stability. But the economies that continental Western Europe claimed to be buffered against instability through heavy job protection and large public sectors, such as those in continental Western Europe, had nothing to show for it: They had low employment and major slumps. And they have paid a steep price: They have little or no dynamism and, as a consequence, underdevelopment, low employment, and not necessarily stable employment at that.

There are plenty of economies in human history that offer more stability and equality than any modern economy ever did. But observation over modern history does not turn up alternatives to the modern economy that deliver less inequality and less instability while delivering no less of the good life.

The modern economy has met new criticisms in recent decades: Portfolios must be balanced; growth must be balanced rather than running in one direction, as in the internet boom; and global imbalances in saving and investment must be corrected. These criticisms seem not to understand that the genius of a well-functioning modern economy is its deployment of the insights and judgment of people immersed in the economy in the economy's decisions about the directions in which a nation should best invest:

> The IMF claims a mandate to address "economic imbalances" . . . because it would be good for world stability. But what is the purpose of a private international credit market if not to permit a nation enjoying an investment boom to borrow abroad and a nation in an investment slump to lend overseas? . . . Next, the IMF speaks of "crisis prevention." The zero tolerance for financial crisis suggests that the IMF has lost sight of the rationale for a well-functioning modern-capitalist economy. Several Western nations have sought to maintain it not because Stalin's Gosplan could not get the relative prices of nuts and bolts right but because the pluralism of entrepreneurs and investors, all with differentiated insights and experiences, is an inspired way to manage the uncertainties that creating new futures entails.[9]

To regard as a flaw the tendency to crash in an economy with the creativity of the American economy—during most of its history, at any rate—is like calling the tendency toward swings between mania and depression in deeply creative people a flaw. It is easy to understand that, in an economy possessing dynamism, a failure to work out new ideas or a dry spell without new ideas may bring on depression. (Of course, the loss of local and regional banks in the past

---

9. Edmund Phelps, "IMF Seems to Have Lost Sight of Rationale for Capitalism," *Financial Times,* letter to the editor, April 25, 2000.

decade and consequent loss of expertise in lending constitute a new dysfunction in economies that had been in the forefront of modern economies. But these pathologies do not represent an injustice in modern economies. The dysfunction can be corrected.)

A provocative critique has arisen in recent years: The good life has been conceived too narrowly. It requires a "balance" between work and home. And the modern economy, which is voracious, leaves not enough time and calm for domestic life and childcare. Here the critics do not want to take issue with the good life so much as to broaden it to the home. They suppose that a new economy can be created in which participants can "have it all"—the rich domestic life and close involvement with children that may have been a feature of the traditional societies centuries ago *without loss* of the dynamism of which a modern economy is capable and the flourishing that is its most important fruit. But talk of a "work-life balance," as if work were not integral to life, casts doubt on whether these critics have understood very well the good life and the conditions on which it depends. A flourishing life in the world of work can come only from an emotional commitment that leads to deep involvement in the work—it cannot be had on the cheap. If going to a four-day workweek or putting a nursery in the offices were found not to lessen employee engagement and effectiveness in many kinds of companies, such companies would have done so. Imposing those practices on companies (through a tax or a fine) would cost companies some employee engagement and thus some of their vibrancy and their dynamism. One company after another has learned that robotic production can be done by employees at home, but innovation requires an office for employee interactions.

A deeper point is that home life cannot be part of the good life unless it too is rich with challenges and hurdles. Some people may at some time find more challenge at home than in business, but they cannot expect to find more flourishing by cutting back on challenges and hurdles. The author Katie Roiphe makes the argument:

> Why is balance necessarily good? Isn't part of the skill or joy of life in the imbalance, in the craziness, in the bizarre or implausible intensity? . . . I am a single mother with three jobs. But I have come to see that there is a kind of exhilaration or happiness in the chaos itself. . . . [T]he human psyche is too complicated, too messy, too elusive, for problems to be solved by "balance," by "healthy environments," by the sheer stubborn physical presence.[10]

10. Katie Roiphe, "There Is No Such Thing as Having It All," *Financial Times*, June 30, 2012.

These visions of an alternative to the modern-capitalist economy all evoke magical thinking—a belief that for any worthy goal there is always a way. But modern thinking tells us that we have to choose among our ends—that we cannot have it all.

The question of the justice of a well and justly-functioning economy is quite different for a society in which one or more elements seek different kinds of life—a life of caring for others or a life of contemplation or a life devoted to family values. Such a pluralism of values—traditionalist ethics alongside modernist ethics—came up in the discussion above of the subsidies to the least-advantaged workers that are required by economic justice in a modern economic system; here we discuss the system required for justice. The crux of the matter is that in any modern society there exists an economy based on exchange, which the modern society supports for the mutual advantage of those who participate in it, while those from the one or more dissenting cultures want to opt out of that exchange system in quest of their dissenting goals. Some social critics appear to believe that it is an injustice of the modern-capitalist economy that it does not provide a space for participants motivated by traditionalist values. In the perspective of this book—the perspective of Kant, Rawls, and some others—justice requires that those who want to pursue a traditional life ought to be free to work and earn in a traditional sector, just as those who aspire to the good life in its classic descriptions must be free to work in the modern sector. (In this diverse society, resources in one economy would be remunerated from what it produces and resources in the other would work without compensation or be paid out of charitable contributions.) It would be a grotesque injustice to consign those with modern values to an unmodern economy relatively devoid of change, originality, and discovery.

Of course, the state will be called upon by people in the original position to protect the ideals of the various traditions, such as traditions of caring. Justice requires tolerance of other lifestyles and thinking, but it does not require those who would pursue the good life to engage in self-denial or to surrender to those styles. Justice does not allow the traditions of the others to so constrict the modern economy as to block the expression of its dynamism in innovative activity and thus modern life.

In this kind of pluralistic society, it might turn out that each ship floats on its own bottom, neither economy cross-subsidizing the other. However we may regard that, it is not an injustice. Justice in the sense of Rawls does not require the modern sector to transfer money to the traditional sector for work subsidies or for any other purpose, since Rawlsian justice in the modern sector is about equity in the distribution of the fruits of that sector. If, however, participants in the modern sector unanimously want the government to subsidize the traditional sector, it would be just to do so. And there is no injustice in individuals donating to that sector. In America, a sector of nonprofit corporations and charitable foundations has become large owing to philanthropy, though some philanthropists acknowledge that their contributions are encouraged by the tax benefits granted by the government, which are apt to lessen the revenue left for the working poor.

We have been discussing justice toward traditionalist elements in a modern society—a society in which modern values have prevailed and created an economy in which the modern sector predominates. Justice is done to those with heavily traditional values by permitting them to operate in a parallel economy and, since that does no harm to the modern economy, justice is done to those with modern values too. (The parallel economy might help the modern economy by drawing away those whose traditional values might make them costly employees and might demoralize the other employees.) It is worth touching on justice toward modernist elements in a heavily traditional society. The problem here is that, unless those with modern values are a tiny minority, allowing them to freely develop and operate a modern sector would have unwelcome impacts on the traditional majority. After all, the counter-revolution of the corporatists against the encroaching modern business economy was set off by the harms that the traditionals felt at the hands of the moderns. Responding to that problem, the state in some European nations—Italy and to a lesser extent France, for example—established penalties and barriers that put a curb on the vibrancy and the dynamism of the modern sector—the sector "parallel" to the sector containing rural industry, state enterprises, the central government, and the church. (And this "parallel" sector was so small in relation to the force of the traditional culture that the latter dragged down entrepreneurship and innovatorship.) The European nations did not generally allow a modern economy to flower, nor did they encourage their citizens to seek lives of nonconformity, creativity, and adventure. Prevailing attitudes and beliefs did serious injustice by blocking and even discouraging the moderns from their pursuit of the good life.

So, though one might think at first that the European nations having strong traditionalist values were perfectly just in installing highly corporatist or socialist economies, much as nations having modernist values were just in welcoming modern economies, the truth is that the traditionalist societies barred ordinary people from chances to pursue the good life—while the modern societies did not bar people from finding traditional lives in nongovernmental organizations, foundations, nonprofits, churches, and the home. And that was unjust.

We do not need to remind ourselves that *actual* modern-capitalist economies do exhibit injustices, as do actual corporatist economies. The most glaring one is the omission of sufficient measures to pull employment and wages of the lowest-paid employees up to much higher levels, though nations with corporatist economies have similarly failed. Another glaring injustice is the practice of inflating disposable incomes through undertaxation and enactment of entitlements that will not be paid, though private and social wealth are puffed up in the corporatist nations too. But these injustices could be corrected if only the beneficiaries understood the fallaciousness of their excuses. However, being neither inherent nor peculiar to a modern-capitalist economy, these injustices do not show that modern capitalism itself is unjustified. It is only marred.

If the argument of this book is right, then, a modern-capitalist economy *is* justified—in nations where it can function well and justly and where modern values are prevalent enough to operate it, at any rate. Of course, it is possible—perhaps likely—that, in the future, some subsequent system will come to be seen as the just system—until such time as it too gives way to another system.

To conclude: The advent of modern economies was a godsend for the fortunate nations to which they came. From the mid-1800s to the mid-1900s, the first modern economies—all of them more-or-less modern capitalist— were marvels of the Western world: They brought economic dynamism, a phenomenon never before seen or imagined, and they brought broad inclusion, which pre-modern capitalism had only begun to do. The new economic system got its dynamism and its inclusion by enlisting the imagination and energy of participants from the grassroots on up. The innovation they caused could not have been so extraordinary had it not engaged the mind and seized the imagination of participants down to craftsmen, day laborers, farmers, traders, and factory workers.

This book finds that, far from being a system of materialism, coarseness, Babbitry, Philistinism, and greed that stands in the way of the good life, the modern economy answered a widespread desire for the good life. It arose out of the modern movement for emancipation from traditional societies with their suffocating feudal economies and from the routine and desolation of mercantile capitalism—a system Smith found uninspiring. The mass engagement in innovation and the mass flourishing that resulted from the modern economy perfectly illustrated the Aristotelian perspective on the highest good and the Rawlsian perspective on justice. This system for mass flourishing was the treasure of the modern era—of the modernist values arising from Pico, Luther, and Voltaire to Hume and Nietzsche.

Yet the older myths of economic success have not gone away. They do not see the possibility of dynamism in private enterprise. In one such story, a nation's freedom relative to freedom in other nations determines its relative economic success. But while freedom is obviously necessary for innovation, it is not sufficient. Freeing people to do a thing may not prompt them to do it. Often one has to *make* one's freedom by taking the plunge. Another story lays economic success to the discoveries of science, not those of business. But this story fails to explain why some nations "took off" and other advanced economies did not, and why the take-offs began in a lackluster period for science. Yet another story says that fast innovation in a nation can be achieved by the public sector—faster than what, if any, the private sector can do. It is not seen as significant that no nation has done any such thing yet—unless we relabel Bismarck's German economy as state-driven rather than modern capitalist.

Getting our theories right is going to be crucial for the West and the East too in the next decades. America is unlikely to recover the dynamism and resulting prosperity it had up to the 1970s as long as it operates on the belief that freedom is sufficient to do so, and that freedom can always be dialed up by a downward adjustment of tax rates as required—this is a great mistake. Modern values and traditional values are both consequential. The modern values that fueled the dynamism of old may have declined—and the opposing values of traditionalism have surely surged—more than fiscal policy can manage to offset. The cry of politicians for a rebirth of traditional values is about as loud as their cry for a rebirth of economic dynamism. As a result, the political parties continue to talk as if prosperity will return once agreement has been reached on fiscal measures of sufficient strength.

Europe will not recover to the respectable levels of employment it had in the 1990s, let alone regain the high prosperity of the early 1900s, as long as it clings to the belief that a corporatist economy—with the right state control over private capital—can achieve the stability and harmony that capitalism cannot, and can do so without any loss of the dynamism it had when its economy was more modern. These beliefs have not met the test. Yet Europe continues to operate a stultifying corporatist economy under the tyranny of traditionalist values.

If modern values are so important for careers of creators, inquirers, and explorers in the economic sphere, thus for a good economy, it might be wondered whether they are also important elsewhere in society. De Tocqueville noticed that they were. He recognized that America, a nation most conspicuous for its broad and intense engagement in the economic system, was also remarkable for its broad and intense engagement in the political system. As a result, there was flourishing in both spheres. For flourishing to occur in the political sphere there had to be a grassroots democracy that was in many ways the counterpart of the grassroots dynamism.

Anyone living today may have noticed that, in this respect, Europe is in a bad way in its political sphere as much as in its economic sphere. As Amartya Sen writes in "The Crisis of European Democracy":

> Europe cannot hand itself over to the unilateral views—or good
> intentions—of experts without public reasoning and informed consent
> of its citizens. Both democracy and the chance of creating good policy are
> undermined . . . when ineffective policies are dictated by leaders.

Similar points apply to economic dynamism, some of which have been made in this book. Innovation and broad flourishing are undermined when many of the directions taken by business are set by economic policy, when the formation of new businesses looks increasingly limited and managers are selected from elites to negotiate with government and community, and when companies are so large and hierarchical that workers of ordinary skill have no way to express innovative ideas and no incentive to conceive them.

In a society capable of modernity, then, the standard for a good and just political system is the standard for a good and just economy. The requirement for the good and the just in a modern society is the same in both the political and economic spheres.

Regaining the Modern

Society's course will be changed only by a change of ideas.

FRIEDRICH HAYEK

The coming generation of leaders and creators will have to rekindle the spirit of risk. Real innovation is difficult and dangerous but living without it is impossible.

GARRY KASPAROV and PETER THIEL

I N THE WEST THERE IS A SENSE THAT THE "glorious history of desire and dreams" has wound down. Most Western economies have been nearly stagnant—America since the mid-1970s and much of Western Europe since the late 1990s. While advances in information and communications, largely made in America, have given many the impression that such advances are endemic, labor productivity in the economy as a whole plodded from 1972 until the rollout of the internet began in 1996 and plodded again after the rollout was over in 2004. Wide damage has resulted. Employee compensation has barely grown. The employment rate of white men fell from 80 percent of their working-age population in 1965 to 72 percent in 1995 and 70½ percent at the end of 2007; that of black men fell even more. Total output thus slowed on both counts— labor productivity and labor input. Investment-good output for enterprises, private and public, was hard hit—falling relative to the total from 16 percent in the 1960s to 14.7 percent in the 1990s and 14.3 percent in the 2000s. Output for consumers did better, but jobs are tied more to the former than to the latter.

What can be done to try to restart the system of desire and dreams? The question has barely been discussed. The crisis of the year gets all the attention. Yet the fiscal crises hovering over several of these nations, America, Italy, and France among them, are traceable to the stagnation. So are the financial crises at the banks that had the misjudgment to finance Europe's fiscal profligacy and America's officially promoted and subsidized housing boom.

Fiscal crises arose because economic growth, after picking up the pace somewhat for a few years, slowed again early in the past decade—returning, in America, to the pace of the 1970s and 1980s. This dimmed the prospects for steeply rising tax revenues on which governments had been counting to scale the mountain of social insurance entitlement claims by the bulge of baby boomers. Did governments then rush into the breach with tax hikes or spending cuts? No, they widened the breach. In America, George W. Bush's tax cuts of 2001 and 2003 removed 600 billion dollars from revenues per annum—5 percent of GDP—and "compassionate conservatism" extended Medicare to free pills, adding trillions of dollars to entitlements. In Europe, official fiscal deficits were allowed to rise from around 1.5 percent of GDP over 1999–2000 to around 4 percent over 2003–2005 in Italy and France. And the true deficits, which would take into account that the day of reckoning when benefits soar above revenues was fast approaching, were much higher. This pandering to voters by cutting revenue rather than starting it on the long climb needed to finance existing entitlements was stark fiscal irresponsibility. This irresponsibility was flagrant, since unemployment rates, often given as an excuse for deficits even in times of dire fiscal straits, though rising a bit after the internet boom, were not trending above the normal levels of the 1990s. This irresponsibility contributed to weak exchange rates, a reduced share of world exports (despite exchange depreciations), depressed stock markets, and weak business investment. Corporations have amassed reserves rather than invest. They fear undertaxation in the past will bring supertaxation in the future.

The *financial* crises arose out of the slow growth, the attendant unemployment, and the resulting fiscal deficits. Following the slowdown, several governments in Europe, rather than rein in their deficits, ran the deficits as long as European banks would buy them at low interest rates; and the banks were content to buy them so long as sovereign debt was rated AAA by credit agencies requiring banks to hold little capital against such debt. The U.S. government, while continuing to borrow, encouraged others to borrow as well. It coaxed government-sponsored enterprises (GSEs) in the home mortgage market and commercial banks to establish reduced interest rates on subprime mortgages. It also encouraged a huge volume of student loans. The GSEs, banks, and other lenders went on financing the resulting explosion of demand for loans by speculators and new buyers as long as home prices kept on rising—while failing to appreciate the risk.

After the 2008 crisis and the onset of panic, unemployment rose, eventually peaking and receding only very slowly. A huge debate began over why the unemployment rate, nearing 8 percent, was falling back so weakly and erratically that it looked unlikely to go below 7 percent—far above the "old normal" of 5½ percent in 1995–1996 and even farther above the older normal of 4½ percent in 1965. The standard theories of economics purported to explain the weakness of employment, aside from the brief booms, with no reference to the post-1970 stagnation. Crude Keynesians parroted "deficient aggregate demand," never squaring that "deficiency" with the absence of deflation that their textbooks said was a telltale sign of such a deficiency. Supply siders blamed "high" tax rates, never noting that employment failed to rise after George W. Bush's massive 2001 and 2003 tax cuts—it rose only with his housing boom. But it is odd to speak either of low spending by consumers or high tax rates on wages as the cause of the employment slump when so many other causes are operating: technology is doing less than usual to increase supply; retirements are decreasing the supply; households are bursting with social benefits and tax credits, present and prospective, that further reduce supply; and the fiscal crunch ahead will send interest rates skyward. The toll of all this on business confidence undoubtedly lies behind the depressed valuations put on a range of business assets, from machine to customer and employee, by enough to account for all or most of the present slump—though the prevailing trickle of innovation may well be strong enough to lower somewhat further the unemployment rate.

The crude Keynesians bent on keeping up spending and the crude supply siders bent on holding down tax rates would blithely create high fiscal deficits and thus ever-rising public debt (on top of the entitlements) as long as the stagnation of productivity and wages persisted. They do not worry for, in their models, there is no public debt level too high for the economy to "grow out of," since, for them, growth is forever: if it pauses, it will resume—it always does. They cannot comprehend that stagnation is not impossible. (They do not really comprehend that the opposite of stagnation—the flowering that comes from dynamism—is not impossible either.)

The standard theories offer no inkling of what policy initiatives might solve the stagnation of productivity and wages, thus their toll on employment. Their models were conceived to show how short-term fiscal interventions could shave off peaks and troughs of a short cycle around a rising trend path—not to address a sea change in dynamism bringing stagnation.

Thus the policy responses in Washington and other capitals have merely treated symptoms with make-work or offered palliatives with benefits and tax cuts. As Howard Stringer, head of Sony, in a March 2011 interview with

Fareed Zakaria, cried out, "It's fine to take care of the passengers and crew, but somebody has to save the ship!" There was nothing in the policy responses in America—in Bush's two terms or Obama's first term—or in Europe that could be seen as a transformational change intended to reverse the stubborn slow-down of innovation, hence productivity, that lay *behind* the drift of wages onto a lower path, the loss of jobs, and the sense of a setback in economic inclusion. Policy circles have not taken any steps they thought or said would restore the spirit of "desire and dreams" that animated the West's best econ-omies in their best times.

If the Western nations are to regain their pre-stagnation levels of employ-ment, inclusion, and job satisfaction, they will need to find ways to end their respective stagnations. The solution is indeed to step up "innovation," as some economists and others have said. But the term has a variety of mean-ings, and the discourse on how nations might go about increasing innovation (in the appropriate sense) has barely started. Finding policies to speed inno-vation will require nations to have a basic understanding of the roots of inno-vation over modern history.

I believe that the perspective of this book, which is new in its focus on grass-roots innovation and the social values behind it and new also in its empha-sis on the rewards of the working life to which it gives rise, can shed light on how we got into the state we are in. More importantly, it can show us paths back to the exploration, challenge, and expression—and the daily discoveries and innovations—that were the West's most profound achievement.

The book is at one level a narrative of the modern economies that sprang up in the 19th century and struggled in the 20th—economies possessing the grassroots dynamism to generate homegrown innovation. I first conceived the book as setting out an understanding of the core of the modern system that lay behind the torrent of innovation, believing that this understanding would help to preserve it where still functioning. During the writing, though, I came to see that the system had seriously deteriorated—putting itself in danger and the "glorious history" with it. So the resulting book had to tell not only the story of the rise of modern economies in the West nearly 200 years ago: their material progress, economic inclusion, and human flourish-ing. It had also to relate the decline of the modern economy. In America, that decline set in about 40 years ago: a stubborn slowdown of growth, a shrink-age of inclusion—first among the working class, then middle-income work-ers—and a loss of job satisfaction—the symptoms of a decrease of dynamism and thus of the average rate of innovation. In Europe the loss of indigenous innovation was earlier and more profound, though masked by technological transfer from overseas. Hence, the reduced innovation in America ultimately forced severe slowdowns, especially in Italy and France. Searching for causes, the book looks at both institutions that enable or disable dynamism and values that encourage or discourage it.

The dynamism of the modern economy drew on a set of modern institutions. In the private sector, the accrual of property law and company law enabled people wishing to be innovators to start up new companies and close them down as fast, unfettered by society's views, if it had any. Stock markets, banks, and patents were open to long-term visions, thus to innovations, large and small. In the public sector, the few institutions and policies it had were oriented toward the far future. A series of actions over several decades expanded the resources available for investment and innovation, from loans for visionary projects and land grants to pioneering settlers to freeing slaves and writing laws to protect investors and creditors. There was political pork and graft, but they did not hobble enterprise and choke innovation. All that changed.

Now there is much rot in the once-modern institutions. Short-termism is rife in business and finance—not just governments. In the private sector, CEOs have no long-term interest in their companies, and mutual funds have only a short-term interest in holding the shares. The result is that virtually all innovation can come only from outsiders—start-ups and angel investors—competing with established companies and industries. This short-termism reduces the *supply* of innovation—the innovatorship, risk capital, and venturesome end-users that innovation requires. In the public sector, corporatism has spread from Europe to America and metastasized into clientelism, cronyism, and pandering—graft is the least of it. Corporatism has also brought an explosion of regulations, grants, loans, guarantees, taxes, deductions, carve-outs, and patent extensions intended mainly to serve vested interests, political clients, and cronies. The protection of vested interests chokes off the opportunity that outsiders with new ideas would have to break into the market. All this has further reduced the supply of innovation. There is more. The corporatist government's contacts with political supporters and lobbyists shrink the size of the market left to innovators. In the past decade, large banks, large companies, and large government formed a nexus to pump up home mortgage debt in America and to create unchecked sovereign debt and unfunded entitlements in several nations in Europe. So America has joined Europe in having a parallel economy that draws its nourishment from the ideas of political elites, whatever their motives, rather than from new commercial ideas. All this reduces the rewards of innovation—the *demand* for innovation.

This book also sees the reprise of a surfeit of traditional values— restraining and suffocating attitudes and beliefs originating in pre-modern times. With the modern era, stretch version, a series of *modern* values arose from the 1500s onward that fueled grassroots dynamism by bringing out in people their need for the freedom to make a mark, create, explore, and pioneer: A good life is one lived to the fullest. People possess the imagination to create new things and the judgment to think for themselves. Advances in understanding are promoted if established ideas have to compete with new ideas. Economies work better if one has a right to own property. And everyone has a right to work for one's own gain, one's own property—not to be used as a means to the ends of others—of society or one's spouse. Advances in the economy are promoted if established companies and job holders have to compete with newcomers. The creativity and evolving desires of a modern world make its future indeterminate. So the modern world is open for us "to act on"! In a few nations, the modern notions prevailed over absolutism, determinism, antimaterialism, scientism, elitism, and the primacy of the family. These fortunate few supported modern-capitalist economies in the 19th century until their decline in the 20th. This too has changed.

Now, the balance between modern and traditional values appears on the whole to have swung back significantly. There may have been no loss in the intensity with which modern values are held nor in the prevalence of those holding them. Some scant survey evidence suggests that modern values gained or regained some ground between the decadal data wave of the early 1990s and the wave in the early 2000s, perhaps brought by the excitement of the internet boom. However, survey data record a strong increase of *traditional* values. These include family values and community values, of course, and some age-old ethical dogma: advance in lockstep, take no action (like competing) that would harm others, and the right to be compensated for every reversal at the hand of the market or the state.

There is also evidence that these values have won heightened influence over Western economies. The resurgence of family values and community values has drained companies of some of their innovative spirit and pressured them to serve community life and family life more and the bottom line less. With the rise of stakeholderism, anyone deciding to start up an innovative company would have to expect that its property rights would be diluted as it copes with an array of figures—its own workforce, interest groups, advocates, and community representatives—who ardently believe they have a legitimate "stake" in the company's results. Many employees feel they have the right to hold on to their jobs—no matter that many others would do the job for far less money—so long as they add something to profit or the company makes a profit from other divisions that can cover the loss. With the rise of solidarism, entrepreneurs seeking profits from successful innovations must expect that any profits will be shared through corporate profit taxes. The broad classes of income are to move in lockstep, so if upper incomes soar higher, the schedule of tax rates on high income is to be shifted up to share the wealth with the middle class—no matter if those tax rates become so high they lose more revenue than they gain. The backslide to a pre-modern fixation on wealth—which was harmless in Europe's corporatist societies, since their high tax rates effectively barred people from becoming rich—has poisoned America. It lured a generation away from voyages of creativity and discovery like those of their forebears to careers in banking or consulting. With the rise of a premodern culture of medieval entitlement, self-importance, conformism, and group dependence, there has been a palpable decline in vitalism—in "doing," as Thatcher or Sen might term it. Thus, even if modern values are intact, premodern notions have regained influence over business and the government. This accounts in part, if not in full, for how America and earlier Europe lost some of their dynamism and thus their indigenous innovation.

What can be done? Western societies will have to work on both their institutions and culture to restore their economic dynamism if they are to improve markedly their performance in employment, productivity, and, crucially, the work experience. While the universities and the press can help, many reforms and new forms will require governments at various levels—central, state, and local. Hayek said that no state could create a system for economic efficiency—though Lenin came pretty close. It is even truer that no state can create from scratch a set of institutions and values that would generate the dynamism for high indigenous innovation: In large part, our institutions and values evolved, then decayed, through the trial and error of entrepreneurs, financiers, and adopters. Yet governments in the past were at times activist in the formation of institutions and values—imperfect interventions resulting from inherently imperfect knowledge. So it will not be a widening of the scope of governments if, desiring to restore dynamism, they undertake *new* interventions and rescind *old* ones.

Governments will not act to restore dynamism until they become aware of the importance of the role played by dynamism in a modern-capitalist economy. At present, they are still in thrall to pre-modern notions that have been resurgent for several decades. In America, the Democratic Party voices a new corporatism well beyond Franklin Roosevelt's New Deal or Lyndon Johnson's Great Society. Geraldine Ferraro, the vice-presidential candidate in 1984, encapsulated it in what has become the party's mantra: "The promise of our country is that the rules are fair. If you work hard and play by the rules, you can earn your share of America's blessings." It suggests that America's century of mass flourishing was somehow the product of a pre-modern, mechanical economy in which people's wage rates could be relied on to rise in parallel, and all people had to do was put in the hours best for them. There was no such thing as particular individuals, enterprises, or industries, with their special insight, vision, and good fortune, driving up *their own* wages and profits disproportionately through innovations. And if perchance some industry or occupation did face wages falling off the pace, the government would award special projects to pull those wages up. The Republican Party has come just as deeply under the influence of traditional values. Bush's "compassionate conservatism" conceives the good economy as mercantile capitalism plus social protection and social insurance. Seeing the economy as a servomechanism pinged by shocks, the party has no thought of trying to guard and nourish dynamism in the economy and no desire to shape it for indigenous innovation. One can hardly believe this is the party of Lincoln. In Europe, birthplace of solidarity and security, there is a failure to grasp that most innovation, as in the past, must be indigenous either in Europe or America or both—little of it will be Schumpeterian manna from heaven or the state. They fail too to grasp that Europeans would have more engaging economies if they stopped depending on America to make their innovations for them.

The present crisis of the West can be laid to its leaders' unawareness of the importance of dynamism: A breadth of dynamism is the main source of innovative activity and its engaging jobs, and this activity—its extent, insights, and luck—is the main source of growth in productivity and income. Thus grassroots dynamism was crucial to the good economy of the past: to material progress, inclusion, and job satisfaction. And restoration of that dynamism will be crucial to the rebirth of the good economy. The parlous finances of most Western governments at the present time only make this restoration more urgent.

To take action—well-judged actions—governments must also have a sense of the way forward. They will have to have an elementary understanding of *how* the business sphere of a well-functioning modern economy generates dynamism. It is not mechanical: It is organic, in Bergson's and Barzun's terminology. It is not an ordered system: It is turned topsy-turvy by homegrown innovation and the crazy scramble to try to create innovation. Interventions will benefit from intuition and experience and will be dangerous without them. Now, however, Washington has little business background. Few regulators have worked much in business, and reportedly some have never been inside a business office! Few legislators have spent a substantial part of their careers in businesses other than in their own law firms. Washington's naïvete was demonstrated in 2012 when Congress estimated that expiration of the Bush tax cuts (worth about 500 billion dollars annually) would cost 800 billion dollars in annual domestic output if no tax cuts were put in their place. Without an estimate of how much the reckless deficits caused by the Bush cuts cost innovation and thus investment in the past, let alone how the resulting reduction of the deficits would boost innovation in the future, it is indeterminate whether expiration would weigh heavily on employment or whether jobs would soon be buoyed up by entrepreneurs' new confidence. "We simply don't know," as Keynes commented on a similar issue.

Orienting the state toward dynamism, then, is going to need personnel in government with some practical knowledge of how innovation is generated and how it is deterred in the various industries—from manufacturing and banking to health care and schooling. America's founders envisioned that Congress would consist primarily of persons pausing for an interlude from their private endeavors, primarily businesses ranging from large farms to urban factories, offices, and shops. Thus senators and representatives would come from the world of business and go back when their term was up.

But if that method is out of reach, another approach is needed. Consider regulators. It would be desirable to require them to have an internship in one or two industries or specialties. Such regulators, with training costs comparable to those of business experts, accountants, and similar professionals, would have to expect comparable income, otherwise few would enter the field. Interns would acquire experience and insight. Maybe they would not penetrate to the depths of dynamism, but they would gain a working understanding of the costs as well as the benefits various regulatory restrictions might bring.

Legislators could gain from interning too, but they need a more general background. If legislators are to be apt stewards in guiding the refitting of the business economy for high dynamism, they will have to have insight and judgment. This will require some sort of education. Keynes once remarked that one studies economics not because any particular theoretical result in the standard works has a great deal of substantive value but because it is the way that a practitioner learns to ask the right questions. Imaginably, something like France's *grande école* for politics and economics, Science Po, or China's postgraduate programs for its leaders could be instituted in other countries, including America. But there is something worrying about the prospect of legislative leaders under the spell of a guru of unknown insight. Better a system encouraging them to read and to discuss by themselves. Legislators can find a body of literature with which to start that will give them a feel for how innovation has worked in the past and, with little doubt, how it will have to work in the future. On the history of grand innovation they may read Harold Evans's *They Made America* and *The Dawn of Innovation* by Charles Morris. On the innovation system they may read Hayek's classic "Competition as a Discover Procedure," Richard Nelson's "How Medical Know-How Progresses," and *The Venturesome Economy* by Amar Bhidé. On corporatism they may start with *The Rise and Decline of Nations* by Mancur Olson. My book, while weighing in on these aspects, points to the cultural values behind dynamism and to the forces arrayed against it.

With a background in matters of innovation, legislators and regulators would have dynamism on their minds and could usefully ask of every bill and regulatory directive: How would it impact the dynamism of our economy? Legislators would not approve or let slide fiscal deficits as massive as the West has seen for a decade on the thinking that to act against them would cost jobs. Instead they would grasp that massive deficits over many years ultimately threaten increased costs of credit and depressed valuations of business assets and are thus bad for innovation and investment—hence bad for employment, productivity, and job satisfaction.

A background in innovation would contribute to improved governance over the economy. In America and in much of Europe the fall in the share of jobs in manufacturing has led many legislators to favor an industrial policy of stimulating some manufacturing industries through subsidies, mandates, or private-public partnerships, and GSEs in preference to other parts of the economy, reopening a fight over political economy—over the governance of the economy—that goes back to Colbert, Hamilton, List, Keynes, and Prebish. They make the discredited argument that subsidies in the directions proposed increase economic growth, and the harvest of additional tax revenue makes it safe for the government to engage in the practice. As a French businessman recently exclaimed, referring to the grandiose pretensions of French politicians, "they would create value from their ministries!" It is far better to leave the directions of the economy to the competition of the market, since the state does not have the knowledge or judgment to improve the efficiency of the market's allocation of investment. In fact, subsidies, mandates, and GSEs have a sorry record of unintended consequences in agriculture, construction, energy, and finance: subsidies for growing soy for biofuels, for the purchase of solar panels, for profitless green energy companies, and for the ventures of Fannie Mae and Freddie Mac. Legislators with innovation on their minds would shrink from extending these initiatives to manufacturing. They would grasp that more start-up companies will form and succeed in a country if the legislature does not handicap them by encouraging less-innovative companies and industries to use up fuel, land, labor, and finance capital— companies and industries that would not otherwise have gotten in the way.

In general, public policies and all the governmental institutions and practices of the corporatist economy must be shrunk and some of them terminated. A government is needed for a well-functioning modern economy, of course, and conceivably some circumstances might demand a large one. What is important to keep small is special interest legislation. To that end the government could be required to finance all special interest legislation through special funds earmarked for the purpose, while public expenditure in the general interest would come from general revenue. The requirement of special funds would serve to call attention to the outlay and to ensure that the benefit level is geared to what the beneficiaries are willing to pay. At present, much special interest legislation exists in the form of tax deductions, exemptions, and carve-outs of which the public is not aware or in the form of general-interest legislation. My book argues that the provision of private benefits to special interest groups leads not simply to some inefficiency but to a culture that undermines the spirit of aspiration and discovery that is required for economic dynamism. Putting an end to a wanton disregard for the costliness of special interest legislation is likely to be a necessary condition for sustained dynamism. The relatively good performance of Sweden and Norway does not refute this proposition, since on most evidence they possess little dynamism and not a great deal of satisfaction either. I would add that my book is far from suggesting that government "limited" in this way is a *sufficient* condition for economic dynamism.

Once a nation has made it a goal to return to dynamism it will find a great deal of reform to undertake in the private sector too. The formerly dynamic economies will have to be refitted with some new institutions. Few changes are more needed than reforms to stop the corporate practice of paying CEOs very high salaries over a term expected to be very short, which induces them to dis-regard innovative projects that could pay off only in the long term. Company law could be amended to forbid corporations from using their capital to bestow golden parachute payments to CEOs every time they are dismissed, which similarly pushes CEOs to go for short-term gains rather than long-term gains from innovations that would be far more valuable to shareowners, since share prices reflect prospects over the whole of the company's future. (It may seem that making it harder for CEOs to select the directors on their corporate board would also serve to hold them to a higher standard, but while it might save soci-ety and the shareowners from CEO incompetence, it could also stimulate the CEOs to even more short termism before they are changed for another CEO.)

Also high on the list is reform of the mutual funds. They must be stopped from threatening a CEO with dumping her company's stock unless she fixes her attention on hitting the next quarter's earnings target. This extortion is legal at present, but it could be made an offense for mutual fund managers to threaten officials of a company with such financial damage and an offense for CEOs not to report them. (In some countries it is illegal to pay ransom to kidnappers.) Another problem is the rise of mutual funds that attract retail investors on the selling point that they offer minimum risk via a highly diversified portfolio of stocks. If all stocks were picked that way, new shares issues aimed at financing relatively unprofitable corporate expansions would receive as much financing as new issues aimed at profitable expansions.[1]

Restoration of grassroots innovation will require an overhaul of the bank-ing industry. That will require a wealth of start-up companies with unfamil-iar ideas, and such companies receive financing only from someone with the personal knowledge that comes from up-close observation and reflection. So the restoration of high dynamism will require the revival of financing the old-fashioned way—"relational banking" in which the lender or investor through accumulating experience comes to have a sense of the chances of the com-pany it is financing that is about as good as the company does. Governments mindful of innovation could redraw the map of financial institutions so as to provide vastly more finance for innovative projects and start-ups.

To this end, governments in Europe and America could restructure some of the existing banks. To date, discussions of the banking industry since the

---

1. It is argued in reply that hedge fund managers do a reasonably good job of judging the worth of shares, so if the government will see to it that there is enough of them, the dynamism of the economy will not suffer from the mechanical diversification among the general pub-lic. But it is doubtful that there could be enough talented hedge fund managers for this task.

2008 crisis have been centered around correcting banking's tendency to instability, thus insolvency. Thus far, legislatures have enacted regulations largely intended to restrict risky practices, such as excessive short-term borrowing. But there is fear that the banks will be able to keep one step ahead of the regulators, thus exposing the economy yet again to the risks of financial crisis. A more reliable approach to instability seeks instead to restructure banks for a narrower mission, leaving risky assets to financial markets with the appropriate expertise. This route could also be an approach to the acute deficiency of risk capital, or angel finance, for start-up companies and innovative projects generally. If Europe and America begin restructuring the banking behemoths of the present day into smaller units with much less latitude, governments that are mindful of the need for dynamism can then seek to ensure that the new narrow banks are oriented toward lending to business, especially innovative business.

In addition, a government mindful of innovation will want to license and encourage formation of new financial companies designed for relational banking ("banks" if they do not take big equity positions, "merchant banks" if they do). The government will want to see the landscape of the economy dotted with local investors and lenders. (Never mind George Bailey, the small town mortgage banker in Frank Capra's film *It's A Wonderful Life.* He only lent to home buyers.) Imaginably, such a system might prove limited or slow to develop, though. In 2010, Leo Tilman and I proposed a national bank specializing in extending credit or equity capital to start-up firms. Our proposal was modeled after the highly successful Farm Credit System. Although it would entail only a modest investment by the U.S. government, with the rest of the capital being borrowed under government guarantees, the main worry with any such GSE is the moral hazard that officials will succumb to pressure from politicians to use it to supply patronage. The fact that some sovereign debt agencies have operated without charges of politicization is encouraging. Meanwhile, the market itself has come to the rescue with resources that, though not large, are very welcome: the super-angel funds formed in California.

Some other institutions in the private sector are overdue for a reexamination. Labor unions and professional associations are capable of raising uncertainties for anyone contemplating an innovative venture. In Europe, the medical and legal associations have great power. Union "manifestations" and wildcat actions are still awesome. In France, President François Hollande demanded in November 2012 that Lakshmi Mittal guarantee the long-term future of workers at his steel plant in Florange, France. Earlier, bands of workers took their managers hostage—a practice known as bossnapping. In America, the unions, now more important in the public sector than the private, are not thought to impair innovation. But the fact that unionized construction takes a year in New York to build office buildings that Shanghai builds in a few months puts that faith in doubt. The lawsuit of the U.S. government against Boeing for opening a plant in a right-to-work state must give pause to innovators. The financial reorganization of General Motors, which put the labor union's trust fund ahead of the claims of bondholders, must give pause to those lending to innovators. It is thought that the legal and medical associations serve to uphold quality. But, whatever their overall effects, the restrictions they impose on new entrants surely operate to reduce innovation. It would be of symbolic importance for the spirits of innovators and entrepreneurs generally if the powers of labor unions and professional associations entered into the public debate.

Though reform of the institutions of the private sector is of the greatest importance for the revival of its dynamism, it will also be important to strengthen the modern values—the desire for challenge, expression, and the rest—that nourish and enlist the human resources that go into dynamism, resources such as creativity, curiosity, and vitality. It was the heady mix of modern values that brought forth and continued to fuel the world's first modern economies. These economies launched a marvelous take-off of productivity, lifting wages and wealth in their train, in the process of transforming work from little more than a means of income to a fount of mental stimulus, challenge, and adventure for more and more people. The modern peoples wanted that modern kind of life. If the modern economies flowed from the values of the modern era, it is reasonable to think that a revival of the modern economy would benefit from a reaffirmation and wider spread of modern values. Once, entrepreneurs were wedded to seeing how far their companies could go. Would today's CEOs follow short-termist policies if they cared more about building companies than building their dream houses? Moreover, there is no compelling reason to suppose that the modern spirit will survive if the West does not go back repeatedly to its greatest expressions.

In *Lost in Transition,* Christian Smith finds evidence from his interviews with young adults that they have not found their way. Their difficulties arise not from any failure of their own but from society's failure to provide them the cultural resources to help them in their journey to adulthood and help them thrive. Asked about the consumerism around them, most are positive— some justifying it as good for the economy. Asked to talk about what sort of a life they would like to lead, they speak about working for the money—working to have "nice things," a family, and financial security. Very few spoke of the nature of the work they wanted to do. The words "challenge," "exploration," "adventure," and "passion" were not in their vocabulary. They are lost.

We must reintroduce the main ideas of modern thought, such as individualism and vitalism, into secondary and higher education both to refuel grassroots dynamism in the economy and to preserve the modern itself. Americans are now debating the Common Core State Standards recently introduced in most states into grades K-12. The English Standards reemphasize expository writing and "informational" texts like essays and biographies, which had been displaced by fiction aimed more at communicating feeling and compassion. The argument is that young people will need expository writing in their careers and the economy needs it too. But what a modern economy needs more than personnel with expository skills is people eager to exercise their creativity and venturesome spirit in ever-new and challenging environments. It needs people who when they were young read the intriguing and uplifting works of the imagination by the likes of Jack London, H. Rider Haggard, Jules Verne, Willa Cather, Laura Ingalls Wilder, Arthur Conan Doyle, and H. P. Lovecraft.

Can the nations of the West regain the high dynamism of their best times? A nation's corporate and financial institutions could be reformed to play the role they once did in the innovative process. The haze of regulation and pork barrel contracts could be curbed so that businesses across the economy would once again have the freedom and incentive to attempt innovation. Fiscal responsibility could be reestablished to allay business fears that profit from innovation would be taxed away. But without a supportive culture, these steps will not be sufficient; they will not even be taken. The genius of high dynamism was a restless spirit of conceiving, experimenting, and exploring throughout the economy from the bottom up—leading, with insight and luck, to innovation. This grassroots spirit was driven by the new attitudes and beliefs that defined the modern era, and a full return to high dynamism will require that those modern values prevail again over traditional ones: Nations will have to push back against the resurgence of traditional values that have been so suffocating in recent decades and revive the modern values that stirred people to go boldly forth toward lives of richness. Nations can hope to regain their past brilliance if they have the will do so. A future of mass flourishing depends on it.

TIMELINE: MODERNISM AND MODERNITY

Age of Antiquity

500,000 years ago	The construction of shelters spreads; fire used for cooking and heating
35,000 BC	Flutes made out of a vulture bone used in southern German cave
10,000 BC	Wooden knives set with flint blades used in Palestine
7500 BC	Jericho adopts weaving, fortification, cultivated cereals
6000 BC	Farming spreads through Macedonia
3300 BC	Writing, sailboats, wheeled vehicles, and animal-drawn ploughs begin to be used in Sumer
2400 BC	Sumerian king declares debt cancellation within his kingdom and makes the first political reference to "freedom"
1760 BC	Code of Hammurabi in Babylonia outlines laws on private property
ca. 1500 BC	Egypt develops glass technology and industry; Egyptian glass beads become a popular trading commodity
ca. 450 BC	Socrates founds Western philosophy and with his student, Plato, introduces the dialogue as a device for exploring questions in philosophy, politics, and management

385 BC	Plato founds the Academy in Athens, the West's first institution of higher learning
ca. 350 BC	Aristotle creates a comprehensive system of philosophy, covering ethics, aesthetics, logic, science, politics, and metaphysics
105 BC	Paper developed in ancient China

Early Middle Ages ca. 500–800

ca. 500	Greek mathematician Anthemius of Tralles uses camera obscura
ca. 800	Chinese alchemists discover gunpowder, but innovation does not follow

High Middle Ages ca. 800–1300

ca. 1088	Use of movable type system recorded in *Chinese Dream Pool Essays*
1215	King John of England issues the Magna Carta Libertatum outlining rights against the king
1282	Mechanization of papermaking (paper mill) in Xàtiva, Kingdom of Aragon

Late Middle Ages ca. 1300–1500

1400s	Trade spreads via Hanseatic routes and Silk Road
ca. 1444	Gutenberg's printing press first assembled
1455	Gutenberg's printing press is used for mass production of the Gutenberg Bible, enabling thousands to read it for the first time
1480s	Portuguese sailors use astrolabe to circumnavigate Africa
1486	Giovanni Pico della Mirandola publishes *Oration on the Dignity of Man,* a manifesto of the Renaissance, arguing that mankind possesses creativity
1492	Columbus opens sea routes to the Western hemisphere

Early Modern Age ca. 1500–1815

late 1400s–1500s	With Pico on human creativity, Erasmus on expanding possibilities, and Luther on the liberty of Christians to read

	and interpret the Bible for themselves, the modern era (1500–2000) begins
1500	Foreign trade extends via the Hanseatic routes, Silk Road, and ocean lanes
1509	*The Praise of Folly* by the humanist Erasmus is first published in Paris
1517	Luther posts the "95 Theses" demanding a wider role for the individual in the practice of religion
1540s	Calvinism views secular vocations as having religious value and extending God's providential governance
1553	In a setback to free thinking, Michael Servetus, first European to describe the circulation of the blood, is burned at the stake as a heretic by John Calvin and the Geneva council
1580	Michel de Montaigne's *Essais*, chronicling his own inner life and the personal growth he calls "becoming," first published in Paris
1600	Giordano Bruno, a precursor of the modern cosmologist, is similarly put to death by the Inquisition
1600–1760	Baroque composers develop the basic building blocks of tonal music
1603	Shakespeare publishes early text of *Hamlet*
1614	Miguel de Cervantes's *Don Quixote* is published
1620	Francis Bacon outlines a new logic in his *Novo Organum*, developing the modern scientific method
1628	William Harvey uses logic to deduce the circulation of the blood, ushering in Western medicine
1688	Glorious Revolution takes place in England, in which Parliamentarians unite with William of Orange to expel King James II
1689	English Bill of Rights puts the rights first proposed by the Magna Carta into actual effect
1698	John Castaing, a broker operating out of an Exchange Alley coffeehouse in London, begins posting lists of prices for stocks and commodities, constituting thereby the beginnings of the London Stock Exchange
1719	Daniel Defoe's *Robinson Crusoe* is published in London

1740	David Hume publishes *Treatise of Human Nature*
1748	David Hume publishes *An Enquiry Concerning Human Understanding* on how knowledge is increased
1750s	Neoclassical art is practiced by Jacques-Louis David, Thomas Gainsborough, and Joshua Reynolds
1750–1810	Wages in Britain fall
1759	Adam Smith's *Theory of Moral Sentiments* first published in London
1759	Voltaire's *Candide*, celebrating individual enterprise, first published in France
1760s	Adam Smith delivers what became *Lectures on Jurisprudence*
1776	James Watt installs first steam engine in a British factory
1776	Thomas Paine's *Common Sense* opposes British rule as an obstacle to America's prosperity
1776	America's Declaration of Independence proclaims the right of people to self-government and the "pursuit of happiness"
1776	Adam Smith's *Wealth of Nations* first published in London
1781	Immanuel Kant's *Critique of Pure Reason* argues for the intimate connection of reason and experience
1785	Immanuel Kant's *Foundations of the Metaphysics of Morals* rejects an older idea of liberty in Hobbes and Smith, in which men treat each other as means instead of ends
1780s	Pig iron frame is developed by the iron mill of Cort & Jellicoe
1787	Contracts Clause is added to the U.S. Constitution
1788	U.S. Constitution creates a House of Representatives and Senate and opens federal voting to all males with property qualifications
1789	French Revolution begins
1791	Polish-Lithuanian Constitution calls for political equality between townsfolk and nobility
1792	Wall Street's first crisis occurs
1792	Mary Wollstonecraft writes *A Vindication of the Rights of Woman*

1796–1797	Financial panic takes place in the United Kingdom and America
1803	Beethoven's Second Symphony expresses the experience of successive trials
1803	Jean-Baptiste Say, in his *Traité d'économie politique* in Paris, contrasts entrepreneurs with rent-seekers
1804	William Blake writes of "dark Satanic mills," of which there were then only very few
1812	U.S. vote is extended to white men without property
1814	Bourbon Restoration restores Kingdom of France after the First Empire under Napoleon

High Modern Age ca. 1815–1940

1815	The Napoleonic Wars and the War of 1812 end; the modern economy is born in Britain
1815	Output per worker begins its "take-off" in England, making it the first modern economy
1818	Mary Shelley's *Frankenstein; or, The Modern Prometheus* is published in London
1819	U.S. Supreme Court, in a suit with the Corporation of Dartmouth College, rules that all corporations have rights, including the right not to have their charter rewritten by new state laws
1819	Financial panic occurs in America
1820	Output per worker begins its "take-off" in America, making it the second modern economy
1820	Percy Bysshe Shelley's *Prometheus Unbound* is first published
1820–1840s	German wages decrease
1821	Hegel's *Grundlinien der Philosophie des Rechts* (*Elements of the Philosophy of Right*) is published in Berlin, arguing that rules are necessary to enable people to do the creative things for their self-actualization—to "act on the world"
1820s	In Britain, wages take off as innovation sweeps the country, while in Germany wages fall until 1848

1820s	French Romantic movement in painting begins
1823	Samuel Brown patents the first industrially used internal combustion engine
1824	Beethoven's Ninth Symphony, with passages of frenzy and near chaos, premiers in Vienna
1830s	France and Belgium, following Britain, begin sustained growth of output per head
1830–1860s	Britain's output per head rises markedly
1830	Massachusetts legislature extends charters beyond public works like canals and colleges
1830	July Revolution in France overthrows Bourbon King Charles X and instates Louis-Philippe
1830	Belgian Revolution establishes a parliamentary democracy
1830	Output per worker begins to "take-off" in France and Belgium
1832	The English Reform Act extends the vote for the House of Commons to men without reference to property qualifications and redistributes seats to urban areas
1833	The Slavery Abolition Act emancipates slaves in the British West Indies
1833	Federal imprisonment for debtors is abolished in America
1835	Alexis de Tocqueville's *Democracy in America* is first published in France
1836	A lithograph depicts nine firms on New York's Liberty Street, four of which will be bankrupt within five years
1836	Samuel Colt introduces the revolver
1836	Samuel Morse develops the electrical telegraph system and Morse code
1837	Connecticut permits companies to incorporate without a legislative act
1837	Financial panic occurs in America
1839	Dickens's *Oliver Twist* is published in London
1841	U.S. Bankruptcy Act of 1841 eases penalties of default; it is repealed in 1843

1842	Musikverein is founded to support the Vienna Philharmonic Orchestra
1842	Philharmonic Society of New York is founded to create a top orchestra
1843	Søren Kierkegaard publishes in Copenhagen under a pseudonym his *Either/Or* on the necessity of leaps of faith
1844	Joint Stock Companies Act in England permits incorporating though without limited liability
1844	J. M. W. Turner paints *Rail, Steam and Speed*
1846	Financial panic occurs in Europe
1847	Emily Brontë's *Wuthering Heights* is published under the pseudonym Ellis Bell
1848	Charlotte Brontë's *Jane Eyre* is published in London
1848	King Louis-Philippe of France is overthrown; popular uprisings sweep Europe
1848	Karl Marx and Friedrich Engels's *The Communist Manifesto* is published
1851	Herman Melville's *Moby-Dick* is published in New York
1852	Robert Schumann premiers *Manfred Overture* in Leipzig
1854	Franz Liszt premiers *Les preludes* in Weimar
1854	Charles Dickens's *Hard Times* is published in London
1856	Joint Stock Companies Act of 1856 in England grants corporations limited liability
1857	Herman Melville's *The Confidence-Man* is published in New York
1857	Financial panic occurs in Europe and America
1858	Charles Dickens's *David Copperfield* is published in London
1859	Samuel Smile's *Self-Help* is published in London
1859	*On the Origin of Species* by Charles Darwin describes the natural selection among variants of a species thrown up by "chance"
1863	Abraham Lincoln delivers the Emancipation Proclamation
1863	France allows companies to incorporate with limited liability

1864	Fyodor Dostoevsky's *Notes from the Underground* is published in Russia
1866	German states lose unification under the Austrian Empire
1867	U.S. Bankruptcy Act of 1867 eases penalties for default; it is repealed in 1878
1869	Debtors Act abolishes imprisonment for debt in England
1870	"High Modernism" begins in the arts and goes on to 1940
1870	U.S. vote is extended to non-white men
1870	Germany allows companies to incorporate with limited liability
1870	Western European output per head is up 63 percent over the 1820 level; the U.S. level is up by 95 percent
1870s–1940s	The period of high modernism in painting emerges
1871	Otto von Bismarck unifies German states and Prussia under Kaiser Wilhelm's Empire
1872	Nietzsche publishes *The Birth of Tragedy*
1873	Financial panic takes place in Europe and America
1876	Mark Twain's *The Adventures of Tom Sawyer* is published in America
1876	Richard Wagner premieres *Der Ring des Nibelungen* at the Bayreuth Festival
1880	Fyodor Dostoevsky publishes *The Brothers Karamazov*
1887	Sociologist Ferdinand Tönnies's *Community and Society* is published in Germany
1888	Vincent van Gogh paints *Sower with Setting Sun*, *The Painter on the Road to Tarascon*, and *Café Terrace on the Place du Forum*
1893	Financial panic occurs in Europe and America; unemployment in America is over 12 percent from 1893 to 1898
1894	Building off of Eadweard Muybridge's proto-film experiments, Thomas Edison undertakes the first commercial exhibition of films with his Kinetoscope parlors
1898	U.S. Bankruptcy Act of 1898 gives companies the option of being protected from creditors
1900	Fifty towns in Germany qualify as cities (up from four in 1800)

1901	Thomas Mann's *Buddenbrooks* is published in Germany
1902	Ransom Olds's Oldsmobile production-line manufactures affordable automobiles
1902	Arnold Schoenberg's *Verklärte Nacht* premieres in Vienna
1907	Henri Bergson's *L'évolution créatrice* is published in Paris, translated into English four years later as *Creative Evolution* and published to great acclaim
1910s	Franz Kafka writes *The Trial*, "In the Penal Colony," and *The Castle,* depicting the oppressiveness of totalitarianism and the hierarchical state
1912	Futurist Giacomo Balla paints *Dynamism of a Dog on a Leash*
1912	Joseph Schumpeter publishes in Leipzig his landmark book, *Theorie der wirtschaftlichen Entwicklung,* translated as *The Theory of Economic Development* in 1934
1913–1915	Ernst Ludwig Kirchner paints half a dozen paintings titled *Berlin Street Scene*
1913	Igor Stravinsky premieres *The Rite of Spring* in Paris
1914	Henry Ford's assembly line makes a Model T car in 1 hour 33 minutes
1919	Walter Gropius founds Bauhaus in Weimar
1919	Ludwig von Mises's *Nation, State, and Economy* is published in Vienna
1920	By this year, most Americans live in cities
1920	U.S. vote extends to women
1921	John Maynard Keynes publishes *A Treatise on Probability*
1921	Frank Knight's *Risk, Uncertainty and Profit* is published
1922	Le Corbusier presents his plan for Ville Contemporaine
1922	Max Weber's *Economy and Society* is published posthumously in Tübingen
1922	Ludwig von Mises's *Socialism: An Economic and Sociological Analysis* is published
1923	C. S. Peirce's *Chance, Love, and Logic: Philosophical Essays* is published

1927	Werner Heisenberg's "Über den anschaulichen Inhalt der quantentheoretischen Kinematik und Mechanik" ("On the Perceptual Content of Quantum Theoretical Kinematics and Mechanics") sets out the first version of the Uncertainty Principle
1927	First talkie film, *The Jazz Singer,* is released
1930	Sigmund Freud's *Civilization and Its Discontents* is published in Germany
1930	P. T. Farnsworth patents the television; World War II prevents its spread in the United States until 1948
1931	*M* directed by Fritz Lang is released
1933	George Balanchine and Lincoln Kirstein form the New York City Ballet
1935	Frank Lloyd Wright completes Fallingwater
1935–38	Alfred Hitchcock's *The 39 Steps* and *The Lady Vanishes* dramatize how little we understand of the world
1935	*Collectivist Economic Planning*, edited by Friedrich Hayek, is published in London
1935	Oskar Morgenstern's "Volkommene Voraussicht und Wirt-schaftliches Gleichgewicht" ("Perfect Foresight and Economic Equilibrium") appears in *Zeitschrift für Nationalökonomie*
1936	John Maynard Keynes's *General Theory* is first published
1937	Charlie Chaplin's *Modern Times* satirizes the assembly line
1938	Jean-Paul Sartre's *Nausea* is published in Paris
1939	Raymond Chandler's *The Big Sleep* is published
1940s	Robert Merton introduces the law of unexpected consequences and the "latent function" a law may have
1940	Charles Ives' *The Unanswered Question*, drafted in 1906, is published and performed

Late Modern Age ca. 1941 to the present

1944	Friedrich Hayek's *The Road to Serfdom* is published in London
1945	Karl Popper's *The Open Society and Its Enemies* is published in London

1951	Ludwig Mies van der Rohe completes the Farnsworth House
1953	In *Waiting for Godot,* Samuel Beckett draws a surreal portrait of modern-day anxiety
1955	Former trucking company owner Malcom McLean designs the modern intermodal container with engineer Keith Tantlinger and gives the patented designs to industry
1957	Karl Popper's *The Poverty of Historicism* is published in London
1958	Michael Polanyi's *Personal Knowledge*, from the 1951–1952 Gifford Lectures, is published
1960s	Harold Pinter's play *A Slight Ache* dramatizes how little we know about the social world around us
1961	Friedrich Hayek's "The Non-Sequitur of the 'Dependence Effect'" is published
1961	Jane Jacobs's *The Death and Life of Great American Cities* is published in New York
1966	Tom Stoppard's play *Rosencrantz and Guildenstern Are Dead* suggests that each person is limited by his or her position
1968	Friedrich Hayek's "Competition as a Discovery Procedure" is published
1969	Jane Jacobs's *The Economy of Cities* is published
1970	*Microeconomic Foundations of Employment and Inflation Theory*, a volume from a conference organized by Edmund Phelps, introduces wage and price expectations into employment determination
1989	Thomas Nagel's *The View from Nowhere* is published
1991	Paul Johnson's *The Birth of the Modern: World Society 1815–1830* is published
1992	Following protocols agreed upon earlier in the 1990s, Netscape's initial public offering launches the internet into widespread use
2006	Edmund Phelps gives Nobel Prize Lecture on understanding economies of dynamism

2006	In a conference, *Perspectives on the Performance of the Continental Economies,* Edmund Phelps reports that the differences in nations' economic values largely account for differences in their productivity and employment.
2007	Roman Frydman and Michael Goldberg's *Imperfect Knowledge Economics* is published
2008	Amar Bhidé's *The Venturesome Economy* is published
2009	Mark C. Taylor's *Field Notes from Elsewhere* reflects on living in modern times
2011	Martin Seligman's *Flourish: A Visionary New Understanding of Happiness and Well-being* is published

BIBLIOGRAPHY

Abelshauser, Werncr. "The First Post-Liberal Nation: Stages in the Development of Modern Corporatism in Germany." *European History Quarterly* 14, no. 3 (1984): 285–318.

Abramovitz, Moses. "Resource and Output Trends in the United States since 1870." *American Economic Review* 46 (1956): 1–23.

Aghion, Philippe, and Enisse Kharroubi. "Stabilization Policies and Economic Growth," in Roman Frydman and Edmund Phelps (eds.), *Rethinking Expectations: The Way Forward for Macroeconomics.* Princeton, N.J.: Princeton University Press, 2013.

Alda, Alan. *Things I Overheard While Talking to Myself.* New York: Random House, 2007.

Allen, Robert C. "The Great Divergence in European Wages and Prices." *Explorations in Economic History* 38 (2001): 411–447.

Ammous, Saifedean, and Edmund Phelps. "Climate Change, the Knowledge Problem and the Good Life." Working Paper 42, Center on Capitalism and Society, Columbia University, New York, September 2009.

———. "Blaming Capitalism for the Ills of Corporatism," *Project Syndicate*, January 31, 2012. http://www.project-syndicate.org/commentary/blaming-capitalism-for-corporatism.

Andrews, Malcolm. *Dickens on England and the English.* Hassocks, Sussex: Harvester, 1979.

Aristotle. *Aristotle: Nicomachean Ethics*, edited by Terence Irwin. Indianapolis, Ind.: Hackett Publishing, 2nd edition, 1999.

Arnold, Matthew. *The Function of Criticism.* London: Macmillan, 1895.

Austen, Jane. *Sense and Sensibility.* London: Thomas Egerton, 1811.

———. *Mansfield Park.* London: Thomas Egerton, 1814.

Bairoch, Paul. "Wages as an Indicator of Gross National Product," in Peter Scholliers (ed.), *Real Wages in 19th and 20th Century Europe: Historical and Comparative Perspectives.* New York: Berg, 1989.

Balas, Aron, Rafael La Porta, Florencio Lopez-de-Silanes, and Andre Shleifer. "The Divergence of Legal Procedures." *American Economic Journal: Economic Policy* 1, no. 2 (2009): 138–162.

Balleisen, Edward J. *Navigating Failure: Bankruptcy and Commercial Society in Antebellum America*. Chapel Hill: University of North Carolina, 2001.

Banfield, Edward C. *The Moral Basis of a Backward Society*. New York: Basic Books, 1958.

Barzun, Jacques. "From the Nineteenth Century to the Twentieth," in Contemporary Civilization Staff of Columbia College (eds.), *Chapters in Western Civilization*, vol. II. New York: Columbia University Press, 3rd edition, 1962.

——. *A Stroll with William James*. New York: Harper, 1983.

——. *From Dawn to Decadence: 500 Years of Western Cultural Life*. New York: Harper Perennial, 2001.

Bekker, Immanuel. *Aristotelis Opera edidit Academia Regia Borussica*. Berlin, 1831–1870.

Bentolila, Samuel, and Giuseppe Bertola. "Firing Costs and Labour Demand: How Bad Is Eurosclerosis?" *Review of Economic Studies* 57, no. 3 (1990): 381–402.

Berghahn, V. R. "Corporatism in Germany in Historical Perspective," in Andrew W. Cox and Noel O'Sullivan (eds.), *The Corporate State: Corporatism and the State Tradition in Western Europe*. Aldershot, U.K.: Edward Elgar, 1988.

Bergson, Henri. *Creative Evolution*. New York: Henry Holt, 1911.

Berle, Adolf, and Gardiner Means. *The Modern Corporation and Private Property*. New York: Transaction Publishers, 1932.

Bhidé, Amar. "The Hidden Costs of Stock Market Liquidity." *Journal of Financial Economics* 34 (1993): 31–51.

——. *The Venturesome Economy*. Princeton, N.J.: Princeton University Press, 2008.

Bhidé, Amar, and Edmund S. Phelps. "More Harm Than Good: How the IMF's Business Model Sabotages Properly Functioning Capitalism," *Newsweek International*, July 11, 2011, p. 18.

Blanchflower, David, and Andrew J. Oswald. "Well-Being, Insecurity and the Decline of American Job Satisfaction." Working Paper, National Bureau of Economic Research, Cambridge, Mass., 1999.

Bloom, Harold. *The Visionary Company: A Reading of English Romantic Poetry*. New York: Doubleday, 1961.

——. *The Western Canon: The Books and Schools of the Ages*. New York: Penguin Putnam, 1994.

——. *Shakespeare: The Invention of the Human*. New York: Riverhead Books, 1998.

Bodenhorn, Howard. *A History of Banking in Antebellum America: Financial Markets and Economic Development in an Era of Nation-Building*. Cambridge: Cambridge University Press, 2000.

Bojilov, Raicho, and Edmund S. Phelps. "Job Satisfaction: The Effects of Two Economic Cultures." Working Paper 78, Center on Capitalism and Society, Columbia University, New York, September 2012.

Boulding, Kenneth. *Beyond Economics: Essays on Society, Religion, and Ethics*. Ann Arbor: University of Michigan Press, 1968.

Bourguignon, Philippe. "Deux éducations, deux cultures," in Jean-Marie Chevalier and Jacques Mistral (eds.), *Le Cercle des economistes: L'Europe et les Etats-Unis*. Paris: Descartes et Cie, 2006.

Bradshaw, David J., and Suzanne Ozment. *The Voices of Toil: Nineteenth-Century British Writings about Work*. Athens, Ohio: Ohio University Press, 2000.

Brands, H. W. *American Colossus: The Triumph of Capitalism, 1865–1900*. New York: Doubleday, 2010.

Brass, Dick. "Microsoft's Creative Destruction." *New York Times*, February 4, 2010, p. A27.

Braudel, Fernand. *The Mediterranean and the Mediterranean World in the Age of Philip II*, vol. 2. New York: Harper and Row, 1972.

Brontë, Charlotte. *Jane Eyre*. London: Smith, Elder, and Company, 1847.

Brontë, Emily. *Wuthering Heights*. London: Thomas Cautley Newby, 1847.

Caldwell, Christopher. "The New Battle for the Old Soul of the Republican Party." *Financial Times*, February 24, 2012, p. 9.

Calvin, John. *Institutio Christianae Religionis (Institutes of Christian Religion)*. Geneva: Robert Estienne, 1559.

Cantillon, Richard. *Essai sur la Nature du Commerce en Général*. London: Fletcher Gyles, 1755.

Caron, François. *An Economic History of Modern France*, translated by Barbara Bray. London: Methuen, 1979.

Cary, Joyce. *The Horse's Mouth*. New York: Harper, 1944.

Cassirer, Ernst. "Giovanni Pico della Mirandola: A Study in the History of Renaissance Ideas." *Journal of the History of Ideas* 3, no. 3 (1942): 319–346.

Casson, Mark. "Entrepreneurship," in Mark Casson (ed.), *International Library of Critical Writings in Economics*, vol. 13. Aldershot, U.K.: Edward Elgar, 1990.

Cather, Willa. *Death Comes for the Archbishop*. New York: Alfred A. Knopf, 1927.

Cellini, Benvenuto. *The Autobiography of Benvenuto Cellini*. New York: Alfred A. Knopf, 2010.

Cervantes, Miguel de. *Don Quixote*. Madrid: Juan de la Cuesta, 1605–1620.

Chandler, Alfred D., Jr. *Strategy and Structure: Chapters in the History of the American Industrial Enterprise*. Cambridge, Mass.: MIT Press, 1962.

———. *The Visible Hand: The Managerial Revolution in American Business*. Cambridge, Mass.: Harvard University Press, 1977.

———. *The Coming of Managerial Capitalism*. New York: Richard D. Irwin, 1985.

———. *Scale and Scope: The Dynamics of Industrial Capitalism*. Cambridge, Mass.: Harvard University Press, 1990.

Christiansen, G. B., and R. H. Haveman. "Government Regulations and Their Impact on the Economy." *Annals of the American Academy of Political and Social Science* 459, no. 1 (1982): 112–122.

Clark, Gregory. "The Long March of History: Population and Economic Growth." Working Paper 05-40, University of California, Davis, 2005.

———. *A Farewell to Alms: A Brief Economic History of the World*. Princeton, N.J.: Princeton University Press, 2007.

Coke, Edward. *The Second [Third and Fourth] Part[s] of the Institutes of the Laws of England*. London: Printed for E. and R. Brooke, 1797 (first written 1641).

Conard, Nicholas J., Maria Malina, and Susanne C. Münzel. "New Flutes Document the Earliest Musical Tradition in Southwestern Germany." *Nature* 460 (2009): 737–740.

Coolidge, Calvin. "Address to the American Society of Newspaper Editors, Washington, D.C.," January 17, 1925. Online by Gerhard Peters and John T. Woolley, The American Presidency Project. http://www.presidency.ucsb.edu/ws/?pid=24180.

Cooper, John M. *Reason and the Human Good in Aristotle*. Cambridge, Mass.: Harvard University Press, 1975.

Crafts, N.F.R. "British Economic Growth, 1700–1831: A Review of the Evidence." *Economic History Review* 36, no. 2 (1983): 177–199.

Crooks, Ed. "US 'Creative Destruction' out of Steam." *Financial Times,* December 12, 2011.

Dahlhaus, Carl. *Nineteenth-Century Music.* Berkeley: University of California, 1989.

David, Paul A. "The Growth of Real Product in the United States before 1840: New Evidence, Controlled Conjectures." *Journal of Economic History* 27, no. 2 (1967): 151–197.

Defoe, Daniel. *Robinson Crusoe.* London: W. Taylor, 1719.

——. *Moll Flanders.* London: W. Taylor, 1721.

Demsetz, Harold. "Toward a Theory of Property Rights II: The Competition between Private and Collective Ownership." *Journal of Legal Studies* (June 2002): 668.

Denning, Peter J., and Robert Dunham. *The Innovator's Way: Essential Practices for Successful Innovation.* Cambridge, Mass.: MIT Press, 2010.

Dewey, John. *Human Nature and Conduct.* New York: Holt, 1922.

——. "The House Divided against Itself." *New Republic,* April 24, 1929, pp. 270–271.

——. *Individualism Old and New.* New York: Minton, Balch, and Company, 1930.

——. *Experience and Education.* New York: Simon and Schuster, 1938.

Diamond, Jared M. *Guns, Germs, and Steel: The Fates of Human Societies.* New York: W. W. Norton, 1997.

Dickens, Charles. *Sketches by Boz.* London: John Macrone, 1836.

——. *Oliver Twist.* London: Richard Bentley, 1837.

——. *David Copperfield.* London: Bradbury and Evans, 1850.

——. *Hard Times.* London: Bradbury and Evans, 1854.

——. *Speeches, Letters and Sayings.* New York: Harper, 1870.

——. *The Uncommercial Traveler and Reprinted Pieces.* Philadelphia: John D. Morris, 1900.

Dods, Marcus. *Erasmus, and Other Essays.* Longdon: Hodder and Stoughton, 1891.

DuBois, Armand Budington. *The English Business Company after the Bubble Act, 1720–1800.* New York: Octagon, 1971.

Edlund, Lena. "Big Ideas." *Milken Institute Review* 13, no. 1 (2011): 89–94.

Eggertsson, Thrainn. *Imperfect Institutions: Possibilities and Limits for Reform.* Ann Arbor: University of Michigan Press, 2006.

Erhard, Ludwig. *Wohlstand für Alle.* Dusseldorf: Econ-Verlag, 1957.

——. *Prosperity through Competition.* New York: Praeger, 1958.

Evans, Harold. *They Made America.* New York: Little Brown, 2004.

——. "Eureka: A Lecture on Innovation." Lecture given at the Royal Society of Arts, London, March 2011.

Ferguson, Adam. *Essay on the History of Civil Society.* Dublin: Grierson, 1767.

Ferraro, Geraldine. "Inspiration from the Land Where Dreams Come True." Speech, San Francisco, July 19, 1984. Available at http://www.cnn.com/ALLPOLITICS/1996/conventions/chicago/facts/famous.speeches/ferraro.84.shtml.

Finley, M. I. *The Ancient Economy.* Berkeley: University of California Press, 1999.

Fitoussi, Jean-Paul, and Edmund S. Phelps. *The Slump in Europe.* Oxford: Blackwell, 1988.

Fogel, Robert William. *Railroads and American Economic Growth: Essays in Econometric History.* Baltimore: Johns Hopkins University Press, 1964.

Foster, John Bellamy, Robert W. McChesney, and Jamil Jonna. "Monopoly and Competition in Twenty-First Century Capitalism." *Monthly Review* 62, no. 11 (2011): 1–23.

Foster-Hahn, Francoise, Claude Keisch, Peter-Klaus Schuster, and Angelika Wesenberg. *Spirit of an Age: Nineteenth-Century Paintings from the Nationalgalerie, Berlin.* London: National Gallery, 2001.

Freud, Sigmund. *Das Unbehagen in der Kultur.* Vienna: Internationaler Psychoanalytischer Verlag, 1930.

———. *Civilization and Its Discontents,* translated by James Strachey. New York: W. W. Norton, 1989.

Fry, Stephen. "Lady Gaga Takes Tea with Mr Fry." *Financial Times* (London), May 27, 2011, p. 12.

Frydman, Roman, and Michael Goldberg. *Imperfect Knowledge Economics: Exchange Rates and Risk.* Princeton: Princeton University Press, 2007.

Frydman, Roman, Marek Hessel, and Andrzej Rapaczynski. "When Does Privatization Work?" *Quarterly Journal of Economics* (1999): 1153–1191.

Geddes, Rick, and Dean Lueck. "Gains from Self-Ownership and the Expansion of Women's Rights." *American Economic Review* 92, no. 4 (2002): 63–83.

Gibbon, Edward. *The History of the Decline and Fall of the Roman Empire.* London: Strahan and Cadell, 1776–1789.

Giffen, Robert. "The Material Progress of Great Britain." Address before the Economic Sector of the British Association, London, 1887.

Gombrich, E. H. *The Story of Art.* London: Phaidon, 4th edition, 1951.

Gordon, Robert J. "U.S. Productivity Growth over the Past Century with a View to the Future." Working Paper 15834, National Bureau of Economic Research, Cambridge, Mass., March 2010.

———. "Is U.S. Economic Growth Over? Faltering Innovation Confronts the Six Headwinds." Working Paper 18315, National Bureau of Economic Research, Cambridge, Mass., August 2012.

Gray, Henry. *Anatomy, Descriptive and Surgical.* Philadelphia: Blanchard and Lea, 2nd American edition, 1862.

Greenwald, Bruce C. N., and Judd Kahn. *Globalization: The Irrational Fear That Someone in China Will Take Your Job.* Hoboken, N.J.: John Wiley and Sons, 2009.

Groom, Brian. "War Hero Who Became Captain of British Industry." *Financial Times,* October 2–3, 2010, p. 7.

———. "Gloom and Boom." Books Section, *Financial Times,* October 2–3, 2010, p. 16.

Gwartney, James, Robert Lawson, and Joshua Hall. *Economic Freedom of the World: 2011 Annual Report.* Vancouver: Fraser Institute, 2011.

Hall, Robert, and Charles I. Jones. "Why Do Some Countries Produce So Much More Output per Worker Than Others?" *Quarterly Journal of Economics* 114, no. 1 (1999): 83–116.

Hansard, Thomas C. (ed.). *Hansard's Parliamentary Debates.* Third series, second volume of the session. London: Cornelius Buck, 1863.

Hayek, Friedrich. "The Trend of Economic Thinking." *Economica* 13 (1933): 127–137.

———. "Socialist Calculation: The State of the Debate," in Friedrich Hayek (ed.), *Collectivist Economic Planning; Critical Studies on the Possibilities of Socialism.* London: Routledge, 1935.

———. *The Road to Serfdom.* London: Routledge, 1944.

———. *Individualism and Economic Order.* Chicago: University of Chicago Press, 1948.

Hayek, Friedrich. *The Counter-Revolution of Science; Studies on the Abuse of Reason.* Glencoe, Ill.: Free Press, 1952.

———. "The Non-Sequitur of the 'Dependence Effect.'" *Southern Economic Journal* 27 (1961): 346.

———. "Competition as a Discovery Procedure," in *New Studies in Philosophy, Politics, Economics and the History of Ideas.* Chicago: University of Chicago Press, 1978.

Heckman, James J., and Dimitriy V. Masterov. "The Productivity Argument for Investing in Young Children." *Applied Economic Perspectives and Policy* 29, no. 3 (2007): 446–493.

Henley, William Ernest. *Poems.* New York: Charles Scribner's Sons, 1898.

Hewlett, Sylvia Ann. *A Lesser Life: The Myth of Women's Liberation in America.* New York: Morrow, 1986.

Hicks, John. *A Theory of Economic History.* Oxford: Oxford University Press, 1969.

Hoon, Hian Teck, and Edmund Phelps. "Payroll Taxes and VAT in a Labor-Turnover Model of the 'Natural Rate.'" *International Tax and Public Finance* 3 (June 1996): 185–201.

———. "Growth, Wealth and the Natural Rate: Is Europe's Jobs Crisis a Growth Crisis?" *European Economic Review* 41 (April 1997): 549–557.

———. "Effects of Technological Improvement in the ICT-Producing Sector on Business Activity." Columbia University Department of Economics Discussion Paper 0506-21, February 2006.

Howard, Philip K. *The Death of Common Sense: How Law Is Suffocating America.* New York: Random House, 1995.

———. *The Collapse of the Common Good: How America's Lawsuit Culture Undermines Our Freedom.* New York: Ballantine, 2001.

Hume, David. *A Treatise on Human Nature.* London: John Noon, 1739–1740.

———. *Philosophical Essays Concerning Human Understanding.* London: A. Millar, 1748. Subsequently republished as *An Enquiry Concerning Human Understanding.*

Huppert, Felicia A., and Timothy T. C. So. "What Percentage of People in Europe Are Flourishing and What Characterises Them?" Retrieved January 4, 2013, from www.isqols2009.istitutodeglinnocenti.it/Content_en/Huppert.pdf.

Ibison, David. "The Monday Interview: Carl-Henric Svanberg." *Financial Times,* October 1, 2006, p. 11.

Ibsen, Henrik. *Peer Gynt,* translated by Rolf Fjelde. Minneapolis: University of Minnesota Press, 1980.

Inglehart, Ronald, and Christian Welzel. *Modernization, Cultural Change, and Democracy: The Human Development Sequence.* Cambridge: Cambridge University Press, 2005.

Irving, Washington. *The Sketch Book of Geoffrey Crayon, Gent.* London: John Murray, 1820.

Jackman, Richard, Richard Layard, and Stephen Nickell. *Unemployment: Macroeconomic Performance and the Labour Market.* Oxford: Oxford University Press, 1991.

Jackson, R. V. "The Structure of Pay in Nineteenth-Century Britain." *Economic History Review* 40, no. 4 (1987): 561–570.

Jacobs, Jane. *The Death and Life of Great American Cities.* New York: Random House, 1961.

———. *The Economy of Cities.* New York: Random House, 1969.

James, Harold. *Europe Reborn.* Princeton, N.J.: Princeton University Press, 2009.

Jamison, Kay Redfield. *Exuberance: The Passion for Life.* New York: Alfred A. Knopf, 2004.

Jefferson, Thomas. *The Works of Thomas Jefferson,* vol. 2. New York: G. P. Putnam and Sons, 1904.

Johnson, Paul. *The Birth of the Modern: World Society 1815–1830.* New York: Harper Collins, 1991.

Jones, Jonathan. "Other Artists Paint Pictures, Turner Brings Them to Life." *Guardian,* May 6, 2009. Available at www.guardian.co.uk.

Karakacili, E. "English Agrarian Labour Productivity Rates before the Black Death: A Case Study." *Journal of Economic History* 64 (March 2004): 24–60.

Keats, John. *The Poems of John Keats,* edited by Jack Stillinger. Cambridge, Mass.: Belknap Press of Harvard University Press, 1978.

Kellaway, Lucy. "Jobs, Motherhood and Varieties of Wrong." *Financial Times,* July 29, 2012, p. 16.

Kennedy, Maev. "British Library Publishes Online Archive of 19th Century Newspapers." *Guardian,* June 18, 2009, p. 18.

Keynes, John Maynard. *A Treatise on Probability.* London: Macmillan, 1921.

——. *General Theory of Employment, Interest and Money.* London: Palgrave Macmillan, 1936.

——. "Economic Possibilities for Our Grandchildren," in *Essays in Persuasion.* New York: W. W. Norton, 1963.

Kindleberger, Charles Poor. *A Financial History of Western Europe.* New York: Oxford University Press, 1993.

Kirby, William C. "China Unincorporated: Company Law and Business Enterprise in 20th Century China." *Journal of Asian Studies* 54 (February 1995): 43–46.

Kling, Arnold, and Nick Schulz. "The New Commanding Heights." *National Affairs* 8 (Summer 2011): 3–19.

Knight, Frank. *Risk, Uncertainty and Profit.* Boston: Hart, Schaffner and Marx; Houghton Mifflin, 1921.

Koestler, Arthur. *The Act of Creation.* New York: Macmillan, 1964.

——. *The Sleepwalkers.* New York: Macmillan, 1968.

Kronman, Anthony T. *Education's End: Why Our Colleges and Universities Have Given Up on the Meaning of Life.* New Haven, Conn.: Yale University Press, 2007.

Krugman, Paul R. *Geography and Trade.* Cambridge, Mass.: MIT Press, 1992.

Kuczynski, Jürgen. *Labour Conditions in Western Europe.* London: F. Muller, 1937.

——. *A Short History of Labour Conditions under Industrial Capitalism.* London: F. Muller, 1942–1945.

Kuznets, Simon. "Population Change and Aggregate Output," in *Demographic and Economic Change in Developed Countries, a Conference of the Universities–National Bureau Committee for Economic Research.* Princeton, N.J.: Princeton University Press, 1960.

Lange, Oskar. "On the Economic Theory of Socialism," in Oskar Lange, Benjamin E. Lippincott, and Frederick M. Taylor (eds.), *On the Economic Theory of Socialism.* Minneapolis: University of Minnesota Press, 1938.

Layard, Richard. *Happiness: Lessons from a New Science.* London: Penguin, 2007.

Layard, Richard, and Stephen Nickell. *Handbook of Labor Economics.* Amsterdam: North-Holland, 1999.

Leroux, Pierre. *De l'égalité; précédé de l'individualisme et du socialisme.* Paris: Slatkine, 1996.

Lincoln, Abraham. "Second Lecture on Discoveries and Inventions" (1859). In *Collected Works of Abraham Lincoln,* vol. 3. New Brunswick, N.J: Rutgers University Press, 1953, 356–363.

Lindert, Peter H., and Jeffrey G. Williamson. "English Workers' Living Standards during the Industrial Revolution: A New Look." *Economic History Review* 36, no. 1 (1983): 1–25.

Lippmann, Walter. *The Good Society.* New York: Little Brown, 1936.

Litan, Robert E., and Carl J. Schramm. *Better Capitalism: Renewing the Entrepreneurial Strength of the American Economy.* New Haven, Conn.: Yale University Press, 2012.

Loasby, Brian J. *The Mind and Method of the Economist: A Critical Appraisal of Major Economists in the 20th Century.* Aldershot, U.K.: Edward Elgar, 1989.

Lovecraft, H. P. *The Dream-Quest of Unknown Kadath* (1926), in *At the Mountains of Madness and Other Novels.* Sauk City, Wisc.: Arkham House, 1964.

Lowenstein, Louis. *The Investor's Dilemma: How Mutual Funds Are Betraying Your Trust and What to Do about It.* Hoboken, N.J.: John Wiley and Sons, 2008.

Lubasz, Heinz. *Fascism: Three Major Regimes.* New York: John Wiley and Sons, 1973.

Maddison, Angus. *The World Economy: Historical Statistics.* Paris: OECD, 2006: table 1b, p. 439, and table 8c, p. 642.

Mann, Thomas. *Buddenbrooks.* Berlin: S. Fischer Verlag, 1901.

Marr, Andrew. *The Making of Modern Britain.* London: Macmillan, 2009.

Marshall, Alfred. *Elements of Economics.* London: Macmillan, 1892.

——— . *Principles of Economics: An Introductory Volume.* London: Macmillan, 1938.

Marx, Karl. *Grundrisse der Kritik der politischen Ökonomie* (1858). Frankfurt: Europäische Verlagsanstalt, 1939–1941.

——— . *Critique of the Gotha Program* (1875). Moscow: Moscow Foreign Languages Publishing House, 1947.

Marx, Karl, and Friedrich Engels. *The Communist Manifesto.* London: 1848.

Maslow, Abraham. "A Theory of Motivation." *Psychological Review* 50 (1943): 370–396.

Maugham, W. Somerset. "The Man Who Made His Mark." *Cosmopolitan,* June 1929.

Melville, Herman. *Moby-Dick.* New York: Harper and Brothers, 1851.

——— . *The Confidence-Man.* New York: Dix, Edwards, 1857.

Mickelthwait, John, and Adrian Wooldridge. *The Company: A Short History of a Revolutionary Idea.* New York: Modern Library, 2003.

Milanović, Branko. *Liberalization and Entrepreneurship: Dynamics of Reform in Socialism and Capitalism.* Armonk, N.Y.: M. E. Sharpe, 1989.

Mill, John Stuart. "The Law of Partnership" (1851), in John M. Robson (ed.), *Essays on Economics and Society Part II.* London: Routledge and Kegan Paul, 1967.

Mises, Ludwig von. "Die Wirtschaftsrechnung im sozialistischen Gemeinwesen." *Archiv für Sozialwissenschaften und Sozialpolitik* 47 (1920): 86–121.

——— . *Die Gemeinwirtschaft: Untersuchungen über den Sozialismus.* Jena: Gustav Fischer Verlag, 1922.

——— . "Economic Calculation in the Socialist Commonwealth," in Friedrich Hayek (ed.), *Collectivist Economic Planning; Critical Studies on the Possibilities of Socialism.* London: G. Routledge, 1935.

——— . *Socialism: An Economic and Sociological Analysis,* translated by J. Kahane. London: Jonathan Cape, 1936.

Mokyr, Joel. "The Industrial Revolution and Modern Economic Growth." Max Weber Lecture given at the European University, San Domenico di Fiesole, Italy, March 2007. Revised June 2007.

——. "Intellectual Property Rights, the Industrial Revolution, and the Beginnings of Modern Economic Growth." *American Economic Review* 99, no. 2 (2009): 349–355.

Montaigne, Michel de. *Essais*. Paris: Garnier, 1962.

Morris, Charles. *The Dawn of Innovation: The First American Industrial Revolution*. New York: Public Affairs, 2012.

Muller, Jerry Z. *The Mind and the Market: Capitalism in Modern European Thought*. New York: Alfred A. Knopf, 2002.

Mussolini, Benito. *Quatro Discorsi sullo Stato Corporativo*. Rome: Laboremus, 1935.

——. *Four Speeches on the Corporate State*. Rome: Laboremus, 1935.

Mynors, R.A.B. *Georgics by Virgil*. Oxford: Clarendon Press, 1990.

Myrdal, Gunnar. *The Political Element in the Development of Economic Theory*. London: Routledge and Kegan Paul, 1953.

Nagel, Thomas. "Aristotle on Eudaimonia." *Phronesis* 17, no. 3 (1972): 252–259.

——. "What Is It Like to Be a Bat?" *Philosophical Review* 83, no. 4 (1974): 435–450.

——. *The Possibility of Altruism*. Oxford: Oxford University Press, 1978.

Nelson, Richard. "How Medical Know-How Progresses." Working Paper 23, Center on Capitalism and Society, Columbia University, New York, January 2008.

Nicholls, A. J. "Hitler's Success and Weimar's Failure," in *Weimar and the Rise of Hitler*. Houndmills, Basingstoke, U.K.: Palgrave Macmillan, 1968.

Nickell, Stephen. "Fundamental Changes in the UK Labour Market." *Oxford Bulletin of Economics and Statistics* 63 (2001): 715–736.

Nietzsche, Friedrich. *Der Wille zur Macht,* edited by Heinrich Köselitz, Ernst Horneffer, and August Horneffer. Leipzig: Naumann, 1901.

——. *The Will to Power*, translated by Walter Kaufmann. New York: Vintage, 1968.

Nocken, Ulrich. "Corporatism and Pluralism in Modern German History," in Dirk Stegmann et al. (eds.), *Industrielle Gesellschaft und politisches System*. Bonn: Verlag Neue Gesellschaft, 1978.

OECD (Organisation for Economic Co-operation and Development). *Historical Statistics 1960–81*. Paris, 1983.

——. *The OECD Jobs Study: Facts, Analysis, Strategies*. Paris, 1994.

OECD (Organisation for Economic Co-operation and Development) and Jean-Philippe Cotis. *Going for Growth: 2007*. Paris, 2007.

Olson, Mancur. *The Rise and Decline of Nations*. New Haven, Conn.: Yale University Press, 1982.

Paganetto, Luigi, and Edmund S. Phelps. *Finance, Research, Education, and Growth*. Houndmills, Basingstoke, U.K.: Palgrave Macmillan, 2005.

Paine, Thomas. *Common Sense*. London: H. D. Symonds, 1792.

Paxton, Robert. *The Anatomy of Fascism*. New York: Alfred A. Knopf, 2004.

PBS. "The Planning Debate in New York, 1955–1975." *American Experience: New York Disc 7; People & Events*. Television.

Phelps, Edmund S. *Fiscal Neutrality toward Economic Growth*. New York: McGraw-Hill, 1965.

——. "Population Increase." *Canadian Journal of Economics* 1 (1968): 497–518.

Phelps, Edmund S. "Taxation of Wage Income for Economic Justice." *Quarterly Journal of Economics* 87 (August 1973): 331–354.

—— (ed.). *Altruism, Morality and Economic Theory.* New York: Basic Books, 1975.

——. "Arguments for Private Ownership," in *Annual Economic Outlook.* London: European Bank for Reconstruction and Development, 1993.

——. *Structural Slumps: The Modern Equilibrium Theory of Employment, Interest and Assets.* Cambridge, Mass.: Harvard University Press, 1994.

——. *Rewarding Work: How to Restore Participation and Self-Support to Free Enterprise.* Cambridge, Mass.: Harvard University Press, 1997 (2nd printing 2007).

——. "Behind This Structural Boom: The Role of Asset Valuations." *American Economic Review (Papers and Proceedings)* 89, no. 2 (1999): 63–68.

Phelps, Edmund S. "The Importance of Inclusion and the Power of Job Subsidies to Increase It." *OECD Economic Studies* 31 (2000/2): 86–113.

——. "The Unproven Case for Tax Cuts." *Financial Times,* February 2, 2001, p. 13.

——. "Reflections on Parts III and IV," in Philippe Aghion, Joseph Stiglitz, Michael Woodford, and Roman Frydman (eds.), *Knowledge, Information, and Expectations in Modern Macroeconomics: In Honor of Edmund S. Phelps.* Princeton, N.J.: Princeton University Press, 2003.

——. "The Good Life and the Good Economy: The Humanist Perspective of Aristotle, the Pragmatists and Vitalists; And the Economic Justice of John Rawls," in Kaushik Basu and Ravi Kanbur (eds.), *Arguments for a Better World*: *Essays in Honor of Amartya Sen.* Oxford: Oxford University Press, 2008.

——. "Economic Culture and Economic Performance," in Hans-Werner Sinn and Edmund S. Phelps (eds.), *Perspectives on the Performance of the Continental Economies.* Cambridge, Mass.: MIT Press, 2011.

Phelps, Edmund S., and Richard R. Nelson. "Investment in Humans, Technological Diffusion, and Economic Growth." *American Economic Review* 56, no. 1–2 (1966): 69–75.

Phelps, Edmund S., and Robert Reich. Radio interview, National Public Radio, October 17, 2006.

Phelps, Edmund S., and Gylfi Zoega. "The Search for Routes to Better Economic Performance in Continental Europe: The European Labour Markets." *CESifo Forum* 5, no. 1 (2004): 3–11.

——. "Entrepreneurship, Culture and Openness," in D. B. Audretsch, Robert J. Strom, and Robert Litan (eds.), *Entrepreneurship and Openness.* Cheltenham, U.K.: Edward Elgar, 2009.

——. "Job Satisfaction: The Effect of Modern-Capitalist and Corporatist Institutions." Working Paper 77, Center on Capitalism and Society, Columbia University, New York, December 2012.

Phillips, A. W. "The Relationship between Unemployment and the Rate of Change of Money Wage Rates in the United Kingdom, 1861–1957." *Economica* 25 (1958): 283–299.

Polanyí, Karl. *The Great Transformation.* New York: Farrar and Rinehart, 1944.

Polanyí, Michael. *Personal Knowledge*: *Towards a Post-Critical Philosophy.* Chicago: University of Chicago Press, 1958.

Popper, Karl R. *The Poverty of Historicism.* London: Routledge and Kegan Paul, 1957.

Prescott, Edward, and Stephen Parente. *Barriers to Riches.* Cambridge, Mass.: MIT Press, 2000.

Rapaczynski, Andrzej. *Nature and Politics: Liberalism in the Philosophies of Hobbes, Locke and Rousseau.* Ithaca, N.Y.: Cornell University Press, 1987.

Rawls, John. *A Theory of Justice.* Cambridge, Mass.: Harvard University Press, 1971.

——. *Justice as Fairness: A Restatement,* edited by Erin Kelly. Cambridge, Mass.: Harvard University Press, 2001.

Razzell, Peter, and Christine Spence. "The History of Infant, Child and Adult Mortality in London, 1550–1850." *London Journal* 32, no. 3 (2007): 271–292.

Robb, Richard. "Nietzsche and the Economics of Becoming." *Capitalism and Society* 4, no. 1 (2009).

Roh, Franz. "After Expressionism: Magic Realism," in Lois Parkinson Zamora and Wendy B. Faris (eds.), *Magical Realism: Theory, History, Community.* Durham, N.C.: Duke University Press, 1995.

Roland, Gérard. "Understanding Institutional Change: Fast-Moving and Slow-Moving Institutions." *Studies in Comparative International Development* 38, no. 4 (2004): 109–131.

Rosenberg, Nathan, and L. E. Birdzell. *How the West Grew Rich: The Economic Transformation of the Industrial World.* New York: Basic Books, 1986.

Rostow, W. W. *The Process of Economic Growth.* Oxford: Clarendon, 1953.

——. *The Stages of Economic Growth, a Non-Communist Manifesto.* Cambridge: Cambridge University Press, 1960.

Rothschild, Emma. *Economic Sentiments: Adam Smith, Condorcet, and the Enlightenment.* Cambridge, Mass.: Harvard University Press, 2001.

Rousseau, Jean-Jacques. *Émile, ou de l'Education.* Paris: Garnier-Flammarion, 1966.

Rylance, Rick. "Getting on," in Heather Glen (ed.), *The Cambridge Companion to the Brontës.* Cambridge: Cambridge University Press, 2002.

Sadka, Efraim. "On Progressive Income Taxation." *American Economic Review* 66, no. 5 (1976): 931–935.

Saint-Simon, Henri de. *Lettres d'un habitant de Genève à ses contemporains.* Paris: Librairie Saint-Simonienne, 1803.

——. *Nouveau Christianisme.* Paris: Bossange, 1825.

Sassoon, Donald. "All Shout Together." *Times Literary Supplement,* December 6, 2002, p. 5.

Say, Jean-Baptiste. *Traité d'économie politique.* Paris: Rapilly, 1803.

Schlesinger, Arthur Meier. *The Coming of the New Deal: 1933–1935.* Boston: Houghton Mifflin, 2003.

Schlicke, Paul. *Oxford Reader's Companion to Dickens.* Oxford: Oxford University Press, 1999.

Schmitter, Philippe C. "Still the Century of Corporatism?" *Review of Politics* 36, no. 1, The New Corporatism: Social and Political Structures in the Iberian World (1974): 85–131.

Schumpeter, Joseph A. *Theorie der wirtschaftlichen Entwicklung.* Leipzig: Duncker and Humblot, 1912.

——. *The Theory of Economic Development.* Cambridge, Mass.: Harvard University Press, 1934.

——. *Capitalism, Socialism and Democracy.* New York: Harper and Brothers, 1942.

Seligman, Martin. *Flourish: A Visionary New Understanding of Happiness and Well-Being.* New York: Free Press, 2011.

Sen, Amartya. *Inequality Reexamined.* New York: W. W. Norton, 1992.

Sen, Amartya. *Commodities and Capabilities.* New York: Oxford University Press, 1999.

———. "The Crisis of European Democracy." *New York Times,* May 22, 2012.

Sennett, Richard. *The Culture of the New Capitalism.* New Haven, Conn.: Yale University Press, 2006.

Shelley, Mary Wollstonecraft. *Frankenstein; or, The Modern Prometheus.* London: Lackington, Hughes, Harding, Mavor and Jones, 1818.

Shelley, Percy Bysshe. *Prometheus Unbound: A Lyrical Drama with Other Poems.* London: C. and J. Ollier: 1820.

Sidorsky, David. "Modernism and the Emancipation of Literature from Morality." *New Literary History* 15 (1983): 137–153.

———. "The Uses of the Philosophy of G. E. Moore in the Works of E. M. Forster." *New Literary History* 38 (2007): 245–271.

Silver, Kenneth E. *Esprit de Corps: The Art of the Parisian Avant-Garde and the First World War, 1914–1925.* Princeton, N.J.: Princeton University Press, 1992.

———. *Chaos & Classicism: Art in France, Italy, and Germany 1918–1936 [published on the Occasion of the Exhibition Chaos and Classicism: Art in France, Italy, and Germany, 1918–1936].* New York: Guggenheim Museum, 2010.

Slaughter, Anne-Marie. "Why Women Still Can't Have It All." *Atlantic Monthly,* July/August 2012, pp. 85–90, 92–94, 96–98, 100–102.

Smiles, Samuel. *Self-Help with Illustrations of Character and Conduct.* London: John Murray, 1859.

Smith, Adam. *Inquiry into the Nature and Causes of the Wealth of Nations.* London: W. Strahan and T. Cadell, 1776.

———. *Lectures on Jurisprudence* (1762–1763). Oxford: Clarendon Press, 1978.

———. *The Theory of Moral Sentiments* (1759). New York: Penguin, 2009.

Smith, Christian (with Kari Christoffersen, Hilary Davidson, and Patricia Snell Herzog). *Lost in Transition: The Dark Side of Emerging Adulthood.* New York: Oxford University Press, 2011.

Snow, C. P. *The Two Cultures and the Scientific Revolution.* New York: Cambridge University Press, 1959.

Spengler, Oswald. *The Decline of the West.* New York: Alfred A. Knopf, 1926.

Spiegelman, Willard. "Revolutionary Romanticism: *The Raft of the Medusa.*" *Wall Street Journal,* August 15, 2009, p. W14.

Starr, Frederick S. "Rediscovering Central Asia." *Wilson Quarterly,* Summer 2009, pp. 33–43.

Stewart, Barbara. "Recall of the Wild: Fighting Boredom, Zoos Play to the Inmates' Instincts." *New York Times,* April 6, 2002, p. B1.

Stone, Irving. *Lust for Life.* New York: Doubleday, 1937.

Tanzi, Vito. *Government versus Markets: The Changing Economic Role of the State.* New York: Cambridge University Press, 2011.

Taylor, Mark C. *Field Notes from Elsewhere: Reflections on Dying and Living.* New York: Columbia University Press, 2009.

Theil, Stefan. "Europe's Philosophy of Failure." *Foreign Policy,* January–February 2008, pp. 55–60.

Thurm, Scott. "Companies Struggle to Pass on Knowledge That Workers Acquire." *Wall Street Journal,* January 23, 2006, p. B1.

Titmuss, Richard. *The Gift Relationship: From Human Blood to Social Policy.* New York: Pantheon Books, 1971.

Tocqueville, Alexis de. *Democracy in America.* London: Saunders and Otley, 1835.

———. "Letters from America," translated by Frederick Brown. *Hudson Review* 62, no. 3 (2009): 375–376.

Tönnies, Ferdinand. *Community and Civil Society,* translated by Jose Harris. Cambridge: Cambridge University Press, 2001.

Tooze, J. Adam. *The Wages of Destruction: The Making and Breaking of the Nazi Economy.* New York: Viking, 2007.

Toynbee, Arnold. *A Study of History.* New York: Oxford University Press, 1947–1957.

Trilling, Lionel. *The Liberal Imagination.* New York: Doubleday, 1950.

Twain, Mark. *The Adventures of Tom Sawyer.* Hartford, Conn.: American Publishing, 1876.

Van Gogh, Vincent. *The Letters: The Complete Illustrated Edition,* edited by Leo Jansen, Hans Luitjen, and Nienke Bakker. London: Thames and Hudson, 2009.

Vincenti, Walter G. "The Retractable Airplane Landing Gear and the Northrop 'Anomaly.'" *Technology and Culture* 35 (January 1994): 1–33.

Volpi, Giulio. "Soya Is Not the Solution to Climate Change." *Guardian,* March 16, 2006.

Voltaire. *Candide, ou l'optimisme.* Paris: Sirène, 1759.

Weber, Adna Ferrin. *The Growth of Cities in the Nineteenth Century: A Study in Statistics.* Ithaca, N.Y.: Cornell University Press, 1899.

Weber, Max. *Wirtschaft und Gesellschaft.* Tübingen, Germany: J.C.B. Mohr (P. Siebeck), 1922.

———. *The Protestant Ethic and the Spirit of Capitalism,* translated by Talcott Parsons. London: Unwin, 1930.

———. *Economy and Society,* edited by Guenther Roth and Claus Wittich. Berkeley: University of California Press, 1978.

Wells, David Ames. *Recent Economic Changes and Their Effect on the Production and Distribution of Wealth and the Well-being of Society.* New York: D. Appleton, 1899.

Wuthering Heights. Dir. William Wyler. Perf. Merle Oberon, Lawrence Olivier. Samuel Goldwyn. Film, 1939.

Zingales, Luigi. *A Capitalism for the People.* New York: Basic Books, 2012.

ACKNOWLEDGMENTS

I N MY CAREER I HAVE HAD many advantages—parents, teachers, colleagues, and a happy marriage with my wife Viviana. This book is dedicated to four giants who for decades inspired and influenced me: Paul Samuelson, William Fellner, John Rawls, and Robert Merton.

The book grew from several ideas, one of them being the importance of a nation's attitudes and beliefs. In the 1980s Viviana sometimes remarked to me in our travels that we shouldn't be surprised that people in other countries behave in ways different from my country of birth, America, and hers, Argentina. Nations differ in their attitudes and beliefs. This perspective stayed with me as we visit or work in countries overseas. I also remembered a fascinating dinner, probably in the 1990s, with the sociologist Seymour Martin Lipset at which he told me of his work on values in America that were less pronounced elsewhere. In a course I gave at Columbia from 1992 to 2006, World Economic Problems, I began to suggest that differences in values give rise to the differences in economic institutions and economic performance we observe in the West. Research on the hypothesis started in May 2006 when I had the good fortune to find two graduate students, Luminita Stevens and Raicho Bojilov, who were eager to test the hypothesis against data. They hit upon the World Values Survey, which proved in a 2006 report to be a gold mine.

(In 2010 I was delighted to be able to tell the WVS founder Ronald Inglehart about some of our statistical results.)

In that same course and a later seminar, two research assistants helped me by reading and distilling a range of materials that improved my book at many places: Eleanor Dillon and Valeria Zhavoronkina. More informally, three other students, Oren Ziv, Edward Fox, and Jonathan Krueger engaged me in discussion. My Chapter 1 quotes Jonathan's term paper. (I learned one day that the acuteness of his comments on my text came from reading scripts for a Hollywood studio. I was sad to see him die so young and talented.)

No work as different from standard texts as this one could have been written by a committee, but it could not have been written without numerous, often continuing, interactions with others. During the four years of writing, I benefitted enormously from the generous help on a range of issues of Richard Robb, Gylfi Zoega, Raicho Bojilov, Amar Bhidé, Roman Frydman, Saif Ammous, and Juan Vicente Sola—all colleagues of mine at Columbia's Center on Capitalism and Society. Richard and Saif kindly read chapters of the book. Jeff Sachs and Amartya Sen were there for me in times of need. Peter Jungen was a great supporter of my message in recent years, as was Luigi Paganetto from early days at the Consiglio Nazionale delle Ricerche. Esa Saarinen made me see how valuable it is to write with all the empathy and passion I feel. hConversations with Barnaby Marsh and Mark C. Berner of the Templeton Foundation and with Seth Ditchik of Princeton University Press were also a boost. I am also grateful to Robert J. Gordon for providing me with the calculations that made it possible to chart in Chapter 9 the slowdown of total factor productivity alongside his chart showing the lesser slowdown of labor productivity.

I am very grateful to the Kauffman Foundation, particularly to Carl Schramm, Robert Litan, and Robert Strom, for their consistent financial and intellectual support of my research on modern capitalism. I am glad too that Andrew Wylie took on the book and gave its publication the benefit of his advice.

I have been blessed with the help of an extraordinarily talented group who came out of Literature and Classics at Harvard. It was perfect. They knew much that I did not know. Miranda Featherstone, a writer, edited chapters in 2008 and 2009. Francesca Mari, also a writer, followed in 2010. Jeff Nagy, a poet, came in 2012. They not only did their work at a high level. They put their hearts into it. Their spirit made my years on the project a special pleasure.

INDEX

Page numbers for entries occurring in figures are followed by an *f*, those for entries in notes, by an *n*, and those for entries in tables, by a *t*.

attainments, in modern experience of work, 59–60

Austen, Jane, 65–66; *Mansfield Park*, 67; *Sense and Sensibility*, 66

Australia: corporatism in, measurement of, 181; economic performance of, recent, 171–73; hours spent on household chores in, 299

Austria: corporatism in, interwar, 151; corporatism in, measurement of, 180–82; corporatism in, performance of, 182–85; economic performance of, recent, 171–73, 182–85; infectious diseases in, decline of, 49; job satisfaction in, 207, 214; mercantile capitalism in, 5; in World War I, 144

Austrian Empire, 149

Austrian school of economics, 30, 121, 129–30

authoritarianism, loss of freedom under, 133

autocracy, vs. democracy, in formation of modern economies, 93–95

automobile industry, 32–33, 156, 160

Babbage, Charles, 27

baby boomers, 227, 259, 311

Babylonia: credit institutions in, 91; private property in, 84

Bach, Johann Sebastian, 13, 286

Bacon, Francis, *Novo Organum*, 10

Bairoch, Paul, 6n8, 45n3

Balanchine, George, 75

Balla, Giacomo, 71

Balleisen, Edward J., 91n10

ballet, 75

Balzac, Honoré de, 67

bank(s): concentration of industry, 256; government debt held by, 251–52; government relationship with, 251–52; Italian, bailouts of, 144; local and regional, decline of, 303–4; merchant, 91–92, 322; origins and rise of, 91–92; as partnerships vs. corporations, 244; reform of, for recovery of dynamism, 321–22; structural faults of, as source of post-1960s economic decline, 244–46; U.S. reform of, 154, 245, 321–22

bankruptcy, origins of, 91

Bankruptcy Acts (U.S.), 91

Baring family, 91

Baroque music, 72

Barre, Raymond, 157

Barres, Maurice, 151

Barzun, Jacques: *From Dawn to Decadence*, 98, 217; humanities courses taught by, 296; on James (William), 281n14; on modern era, 98,

203; on organic generation of innovation, 318; on vitalism, 99n13, 279

Becker, Gary, 208n16

Beethoven, Ludwig van, 72–73

Belgian Revolution, 96

Belgium: corporatism in, measurement of, 179–82; corporatism in, performance of, 182–86; democracy in, development of, 95–96; economic knowledge in, 11; economic performance of, recent, 174, 182–86; mercantile capitalism in, 5; output per worker in, 5, 6; population growth in, 107–8; real wages per worker in, 44; urbanization in, 108

Benedict, Ruth, 194

Bentham, Jeremy, 290, 291

Bentolila, Samuel, 201n6

Bergson, Henri, 318; *Creative Evolution*, 282, 282n17

Berle, Adolf, *The Modern Corporation and Private Property*, 243

Berlin (Germany), March Revolution in, 117

Berners-Lee, Tim, 27

Bernstein, Leonard, 276

Bertola, Giuseppe, 201n6

Beveridge, William, 132n15

Bhidé, Amar, 29n6, 244; *The Venturesome Economy*, 319

Bill of Rights (1689, England), 86, 287

biofuels, 130–31

Birth of the Modern (Johnson), 98

Bismarck, Otto von, 149, 157, 170

black activism, in 1960s, 291

Black Death, 3, 4

Blake, William, 51, 67

Blanchflower, David, 196, 231, 231n10

Bloom, Harold, 99n13, 279; *Shakespeare: The Invention of the Human*, 280

Blowup (film), 78n2

blue collar workers. *See* working class

Bodenhorn, Howard, 92, 92n11

Boeing, 323

Boer War, 53n15

Bojilov, Raicho, 212

Bolshevik revolution, 134

booms: construction, 234, 261; dot.com, 201, 226; housing, 226, 245, 252–53, 310, 312; internet, 219, 261, 303, 311, 315; in mercantile capitalism, 115

borrowing, short-term, by banks, 244–45, 322

bossnapping, 162–63, 323

Boulton, Matthew, 12, 13, 89

bourgeoisie: in mercantile economies, 97; in modern economies, 97, 114
Bourguignon, Philippe, 209, 210
Bradley, Harold, 32
Bradley, Owen, 32
Bradshaw, David J., 66
Brass, Dick, 242, 242n5
Braudel, Fernand, 1, 44, 44n2
Brazil, corporatism in, 151–52
bribery, in corporatism, 178
Britain: art depicting modern life in, 69–70; bankruptcy in, 91; commerce in, rise of, 96–97; common law in, 84, 85, 87n8; competition in, 195; corporatism in, interwar, 152, 155–56; corporatism in, measurement of, 179, 179–82; corporatism in, postwar, 163–64, 165; democracy in, development of, 95; economic culture of, 195; economic knowledge in, sources of, 11, 12; economic performance of, interwar, 155, 156; economic performance of, recent, 171–76; financial panics in, 115; formation of modern economy in, 79, 84, 95, 102; infectious diseases in, decline of, 49; intellectual property rights in, 85; inventions of First Industrial Revolution in, 12, 13, 14; job satisfaction in, 199, 233; joint-stock companies of, 89–90; literature on modern life in, 63–67; mercantile capitalism in, 2, 5, 115; output per worker in, 5–6, 7n9, 43; population growth in, 107–8; post-1960s economic decline in, 222, 233; poverty in, decline of, 48; productivity growth in, 19th-century, 5–8; property rights in, 85; public opinion in establishment of capitalism in, 113; real wages per worker in, 5, 6, 6n8, 44, 45, 46–47; rule of law in, 86–87; socialism in, 120, 132n15, 163; unemployment in, 50, 51, 132n15; urbanization in, 61, 108; wage-productivity ratio in, 44, 47; wars of, 53n15; working class wages in, 46–48. See also England; Ireland; Scotland
British Parliament. See Parliament, British
Brontë, Charlotte, *Jane Eyre,* 66
Brontë, Emily, *Wuthering Heights,* 64, 64n6
Brooks, David, 239, 280
bubbles, in mercantile capitalism, 115. See also booms
bubonic plague, 3, 4
Buddenbrooks (Mann), 67
Buffett, Warren, 287
Burckhardt, Jacob, 111

bureaucratic red tape, as measure of corporatism, 162, 162n26, 164, 180
Bush, George H. W., 226, 252
Bush, George W.: compassionate conservatism of, 311, 317; expansion of Medicare under, 259–60; policy response to stagnation, 313; tax cuts of, 226, 247, 263, 311, 312, 318
business knowledge: growth in, 34; in recovery of dynamism, 318–19
business sector. See companies; corporations
Butler, Nicholas Murray, 296
Byron, Lord, 63n5

Calmfors, Lars, 202n8
Calvin, John, 100, 286
Calvinism, and economic culture, 78
Cameron, David, 205
Canada: corporatism in, measurement of, 179–82, 180n6; economic performance of, recent, 171–74, 182–86; job satisfaction in, 198, 201, 214; modernization of economy of, 41–42
Candide (Voltaire), 101–2, 275–76
Cantillon, Richard, 106
capital: definition of, 7; of entrepreneurs, 25; vs. labor, in innovative activity, 23–24; 19th-century growth of, 7–8; physical, in value of companies, 187; population growth in returns on, 108n23; socialist approach to allocation of, 120
capital access index, and job satisfaction, 204
capital goods, vs. consumer goods, in post-1960s economic decline, 224, 224n4, 225n5, 228n7
capitalism: antipathy for, 301; competition in, repression of, 26; corporatism's critique of, 150; definition of, 41n1; introduction of innovation into, 26; mercantile (See mercantile capitalism); modern (See modern capitalism); mutual gain from exchange of services in, 289–90; origins of, 2, 108; scholarship on rise of, 77–78, 108–9; socialism's critique of, 117–20; use of term, 41n1, 266. See also specific countries
Capitalism, Socialism and Democracy (Schumpeter), 10, 10n12, 27n4, 207
careers. See employment; job(s); work
caregiving, fulfillment through, 298
Carlyle, Thomas, 67, 117n2
cartels, in corporatism, 143, 148, 151
Casanova, Giacomo, 286
Cassel, Gustav, 9n11

Casson, Mark, 28

Catherine the Great, 297

Catholic Church, on corporatism, 139, 151

Cavalleria Rusticana (Mascagni), 137

CBI. *See* Confederation of British Industry

Cellini, Benvenuto, *Autobiography,* 100, 279–80

Celsus, Publius luventius, 289

Census Bureau, U.S., 229, 234n13

centralization, in socialism, 119–20

CEOs, salaries of, 320–21

Cervantes, Miguel, *Don Quixote,* 63, 100, 280

Cézanne, Paul, 71

challenges, in the good life, 280–82, 283–84

Chandler, Alfred, *The Visible Hand,* 241, 241n4

change, continual, in modern experience of work, 57

Chaplin, Charlie, 52

charitable foundations, 306

Charles Albert (king of Sardinia), 144n7

chartered joint-stock companies, 89

Chicago, jazz in, 75

child mortality, effects of modern economies on, 48–49, 48n9, 55

China: dynamism of, 22; economic culture of, 195; economic reformation of 1978 in, 195; education of leaders of, 319; manufacturing in, 52, 234–35; population density of, and rise of innovation, 105–6; productivity growth in, 43; recession of 2008–2009 in, 175; socialism in, 130; wealth accumulation in, 286, 287

choice, in the good life, 278

Christian socialism, 118

Christian Social Party, 141n5

Churchill, Winston, 147

cities: art depicting life in, 70–71; creativity in, 106–7, 107n21; diversity of, 106–7, 116; formation of, 106, 108; population density of, in formation of modern economies, 104–8. *See also* urbanization

Civilian Conservation Corps, 153

Civilization and Its Discontents (Freud), 139

Clark, Gregory, 3, 3n3, 4, 6n8, 46

classical economics: dominance of, 10; on economic knowledge, 9, 10; on freedom, 59

classical music, 72–73

classic corporatism, 166

ClearType, 242

Cleminson, James, 164, 164n27

Clinton, Bill, 226, 252

Coase, Ronald, 85n6

codetermination, 138, 141, 166

Coke, Edward, 87n7

Colbert, Jean-Baptiste, 162

Coleridge, Samuel, 66–67

collective bargaining, 202, 202n8, 207

colonialism, in mercantile capitalism, 2

Columbia College, 296

Columbia University, Center on Capitalism and Society at, 210–11

commercial banks, 92, 154, 245

commercial economies: culture of, 98; rise and spread of, 2, 96–97. *See also* mercantile capitalism; traditional economies

Common Core State Standards, 324

common law: development of, 84, 85, 87n8; vs. Roman law, 85, 202

Common Sense (Paine), 136

communism, vs. other types of socialism, 118, 120

Communist Manifesto, The (Marx and Engels), 41n1, 109, 117, 119

communitarianism, in cities, 116

companies: creation of ideas in, 30–31; culture of, 208; development of forms of, 88–90; joint-stock, 89–90, 105; measurement of value of, 187–88; right to ownership of, 83; short termism in management of, 243–44, 314, 320–21; structural faults of, as source of post-1960s economic decline, 241–46. *See also* corporations

Company, The (Mickelthwait and Wooldridge), 90n8

company law: in modern capitalism, 205–6; in recovery of dynamism, 321

compassionate conservatism, 311, 317

competition: in capitalism, 26; in corporatism, 24, 26, 142–43, 168, 180; in economic culture, 195; of ideas, 24; measurement of, 180; and postwar economic growth, 158–59, 159n23; in relationship between innovation and employment, 222; repression of, 26; ruinous, 245–46; in socialism, 24, 124–25

"Competition as a Discovery Procedure" (Hayek), 34n9, 37n14, 319

Conard, Nicholas, 1n1

concentration, of banking industry, 256

Condorcet, Nicolas de, 101

Confederation of British Industry (CBI), 164

Confederation of Industry (Italy), 145–46

Confindustria (Italy), 146

conformism, rise of, 250

Congress, U.S.: banking reform by, 154, 245; business knowledge in, lack of, 318–19;

on copyright, 254; democracy in, 95; on
mortgages, 252; reaction to post-1960s
economic decline in, 226, 228–29
consensual corporatism, in Germany, 149–50
conservatism, compassionate, 311
Constable, John, 69n14, 71
constitution(s): German, 157; Italian, 156–57;
lack of, in Europe, 144; in measurement of
corporatism, 181–82; Polish-Lithuanian, 93;
U.S., 87, 89
constitutional democracy, moral hazards in,
178
constitutional government, origins of, 86–87
construction boom, 234, 261
consumer goods, vs. capital goods, in post-
1960s economic decline, 224, 224n4, 225n5,
228n7
contracts: enforcement of, 81; limitations
of, 206; social, 140, 166, 166n29, 291; U.S.
Constitution on, 87, 89
Coolidge, Calvin, 136
Cooper, John, 284
copyrights: origins of, 85, 253; problems caused
by, 253–54
corporate welfare, 254, 267
corporations: concentration of sector in large,
256; culture of, 208; governance of, flaws
in, 243; origins and development of, 89–90,
105; vs. partnerships, banks as, 244; short
termism in, 243–44, 314, 320–21; structural
faults of, as source of post-1960s economic
decline, 241–46; U.S. Supreme Court on
rights of, 89, 266
corporatism, 135–69; agenda of, 141–43, 166;
classic, 166; competition in, 24, 26, 142–43,
168, 180; critique of modern economy in,
135–43, 150; current status of, 314; dark
side of, 168–69; definition of, 26, 143n6;
economic justice in, 186, 301, 302, 306–7;
future of, 308–9, 320; the good life in, 269,
270; innovation in, lack of, 167–68, 186–92,
314; job satisfaction in (See job satisfaction);
measurement of, approaches to, 159, 179–82,
180n6; modern elements in, suppression
of, 306–7; moral hazards of, 178–79; new
version of, 166–68, 265–66; origins of, 137–
41; in post-1960s economic decline, 251–58,
265–66; postwar evolution of, 150, 157–65; as
third way, 150; between world wars, 143–57.
See also specific countries
corporatism, performance of: assumptions in
scholarship on, 201–3; claims vs. evidence

on, 178–86, 268–69; interwar, 155–57; in new
version, 265–66
corporazioni (ancient guilds), 145–46
corruption, as sign of corporatism, 181
Cort, Henry, 12
Cortés, Hernán, 280
Cotis, Jean-Philippe, 180n6
Counter-Revolution of Science, The (Hayek),
34n10
courage, in creation of ideas, 28
Craft, Robert, 30
crashes, in mercantile capitalism, 115
Creative Evolution (Bergson), 282, 282n17
creativity: in cities, 106–7, 107n21; drivers of,
26–36; in dynamism, 28, 35; in the good life,
282–83; imagination in, recognition of role
of, 101
credit institutions, origins of, 91
Crimean War, 53n15
crises. See financial crises
critical mass, populations at, 108
Cubism, 71
culturalism, in corporatism, 142
culture(s): company, 208; in economics, lack
of consideration of, 194–95; vs. institutions,
195n1; political, 194; significance of
international differences among, 194
culture, economic, 96–104; definition of, 96,
194, 207–8; in economic performance,
103–4, 210–11; in formation of modern
economies, 96–104, 109; international
differences in, 103–4, 209–11; in job
satisfaction, 194, 207–15, 213f, 214f; of
mercantile capitalism, 97; modern values
in, 98–104; in post-1960s economic decline,
246–50; Protestantism and, 78; in recovery
of dynamism, 323–24; of socialism, 120;
traditional vs. modern, corporatism on,
137–39. See also values; specific countries
curiosity, in creation of ideas, 28, 29
currency speculation, 144, 244

Dartmouth College, 89
Darwin, Charles, 38
Daumier, Honoré, 45
Dawn of Innovation, The (Morris), 319
Debtors Act of 1869 (Britain), 91
debtors' prisons, 91
Declaration of Independence, U.S., 93, 136
Decline and Fall of the Roman Empire (Gibbon),
79n3
Decline of the West, The (Spengler), 79n3

Decree of July 1926 (Italy), 146
deficits. *See* government deficits
Defoe, Daniel: *Moll Flanders,* 63; on need for copyrights, 253; *Robinson Crusoe,* 37, 39, 63, 279n13
democracy: and corporatism, coexistence of, 157; European, development of, 95–96; in formation of modern economies, 93–96, 105, 109; grassroots, 309; modern values in origins of, x; moral hazards in, 178; scholarship on rise of, 77; U.S., development of, 94–95
Democracy in America (Tocqueville), 79n3
Democratic Party (U.S.): on social welfare, 260; traditional values in, 260, 317
Demsetz, Harold, 84–85, 85n6
Deng Xiaoping, 52, 195, 286
Denmark: corporatism in, measurement of, 180–82; corporatism in, performance of, 182–84; economic performance of, recent, 171–73, 176, 182–84; job satisfaction in, 198, 199, 213–14; mercantile capitalism in, 5
depressions, economic: of 1893–1898, 116; in Germany, 148; modern history of, 116. *See also* Great Depression
derivatives, 266, 267
desires, hierarchy of, 275
determinism: creativity and, 282; historical, 9, 10, 37
Dewey, John, 58n3, 246–47, 276, 276n7
Diamond, Jared, 77, 79; *Guns, Germs and Steel,* 78n1
Dickens, Charles: *David Copperfield,* 65–66; on debtors' prisons, 91; *Hard Times,* 64–65; on modern experience of work, 64–66, 66n10; *Oliver Twist,* 45, 64; *Sketches by Boz,* 65, 65n9; *Speeches, Letters and Sayings,* 65n9; *The Uncommercial Traveller,* 65n9
diet, effects of modern economies on, 49, 49n13
difference, making a, 285
dignity, 52, 81, 118
diminishing returns, 3, 7
directedness, in corporatism, 138, 166
discoveries, in modern experience of work, 59, 62
Discovery, Age of, 100
discovery procedure, 34, 34n9. *See also* Hayek, Friedrich
disease: effects of modern economies on, 48–50; population density in spread of, 106
distributive justice, 291–95, 299–300, 305–6. *See also* Rawls, John

diversity: of cities, 106–7, 116; in dynamism, 38; of human nature, 297–98; and wage inequality, 186
division of labor, in innovation, 23
Doctors without Borders, 286
Doctrine of Fascism, The (Mussolini), 145
Dolfuss, Engelbert, 151
D1/D5 ratio, 186n12
Don Quixote (Cervantes), 63, 100, 280
Dornbusch, Rudi, 174
dot.com boom, 201, 226
Douthat, Ross, 238
Draghi, Mario, 174
due process, development of, 86–87, 87n8
Dupont, 241n4
Durkheim, Émile, 147
Duyckinck, Evert, 68n12
dynamism, 19–40; definition of, ix, 20, 194; in definition of modern economies, ix, 19; diversity in, role of, 38; drivers of creation of ideas in, 26–36; economic culture in, 194, 323–24; economic freedoms in, x, 29, 308; emergence of first economies with, 14–15, 307; growth in relation to, 19–22; human resources needed for, 28, 29, 31, 35; measurement of, approaches to, 21–22; pecuniary and nonpecuniary motives in, 25, 25n3, 29; recognition of role of, in modern capitalism, 317; recovery of, approaches to, 316–24; recovery of, prospects for, 308–9, 316–17; rise of (*See* modern economies, formation of); selection mechanisms for ideas in, 24–26; social system in, 36–40; understanding of mechanisms of, need for, 317–19

Earned Income Tax Credit (EITC), 177n3, 206, 228–29
East India Company, 89
eBay, 205
economic growth: in corporatism, 144–45, 158–59, 161, 178; dynamism in relation to, 19–22; in financial crises, origins of, 311; first economies with sustained, 6–15; postwar comparison of, 158–59, 159n23, 161. *See also* performance
"Economic Possibilities for Our Grandchildren" (Keynes), 274
Economic Reform of 1948 (Germany), 158
economics, Keynes on study of, 319
"Economics and Knowledge" (Hayek), 31n7
economies. *See specific countries and types of economies*

economies of scale, in 19th-century productivity growth, 7–8

Economy and Society (Weber), 78n2

Edison, Thomas, 33

education: in economic justice, 295–96, 296n4; government role in, 255, 295, 296n4; humanities courses in, 296–97; of legislators and regulators, 318–19; modern values in, 324; in socialist economies, 177

efficiency: economic freedoms and, 81; in economic justice, 291, 300; government role in, 316; in socialism, 121, 123, 129–30, 132–33

Einaudi, Luigi, 157

Einstein, Albert, 113

Eisenhower, Dwight, 251

EITC. *See* Earned Income Tax Credit

Eliot, Charles, 296

Elmeskov, Jørgen, 201n6

employee engagement, 58, 62, 304

employers' associations: in German corporatism, 149, 150, 160; in Italian corporatism, 145

employment protection, in corporatism, 180, 190–91, 190f, 191f, 201

employment protection legislation (EPL), 180, 191, 201, 201n6

employment rates: in corporatist economies, 188–91; entitlements' impact on, 260–63; growth as synonym for high, 222; innovation rate and, 188–91, 222–23; market-cap-to-output ratio as predictor of, 188–89, 189f; of men, decline in, 310; productivity growth rate and, 190n14. *See also* job(s); unemployment

enclosure movement, 108

end-users: adoption of innovation by, 29, 29n6; diversity among, 38; uncertainty about, 37

energy production, capital in, 24

engagement: employee, 58, 62, 304; in the good life, 284; political, 309

Engels, Friedrich, 117n2; *The Communist Manifesto*, 41n1, 109, 117, 119

England: Bill of Rights in, 86, 287; copyrights in, 253; economic knowledge in, 3–5; mercantile capitalism in, 2, 3–5; poverty in, decline of, 48

Enlightenment: definition of, 10; the good life in, 280, 287; headline inventions of, 12; origins of modernism in, 100–101; scientific advances in, 10–11

Enquiry Concerning Human Understanding, An (Hume), 28n5, 101

entitlement, culture of, 249

entitlements: employment affected by, 260–63; expansion of, 229–30, 258–60

entrepreneur(s): angel investors and, 35–36; definition of, 25; diversity among, 38; early recognition of value of, 100–101, 276; economic freedoms needed by, 29, 82; initiative taking by, 58–59, 98, 98n12; vs. innovators, 28; pecuniary vs. nonpecuniary returns for, 25, 25n3; pre-modern vs. modern, 28; scientific advances used by, ix, 9–10, 28; in selection process for ideas, 25; social, 25, 286; uncertainty of, 37

"entrepreneurial spirit," coining of term, 78n2

EPL. *See* employment protection legislation

equilibrium: in market economies, 9; punctuated, 22–23

equity, and wages in free market, 290. *See also* justice

Erasmus, Desiderius, 99–100

Erhard, Ludwig, *Prosperity through Competition*, 158

Ericson, Leif, 59, 297

Erskine, John, 296

ESOPs, 128–29

Espejo, Eugenio, 11

Essais (Montaigne), 100

ethics: Aristotelian, 286–88; modern, 211; vs. morality, 208; socialist, 118–20, 123; work, 123. *See also* values

ethnic diversity, and wage inequality, 186

ethnicity, in corporatism, 141n5

eudaimonia, 272, 273, 284, 288

Eurasia, specialization of labor in, 77

Europe: constitutions in, lack of, 144; debate over alternatives to capitalism in, 110; democracy in, development of, 95–96; distribution of modern economies in, 77–78; economic culture of, vs. U.S., 209; financial crises in, origins of, 310–11; financial panics in, 115; job satisfaction in, 232–33; music depicting modern life in, 72–74; political engagement in, 309; post-1960s economic decline in, 221–22, 232–33, 314; recovery of dynamism in, approaches to, 316–24; recovery of dynamism in, prospects for, 308–9, 317; revolutions of 1848 in, 116, 117; social welfare in, 258–59. *See also specific countries*

European Economic Commission, 158

European Union, establishment of, 158

Evans, Harold: "Eureka," 32–33; *They Made America*, 33, 319

Evans, Oliver, 33
evolution, theory of, 38
evolutionary socialism, 118
Expressionism, 55, 70–71

Fabian socialism, 118, 120
Facebook, 243, 249
factories: Dickens on, 64, 65; rise of, 51–52. *See also* manufacturing
"factory councils" movement, 146
failures, social value of, 38
family satisfaction, 197–98
family values, 250, 315
Fannie Mae, 252–53, 254
Farm Credit System, 322
farm workers, output of, 3–4, 3n3
Fascist Manifesto of 1919, 144
Fascist Party (Italy), 144, 146
February Revolution (1848), 117
Federal Register of Regulations, 164
Federal Reserve, U.S., 175
Ferguson, Adam, *Essay on the History of Civil Society,* 2n2
Ferraro, Geraldine, 317
feudal system: decline of, 80, 108; wealth accumulation in, 104
Feynman, Richard, 113
Field Notes from Elsewhere (Taylor), 71
50-10 ratio, 186n12, 227
financial crises: of 2007–2008, 185, 186, 311–12, 322; origins of, 310–11
financial institutions: in job satisfaction, 204–5; reform of, in recovery of dynamism, 321–22; rise of, 91–92. *See also* bank(s)
financial panics, 115
financiers: angel investors as, 35–36; pluralism of views among, 38
Finland: corporatism in, 180, 185; economic performance of, recent, 171–73, 176; job satisfaction in, 213–14
Finley, M. I., *The Ancient Economy,* 1
Fiscal Neutrality toward Economic Growth (Phelps), 263
Fitch, John, 12
Five-Year Plans, of France, 151
Fleming, Alexander, 33
Flexicurity, 198
Flourish (Seligman), 285
flourishing. *See* mass flourishing; personal flourishing
Fogel, Robert, 14
food production, labor vs. capital in, 23–24

Ford, Henry, 32–33
Ford Motor Company, 156
foreign trade. *See* trade
Forster, E. M., 136
Foster, John, 256
Four Speeches on the Corporate State (Mussolini), 145, 145n8, 146
Four-Year Plans, of Italy and Germany, 151
framework conditions, 81. *See also* institutions, economic
France: art depicting modern life in, 69; corporatism in (*See* French corporatism); democracy in, development of, 95; dynamism of, loss of, 41; economic culture of, 209–10, 246; economic knowledge in, 11; economic performance of, recent, 171–76, 182–87, 192; emigration from, 185; entrepreneurs in, recognition of value of, 100–101, 276; February Revolution in, 117; intellectual property rights in, 85; job satisfaction in, 199, 201, 214, 233; joint-stock companies of, 90; labor force participation in, 51; labor unions in, 162–63, 322–23; literature on modern life in, 67; mercantile capitalism in, 5, 115; music depicting modern life in, 74–75; output per worker in, 5–6; population growth in, 107; post-1960s economic decline in, 222, 233; productivity growth in, 19th-century, 5–8; property rights in, 85; real wages per worker in, 5, 6, 44, 45; socialism in, 134, 151; social welfare in, 259; tax code of, 165; unemployment in, 222; unemployment insurance in, 50; urbanization in, 61, 108; wage-productivity ratio in, 44–45, 47; wars of, 53n15
Franco, Francisco, 151
Frankenstein (film), 64
Frankenstein (Shelley), 63–64
Fraser Institute, 204, 204n14
Freddie Mac, 252–53, 254
freedom(s): in dynamism, x, 29, 308; in economic success, 308; in formation of modern economies, 81–85, 105; in the good life, 272, 273; international differences in, 104; in justice, 292; in modern experience of work, 59; in socialism, 133
free market, wages in, 290
French corporatism: measurement of, 179–82, 180n6; origins of, 151, 162; performance of, 182–87; postwar, 162–63
French Revolution of 1789–1799, 45, 85, 93, 95
French Revolution of 1830, 95

French Revolution of 1848, 95
Freud, Sigmund, 138, 138n3, 287; *Civilization and Its Discontents,* 139
Fromm, Erich, 194
frontier, U.S., economic role of, 102, 108n23
Fuggers, 91
future: in historicism, 9; unknowability of, 37–38
Futurist art, 71

Gainsborough, Thomas, 68
Galbraith, John Kenneth, 34, 129n12, 267
Gallup, 231, 233
Gandhi, Mahatma, 292n2
Gates, Bill, 193, 242, 286, 290
Gaulle, Charles de, 151
GDP: government outlays as percentage of, 162, 162n25, 164, 179–80; per employee, international comparison of, 182–83, 183f; per hour worked, international comparison of, 183–84, 184f; state-owned enterprises in, 171, 177
gender: barriers based on, effects of modern economies on, 74; and housework, 299; and human fulfillment, 298; and job satisfaction, 231, 231n10; and wage inequality, 227. *See also* men; women
General Motors, 241n4, 323
General Social Surveys, 62, 231, 232n11, 233
General Theory (Keynes), 37n14
Gentile, Giovanni, 145
Georgics (Virgil), 275
Géricault, Théodore, 69, 69n13
German corporatism: interwar, 141n5, 147–50, 155–57, 170; measurement of, 179–82, 180n6; origins of, 137; performance of, 182–87; postwar, 157–63, 162n25
German Historical School of Economics, 9–10, 9n11, 27
German Workers Party, 147. *See also* Nazi Germany
Germany: anti-Semitism in, 141n5, 147; art depicting modern life in, 70–71; constitution of, 157; corporatism in (*See* German corporatism); democracy in, development of, 96; dynamism of, loss of, 41; economic culture of, 209–10; economic growth in, postwar, 158–59, 161; economic knowledge in, 11; economic performance of, interwar, 155–57; economic performance of, recent, 171–76, 182–87, 192; job satisfaction in, 199, 201, 214, 233; joint-stock companies

of, 90; literature on modern life in, 67; March Revolution in, 117; mercantile capitalism in, 5; music depicting modern life in, 72–74; Nazi (*See* Nazi Germany); output per worker in, 5–6; population growth in, 107; post-1960s economic decline in, 222, 233; productivity growth in, 19th-century, 5–8; real wages per worker in, 5, 6, 44, 45; socialism in, 118, 119n5, 134, 147; social welfare in, 258; unemployment in, 222; unification of (1871), 149; urbanization in, 60; wage-productivity ratio in, 45, 47; wars of, 53n15; women in labor force of, 195; World War I reparations by, 148
Gibbon, Edward, *Decline and Fall of the Roman Empire,* 79n3
Giersch, Herbert, 157
Giffen, Robert, 47, 47n7, 48
Giffen good, 47n7
Gilbert, W. S., 283
Gladstone, William Ewart, 46
Glass, Philip, 75
Glass-Steagall Banking Act of 1933 (U.S.), 154, 245
global economy: dynamism in rise of, 22; in "golden age" narratives, 238; internationalization of innovation in, 20; measurement of dynamism in, 21; money culture in, 247
Glorious Revolution of 1688, 86
Godwin, William, 63n5
Goethe, Johann Wolfgang von, 67
Gogh, Vincent van, 70
"golden age" narratives, 237–40
golden parachute payments, 321
gold standard, 175
Goldwyn, Samuel, 64n7
Gombrich, E. H., 69, 69n14
good, the, Aristotle on, 271, 272
good economy: Democrats' conception of, 317; dynamism in restoration of, 317; the good life in proper definition of, 269–70, 288; as modern economy, 293, 309; Republicans' conception of, 317
good life, the, 268–88; ancient concepts of, xi; Aristotle on, 271–75, 277, 284, 288; in corporatism, 269, 270; definition of, 271, 272; economic justice and, 293; humanism on, 270–73; in modern capitalism, 301; in modern economies, xi–xii, 307–8; pragmatists on, 274–79, 281, 283–84; in socialism, 270; universality of goal of, 296; vitalists on, 279–88; work-life balance and, 304

Gordon, Robert J., 220n1
Gotha Program, 119n5
government: constitutional, origins of, 86–87;
    expansion of powers of, 86; joint-stock
    companies chartered by, 89
government debt. *See* sovereign debt
government deficits: in financial crises, 311;
    lack of understanding of, 318; need for
    understanding of, 319; tax rates and, 226,
    227n6, 311, 318
government institutions. *See* institutions
government outlays: and job satisfaction,
    206–7, 207n15; as measure of corporatism,
    161–62, 162n25, 163, 164, 179–80
government regulations: business knowledge
    underlying, lack of, 318–19; effects on
    innovation, 82–83; harm vs. benefits of,
    82–83, 206; and job satisfaction, 206, 207;
    in new corporatism, 167; rise in number of,
    253, 253n10
government (state) role: in efficiency, 316; in
    modernism, 136–37; in post-1960s economic
    decline, 251–64, 266–67; in recovery of
    dynamism, 316–24
grassroots democracy, 309
Great Books programs, 296
Great Depression: corporatism and, 150, 152,
    153, 155; productivity growth in, 8, 222;
    recovery from, 235; Second, 175
Great Divergence, 11
Great Moderation, 116n1
Great Recession of 2008–2009, 235, 236
Great Transformation of 1820–1930, 264–65
Greece, ancient: infrequent innovation in, 1;
    rule of law in, 87
Greece, modern, bailout of, 252
Groom, Brian, 163–64
gross domestic product. *See* GDP
Grosz, George, 71
growth, as synonym for high employment, 222.
    See also specific types
guilds, 26, 140, 149
guild socialism, 118
Gutenberg, Johannes, 77

Hamburg (city-state), commercial economy
    of, 2
Hamlet (Shakespeare), 100, 280
Hammurabi, Code of, 84
happiness: Aristotle on, 284; in the good life,
    277–78, 284; income in relation to, 52–53;
    literature on, 71–72; neoclassical economics

on, 277–78; productivity growth and, 274n4;
    pursuit of, in U.S., 101, 280, 284
Hard Times (Dickens), 64–65
Hargreaves, James, 12
Harris Interactive, 231n9
Hart, Lorenz, 153n16
Harvey, William, 10, 100
"having it all," 304–5
Haydn, Joseph, 72
Hayek, Friedrich, ix; on adaptations, 31; in
    Austrian school, 30, 121; counter-revolution
    of science, 34n10; "Dependence Effect,"
    34n9, 129n12; on discovery procedure,
    34, 34n9, 37n14, 319; "Economics and
    Knowledge," 31n7; on efficiency, 316;
    on feasibility of socialism, 125–32, 133;
    on German corporatism, 149, 156n21;
    Individualism and Economic Order, 31n7; on
    laissez-faire, 132n15; Mises as teacher of, 121;
    on personal knowledge in innovation, 30–31,
    31n7, 101; in recognition of indigenous
    innovation, 128, 129, 129n12; *The Road to
    Serfdom*, 129n12, 131–32, 132n15, 133, 149,
    156n21; Schumpeter influenced by, 10n12;
    on social change, 310; on unknowns in
    innovation, 34; use of knowledge in society,
    31n7
healthcare industry: government role in, 255,
    258; improvements in, with rise of modern
    economies, 50; in U.S. vs. Europe, 258
Hecht, Ben, 64n7
Heckman, James, 295
hedge funds, 243–44, 321n1
Henley, William Ernest, *Invictus*, 280
Henry V (Shakespeare), 278
"heroic spirit," 2, 2n2, 15
Hewlett, Sylvia Ann, 299
Hicks, John, 7n10
historicism, 9, 10, 26, 37
Hitchcock, Alfred, 78n2, 224n4, 248
Hitler, Adolf, corporatism under, 147, 148, 155,
    155n18, 156, 156n21, 170
Hobbes, Thomas, 37
Hockney, David, vii
holding companies, 88
Holland. *See* Netherlands
Hollande, François, 322
Holocaust, 141n5
home: balance between work and, 304; in the
    good life, 304; management of, 298, 299;
    working from, innovation impeded by, 39,
    250, 304

home mortgages, government role in, 252–53, 311

Homer: *Iliad*, 279; *Odyssey*, 279

Hoon, Hian Teck, 222

Hoover, Herbert, 155, 175

Hopper, Edward, 248

hospital practice, improvements in, with rise of modern economies, 50

housework, 298, 299

housing, in recession of 2008–2009, 236, 311

housing boom, 226, 245, 252–53, 310, 312

Howard, Philip K., 165

"How Medical Know-How Progresses" (Nelson), 319

Hubble, Edwin, 248

Hudson's Bay Company, 89

Hugo, Victor, *Les Misérables*, 45

human fulfillment, 297–98

humanism: in economic culture of modern economies, 98; on the good life, 270–73; vs. socialism, 132, 133

humanities, in core curriculum, 296–97

human nature: economic justice and, 296–300; as universal vs. diverse, 297–98

Hume, David: *An Enquiry Concerning Human Understanding*, 28n5, 101; on the good life, 280; on imagination, 28, 28n5; on mercantile capitalism, 97; *Treatise on Human Nature*, 97

"hundred years' peace," 53n15

Hungary: job satisfaction vs. security in, 233; market socialism in, 125

Hutchens, Robert, 296

hygiene, effects of modern economies on, 49

Ibert, Jacques, 74–75

Ibsen, Henrik, 282

Iceland: corporatism in, measurement of, 181; job satisfaction in, 214; population density of, 105; vitalism in, 286

ICT. *See* information and communications technologies

ideas: competition of, 24; drivers of creation of, 26–36; failed, value of, 38; in modern economies, 23–27; population density in spread of, 106; science as source of, 26–27; selection mechanisms for, 24–26; society's role in, 36–40

ideas sector, 23

imaginarium, modern economy as, 27–28

imagination: in creativity, recognition of role of, 101; in dynamism, 28, 29, 32; in the good life, 280

IMF. *See* International Monetary Fund

imitation, vs. innovation, 20; in corporatist economies, 187; in global economy, 20, 21

immigration: economic performance and, 185–86; job satisfaction and, 201

importance of job, in job satisfaction, 199–201, 200t

incentives: in joint-stock companies, 90; short-term, at corporations, 243–44, 314, 320–21; in socialism, 122–26, 123n7

inclusion, economic: definition of, 173, 227; international decline of, 176; in modern capitalism, 307; in nineteenth-century London, 64n6; in post-1960s economic decline, 227–30; as social benefit of wage growth, 47; in socialism, 173, 176; subsidies for, 240, 292

income: control of, in corporatism, 159; extraordinary, 293; vs. flourishing, vii; and the good life, 271–72, 273–74; growth of, in expansion of social welfare, 260; happiness in relation to, 52–53; justice in distribution of, 291–95, 299–300, 305–6. *See also* wage(s)

income inequality. *See* wage inequality

income tax. *See* tax(es)

Index of Social Infrastructure, 181n8

India, employment subsidies in, 292n2

indigenous innovation: capacity for (*See* dynamism); in corporatism, evidence on lack of, 187–92; definition of, ix, 9; emergence of economies based on, 14–15; Hayek's role in recognition of, 128, 129, 129n12; as source of economic knowledge, 14–15

individualism: in corporatism, 147, 151, 166, 168; in modernism, 99–100, 135–36; origins and development of, 99–100; in socialism, 132–33

Individualism and Economic Order (Hayek), 31n7

industrialization: Dickens's views on, 65; as stage of modernization, 108–9

Industrial Revolution, First: dates of, 12, 13n13; headline inventions of, 12–14

Industrial Revolution, Second, 13n13

infectious diseases, effects of modern economies on, 48–50

informal sector, in socialist economies, 174

information and communications technologies (ICT), 180n6, 225n5, 228, 228n7

Inglehardt, Ronald, 285

initiative, taking, in modern vs. traditional economies, 58–59, 98, 98n12

innovation(s): vs. adaptation, 31–32; in ancient world, 1, 1n1; current status of, 313–16; definition of, vii, 1, 20, 20n1; development vs. adoption of, 20, 20n1; division of labor in, 23; employment in relation to, 188–91, 222–23; end-users' role in, 29, 29n6; indigenous (*See* indigenous innovation); international differences in distribution of, 77–78, 105; vs. invention, 20n1; mass, in modern economies, 53–54, 308; need for, to reverse stagnation, 313; in post-1960s economic decline, 225, 228, 263–64; public recognition of role of, vii–viii; during recessions, 235, 235n14; regulations' effects on, 82–83; Schumpeter's account of, ix, xi, 10, 10n12; vs. scientific discoveries, 11, 12–13; scientific discoveries as cause of, ix, xi, 9–12, 26–27; selection mechanisms for, 24–26; short termism and, 314; in socialist economies, lack of, 127–29, 130; as source of economic knowledge, 12–14; stages in process of, 23; understanding of mechanisms of, need for, 317–19; use of term, 20n1; variations in volume of, 20–21
innovation system, national economy as, 20
input. *See* productivity
insiders, in corporatism, 178–79
insight, in dynamism, 28, 29, 32
institutions: vs. culture, 195n1; financial (*See* financial institutions); German Historical School on role of, 9n11; political, 93–96, 142–43; in rise of innovation, vii, 79–80
institutions, economic: of capitalism, 204–7; in economic performance, 104; financial institutions as, 91–92; in formation of modern economies, 81–92, 314; freedoms as, 81–85; international differences in, 104; in job satisfaction, 201–7; private property as, 83–86, 204; in representative democracies, 93–94; of socialism, 120
insurance: social, 206–7, 258; unemployment, 50, 201–2
intellectual property rights: in formation of modern economies, 85–86; origins of protections for, 85–86, 253; problems caused by, 253–54
interactivity: in dynamism, 38–39; in modern experience of work, 58, 60–61
interchange, in modern experience of work, 58, 60–61
interest rates, expansion of entitlements and, 261

international differences: in economic culture, 103–4, 209–11; in economic knowledge, 11–12; in innovation, rise of, 77–78, 105; in job satisfaction (*See* job satisfaction); in modern values, 103–4, 285–86
International Monetary Fund (IMF), 303
International Social Survey Programme, 199
international trade. *See* trade
internet boom, 219, 261, 303, 311, 315
internet revolution, 188, 226
internships, for regulators and legislators, 318
inventions: accidental innovations, 33; characteristics of inventors, 12–13; headline, of First Industrial Revolution, 12–14; vs. innovation, 20n1; as source of scientific knowledge, 12–13
investment banks: and commercial banks, separation of, 154, 245; origins of, 92; as partnerships, 88; structural faults of, as source of post-1960s economic decline, 244–46
Ireland: corporatism in, interwar, 151; corporatism in, measurement of, 180–82; corporatism in, performance of, 182–86; economic performance of, recent, 182–86; job satisfaction in, 196, 198, 201, 214; pauperism in, 48
Irving, Washington: "The Legend of Sleepy Hollow," 68; *The Sketch Book of Geoffrey Crayon, Gent.,* 68
isolation, innovation impeded by, 39
Israel, modernization of economy of, 42
Italian corporatism: interwar, 141–42, 143–47, 155–56; measurement of, 179–82, 180n6; performance of, 182–87; postwar, 160–63
Italy: art depicting modern life in, 71; authoritarianism in, 133; bribery in, 178; capitalism in, rejection of, 144–45; constitution of, 156–57; corporatism in (*See* Italian corporatism); dynamism in, 21; economic knowledge in, 12; economic performance of, interwar, 155–56; economic performance of, recent, 171–77, 182–87, 192; job satisfaction in, 199, 201, 214, 233; mercantile capitalism in, 5, 144; music depicting modern life in, 74; 19th-century productivity in, 8, 21; post-1960s economic decline in, 233; scientism in, 142; socialism in, 134, 144; in World War I, 144

Jacobs, Jane, 106–7, 107n21
James, William, 58n3, 280–81, 281n14, 282

James I (king of England), 253
Jane Eyre (Charlotte Brontë), 66
Janicek, Joseph, 77
Japan: corporatism in, 152, 181; dynamism of, 22
jazz, 74–75
Jefferson, Thomas, 101, 136, 248, 280, 284
Jellicoe, Samuel, 12
Jewish law, 84, 87
Jews: anti-Semitism against, 141n5, 147; corporatism on, 141n5
Jhunjhunwala, Bharat, 292n2
job(s): access to, socialism on, 118; employee engagement in, 58, 62, 304; importance of, in job satisfaction, 199–201, 200t. *See also* employment rates; unemployment
job creation, decline in, 234, 256, 257f
job destruction, decline of, 234, 256, 257f
jobless recovery: of 2010–2011, 222; definition of, 234
Jobs, Steve, 28, 228, 268
job satisfaction, 193–215; cultural cause of differences in, 194, 207–15, 213f, 214f; institutional cause of differences in, 201–7; international differences in, 195–201, 196f, 197f, 198f, 200t; vs. job security, 233; in post-1960s economic decline, 230–33, 231n9, 232f; in socialist economies, 120; value of measuring, 196–97; among working class, 62. *See also* work, experience of; *specific countries*
job security: and discontent with modern economies, 115–16, 116n1; in post-1960s economic decline, 233–34, 234n12; in socialist economies, 174–75
John (king of England), 86
Johnson, Paul, 1, 12–13; *Birth of the Modern,* 98
Johnson, Samuel, 107
joint-stock companies, origins of, 89–90, 105. *See also* corporations
Joint Stock Companies Act of 1844 (Britain), 89
Joint Stock Companies Act of 1856 (Britain), 89–90
Jonna, Jamil, 256
Judah, Anna, 33
Judah, Theodore, 33
judgment, in creation of ideas, 28
justice, economic, xii, 289–309; distributive, 291–95, 299–300, 305–6; flawed conception of in corporatism, 186, 301, 302, 306–7; in good economy, 288; human nature and, 296–300; in modern capitalism, 293, 300–307; in modern economies, xii, 292–96;

for nonparticipants in economy, 298–300, 305–6; political systems and, 309; Rawls on, 228, 290–96, 299–300; in socialism, 301, 302, 306–7; wage inequality in, 290, 291–92, 302

Kasparov, Garry, 310
Keats, John, 280
Kellaway, Lucy, 197n3
Kennedy, John F., 219–20, 226
Kennedy, Maev, 50
Keynes, John Maynard, ix; on creation of ideas, 37, 37n14; "Economic Possibilities for Our Grandchildren," 274; *General Theory,* 37n14; on Hayek, 132n15; on importance of ideas, 267; on Italian corporatism, 147; as Marshall's student, 56n1; neoclassical welfarism of, xi; at Spiethoff's retirement, 9n11; on study of economics, 319; *A Treatise on Probability,* 37n13; on uncertainty, 37, 318
kickbacks, 178
Kierkegaard, Søren, 101, 282
Kilby, Jack, 27
king, rights against the, 86–87
King, Larry, 33
King Lear (Shakespeare), 100
Kirchner, Ernst Ludwig, 71
Klein, Felix, 19
Kling, Arnold, 255
Knight, Frank, ix, 36–37; *Risk, Uncertainty and Profit,* 37n13
knowledge, business: growth in, 34; in recovery of dynamism, 318–19
knowledge, economic, 1–15; in ancient world, 1; definition of, 1; German Historical School on, 9–10; indigenous innovation as source of, 14–15; international differences in, 11–12; inventions as source of, 12–14; measurement of, approaches to, 3–4; in mercantile era, 2–5; 19th-century explosion of, 5–8; in productivity growth, 3, 8; in Renaissance, 1; scientific advances as source of, 9–12; in socialist economies, 125–27
knowledge, personal: in creation of ideas, 30–31, 31n7, 101; in the good life, 273–77, 284
knowledge economy, 31, 109, 128–29
Koestler, Arthur: *The Act of Creation,* 283; *The Sleepwalkers,* 283
Kokoschka, Oskar, 71
Kroc, Ray, 287
Kronman, Anthony, 296–97
Krueger, Jonathan, 36n12
Kruger, Franz, 70–71

Krugman, Paul, *Geography and Trade,* 7n10

Kuczynski, Jürgen, 6, 6n8, 7; *Labour Conditions in Western Europe,* 6n8; *A Short History of Labour Conditions,* 6n8

Kuznets, Simon, 106n20

labor: vs. capital, in innovative activity, 23–24; division of, 23; specialization of, 77

Labor Charter of April 1927 (Italy), 146

labor force: mercantile-era growth of, 3; migration from subsistence farming to wage labor, 50–51; 19th-century growth of, 7–8

labor force participation: in corporatism, 184–85; effect of wealth on, 260–61, 262f; increase in, with rise of modern economies, 51; in socialism, 173–74; by women, 195

labor productivity. *See* output per worker

labor unions, in corporatist economies: bargaining by, 202, 202n8; Catholic Church on, 139; interwar, 145–46, 148, 149, 150, 152, 154, 160; performance affected by, 202, 202n8; postwar, 160, 162–64, 165; rise in power of, 143, 160, 163, 165

labor unions, reform of, for recovery of dynamism, 322–23

Lady Gaga, 281, 281n15

laissez-faire, 132n15, 144, 158

Lamartine, Alphonse de, 73

land: in mercantile era, 4–5, 4n4; virgin, economic role of, 102, 108n23

Lange, Oskar, 124–25

Laplace, Pierre Simon, 11

large numbers, law of, 94

La Scala opera house (Milan), 142

Lattis, Richard, 61

law: common, 84, 85, 87n8, 202; company, 205–6, 321; Jewish, 84, 87; Roman, 84–85, 137, 202; rule of, 86–87, 94. *See also specific laws*

lawsuits. *See* litigation

Lazear, Edward, 201n6

leadership: in corporatism, 138; in modern economies, lack of, 138

league tables, 21

Lectures on Jurisprudence (Smith), 2n2, 97

Leeuwenhoek, Anton, 10–11

legislators, education of, 318–19

Leigh, Michael, 283

Lenin, Vladimir, 52, 113

Leo XIII (pope), 139, 147, 151

leprosy, 49

Leroux, Pierre, 117n2

Lévi-Strauss, Claude, 194

liability: of corporations, 89–90; of partnerships, 88

liberalism, Italian response to, 144

libertarians, 82, 272

life: the good (*See* good life, the); modern (*See* modern life)

life satisfaction: in the good life, 285; job satisfaction and, 196–98, 198f, 198n4

limited liability, origins of, 89–90

Lincoln, Abraham, 136, 170

Lippmann, Walter, 153, 153n16

Liszt, Franz, *Les preludes,* 73–74

literature: copyright protection for, 253–54; on experience of modern life, 62–68, 71–72; and the good life, 282–83; on happiness, 71–72

litigation: corporatism and, 165, 167; innovation stifled by, 165, 248; on intellectual property rights, 253–54; money culture and, 248; in U.S., rise of, 165, 248

living standards: decreases in, population growth and, 106n20; gains in, as material benefit of modern economies, 40, 43, 52

Loasby, Brian, 34–35

local banks, decline of, 303–4

London (England): Dickens's experience of, 64–65; economic inclusion and dynamism in, 64, 64n6; infectious diseases in, decline of, 49; wages in, 45, 45n3

Long Depression of 1873–1879, 116

longevity, effects of modern economies on, 55

Lorrain, Claude, 68

Louis-Philippe (king of France), 95, 117

Louis XIV (king of France), 162

Lovecraft, H. P., 283

Lowenstein, Louis, 243

Lowenstein, Roger, 243

luck, in innovation, 33

lumpenproletariat, 295

Luther, Martin, 77, 100

Lutheranism, 78

MacArthur, Charles, 64n7

Machlup, Fritz, 24n2

macro uncertainty, 37

Maddison, Angus, *The World Economy,* 3

Magna Carta, 77, 86, 87n7, 94

Mahler, Gustav, *Songs of a Wayfarer,* 273n3

Maillol, Aristide, *Ile-de-France,* 139

majority, tyranny of the, 93

"Make It New!" (Pound), 75

making a difference, 285

Malthus, Thomas, 9

managerial revolution, 241

managers: professional, rise of, 241–43; socialist, incentives of, 124, 125; socialist, innovation by, 127–28

Mann, Thomas, *Buddenbrooks,* 67

manufacturing: in post-1960s economic decline, 234–35; in recovery of dynamism, 319–20

"Man Who Made His Mark, The" (Maugham), 29n6

March on Rome (1922), 144

March Revolution (1848), 117

marginal tax rates, 175, 247n7

market capitalization: definition of, 187; as indicator of innovation, 187–91, 188f, 189f, 190f, 191f; in measurement of job satisfaction, 204–5

market-cap-to-output ratio, 187–91, 188f

market economies: equilibrium in, 9; wage setting in, 290. *See also* capitalism; socialism

Marriage of Maria Braun, The (film), 174

Marshall, Alfred: career of, 56n1; *Elements of Economics,* 56n1; on experience of work, 56–57, 58, 278; *Principles,* 47n7

Martin, Peter, 90

Marx, Karl: *The Communist Manifesto,* 41n1, 109, 117, 119; on dignity of work, 118; on Gotha Program, 119n5; historical determinism of, 10, 37; on institutions, role of, 9n11; on *lumpenproletariat,* 295; on materialism, 97; on modernization, 108–9; on productivity growth, 41; Tönnies compared to, 137, 137n2; working class wages and, 46

Marxian socialism, 118, 120. *See also* communism

Mascagni, Pietro, 74, 137

Maslow, Abraham, 277, 281

mass flourishing (nationwide prosperity): definition of, vii; economic justice in, 308; history of rise and fall of, vii, ix; innovation in (See innovation); personal flourishing in, vii; political engagement and, 309; public memory of experience of, viii; public recognition of mechanisms of, vii–viii

mass innovation, in modern economies, 53–54, 308

mass production, 276n7

mastery, in the good life, 277, 279, 284

material effects of modern economies, 41–54; on disease and mortality, 48–50, 55; on

economic inclusion, 47; on living standards, 40, 43, 52; popular opinion on, 45–48, 51–52; on productivity growth, 40, 41, 42–43; on unemployment, 50–51, 115–16; on wage growth, 43–50, 52, 109, 114; on working class, 45–48

materialism: in commercial era, 97; corporatism's critique of, 139; and the good life, 286–87; in literature, 66–67

Maugham, Somerset, "The Man Who Made His Mark," 29n6

Maurras, Charles, 151

"maximin" criterion, 294n3

Mayer, Marissa, 250

McChesney, Robert, 256

McCloskey, Deirdre, 8

McDonalds, 287

McKinsey & Company (consulting firm), 24

Means, Gardiner, *The Modern Corporation and Private Property,* 243

means to an end: vs. the good life, 271; pragmatists on, 275

median wage, 114, 227–28

medical practice: government role in, 255, 258; improvements in, with rise of modern economies, 50; in U.S. vs. Europe, 258

Medicare, expansion of, 259–60

Medicis, 91

Meeker, Mary, 259

Meistersinger, Die (Wagner), 74, 137

Melville, Herman: *The Confidence-Man,* 67, 68n12; *Moby-Dick,* 67–68, 68n12

men: employment rates of, decline in, 310; wage inequality among, 227

mental stimulation, through work, 56–58, 61–62, 118

mercantile capitalism, 2–5; bubbles and crashes in, 115; chartered companies in, 89; contemporary critics of, 2, 2n2; culture of, 97; definition of, 2; economic knowledge in, 2–5; experience of work in, 36, 59, 60; vs. modern capitalism, 26, 41, 110; vs. modern economies, 36, 59, 60; origins and rise of, 2, 96–97

merchant banks, 91–92, 322

Merton, Robert, 167

Michelangelo, 99

Mickelthwait, John, *The Company,* 90n8

Micklejohn, Alexander, 296

Microsoft, 242, 286, 290

micro uncertainty, 37

middle class: music of, 72; rise of, 52

Milanović, Branko, *Liberalization and Entrepreneurship*, 171, 173
Milhaud, Darius, 74–75
military conflict, in mercantile era, 2
military-industrial complex, 251
Milken Institute, 204
Mill, John Stuart, 90, 194
Mills, Wilbur, 228–29
Mirrlees, James, 294n3
Mises, Ludwig von, on feasibility of socialism, 121–25, 127–29, 131, 133
Mississippi Company, 89, 115
Mitchell, Broadus, 6n8
Mittal, Lakshmi, 322
Mitterand, Danielle, 246
Mitterand, François, 246
Moby-Dick (Melville), 67–68, 68n12
modern, definition of, 98
modern capitalism: company law in, 205–6; creativity in, 35, 35n11; debate over alternatives to, 110, 302–5; definition of, 110; dynamism in, recognition of role of, 317; economic institutions of, 204–7; economic justice in, 293, 300–307; the good life in, 301; Great Transformation to, 264–65; job satisfaction in (*See* job satisfaction); vs. mercantile capitalism, 26, 41, 110; nonmaterial rewards of, 269 (*See also* modern life); nonparticipants in, 305–6; progressiveness of, 41, 41n1, 109; public role in establishment of, 113; selection mechanisms for ideas in, 24–26
Modern Corporation and Private Property, The (Berle and Means), 243
modern economies: capitalist (*See* modern capitalism); corporatism's critique of, 135–43, 150; current decline of, 313–16; definition of, ix, 19, 41n1; discontent with, 114–17; economic justice in, xii, 292–96; experience of working and living in (*See* modern life); formation of (*See* modern economies, formation of); the good life in, xi–xii, 307–8; income and wealth disparities in, 114–15; inner workings of, 22–36; innovation in (*See* dynamism; innovation); material effects of (*See* material effects); modern values in origins of, x; mutual gain from exchange of services in, 289–90, 305; non-capitalist, debate over possibility of, 110; nonmaterial effects of (*See* modern life); progressiveness of, 41, 41n1, 109; selection mechanisms in, 24–26

modern economies, formation of, 77–110; economic culture in, 96–104; economic institutions in, 81–92, 314; end of, 109–10; political institutions in, 93–96; population density in, 104–8; scholarship on, gaps in, 77–79, 108–9
modernism (modernity): corporatism's critique of, 135–43; definition of, 98; economic (*See* modern economies); origins and development of, 1, 99–102
modernization: industrialization as stage in, 108–9; in Italy, 145; national mythologies on, 80; scholarship on history of, 108–9
modern life, ix–x, 55–76; in capitalism vs. corporatism, 269; changes to experience of work in, 55–62; dynamism in origins of, 15; as the good life, xi, 307–8; literature on experience of, 62–68, 71–72; music on experience of, 72–75; paintings on experience of, 68–72; resistance to, viii
modern societies: definition of, 98, 306; origins of, x, 98; traditional elements in, 305–6, 307
Modern Times (film), 52
modern values, 98–104; corporatism's critique of, 135–43; current status of, 315–16; economies based on (*See* modern economies); examples of, x, 98–99; international differences in, 103–4, 285–86; and job satisfaction, 211–15, 214f; measurement of, 212, 215f; origins and development of, x, 99–102, 315; in recovery of dynamism, 308–9, 323–24; struggle between traditional values and, viii, x–xi, 211–12, 308, 315–16; transmission of, 323–24; vitalism in, 285–86
Mokyr, Joel, 11, 14, 14n14
monarchy, British, limits on powers of, 86–87
money culture, in post-1960s economic decline, 246–48
monopolies: chartered companies as, 89; in modern economies, 140; "natural," 241; progressive critique of, 241; U.S. busting of, 154
Montaigne, Michel de, 282, 298; *Essais*, 100
moral hazards: in corporatism, 178–79; in democracy, 178
morality: vs. ethics, 208; modern, 211
Morgenstern, Oskar, 129n12
Morris, Charles, *The Dawn of Innovation*, 319
mortality: effects of modern economies on, 48–50, 55; after retirement, 62
mortgages, government role in, 252–53, 311
Moses, Robert, 106, 107n21

motherhood, 299

multiculturalism, and socialism, 173

multifactor productivity. *See* total factor productivity

music: diversity in, 38; experience of modern life depicted in, 72–75; innovation in, 72–73; interactivity in, 39; source of ideas in, 30

Mussolini, Benito: career of, 143–44; corporatism under, 142, 143–47, 170; *The Doctrine of Fascism*, 145; *Four Speeches on the Corporate State*, 145, 145n8, 146

mutual aid societies, 50

mutual funds: reform of, for recovery of dynamism, 321; structural faults of, as source of post-1960s economic decline, 243–44

Mynors, Roger, 275n5

Myrdal, Gunnar, 56–57, 58, 278

myths: of economic success, 308; national, 80

NAFTA, 266–67

Nagel, Thomas, 99n13, 284; *The Possibility of Altruism*, 208

Napoleon, 95–96, 149

Napoleonic Code of 1804, 85

Napoleonic Wars, 115

National Economic Chamber (Germany), 148

National Economic Council (Germany), 149

national economies, as innovation system, 20. *See also specific countries*

nationalism, German, 147

National Labor Relations Act of 1935 (U.S.), 154

National Labor Relations Board (U.S.), 154

national mythologies, 80

National Opinion Research Center, 231n9

national prosperity. *See* mass flourishing

National Recovery Act of 1933 (U.S.), 152

National Recovery Administration (NRA), 152–53

National Socialist German Workers Party (NSDAP), 147. *See also* Nazi Germany

"natural" monopolies, 241

natural resources, in innovation, 78–79

Nazi Germany: anti-Semitism in, 141n5, 147; authoritarianism in, 133; corporatism in, 147–50, 155–57; economic performance of, 155–57; Hayek's response to, 132n15, 133; women in labor force of, 195

needs, hierarchy of, 277

Nelson, Richard, 142; "How Medical Know-How Progresses," 319

Nelson-Phelps model, 29n6

neoclassical economics: happiness in, 277–78; welfarism of Keynes in, xi

neo-liberalism, 158, 203

neo-neoclassical economics, 11

Netherlands: chartered joint-stock companies of, 89; corporatism in, measurement of, 179–82; corporatism in, performance of, 182–86; economic knowledge in, 12; economic performance of, recent, 171–73, 176, 182–86; mercantile capitalism in, 5, 115; Wassenaar Agreement in, 161

net (after-tax) wage, 227n6, 260–61

new corporatism, 166–68, 265–66

New Deal, 152–54

New Orleans, jazz in, 75

Newton, Isaac, 11

New York, Philharmonic Society of, 72

New Zealand, corporatism in, 181

Nickell, Stephen, 180, 201n6

Nicomachean Ethics (Aristotle), 271, 271n2, 284

Nietzsche, Friedrich, 101, 281–82; *The Will to Power*, 282n16

Nightingale, Florence, 286

NIMBY, 83

Nocken, Ulrich, 149

nonmaterial effects: job satisfaction as (*See* job satisfaction); of modern economies (*See* modern life)

nonparticipants in economy, economic justice and, 298–300, 305–6

nonpecuniary motives, in dynamism, 25, 25n3, 29

nonprofit sector, 298, 299, 306

"Non Sequitur of the 'Dependence Effect,' The" (Hayek), 34n9, 129n12

North American Free Trade Agreement (NAFTA), 266–67

Northrop, 34

Norway: corporatism in, measurement of, 181–82; corporatism in, performance of, 182–84; economic performance of, recent, 171–73, 182–84, 320; job satisfaction in, 207; mercantile capitalism in, 5

Noyce, Robert, 27

NRA. *See* National Recovery Administration

NSDAP. *See* National Socialist German Workers Party

nutrition, effects of modern economies on, 48, 49

Obama, Barack, 313

Oberton, Merle, 64n7

observations, in creation of ideas, 30
Occupy Wall Street protests, 291
OECD. *See* Organisation for Economic Co-operation and Development
OECD Jobs Study, The (OECD), 222
oligarchic economies, as type of corporatism, 26
Olson, Mancur, *The Rise and Decline of Nations,* 319
Omidyar, Pierre, 205
only children, 250
opera, 74–75, 137
opportunity costs, in socialism, 122, 126
Organisation for Economic Co-operation and Development (OECD), 161, 180, 182, 187, 229; *Economic Outlook,* 173; *The OECD Jobs Study,* 222
Organization of National Labor Act of 1934 (Germany), 148
Orwell, George, 65
Oswald, Andrew, 196, 231, 231n10
outliers, 198–99
output, of dynamism, measurement of, 21. *See also* productivity
output per unit of capital, 220
output per worker (labor productivity): in corporatism vs. capitalism, 156, 182–85, 184f; growth in, as material benefit of modern economies, 42–43; market cap in relation to, 187–88, 188f; in mercantile era, 3–5, 3n3, 4n4; 19th-century growth in, 5–8; in socialism vs. capitalism, 177; synonyms for, 42; 20th-century growth in, 8; wages in relation to, 44–45, 47. *See also specific countries*
outsiders, in corporatism, 178–79
Ozment, Suzanne, 66

Paine, Thomas, *Common Sense,* 136
paintings, experience of modern life depicted in, 68–72
Pajama Putsch, 152n15
panics, financial, 115
parallel economies, 306
Paris (France): February Revolution in, 117; wages in, 45, 45n3
Parliament, British: on chartered companies, 89; democracy in, 95; in Glorious Revolution, 86; on patents and copyrights, 253
Parliament, Italian, 144
partnerships, 88, 244

Patent Act (U.S.), 85
patents: origins of, 85, 253; pharmaceutical, 254n11; problems caused by, 253–54
pauperism, reduction in, as social benefit of wage growth, 48
peace, during rise of modern economies, 53n15
Pecora, Ferdinand, 245
Pecora Commission, 154
pecuniary motives, in dynamism, 25, 25n3, 29
Peirce, Charles, 58n3
penicillin, 33
performance, economic: of corporatism (*See* corporatism, performance of); economic culture in, 103–4, 210–11; in good economy, 269–70; of socialism, claims vs. evidence on, 170–78. *See also specific countries*
Perón, Juan, 152
Perry, Claire, 55
personal achievements: in the good life, 284, 285; in modern experience of work, 59
personal flourishing: definition of, vii, 15; desire for, 287–88; *eudaimonia* as, 284; in the good life, 284–85, 287–88; in mass flourishing, vii
personal growth: careers as means to, 65–66; as modern value, 99; in socialism vs. capitalism, 119; in vitalism, 99n13
personal hygiene, effects of modern economies on, 49
personal knowledge: in creation of ideas, 30–31, 31n7, 101; in the good life, 273–77, 284
Petipa, Marius, 75
pharmaceutical industry, 254, 254n11
Phelps, Edmund S., 106n20, 167n30, 177n3, 198n4, 204, 205, 206, 208n16, 212, 222, 224n4, 247n7, 252n9, 261n17, 322; *Fiscal Neutrality toward Economic Growth,* 263; *Rewarding Work,* 240, 292; "The Unproven Case for Tax Cuts," 263
Philharmonic Society of New York, 72
Phillips, A. W., 51
physical capital, in value of companies, 187
Picasso, Pablo, 139
Pico della Mirandola, Giovanni, 99
Pigou, Arthur Cecil, 56n1
Pius XI (pope), 139
Pixar, 33
plague, bubonic, 3, 4
Plato, 37n14, 272
pluralism: in dynamism, 38; of values, and economic justice, 305–6
poems, symphonic, 73–74

Poland, market socialism in, 125
Polanyí, Karl, 9n11, 53n15
Polanyí, Michael, 53n15
policy, economic: impact on innovation, 206; in reaction to post-1960s economic decline, 225–27, 228–30; in reaction to stagnation, 312–13; traditional values in, 260
Polish-Lithuanian Constitution of 1791, 93
political engagement, in U.S., 309
political institutions: in corporatism, 142–43; in formation of modern economies, 93–96
Polo, Marco, 59
Pop Art, 75
Popolo d'Italia, Il (newspaper), 144
Popper, Karl, 9
popular music, 72
popular opinion. *See* public opinion
population density: definition of, 105; in formation of modern economies, 104–8
population growth: and decrease in living standards, 106n20; in formation of modern economies, 104–8; historical records on, 107; in mercantile era, 3, 4–5
Portugal: corporatism in, 151, 181; economic performance of, recent, 171; job satisfaction in, 214
positional goods, 60
Possibility of Altruism, The (Nagel), 208
Pound, Ezra, "Make It New!," 75
poverty reduction, as social benefit of wage growth, 48
Powell, Lewis, 266
powerlessness, in modern economies, corporatism's critique of, 140
practical knowledge, 30–31, 274, 275
pragmatists, on the good life, 274–79, 281, 283–84
Prebisch, Raúl, 39n16
preludes, Les (Liszt), 73–74
prices, in socialist economies, 120–25, 127n11, 131
pride, in job satisfaction, 199–201, 200t
primates, 61
prisons: debtors in, 91; mental stimulation in, 61
private banks, 92
private property. *See* property rights
private sector: in corporatism, 178; in recovery of dynamism, 320–23; in socialism, 119. *See also* companies; corporations
privatization: in Italy, 144; after Soviet collapse, 127

problem solving: in the good life, 275–77, 284; in modern experience of work, 57–58, 58n3, 61
production, state interventions in, in corporatism, 159
productivity: in corporatism vs. capitalism, 156, 182–85; definition of, 3; growth rate of, 190n14; levels of, 22, 42; in socialism vs. capitalism, 120, 122, 177; types of, 220. *See also specific countries*
productivity growth: capital formation and, 7; dynamism in relation to, 22; economic knowledge in, 3, 8; during Great Depression, 8, 222; happiness and, 274n4; vs. level of productivity, 22, 42; as material benefit of modern economies, 40, 41, 42–43; in mercantile era, 3–5; in 19th century, 5–8; and saving, 223–25; slowdown of 1970s in, 192; in 20th century, 8, 222; and wage growth, 44–45
professional associations, in recovery of dynamism, 322, 323
profit motive, lack of, in socialism, 123–24, 125, 128
profits: corporate, 256; social dividends as socialist version of, 120
progressive movement, in U.S., 152, 154, 240–41, 289
progressiveness, of modern economy, 41, 41n1, 109
promethean economies, 71
Prometheus, 63, 63n5, 71
property rights: current status of, 315–16; and economic performance, 177–78; in formation of modern economies, 83–86; and job satisfaction, 204; origins and rise of, 84–85; stakeholderism and, 315–16. *See also* intellectual property
property rights theory, 123
prosperity, national. *See* mass flourishing
Prosperity through Competition (Erhard), 158
Protestant Ethic and the Spirit of Capitalism, The (Weber), 78n2
Protestantism, and economic culture, 78
Prussia: output per worker in, 6; in unification of Germany, 149; urbanization in, 108
public choice theory, 124
public debt. *See* sovereign debt
public health, effects of modern economies on, 48–50
public opinion: in establishment of modern economies, 113; on material effects of modern economies, 45–48, 51–52

public sector: innovation within, 38, 308; labor unions in, 323; as measure of corporatism, 159, 161–63, 164, 178, 179; in recovery of dynamism, 316–20

public works, chartered companies in, 89

Puccini, Giacomo, 74

punctuated equilibrium, 22–23

Quadragesimo Anno (Pius XI), 139

quests, viii, 74, 136, 280, 288

racial diversity, and wage inequality, 186

Raft of the Medusa, The (Géricault), 69, 69n13

railroads: art depicting, 69–70, 71; European, 116; U.S., 14, 33

Rand, Ayn, 82

rational behavior, in socialism, 122

rational-humanism, 63n5

rationalism, 280

Ravel, Maurice, 74–75

Ravitch, Richard, 259

Rawls, John: on justice, 228, 290–95, 299–300, 305–6; on self-realization, viii, 277, 278, 281, 292; student protests of 1960s and, 290, 290n1; *A Theory of Justice*, 228, 289, 290–96; on wealth accumulation, 301

Razzell, Peter, 48n9

Reagan, Ronald, 164, 226, 229, 247

real wages per worker: definition of, 4; economic knowledge and, 4; effects of modern economies on, 43–50; in mercantile era, 4–5, 4n4; 19th-century growth in, 5–8; 20th-century growth in, 8

reason: in the good life, 273; in humans vs. animals, 273, 273n3

recessions: of 2008–2009, 175, 235, 236; innovation during, 235, 235n14; job security in, 234; in mercantile capitalism, 115; in post-1960s economic decline, 235–36; recoveries from, 235–36

redistribution, of income, 292, 293–95, 299–300

Red Scare, 134

red tape, bureaucratic, as measure of corporatism, 162, 162n26, 164, 180

Reform Act of 1832 (Britain), 95

regional banks, decline of, 303–4

regulations. *See* government regulations

Reich, Robert, 62

Reichstag, 148, 149

Reiss, Diana, 61

relational banking, 321, 322

religion, and economic culture, 78

Renaissance: commerce and foreign trade in, 2; origins of modernism in, 99–100; sparse innovation in, 1

representative democracy, in formation of modern economies, 93–96, 105, 109

Republican Party (U.S.): on social welfare, 260; traditional values in, 260, 317

Rerum Novarum (Leo XIII), 139

resource allocation: in socialism, 119–20, 125–26; in U.S., corporatist influence on, 164–65

responsibility: obligations of, in modernism, 136–37; social, in corporatism, 139

retirement, mental stimulation after, 62

revolutions of 1848, 116, 117

Rewarding Work (Phelps), 240, 292

Reynolds, Joshua, 68

Ricardo, David, 9, 194

Richberg, Donald, 153

Riefenstahl, Leni, 139

Riesman, David, *The Lonely Crowd,* 238

rights against the king, 86–87

Ring of the Niebelung, The (Wagner), 74, 119, 141

Rise and Decline of Nations, The (Olson), 319

Risk, Uncertainty and Profit (Knight), 37n13

Road to Serfdom, The (Hayek), 129n12, 131–32, 132n15, 133, 149, 156n21

Robb, Richard, 68n12

Robertson, Dennis H., 56n1, 185

Robinson Crusoe (Defoe), 37, 39, 63, 279n13

Rocco Laws. *See* Sindical Laws

Rodgers, Richard, 153n16

Rodin, Auguste, *The Thinker,* 71

Roiphe, Katie, 304

Romanticism: art of, 68–70; conception of the good life in, 280; literature of, 63–64

Rome, ancient: innovation in, 1; legal system of, 84–85, 137, 202; private property in, 84–85

Rome, March on (1922), 144

Roosevelt, Franklin, 152–55

Roosevelt, Theodore, 154

Rorty, Richard, 58n3

Roscher, Wilhelm, 9n11

Rostow, Walt W., 6, 6n7, 7, 8, 78

Rothschild family, 91

Rousseau, Jean-Jacques, *Émile,* 279n13

Royce, Josiah, 58n3

ruinous competition, 245–46

rule of law: in democracies, 94; development of, 86–87; role in capitalism, 87, 94

rural areas: creativity in, vs. cities, 107, 107n21; depopulation of (*See* urbanization)

Ruskin, John, 69

Russia: Bolshevik revolution in, 134; factories of, 52; music depicting modern life in, 75. *See also* Soviet Union

Rylance, Rick, 66n11

Saalfeld, Diedrich, 6n8

Saarinen, Esa, 39

Sade, Marquis de, 286

Sadka, Efraim, 247n7

Saint-Simon, Henri de, 117, 117n2

Salazar, Antonio, 151

Salgado, Plínio, 151–52, 152n15

Samuelson, Paul, 80, 244

Sandberg, Sheryl, 243

Sarbanes-Oxley law (U.S.), 164

Sardinia, Statuto Albertino of, 144n7

Sassoon, Donald, 117–18

saving: in economic culture, 78; productivity growth and, 223–25; in socialist economies, 174

Say, Jean-Baptiste, 101, 207

Scandizzo, Pasquale Lucio, 286

Schechter v. United States, 153

Schliemann, Heinrich, 287

Schmitter, Philippe, 143n6

Schröder, Gerhard, 161

Schulz, Nick, 255

Schumann, Robert: *Manfred,* 73; piano quartet in E flat major, 73

Schumpeter, Joseph: *Capitalism, Socialism and Democracy,* 10n12, 27n4, 207; on capitalism as culture, 207; on definition of innovation, 20n1; on entrepreneurs, need for, 9–10, 28, 98n12; in German Historical School, 9–10, 9n11; on nonpecuniary returns for entrepreneurs, 25n3; on punctuated equilibrium, 22–23; on science in innovation, ix, xi, 9–12, 10n12, 27; *The Theory of Economic Development,* 10n12; on vibrancy, 20; Weber's influence on, 78n2

science: corporatist view of advances in, 142; in dynamism, x; in economic success, 308; entrepreneurs' use of, ix, 9–10; innovations as separate from discoveries in, 11, 12–13; innovations attributed to discoveries in, ix, xi, 9–12, 26–27; material benefits of modern economies and, 53; publication of findings in, 11; as source of economic knowledge, 9–12

Scientific Revolution, 10–11, 100, 287

scientism, 10–13, 26–27, 142

Scotland: mercantile capitalism in, 2; poverty in, decline of, 48

sculpture, experience of modern life depicted in, 71

Second Great Depression, 175

Second Industrial Revolution, 13n13

Second Transformation, of U.S. economy, 264–65

Securities Act of 1933 (U.S.), 154

Securities and Exchange Commission, 154

Securities Exchange Act of 1934 (U.S.), 154

Seipel, Ignaz, 151

selection mechanisms, for ideas in modern economies, 24–26

self-actualization: in the good life, 277, 281; in modern experience of work, 58

self-affirmation, in modern experience of work, 58–59

self-discovery: in the good life, 281; in modern experience of work, 59; as modern value, 99; in vitalism, 99n13, 281

self-expression, in modern experience of work, 58–59

self-importance, culture of, 249

self-interest: in corporatism, 148, 152n15; in mercantile economies, 97

self-ownership, 81–82

self-realization: in the good life, 277, 278, 281; in modern experience of work, 58; Rawls on, viii, 277, 278, 281, 292

self-respect, 81

Seligman, Martin, *Flourish,* 285

Sen, Amartya, 58n3, 132n15, 133, 277–78, 278n12, 285, 309

Sennett, Richard, 285, 285n21

Severini, Gino, 71

shadow price, in socialism, 122

Shakespeare, William: *Hamlet,* 100, 280; *Henry V,* 278; *King Lear,* 100

shareowning: in formation of modern economies, 83; structural faults of, in post-1960s economic decline, 243–44

Shaw, George Bernard, 147

Shelley, Mary, *Frankenstein,* 63–64

Shelley, Percy Bysshe, 64; *Prometheus Unbound,* 63n5

short-term borrowing, by banks, 244–45, 322

short termism, in management of companies, 243–44, 314, 320–21

Simon, Julian, 106n20

Sindical Laws of 1926 (Italy), 145

Sinn Féin, 151

skilled workers, vs. unskilled workers, wages of, 46, 47

affected by, 230–33, 231n9, 232f; job security affected by, 233–34, 234n12; origins of, 219–20, 313–14; policy reactions to, 225–27, 228–30; productivity slowdown in, 192, 219–25, 220f, 221f; recessions in, 235–36; structural faults as source of, 241–46; structural shifts during, 234–35; unemployment in, 221–24, 226–27, 231–32, 235; wage inequality affected by, 227–30

United States corporatism: current status of, 317; interwar, 152–56; measurement of, 179–82, 180n6; and post-1960s economic decline, 251–58, 265–66; postwar, 164–65; in Second Transformation, 265–66

universal banks, 92

University of Chicago, 296

unknown unknowns, 28, 33–34

"Unproven Case for Tax Cuts, The" (Phelps), 263

unskilled workers: in Dickens's novels, 64–65; vs. skilled workers, wages of, 46, 47

urban areas. See cities

urbanization: emergence of big cities in, 108; and experience of work in modern economies, 60–61; in formation of modern economies, 104–8; and innovativeness, 39–40, 39n16; and unemployment, 50–51

"Use of Knowledge in Society, The" (Hayek), 31n7

users. See end-users

utilitarianism, 290

Valois, Georges, 135

value-added tax, 202

values: corporatist, 159; in the good life, 285–86; in job satisfaction, 208–15; socialist, 118–20, 132–33. See also culture; modern values; traditional values

Van de Velde, Willem, the Younger, 69

van Gogh, Vincent, 70

Vargas, Getúlio, 151, 152n15

Vargas Llosa, Mario, 62

Veblen, Thorstein, 66–67, 194

Velasquez, Diego, 68

Venice (city-state), commercial economy of, 2

Venter, J. Craig, 113

Venturesome Economy, The (Bhidé), 319

Verdi, Giuseppe, 74, 137

Vertigo (film), 78n2

vibrancy: definition of, 20, 194; vs. dynamism, 20, 21, 22; economic culture in, 194

Vichy regime, 151

Vienna (Austria): infectious diseases in, decline of, 49; Philharmonic Orchestra of, 72

Vincenti, Walter, 32

Viner, Jacob, 39n16

Virgil, Georgics, 275

virtues, vs. the good life, 272

Visconti, Luchino, 154

visual arts, experience of modern life depicted in, 68–72

vitalism: decline of, 316; definition of, 99n13; in formation of modern economies, 102–4, 105; on the good life, 279–88; origins and rise of, 100, 279–81; revival of, 284

Vittorio Emanuele III (king of Italy), 144

Volcker, Paul, 175

Volkswagen, 160

Voltaire: Candide, 101–2, 275–76; on the good life, 275–76, 280

voluntary corporatism, in Germany, 149–50

volunteer sector, 299

voodoo economics, 226

wage(s): after-tax (net), 227n6, 260–61; in corporatism, 142–43, 186; effects of modern economies on, 43–50, 52, 109, 114; equal, impossibility of, 290, 291–92; happiness in relation to, 52–53; job satisfaction in relation to, 196, 199, 201; justice in distribution of, 291–95, 299–300, 305–6; median, 114, 227–28; output per worker in relation to, 44–45, 47; ratio of wealth to, 223–24, 223n3, 261, 262f; real (See real wages); in relationship between innovation and employment, 222–23, 223n3; social benefits of growth in, 47–50; in socialism, 119–25

wage inequality: in corporatism, 186; justice of, 290, 291–92, 302; in modern capitalism, 302; in post-1960s economic decline, 227–30; rise of, 114–15, 227–28; in socialism, 176–77

wage-productivity ratio, 44–45, 47

wage-wealth ratio, 223–24, 223n3, 261, 262f

Wagner, Richard, 72–73; Die Meistersinger, 74, 137; Ring of the Niebelung, The, 74, 119, 141

Wagner Act of 1935 (U.S.), 154

Wagner's Law, 260

Wallonia (Belgium), 96

Walt Disney, 254

wars: booms and recessions caused by, 115; during rise of modern economies, 53n15

Wassenaar Agreement (1982), 161

Watt, James, 12, 13, 89

wealth: job satisfaction in relation to, 196, 201; and labor force participation, 260–61, 262f; in money culture, 246–48; ratio of wage to, 223–24, 223n3, 261, 262f; in relationship between innovation and employment, 223, 223n3; social vs. private, 259, 261–63

wealth accumulation: antipathy for, 301; in capitalism, rise of, 108; democratization of, 115; disparities in, rise of, 114–15; in economic culture, 104; as economic freedom, 83–84; in economic justice, 301–2; and the good life, 286–87; motivations for, 286–87; in socialism, 119

wealth effect, 260–63

Wealth of Nations, The (Smith), 2n2, 97

wealthy: income of, vs. working class wages, 47; infectious diseases among, decline of, 49

Webb, James Watson, 91n10

Weber, Max: on economic culture, 78, 97, 194; on economic freedoms, 82; *Economy and Society,* 78n2; on formation of modern economies, 79, 97; in German Historical School, 9n11; on modernization, 108–9; *The Protestant Ethic and the Spirit of Capitalism,* 78n2

Wedgwood, Eli, 89

Weimar Germany, 148, 150, 157

welfare: corporate, 254, 267; social (*See* social welfare)

welfarism, neoclassical, xi

well-being: in the good life, 285; Smith's conception of, xi

Wells, David, 48, 48n8, 49, 49n13

Wen Jiabao, 130

West Germany, corporatism in, 157–62

Whale, James, 64

Whitman, Walt, 281

Wiesel, Elie, 249

Wilde, Oscar, 136

Wilhelm (emperor of Germany), 149

William II (king of England), 86

Williamson, Jeffrey, 6n8

Will to Power, The (Nietzsche), 282n16

Wilson, Woodrow, 154

wisdom, in creation of ideas, 28

Wollstonecraft, Mary, 67

women: labor force participation by, 195; self-ownership of, 81–82

Wooldridge, Adrian, *The Company,* 90n8

work: balance between home and, 304; devaluation of, 229–30; in the good life, 275–78, 304

work, experience of: effects of modern economies on, 55–62; mental stimulation through, 56–58, 118; in mercantile vs. modern economy, 36, 59, 60; modern literature on, 62–68; modern paintings on, 68–72; in traditional vs. modern economy, 57–59, 109. *See also* job satisfaction

workers, in socialism: incentives of, 122–26, 123n7; rights of, 118

work ethic, in socialism, 123

working class: diet of, 49; effects of modern economies on wages of, 45–48, 114; in Italian corporatism, 145–46; job satisfaction among, 62; music of, 72

Works Project Administration, 153

World Bank, *Bureaucrats in Business,* 171

World Economy, The (Maddison), 3

World Values Surveys (WVS), 103, 196, 197–98, 199, 210, 211, 212–13, 233, 285–86

World War I: German reparations for, 148; Italy in, 144

World War II: corporatism after, 156–57; Holocaust in, 141n5

writing, expository, 324

Wullschlager, Jackie, 55

Wuthering Heights (Emily Brontë), 64, 64n6

Wuthering Heights (film), 64, 64n7

WVS. *See* World Values Surveys

Wyler, William, 64n7

Yahoo, 250

zaibatsu, 152

Zakaria, Fareed, 313

Zingales, Luigi, 254

Zoega, Gylfi, 198n4, 204, 205, 206, 261n17, 286

Zola, Émile, 67

zoology, modern views in, 61

Zuckerberg, Mark, 243, 249